ACTION AS AN ORGANIZER OF LEARNING AND DEVELOPMENT

Volume 33 in the Minnesota Symposia
on Child Psychology

ACTION AS AN ORGANIZER OF LEARNING AND DEVELOPMENT

Volume 33 in the Minnesota Symposia on Child Psychology

Edited by

John J. Rieser
Vanderbilt University

Jeffrey J. Lockman
Tulane University

Charles A. Nelson
University of Minnesota

LEA LAWRENCE ERLBAUM ASSOCIATES, PUBLISHERS
2005 Mahwah, New Jersey   London

Lawrence Erlbaum Associates, Inc., Publishers
10 Industrial Avenue
Mahwah, New Jersey 07430
www.erlbaum.com

Cover design by Kathryn Houghtaling Lacey

Library of Congress Cataloging-in-Publication Data

Minnesota Symposia on Child Psychology (33rd : 2002 : University of Minnesota)
Action as an organizer of learning and development / edited by John J. Rieser,
Jeffrey J. Lockman, Charles A. Nelson.
    p.   cm. — (Minnesota symposia on child psychology ; v. 33)
    Includes bibliographical references and index.
    ISBN 0-8058-5030-9 (alk. paper)
    1. Child development—Congresses.   2. Motor ability in children—Congresses.
    3. Developmentally disabled children—Congresses.   4. Child psychology—Congresses.
    5. Cognition in children—Congresses.   6. Developmental disabilities—Congresses.
    I. Rieser, John J.   II. Lockman, Jeffrey J.   III. Nelson, Charles A. (Charles Alexander).
    IV. Title.   V. Series.
RJ131.M545   2002
155.4—dc22   2004047231
                                                                                       CIP

Books published by Lawrence Erlbaum Associates are printed on acid-free paper,
and their bindings are chosen for strength and durability.

Printed in the United States of America
10 9 8 7 6 5 4 3 2 1

IN MEMORIAM

Esther Stillman Thelen
1941–2004

Esther Thelen died on December 29, 2004, at the end of a most courageous year-long battle with cancer, an illness from which she had been in remission for 25 years. She was a renowned scientist, a leader in her profession, and a generous, caring mentor. Beginning with her early meticulous observations of infants' rhythmic movements, she was responsible for a renaissance in the study of motor development. She introduced developmentalists to the utility of dynamical systems principles for understanding the emergent nature of development, especially motor development. (See her chapter in Volume 22 of this series.) Most recently, as exemplified by her chapter in the present volume, she has shown how dynamic field theory can be expanded and applied to understanding more general problems of remembering and learning in development.

Esther's presentations at scientific meetings were always characterized by deeply penetrating arguments delivered with grace and enthusiasm and intellectual rigor. We were pleased and honored when Esther accepted the invitation to participate in the Minnesota Symposium "Action as an Organizer of Learning and Development." We could never have imagined on that occasion that we would be deprived of the joy of many more exhilarating discussions (accompanied by good food and wine) with her over coming years. We are both proud and sad that what is nearly her last major contribution breaking new ground in our understanding of learning and development appears in this volume. Our field has lost a brilliant scholar and we have lost a cherished friend. We are grateful to have known her.

—Anne and Herb Pick
February 2005

Contents

Contributors

Adolph, Karen, E. Department of Psychology, New York University.

Aslin, Richard N. Department of Brain and Cognitive Sciences, University of Rochester.

Banks, Martin S. Department of Visual Sciences, University of California at Berkeley.

Bertenthal, Bennett I. Department of Psychology, University of Chicago.

Bushnell, Emily W. Department of Psychology, Tufts University.

Huttenlocher, Janellen. Department of Psychology, University of Chicago.

Keen, Rachel. Department of Psychology, University of Massachusetts at Amherst.

Lee, David N. Department of Psychology, University of Edinburgh.

Liben, Lynn S. Department of Psychology, The Pennsylvania State University.

Lockman, Jeffrey J. Department of Psychology, Tulane University.

Nelson, Charles A. Institute of Child Development, University of Minnesota.

Newcombe, Nora S. Department of Psychology, Temple University.

Rieser, John J. Department of Psychology and Human Development, Vanderbilt University.

Thelen, Esther. Department of Psychology, Indiana University.

von Hofsten, Claes. Department of Psychology, Uppsala University.

Warren, William H. Department of Cognitive and Linguistic Sciences, Brown University

Whitmyer II, Virgil. Department of Psychology, Indiana University.

Preface

The Minnesota Symposium is always a time for celebration, but when the Symposium celebrates some of its own, the occasion is extra special. So it is the case with the 33rd Minnesota Symposium on Child Psychology, which took place at the University of Minnesota from October 10 to 12, 2002. The Symposium was held to honor the scientific and mentoring contributions of Anne Danielson Pick and Herbert L. Pick, Jr., two long-time and beloved professors of the Institute of Child Development.

For many students and colleagues, Anne and Herb have helped to define the spirit of the Institute. They arrived at the Institute of Child Development in the 1960s: Herb made a slight detour at the University of Wisconsin after finishing his degree at Cornell; Anne's detour from Cornell was at Macalester College. At Cornell, both had studied with James J. and Eleanor J. Gibson, with Anne concentrating on studies of perceptual learning with Eleanor Gibson and Herb also concentrating on studies of perception with Richard Walk and Robbie MacLeod.

In the Picks' subsequent work, individually and together, they did much to shape the emerging field of perceptual development and establish it as a core area within the field of child psychology. Ever mindful of the Gibsonian perspective, they extended it to address questions and topics that were not immediately associated with the field of perception—at least at that time. Consider, for example, Anne's widely cited research on reading and selective attention or Herb's influential work on cognitive mapping. Both programs of research richly illustrate how the Gibsonian ecological perspective can introduce new theoretical and substantive questions about topics not traditionally considered to be problems of perceptual or perception-action development.

Yet these achievements tell only part of the story. Like their own mentors James and Eleanor Gibson, Anne and Herb have been extraordinary teachers and advisors—not just to current or former Institute students, but to colleagues around the nation and across the globe. Anne's and Herb's wisdom and generosity have made them a treasure to all who have had the good fortune to study or consult with them.

For all these reasons and more, many former students and colleagues felt that the time was appropriate, if not past due, to honor Anne and Herb for their contributions to the field. When we began discussing this possibility, it was immediately obvious that a Minnesota Symposium was the ideal way to do so. In the collective memories of all who have passed through the Institute, Anne and Herb are clearly identified with the Symposium series. For many years, Anne organized and edited the Symposia volumes—from 1971 to 1976. At each Symposium, Herb always seemed to be in the audience asking *the* question of a presenter—even if the presenter's topic was far outside Herb's research area. Those lessons were not lost on the fledgling developmental psychologists in the audience. The never flagging intellectual curiosity, the good questions, the joy that comes from hearing about elegant and sound experimental methods: these are all qualities that Anne and Herb displayed at symposium after symposium and that many of us have tried to emulate in our own academic careers long after we exited those symposia audiences.

As might have been predicted, when we first contacted Anne and Herb about the idea of holding a Minnesota Symposium in recognition of their contributions, they were honored, but embarrassed. In their typical selfless way, they were quick to say that if a Minnesota Symposium were to be held in their honor, they did not want it about them or their past work. Rather they were interested in seeing a forward-looking symposium—one that would help set the agenda for the field in the areas that they have cared so deeply about in their own research.

So it is in this spirit that the 33rd Minnesota Symposia on Child Psychology evolved. The topic of the Symposia is "Action as an Organizer of Learning and Development." It is a theme that has been central in the Picks' own research in their more than almost 80 collective years in the field. The goal of this Minnesota Symposium was not to look backward, but to integrate the best and most innovative research on the role of action in perceiving and understanding—in other words, in the research areas that Anne and Herb have helped to define.

Given the honorees, it was an easy task to assemble a stellar group of contributors to this Minnesota Symposium. Perhaps less obvious, but nonetheless equally impressive, Anne and/or Herb have served, at one point or another, as mentors or advisors to most all of the distinguished presenters to the 33rd Minnesota Symposium on Child Psychology. More broadly, the impact that Anne and Herb have had on the field through their mentoring of new generations of developmental scientists has been truly exceptional.

Anne's and Herb's mentoring accomplishments speak both to the past and future, as does the work presented at the 33rd Minnesota Symposium on Child Psychology. The Symposium was organized to consider the general theme of "Action as an Organizer of Learning and Development." Contemporary thinking about the role of action in learning and development is in flux. Recent theoretical advances concerning the relation between the development of perception and action are opening new research questions while posing new conceptual challenges. Theoretical advances associated with the work of the Gibsons and Picks have led developmental scientists to realize that the development of perception and action is inextricably linked: Perception guides action, but new motor skills have important consequences for the way in which the world is perceived. People learn to perceive and perceive in order to learn. Additionally, empirical work over the past decade or so indicates that the role of experience in the emergence of so-called *gross motor skills* has been underestimated. Researchers are increasingly recognizing that the development of locomotor skills involves a complex interplay between maturational and experiential factors.

Against this backdrop, there has also been great controversy about what motor behavior can tell us about conceptual development. In large part, the controversy stems from the interpretation of infant visual habituation and looking time studies. These studies have been hailed by some for uncovering astonishing conceptual capacities in infants, but faulted by others for making rich interpretations of looking time differences in infants. How can it be, go the critics, that infants are credited with abundant physical understanding when toddlers show little evidence of such understanding in their manual actions? Although the present Symposium does not fully resolve this particular question, it does ask researchers to take a step back and ask more basic questions regarding how action may help organize learning and development both in infants and older children.

To address these issues and more, we arranged the presentations and resulting chapters from the 33rd Minnesota Symposium into four sections. The first section is concerned with the general topic of "Using Information to Guide Action." In chapter 1, David N. Lee discusses his foundational research on the informational variable *tau*, which corresponds roughly to time to contact. Dr. Lee's work across a variety of species illustrates how the environment is rich in information to help organisms control action. Based on this work, Dr. Lee argues that there are likely biological universals that organisms may use to act adaptively in their respective environments. In chapter 2, Claes von Hofsten discusses the important problem of prospective control in two basic action systems: looking and reaching. Dr. von Hofsten is at the forefront of efforts to uncover the building blocks of humans' sophisticated perceptuomotor abilities by studying the degree to which infants are able to coordinate perception and action. The problem of prospective control is basic to such coordination. In his chapter, Dr. von Hofsten illustrates how prospective control may be achieved by infants through use of information in the environment, enabling infants to engage in anticipatory looking and, remarkably, catching. Chapter 3 by Karen E. Adolph continues to explore the theme of how infants use information in the environment to control action. Dr. Adolph challenges long-standing maturational views about motor development and highlights the importance of experience and learning to learn. She reports extraordinary data obtained in infants' homes regarding their vast amount of crawling and walking experience—experience that unquestionably helps infants to perfect their new locomotor skills. Finally, in chapter 4, William H. Warren provides a discussion of these chapters. Dr. Warren is a leading expert on the visual control of action and ecological psychology. In his discussion, he places the current chapters in the larger context of past and present research aimed at uncovering regularities in the ways in which organisms and environments physically interact.

Section II represents a reunion of sorts for three Institute alumni. Richard N. Aslin (University of Rochester), Martin S. Banks (University of California, Berkeley), and Emily W. Bushnell (Tufts University) not only overlapped during their years of graduate study at the Institute, but attended at that time the same research group meetings while beginning to make their respective marks on the field of perceptual development. Since that time, each has gone on to make fundamental contributions to the field. Their contributions to the Symposium address the topic of "Computational Complexity and the Integration of Information." In chapter 5, Richard N. Aslin discusses his influential research on statistical learning and the complex problem of object recognition: Organisms may have evolved specialized learning mechanisms to recognize objects based on detecting regularities in informational input. As Dr. Aslin reports, however, statistical learning based on passive perceptual exposure is shown relative to active perceptuomotor responding, which occurs more quickly. This difference, in turn, raises intriguing questions about the nature and extent of object knowledge when perception versus perception and action are involved—an issue that is considered in subsequent chapters as well. In chapter 6, Martin S. Banks describes his recent work on a related problem of object recognition—how individuals combine information about object properties within and across modalities. To address this problem, Dr. Banks proposes that individuals employ a weighting mechanism to solve this fundamental combinatorial problem. In the chapter, Dr. Banks provides support for this proposal through a seamless integration of empirical and modeling studies conducted in his laboratory. As Emily N. Bushnell shows in chapter 7, the processing mechanisms formulated by Aslin and Banks have important implications for understanding the acquisition of a variety of developmental milestones, many of which involve some form of perceptuomotor learning.

The chapters in Section III are devoted to the topic of "Active Learning During Early Development." In chapter 8, Nora S. Newcombe leads off the section with a chapter that considers the roles of language and action in coding spatial location while moving in space. She focuses on recent claims that young children rely on geometric rather than local landmark information to encode an object's location. Her systematic studies illustrate that children's use of such geometric information to code location is not absolute. Rather she favors a cue validity approach based on the values of different types of spatial reference system information given the demands of particular spatial tasks. Note that in a formal sense, the solution via sampling different types of spatial cues advocated by Newcombe shares much in common with the weighting mechanisms advocated by Aslin, Banks, and Bushnell in their chapters on object recognition. Chapter 9 by Esther Thelen and Virgil Whitmyer offers a far-reaching theoretical and empirical synthesis of research on action, perception, and cognition. In their chapter, Drs. Thelen and Whitmyer draw from research on object permanence, visual habituation, and early physical knowledge to present a unified account of how object knowledge is rooted in action. They present a new theoretical approach based on dynamic field theory to integrate these often separate research areas. In so doing, they also account for previously ignored findings and offer new, testable, and exciting predictions. More broadly and like Banks, Drs. Thelen and Whitmyer demonstrate the potential value of combining behavioral and modeling approaches to study the processes that govern learning and development. In chapter 10, Bennett I. Bertenthal discusses the Newcombe and Thelen and Whitmyer chapters in relation to the more general question of what it means to have knowledge of an object. For this purpose, he integrates research from psychology and the neurosciences and argues how the current chapters support the idea that knowledge about what an object is and how to act on an object may be dissociable. As Dr. Bertenthal suggests, understanding how these two basic sources of knowledge become progressively coordinated during development needs to become an explicit goal of future research.

Section IV is organized around the topic of "Using Representations to Guide Action." Throughout the Symposium, a key issue that emerged concerned the different ways in which researchers invoke the notion of representation in their research. The chapters in the present section deal with the particular issue of how children use representations to guide and control action. In chapter 11, Rachel Keen focuses on young children's physical knowledge or lack thereof when attempting to find hidden objects. These difficulties are especially surprising in light of prior research indicating that infants possess sophisticated knowledge about the continuity and solidity of objects—knowledge that should enable preschool children to solve the problems used by Keen. Dr. Keen presents a clever and programmatic series of studies designed to investigate the source of children's difficulties. These studies do much more, however. They go beyond this particular search task and address deep-seated issues about the nature of object knowledge. Dr. Keen's chapter thus raises important questions about how dissociations across different dependent measures of object knowledge—looking versus manual action—should be interpreted, a theme echoed by other contributors to this Symposium volume. In chapter 12, Lynn S. Liben focuses on a different problem of representational use: how children employ external representations to guide action. Dr. Liben reviews her path-breaking research on children's use of maps and other types of place representations. In this connection, she addresses the complementary issues of how human action affects and is affected by external representations of place—issues informed by a consideration of both Gibsonian and Piagetian theoretical traditions. As Dr. Liben notes, conclusions from her studies have important implications for how children should be taught about maps and other graphic representations in school settings. In chapter 13, Janellen Huttenlocher offers not only a commentary on the preceding two chapters, but a cogent distillation of how the term *representation* has been used and perhaps misused in work in developmental psychology over recent years. Dr. Huttenlocher has conducted pioneering research about imagery, spatial representations, and concepts. Her discussion here provides new insights about the relation between motor development and conceptual development, and, more generally, thought and action.

As a reader, you are in for a treat. The chapters that follow certainly capture the intellectual excitement that characterized the 33rd Minnesota Symposium on Child Psychology. If you read between the lines, you may also get a sense of the tributes to Anne and Herb that accompanied each presentation in addition to those from other friends, colleagues, and former students who attended the Symposium. One tribute needs to be highlighted, however. Eleanor J. Gibson, in failing health and shortly before she died a few months after the Symposium, recorded a very special video tribute to her two former students, Anne and Herb. After that surprise tribute was shown at the end of the Symposium, there were no dry eyes in the house, especially the ones of those two former students.

A collective undertaking like the Symposium depends on the contributions of many individuals. Without the help of the staff, graduate students, and faculty of the Institute of Child Development, this Symposium would not have been possible. We are especially grateful to Signe Bobbitt, Claudia Johnston, and Kay O'Geay of the Institute of Child Development for all their efforts connected with making the Symposium seem, well, effortless. We would also like to thank the Institute of Child Development, the Center for Cognitive Science, and the Department of Psychology, all of the University of Minnesota, for their financial support of the Symposium. And we are grateful for the Leveritt-Miller Fund of Vanderbilt University and the Wissenschaftskolleg zu Berlin for providing support for the volume. Additional thanks go to Linda Acredolo, Mervyn Bergman, Andy Collins, Marion Eppler (who traveled to Vermont to prepare the video tribute from Jackie Gibson), Peggy Hagen, Gordon Legge, Anne Masten, Cindy Pick, Karen Pick, Gretchen Pick, and Jerry Siegel. Finally, we must thank Anne and Herb, who have been an inspiration to all of us and to whom we present and dedicate this volume.

Jeffrey J. Lockman
Charles N. Nelson
John J. Rieser

I
▼▼▼▼▼▼▼▼

USING INFORMATION
TO GUIDE ACTION

1

▼▼▼▼▼▼▼

Tau in Action in Development

David N. Lee
University of Edinburgh

ANIMALS ARE BORN TO MOVE

When we watch children take their first steps, a baseball player hit a home run, a pianist play Mozart, birds dive on prey, bees flit from flower to flower, we cannot help but wonder: How do they do that? Understanding movement is central to understanding development. Without movement we—by which I mean the animal kingdom—would not be able to eat, avoid harm, reproduce, or communicate by sound, gesture, or facial expression. We would not be able to perceive because perception is an active process. Consequently, we would not be able to think because there would be nothing to think about. We would not even be able to breathe or pump nutrients around the body. In short, we would be dead.

How is movement controlled and how does the ability develop? I first consider basic principles underlying animal movement. Next I outline a theory (General Tau Theory) of movement guidance based on those principles. Finally, I describe experiments testing the theory and discuss applications of the theory in the study and measurement of development of movement control.

PRINCIPLES OF ANIMAL MOVEMENT

James J. Gibson and Nicholai Bernstein never met and knew little or nothing about each other's work. However, they came to similar conclusions about the nature of animal movement. Separately they pioneered the field of perception and movement control and laid firm foundations for future research. Gibson (1966) approached the problem more from the perceptual angle, Bernstein (1967) more from the movement side. From their work, the following five general principles of animal movement may be distilled:

1. *Movement requires perceptual guidance.* The reason that this must be so is that movements are brought about not simply by muscular forces, but also by external forces such as gravity and friction. Because the external forces are not wholly predictable, they could deviate a movement from its intended course. Therefore, the progress of a movement needs to be monitored perceptually to enable appropriate muscular adjustments to be made. One or more of the perceptual systems may be involved in the monitoring. The articular proprioceptive system, comprising sensors in the joints, muscles, and skin, is constantly active during all movements. The vestibular system is active whenever head movement is part of the action, which it normally is. Hearing is active in movement monitoring whenever controlled sounds are being produced, as when speaking, singing, playing a musical instrument, and guiding movement around the world using echolocation, whether as bat, dolphin, or human. Vision can be active in a multitude of ways in guiding movement. However, one cannot be looking everywhere at once, and to pick up detailed information you need to move your gaze around in an efficient way. Learning to drive, for example, is very much about learning where to look and when. Vision also appears to act as an overseer of the other perceptual systems, keeping them mutually in tune (Lee, 1978).

2. *Movement requires intrinsic guidance.* An animal fashions movements to its purpose, and so movement must also be guided intrinsically. When singing, for example, the music that guides the voice comes from within the singer. Yet, as just mentioned, hearing is required to monitor the voice to make sure it is doing what the inner music directs. Running is another example. The running style comes from within the runner while the eyes guide the progress across the ground.

3. *Movements are prospectively guided.* They flow ahead in time like a melody. This has to be so because an animal has limited power available for making a movement. Therefore, if it does not manage its power resources prospectively, it could end up not having sufficient power available to complete a movement properly. This could have dire consequences if an animal runs out of braking power when trying to stop at a cliff edge.

4. *Movement information embraces the future.* For movements to be guided prospectively, the information guiding the movement, whether

perceptual or intrinsic, must allow adequate extrapolation of the movement into the future. Therefore, the information must have a temporal structure that extends it forward beyond the immediate present.

5. *Movement guidance is simple, rapid, and reliable—and probably follows universal principles.* That movement guidance is rapid and reliable is evident from watching the behavior of any animal. The fact that animals with small nervous systems, such as insects, perform movements with a precision comparable to our own suggests common simple underlying principles of movement guidance.

INFORMATION GUIDING HANDS AND OTHER EFFECTORS

Watching a slow motion film of a fielder catching a fast cricket ball with one hand while diving over the ground brings out two important points. First, the body can move in an indefinite number of ways when directing an effector (the hand in this case) toward something. Even in everyday activities this is the rule rather than the exception. Consider, for example, picking up a coffee cup from a desk. This can be done with equal facility when stepping over to the desk, when swiveling around on a desk chair, or when simply reaching across the desk. In short, reaching is about controlling the movement of the hand relative to the object of the reach. Depending on the circumstances, this can require a variety of different forms of body movement.

The second point concerns the connection between the hand and the object. When watching a fielder catching a ball, one can get the impression that the ball is physically connected to the hand even before the catch is made. It is as if hand and ball are connected by invisible elastic that draws them together. There is, in fact, a physical connection between the hand and the ball before contact is made. It is not, of course, a material connection like a piece of elastic. Rather it is an informational connection more like that between an operator and a radio-controlled model plane. In general, the information that prospectively guides movement is obtained through several perceptual systems. For the fielder, these at least include vision and the articulatory system of sensors in joints, muscles, and skin. For a bat catching an insect on the wing, echolocation is used instead of vision. Whatever the perceptual systems involved, a central component is the information about the changing motion-gap between an effector and its goal (hand and ball for the fielder, wing and insect for the bat) that enables the gap to be prospectively controlled. The motion-gap may be propriospecific, between an effector and part of the body, as when putting food in the mouth, or it may be expropriospecific, between an effector and an external object or surface, as in the ball-catching example (Lee, 1978).

As a general rule, we may think of an effector as anything that is controlled to a goal. It may be a hand as in grasping, a foot as in securing footing, a mouth as in seizing food, or it may be a tool controlled by a person. When manipulating a computer mouse, one reaches with the cursor, not the hand. When holding a laser pointer, one reaches with the laser beam. When using a remote-controlled surgical instrument, one reaches with the remote instrument. In all these examples, the body movements are quite different. Therefore, *the essence of moving an effector to its goal does not reside in the pattern of limb movements that moves the effector. Rather it lies in the form of closure of the motion-gap between the effector (hand, foot, cursor, beam, instrument) and the goal.*

Controlling the closure of the motion-gap between an effector and its goal, as when reaching, is a perceptuomotor act. However, most theories of reaching have primarily addressed just the motor aspects. They have been basically concerned with explaining the dynamics of reaching with the arm and hand in terms of mathematical models of the physiconeural structure of the musculature (Bizzi et al., 1992; Feldman & Levin, 1995; Flanagan et al., 1993). The theories assume that movement of the arm and hand is directed by perceptual information—by shifting the limb's equilibrium point (see Flanagan et al., 1993, for a review of different forms of the equilibrium point hypothesis)—but no explanation of the perceptual component is considered in the theories. However, it is essential that the perceptual component is taken into account when trying to understand control of reaching or any other movement. For example, visual information picked up during reaching can guide the limb and adjust for motion of the goal (Flash, 1990; Georgopoulos et al., 1981; Péllison et al., 1986; Soechting & Lacquaniti, 1983; van Sonderjen et al., 1989).

In short, perceptual information is part and parcel of an act. Thus, if a motion-gap variable, such as its size, is being controlled, there must be a perceptual information variable (or variables) that specifies the value of the motion-gap variable. Conversely, if there is no perceptual information variable that specifies the value of a particular motion-gap variable, then it cannot be controlled. Consider, for example, moving a laser spot to a goal position across a wall that is an uncertain distance away. This can be done quite smoothly and accurately, although there is no perceptual information variable specifying the size of the motion-gap on the wall between the current position of the laser spot and the goal. Therefore, it cannot be the size of the motion-gap that is being controlled in this situation, but some other measure, X. To be sure, if, in another situation, there were perceptual information variables specifying both X and the size of a motion-gap, then the size might be controlled in this case. However, an explanation of control that applies to all situations is to be preferred to a set of ad hoc explanations. Therefore, let us see what General Tau Theory has to offer by way of providing a universal control variable for all situations.

GENERAL TAU THEORY

To summarize thus far, I have argued that an adequate theory of guidance of movement must be based on and adhere to the principles of animal movement outlined earlier. That is, *an adequate theory must explain how movements are perceptually and intrinsically guided. It must explain the form of the guiding perceptual information that enables prospective guidance of movement, and it must be biologically plausible.* So where do we start?

Motion-Gaps

A key aspect of animal movement is that it is goal-directed. Therefore, a basic concept is that of motion-gap. I introduced this concept earlier when discussing the closure of distance motion-gaps, as when catching a ball. However, the concept is more general than this. A motion-gap is the changing gap between the state the animal is currently in and the goal state that it wants to be in. When reaching for a fruit, there is the distance motion-gap between the hand and the fruit. When turning gaze to look at something, there is the angular motion-gap between the current gaze direction and the direction of the object. When thrusting off from a stair, there is the force motion-gap between the current force and the force require for satisfactory lift-off. When singing, there is the pitch motion-gap between the current pitch and the next pitch, which in turn requires controlling other motion-gaps within the vocal system. Note that the dimension of the motion-gap is different in each of these examples—namely, distance, angle, force, and pitch. Thus, the concept of motion-gap is not tied to a particular dimension.

All actions entail closing motion-gaps. Invariably, several motion-gaps need to be controlled at the same time. Running down stairs is an example. You need to coordinate the closure of gaze-stair and foot-stair motion-gaps if you want to get down in one piece. Controlling the closure of a motion-gap requires obtaining perceptual information about the gap and how it is closing. Motion-gaps come in different dimensions (distance, angle, etc.). Yet does this mean that the perceptual information about the gaps has to come in different dimensions also? At first blush, that would appear inevitable. However, it would lead to a complicated system of mixed-dimensions control. Maybe evolution has found a neater solution (it usually does) and measures all motion-gaps in the same dimension.

What might that dimension be? It is unlikely to be one of the dimensions considered so far (distance, angle, force) because that would give one type of motion-gap (distance, say) a privileged position and so would not be a symmetrical solution. Most likely evolution has used the dimension that underlies the process of change of any motion-gap—namely, time.

Tau: A Universal Variable for Controlling Motion-Gaps

Can a single type of temporal variable of a changing motion-gap provide sufficient information for controlling the closure of the motion-gap? It turns out that tau can (Lee, 1998). Tau of a motion-gap is the time to closure of the motion-gap at its current closure rate. [To express it symbolically, suppose that at time t, the size of a motion-gap is x(t) and the rate of change of x(t) is ẋ(t). Then tau of the motion-gap at time t is written as $\tau(x,t)$, and this equals $x(t)/\dot{x}(t)$.] Note that tau is a measure on any motion-gap of any dimension (the dimension of x may be distance, angle, force, etc.), and the value of tau may be sensed, in principle, by any perceptual means (vision, hearing, touch, echolocation, etc.). Thus, to dispel a common misconception, tau is not the inverse of the rate of dilation of an optical image any more than gravity is the apple falling on Newton's head. The apple falling is an example of the general principle of gravity, and the image dilation is an example of the general principle of tau.

Tau-Coupling

Let us now consider how perceiving the tau of a motion gap would benefit an animal. Here a basic concept is *tau-coupling*. Two taus are coupled over a period of time if they remain in constant proportion during that time. Expressed symbolically, the taus (τs) of two gaps, x(t) and y(t), are tau-coupled if

$$\tau(x,t) = K\tau(y,t) \tag{1}$$

for a constant K (the coupling constant). t stands for time. The gaps may be of different dimensions. As an example, consider a bat flying in to land on a perch (Fig. 1.1a). To land properly, the bat has to control the closure of two motion-gaps simultaneously. There is the distance motion-gap, X, between the bat and the perch and the angular motion-gap, A, between the current direction of the line between the bat and the perch and the direction that line needs to lie in during the final approach to the perch. The distance motion-gap, X, needs to be closed to zero in a controlled way to

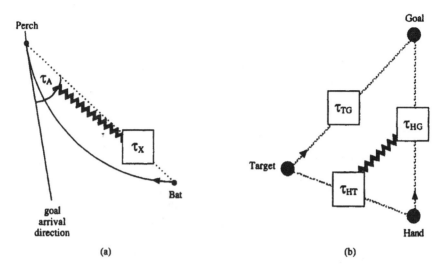

FIG. 1.1.   Tau-coupling. (a) Echolocating bat flying to a perch by keeping τ_A = $K\tau_X$. (b) Human adult intercepting a moving target at a goal zone by keeping $\tau_{HG} = K\tau_{HT}$.

avoid crashing into the perch. Simultaneously, the angular motion-gap, Y, needs to be closed to zero to approach the landing from the right direction (remember that the bat also has to somersault just before landing so that it ends up on the perch upside-down). A film analysis of a bat performing this remarkable feat indicated that it controlled its flight by tau-coupling (Lee et al., 1995). [The coupling equation was $\tau(A,t) = K\tau(X,t)$, written as $\tau_A = K\tau_X$ in Fig. 1.1a.] The tau-coupling automatically ensures that gaps A and X close simultaneously. This is because a gap reaches closure as the tau of the gap becomes zero. [As $\tau(X,t)$ becomes zero, $\tau(A,t)$ becomes zero because $\tau(A,t) = K\tau(X,t)$, and so both A and X also become zero.] However, this is not the whole story on the bat landing. The value of the coupling constant K is also important in determining the dynamics of the movement. We come to this later.

Tau-coupling also applies when intercepting something (Fig. 1.1b). In a recent experiment (Lee et al., 2001), adults had to move a hand cursor up a computer screen by means of a joystick so that it stopped in a goal zone just as a moving target cursor, moving in a straight line with unpredictable speed, reached the goal zone. The relevant motion-gaps here are between hand and goal, hand and target, and target and goal. Analysis of the movement trajectories of hand and target indicated that the participants solved the task by keeping tau of the hand-goal gap coupled onto tau of the hand-target gap [i.e., they kept $\tau(X_{HG},t) = K\tau(X_{HT},t)$, for a constant, K. The equation is written as $\tau_{HG} = K\tau_{HT}$ in Fig. 1.1b].

Tau-G

The last experiment shows how intercepting a moving object such as a ball can be achieved by coupling the tau of the motion-gap between the hand and the ball onto the tau of the motion-gap between the hand and the place of interception. Information about the ball's motion tau-guides the hand. Yet what about reaching the hand out to a stationary ball or playing a note on a piano? In these self-guided movements, again there is the tau of the gap between the effector and its goal. However, there is apparently no other tau to couple onto to guide the movement. At least there is no other extrinsic tau to couple onto. Nonetheless, self-guided movements are well formed both spatially and temporally. Therefore, there must be some information guiding them. Might the tau of the effector–goal gap be coupled onto a (changing) intrinsic tau value generated in the nervous system—by, for instance, a patterned energy flow in the brain? If so, what form might the intrinsic tau take? We might expect that, during the course of evolution, intrinsic taus will have been assimilated by animals while moving in the environment. Because gravity has a ubiquitous influence on an animal's movement, there are likely to be intrinsic taus that reflect the animal's movement under gravity. One common movement is the up-and-down motion of the body during locomotion. Therefore, there might well be an intrinsic tau that corresponds to this up-and-down motion. Such was the line of thought that led me to the tau-G hypothesis.

Tau-G is a changing tau value that, at each moment, has the same value as the tau of the vertical gap to the ground of an object, such as a ball, that is launched from the ground under gravity, reaches its zenith, and then drops down to the ground again (Fig. 1.2). Thus, tau-G is generated by, and could be sensed by, a running animal during each flight phase. Therefore, it is deeply rooted in the ecology of animals.

Let us now consider what would be the consequences of using tau-G for intrinsically guiding a movement. For completeness, we consider the tau of a motion-gap being tau-coupled onto tau-G for the full duration of tau-G (i.e., from "launch" to "landing"). In general, however, coupling may commence partway through tau-G's course. As an illustration, we consider moving a golf club relative to a golf ball. Let the motion-gap between the club-head and the ball at time t be $x(t)$. If tau of the motion-gap is tau-coupled onto tau-G (τ_G), then $\tau(x,t) = K\tau_G(T_G,t)$, where K is a constant and T_G is the duration of tau-G. This equation can be solved to derive the dynamic equations for the motion-gap, $x(t)$ (Appendix 1). Figure 1.3a–f shows plots of $x(t)$ and $\dot{x}(t)$ [the rate of change of $x(t)$] for three ranges of K. (The plots are useful, for example, when eye-balling data, prior to a detailed analysis, to see whether the data might fit the tau-G hypothesis.) The three ranges of K give rise to distinct types of movement.

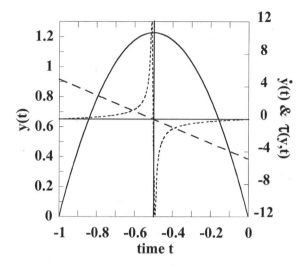

FIG. 1.2. The tau-G guide, $\tau_G(T_G,t)$. Illustrating how the equation for the guide (Appendix 1) would be generated by a ball that is launched from the ground under the gravitational acceleration of 9.81ms^{-2}, rises to its zenith, and then falls back to the ground. The ball is launched at time $t = -1\text{s}$ and lands at time $t = 0\text{s}$. Thus, the duration, T_G, of the tau-G guide is 1s. The solid line represents the height, $y(t)$, of the ball at successive times, t. $y(t)$ increases from 0m at $t = -1\text{s}$ (the launch), reaches its maximum of 1.23m at $t = -0.5\text{s}$ (the zenith), and then decreases to 0 at $t = 0\text{s}$ (the landing). The dashed line represents the vertical component of velocity of the ball, $\dot{y}(t)$. This starts with a value of 4.9ms^{-1} at $t = -1\text{s}$, decreases to zero as the ball reaches its zenith at $t = -0.5\text{s}$, and then becomes negative as the ball drops, reaching a value of -4.9ms^{-1} as it hits the ground at $t = 0\text{s}$. The curves for $y(t)$ and $\dot{y}(t)$ are calculated from Newton's equations, ignoring air resistance. The dotted line represents $\tau(y,t)$, the τ of the gap between the ball and the ground. $\tau(y,t)$ is calculated from $y(t)$ and $\dot{y}(t)$ using the formula $\tau(y,t) = y(t)/\dot{y}(t)$. Like time, t, $\tau(y,t)$ is measured in seconds. $\tau(y,t)$ starts at a value of zero as the ball is launched at $t = 0\text{s}$. It then increases steadily to positive infinity as the ball climbs to its zenith at $t = -0.5\text{s}$. Immediately thereafter, its value switches to negative infinity, and then decreases steadily to reach zero as the ball lands at $t = 0\text{s}$. The plot of $\tau(y,t)$ is the same as that of a general gravity τ_G-guide, $\tau_G(T_G,t)$, of duration $T_G = 1\text{s}$. Note that when a motion-gap, $x(t)$, is τ-coupled onto a gravity τ_G-guide through the equation $\tau(x,t) = K\tau_G(T_G,t)$ for different constants, K, the plots of $\tau(x,t)$ (Fig. 1.3g–i) have the same general shape as the plot of $\tau(y,t)$ (Fig. 1.2). The $\tau(x,t)$s are simply scaled versions of $\tau(y,t)$, the scaling factor being the coupling constant, K. The value of K has a more dramatic influence on the plots of $\dot{x}(t)$ (Fig. 1.3d–f). These vary as a function of the value of K and are quite different in shape from the plot of $\dot{y}(t)$ in Fig. 1.2 (except for the straight line plot in Fig. 1.3f, which corresponds to $K = 1$).

For all values, K, the club-head starts in contact with the ball [at $x(-T_G) = 0$]; it then recedes from the ball until it reaches the end of the backswing [at $x(-T_G/2) = -1$]; finally, it moves forward and contacts the ball [at $x(0) = 0$]. Differences between the three ranges of K occur in the vicinity of the ball [i.e., when x(t) is close to zero].

When $0 < K \leq 0.5$ (Fig. 1.3a & 1.3d), the club-head starts at rest at the ball and moves away with increasing acceleration from a zero value; it then decelerates, reverses direction at the top of the backswing, and accelerates back toward the ball; finally, it decelerates at a decreasing rate and stops at the ball. Thus, when $0 < K \leq 0.5$, the movement ends with touch contact, as when reaching for something light and small. As K increases from 0 to 0.5, the mean absolute force and power involved in moving the club-head increases (Fig. 1.3j & 1.3m) and the maximum velocity of the club-head decreases (Lee, Grealy, Pepping, & Schögler, 2004).

When $0.5 < K < 1$ (Fig. 1.3b & 1.3e), the club-head starts at rest at the ball and moves away with a high initial acceleration (infinite, in theory), which decreases to zero; the club-head then decelerates, reverses at the top of the backswing, and accelerates toward the ball; it then decelerates at an increasing rate until it reaches its maximum deceleration, which is maintained until the ball is hit. Thus, when $0.5 < K < 1$, the movement ends with hard contact with the ball, with the club-head decelerating. The mean absolute force and power involved in moving the club-head are both lowered by increasing K (Fig. 1.3k & 1.3n). The velocity at contact is raised by increasing K (for any given maximum deceleration) or decreasing maximum deceleration (for any given K), and the maximum velocity of the club-head decreases as K increases from 0.5 to 0.66 and then increases as K increases further (Lee, Grealy, et al., 2004).

When $K = 1$, the club-head starts moving away from the ball at speed, decelerates at a decreasing rate (at constant rate when $K = 1$), reverses at the top of the backswing, accelerates at an increasing rate (at constant rate when $K = 1$) until it reaches its maximum acceleration, and finally hits the ball at high velocity. Thus, when $K = 1$, the movement ends with hard contact with the ball, with the club-head accelerating. The mean absolute force and power involved in moving the club-head are both raised by increasing K (Fig. 1.3l, 1.3o). The velocity at contact and the maximum velocity of the club-head are the same when $K = 1$; they are each raised by increasing K, for any given maximum acceleration, or by increasing maximum acceleration, for any given K (Lee, Grealy, et al., 2004).

The duration (T_G) of tau-G and the amplitude of the movement also affect the dynamics of the club-head. (Duration and amplitude were assumed constant earlier.) As duration, T_G, decreases and/or movement amplitude increases, velocity at contact increases, as do absolute force and power involved in moving the club-head (Lee, Grealy, et al., 2004).

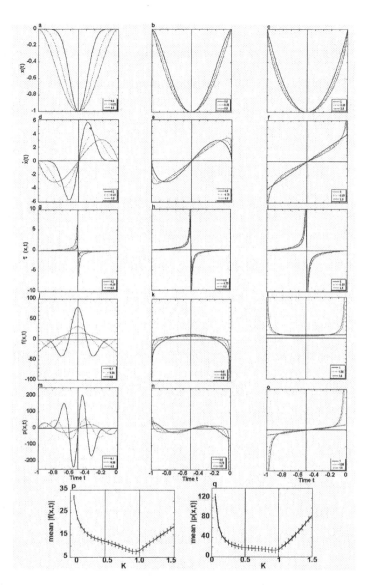

FIG. 1.3. The dynamics of motion-gaps generated by coupling onto a tau-G guide. Three ranges of value of the constant K in the coupling equation $\tau(x,t) = K\tau_G(T_G,t)$ are illustrated. Col. 1: $0 < K \leq 0.5$. Col. 2: $0.5 < K < 1$. Col. 3: $1 \leq K$. At time t, $x(t)$ = size of the motion-gap (m), $\dot{x}(t)$ = the rate of change of the size of the motion-gap (ms^{-1}), $\tau(x,t) = \tau$ of the motion-gap (s). $|f(x,t)|$ (N) is the absolute force, and $|p(x,t)|$ (W) is the absolute power required to move a mass of 1kg and generate the motion-gap. The equations generating the curves are given in Appendix 1. The bottom two plots (p, q) show how the mean absolute force (N) and power (W) required to move a unit mass and generate the motion-gap varies as a function of K. Standard deviation bars are shown.

In summary, if the tau of the motion-gap between an effector and its goal is tau-coupled onto an intrinsic tau-G, the time courses of the velocity, force, and power of the movement, and the velocity of contact at the end of the movement, are all determined by the values of three parameters: the coupling constant (K), the duration of tau-G, and the amplitude of the movement.

Tau-g

An earlier hypothesis about intrinsic guidance of movement from rest postulated that the tau of the motion-gap is tau-coupled onto an intrinsic tau, designated τ_g (Lee, 1998). τ_g corresponds in value to the tau of the motion-gap to a goal of an object accelerating at a constant rate from rest to a goal. Thus, a τ_g corresponds to the second half of a tau-G. Whereas tau-G is generated by both the upward and downward motion of a ball under gravity (Appendix 1), τ_g is generated by just the downward motion. Thus, the τ_g hypothesis is but a special case of the more general tau-G hypothesis. The formula for τ_g is the same as for tau-G (Eq. 1, Appendix 1) except that τ_g only extends over the second half of a tau-G. This means that experiments supporting the τ_g hypothesis also support the tau-G hypothesis. There are a number of such supportive experiments spanning a wide range of activities (Lee, 1998). They indicate, for example, that newborn babies control their suction when feeding from a bottle and golfers control their swing when putting in a similar way by using an intrinsic τ_g or tau-G (Craig & Lee, 1999; Craig et al., 2000).

Tau-Dot

The earliest hypothesis about the use of tau in controlling the closure of a motion-gap was formulated in the context of braking a vehicle to stop at an obstacle (Lee, 1976). The hypothesis is that, during the deceleration phase to an obstacle, the time derivative of the tau of the motion-gap to the obstacle (tau-dot or $\dot{\tau}$) is kept equal to a constant, k. If k is less than or equal to 0.5, this would ensure stopping at the obstacle. Unlike the τ_g hypothesis, the tau-dot hypothesis is not a special case of the tau-G hypothesis. However, it turns out that the two hypotheses make numerically rather similar predictions about the final deceleration phase of a movement to the goal, which is the only phase to which the tau-dot hypothesis applies. Consequently, evidence for the tau-dot hypothesis is also evidence for the tau-G hypothesis. Such evidence spans a wide range of behaviors, including hummingbirds docking on a feeder (Lee, Reddish, &

Rand, 1991), trampolinists somersaulting (Lee, Young, & Rewt, 1992), and drivers braking in a simulator (Yilmaz & Warren, 1995).

Perceiving Tau

Tau-coupling requires perceiving tau: tau is perceptible through tau-coupling. Let me elaborate on this interesting duality. It would be very useful for an evolving organism. For an animal to tau-couple the tau of a motion-gap onto the tau of another motion-gap, or onto a tau-G, it needs to perceive the tau of the motion-gap. Fortunately for the animal, there are naturally occurring tau-couplings that make the perception of tau a relatively easy matter. This is because power laws abound in nature and there is a simple theorem relating power laws and tau-couplings (Lee et al., 1992). For example, suppose we have a motion-gap, $Z(t)$, between a person and a frontal plane containing a tree of height, D (see Fig. 1.4a, bottom). The sensory gap, $r(t)$, corresponds to this physical gap, $Z(t)$. As $Z(t)$ shrinks, $r(t)$ expands. In fact simple geometry reveals that $r(t)$ is a power function of $Z(t)$—namely, $r(t) = DZ(t)^{-1}$. The final step, involving simple calculus, shows that if $r(t) = DZ(t)^{-1}$, then $\tau(Z,t) = -\tau(r,t)$. Thus, the physical tau, $\tau(Z,t)$, is perceptible through the sensory tau, $\tau(r,t)$. Figure 1.4b (and caption) also shows how the tau of a motion-gap in a frontal plane is perceptible through a sensory tau by virtue of the taus being coupled. The general power-law, tau-coupling theorem is this. If a sensory gap, $r(t)$, corresponds to a motion-gap, $Z(t)$, and $r(t) = CZ(t)^{\alpha}$ for constants C and α, then $\tau(Z,t)$ and $\tau(r,t)$ are tau-coupled by the equation $\tau(Z,t) = \alpha\tau(r,t)$. Note that the exponent, α, in the power law relation, $r = CZ^{\alpha}$, becomes the coupling constant, the multiplier in the tau-coupling equation, $\tau(Z,t) = \alpha\tau(r,t)$.

In summary, whenever there is a sensory variable, $r(t)$, that is a power function of a motion gap, $Z(t)$, with exponent, α, the tau of the motion-gap, $\tau(Z,t)$, is, in principle, directly perceptible from the tau of the sensory variable, $\tau(r,t)$, because $\tau(Z,t) = \alpha\tau(r,t)$. Examples of how tau of a motion-gap could be perceived via tau-coupling in echolocation, electrolocation, and other sensory modalities are given in Lee (1998). Examples of experiments showing that tau of a motion-gap can be directly perceived visually from the planar projection of the motion-gap—and therefore without information about the size or rate of change of size of the motion-gap—are given in Yilmaz and Warren (1995) and Lee et al. (2001).

Distance From Tau and Direction

Tau is not everything by way of information needed by an animal to get around in the world, but it is almost everything. Color apart, the other information required is directional information. An animal needs to be able

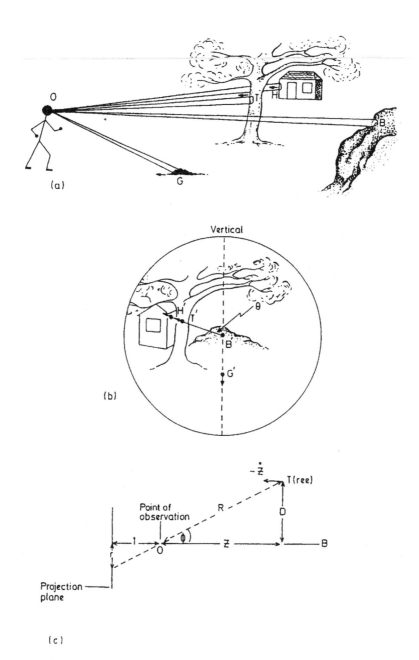

(a)

Vertical

(b)

Point of
observation

Projection
plane

(c)

FIG. 1.4. *(Continued)*

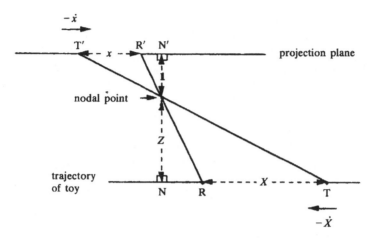

FIG. 1.4.   How the tau of a motion-gap is specified optically through tau-coupling. (a) Forward relative linear movement of point of observation. Upper diagram (a): the optic flow field portrayed as a bundle of narrow optic cones each with its apex at the eye and its base on a surface texture element in the environment. As the eye moves forward, the cones fan out. Middle diagram (b): the optic flow field portrayed as the intercept of the bundle of optic cones with a projection plane in front of the eye and perpendicular to the line of locomotion. Bottom diagram (c): A slice through the optic cone bundle containing the line of locomotion, OB, and the line, OT, to the texture element on the tree. A projection plane perpendicular to the locomotor line is added at unit distance behind O, onto which the image of T is projected, at distance r from the image of O. Tau of the motion-gap $Z(t)$, $\tau(Z,t)$, is specified by $\tau(r,t)$ through the coupling equation $\tau(Z,t) = -\tau(r,t)$. [Proof. From similar triangles, $Z(t)/D = 1/r(t)$. Differentiating with respect to time, t, $(dZ(t)/dt)/D = -(dr(t)/dt)/r(t)^2$. Eliminating D from the two equations, $Z(t)/(dZ(t)/dt) = -r(t)/(dr(t)/dt)$, i.e., $\tau(Z,t) = -\tau(r,t)$.] (b) Sideways relative linear movement of point of observation. $x(t)$ is the projection of the motion-gap $X(t)$. From similar triangles, $X(t)/Z = x(t)/1$. Hence $\tau(X,t) = \tau(x,t)$.

to perceive the direction in which something lies relative to the body to be able to move toward it. Directional information is available visually by virtue of the spatial layout of the retina, acoustically through the time and intensity differences at the ears and the multiple sound reflections in the pinnae, and haptically through the articular receptors in the joints muscles and skin.

Yet surely, you may ask, doesn't an animal also need distance information—about the distance of a surface, the size of an object, its speed of movement, and so on—to judge how hard to thrust to jump over a ditch, how wide a grasp is required to pick something up, or how hard a cross-ball needs to be hit to deflect it into the net? It is true that distance information is needed, but an animal does not require a different form of sensory information for this. Information about tau and direction are sufficient

(Lee, 1980; von Hofsten & Lee, 1994). The basic argument is this. Distance information is necessarily relative. There is no such thing as absolute distance. For distance information about the environment to be useful to an animal (whether in perceiving distance, size, or speed), it has to be scaled relative to the body in some way. This means that perceiving body-scaled distance (e.g., of a surface) requires picking up information about two relative distances: the objective-distance of the surface and a bodily-distance, such as eye-height or stride-length. The ratio of the relative objective-distance to the relative bodily-distance gives the body-scaled distance. Information about tau and direction is sufficient for perceiving both the relative objective-distance and the relative bodily-distance. Thus, body-scaled distance is derivable from information about tau and direction.

Synergic Tau-G Guidance

Suppose you are guiding your gaze toward an object. In general, this involves rotating your eyes in your head and rotating your head on your shoulders, as well as twisting your trunk and maybe shifting your feet. The question is: How do you manage to accurately guide your gaze to the target when it involves so many component movements? The same basic question as to how component movements are organized into a synergy to guide an effector to a goal applies to virtually all movements. This central question has never been satisfactorily answered, however. I propose an answer, or partial answer, by applying General τ Theory to the problem.

According to General τ Theory, the focal aspect in shifting gaze, for example, is tau-G guiding the closure of the angular gap between the current direction of gaze and the direction of the object. This tau-G guidance of gaze is achieved through the combined movements of eyes, head, and so on. However, each of these components also has its own agenda to follow: it has to abide by particular bodily constraints. The eyes and head, for instance, have to be turned in such a way that the muscles and joints are not strained by too abrupt accelerations or decelerations. My suggestion is that this is achieved by independently tau-G guiding the movement of each component (eye, head, etc.) to a goal position lying within the bodily constraints while also tau-G guiding their combination (gaze) to its goal. I refer to this as the tau-G synergy hypothesis. In the tau-G synergy, the movements of the eyes-in-head, head-on-shoulders, and so on may or may not be tau-coupled to the gaze movement or to each other, and the movements may or may not occur over exactly the same time period. What defines a tau-G synergy is simply that all the movements involved in the synergy are tau-G guided. Later, I present evidence in support of the tau-G synergy hypothesis when discussing guidance of gaze. However, before going on to the next section, I should add a caveat. I am not proposing that the component movements that move a bodily effector are invariably accurately tau-G guided any more than the effector is accurately tau-G guided in every instance. Biological control is not perfect, although it can be honed with practice. Even then errors can occur, as in the famous case of the baseball pitcher who snapped his arm by hurling too hard. Indeed it seems likely that many sports injuries are due to errors in tau-G guiding component movements within their bodily constraints.

Stabilizing With a Tau-G Guide

Let us now consider the common problem in movement control of stabilizing an effector within a goal zone. By this I mean keeping the effector within the boundaries of the goal zone. For instance, the effector may be your gaze and the goal zone a moving object that you are inspecting, the effector may be your vehicle and the goal zone the traffic lane you are driving along, or the effector may be the vertical projection of your center of gravity and the goal zone your base of support when you are trying to stand still. Whatever the effector, stabilizing it within a goal zone could be achieved by repeatedly tau-G guiding the gap, X, between the boundary of the effector and the boundary of the goal zone [such that $\tau(X,t) = K\tau_G(T_G,t)$, for $0 < K < 1$], with the tau-G guidance including some bounceback. This would cause the effector to stop momentarily within the goal zone and then reverse direction. At this point, another tau-G would guide it to another momentary stop within the goal zone, followed by reversal, and so on. Later I present evidence for this with regard to stabilizing gaze on a moving object.

Tau-G Guidance in Developing Skill

Skilled movement requires controlling the closure of a set of motion-gaps in a concerted manner. My hypothesis is that this is attained by coupling the taus of the motion-gaps onto the taus of other motion-gaps and onto tau-G guides. Thus, skilled movement comprises a balanced ensemble of tau-couplings. Controlling a tau-coupling requires constantly determining the power that needs to be pumped to the muscles to regulate the closure of the motion-gaps involved in the tau-coupling. For example, if you follow an object with your eyes, you not only need to sense the motiongap between your gaze and the target, you also need to know how to adjust the power to your muscles to move your gaze back onto the target when it wanders off. Thus, calibrating the process of regulating power to the muscles on the basis of prospective sensory information about the taus of motion-gaps is an essential aspect of learning to move skillfully. Because of changing dynamical circumstances (growth, joint stiffness, injury, wearing new spectacles, etc.), the calibration needs to be constantly adjusted. Recalibration experiments (e.g., Hay & Pick, 1966; Pick et al., 1999; Rieser et al., 1995) indicate that calibration takes place in both sensory information pick-up and the regulation of power to the muscles.

Tau Within and Without

I conclude this introduction with a summary of some of the main points of General Tau Theory and then briefly discuss how tau might be embodied in the nervous system. As an illustration, consider someone playing a tune from memory on the piano. This clearly involves both intrinsic and sensory guidance (Fig. 1.5). According to General Tau Theory, controlling the finger movements to play expressively requires guiding the closure of the motion-gaps between the fingers and keys using information about the tau of the motion-gaps. This tau information is picked up by the perceptual systems by detecting corresponding taus in the patterns of sensory input to the eyes and/or ears and/or skin. The perceptual systems translate this tau information into neural tau information in the nervous system. Using the principle of tau-coupling, whereby one tau is kept proportional to another, this tau information, together with intrinsically generated neural tau information in the form of tau-G guiding functions, directs the muscles to change the taus of motion-gaps in the desired way.

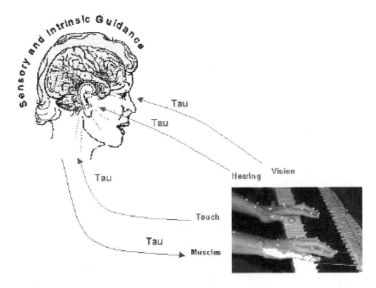

FIG. 1.5. Tau information flowing around a perceptuomotor cycle and coupling with intrinsically generated tau information.

These changes are detected by the perceptual systems and provide feedback, and so the cycle continues.

What form does tau information take in the nervous system? It must be some function of the rate of flow of electrical energy in ensembles of neurons. I refer to this rate of flow of energy as *neural power*. (In the mammalian central nervous system, neural power flows as trains of homogeneous electrical pulses [spike trains] and is often referred to as *neural spike-rate*. I think the term *neural power* is better because it is more general and can be applied to any form of flow of information as electricity within an animal, whether continuous or discontinuous.) However, tau cannot correspond to neural power as such because the dimensions do not match—tau is measured in time units, whereas neural power is measured in power units. However, tau could be specified neurally by the *tau* of the neural power (measured relative to a base level) flowing through ensembles of neurons in the brain. We tested this hypothesis by analyzing neural power data collected from monkey motor cortex and parietal cortex area 5 during a reaching experiment (Lee, Pepping, Lee, & Georgopoulos, 2004). We found that the tau of the motion-gap between the monkey's hand and the target stayed in constant proportion to the tau of neural power in motor cortex and parietal cortex. The tau in motor cortex preceded the motion-gap tau by a few milliseconds, whereas the tau in parietal cortex followed the movement by a few milliseconds. This indicates that the tau of neural power in the motor cortex prescribed the hand movement, whereas the tau of neural power in the parietal cortext monitored it. The tau of the motion-gap and the taus of neural power in motor and parietal cortex each stayed in constant proportion with a tau-G guide, suggesting that the tau-G guide was the underlying base of the movement.

TAU IN DEVELOPMENT

In the remainder of this chapter, I consider how General Tau Theory might help in understanding the development of some basic skills—feeding, breathing, vocalizing, guiding the head and gaze, guiding the hand, and guiding the feet when walking and running. For the most part, each section starts with an analysis of adult skill and moves on to consider how the developing child progresses toward the adult level.

Feeding, Breathing, and Vocalizing

Fueling the body is essential for movement and involves skilled movement. Therefore, it is not surprising that most skilled actions of young babies center around the mouth and nose. Infants start their life outside the womb with a controlled gusty outflow of air with which they announce their needs. Shortly later they are again busy with their mouths, this time regulating the inflow of milk. Crying and sucking are sophisticated skills, and babies practice them a lot. They have pretty good command of these skills from the start, in contrast to their ability to pick up objects. This makes sense, of course, because they have to cry and suck to get food. Yet how do they do it?

Tau-G Guidance of Nutritive Sucking

Let us start with sucking. Sucking milk from a breast or bottle basically requires creating suction pressure in the mouth so that the milk is drawn in. This involves a number of coordinated movements in and around the mouth (Bu'Lock et al., 1990). The lips close tightly around the nipple to form an airtight seal. The jaw lowers and the tongue, which is cradling the nipple, moves forward in the mouth and hollows in the middle. The action results in steadily increasing the size of the oral cavity and hence progressively increasing the suction. When an adequate level of suction has been reached and milk is drawn into the mouth, the suction is then steadily lowered by the reverse action of raising the jaw, flattening the tongue, and moving it back in the mouth. This movement also draws the tongue along the nipple and squeezes further milk from it. Not only is the whole action a wonder of coordination, but newborn babies can even regulate the degree and duration of their sucks to fit with naturally occurring changes in the flow rate and fat composition of the milk (Mathew, 1991; Woolridge et al., 1980).

If you think this sounds as sophisticated as an adult skill such as reaching, you would be right. Certainly the root elements are there. Both baby and adult are controlling motion-gaps by coordinating a number of muscles and joints. The baby when sucking is controlling a pressure motion-gap, and the adult when reaching is controlling a distance motion-gap. Yet does it go further than that? Do babies intrinsically tau-guide their sucking movements in the same way as adults tau-guide their reaches (Lee, Craig, & Grealy, 1999)? A recent study indicates that indeed they do (Craig & Lee, 1999). The changing suction was recorded in the mouths of full-term newborns between the ages of 28 and 82 hours while they were bottle-feeding. The hypothesis, illustrated in Fig. 1.6a, was that the baby would continually sense, τ_p, the tau of the pressure gap between the intra-oral suction and its end value, and would continually adjust its sucking pressure so as to keep τ_p coupled to an intrinsic tau-G guide (symbolized as τ_g in Fig. 1.6) by maintaining the relation $\tau_p = k\tau_g$ for a constant, k. To test the hypothesis, first the pressure and its time derivative, rate of closure of pressure gap, were plotted against time. Figure 1.6b, left panel, shows typical plots for a full-term infant. From these data, τ_p was calculated at each time point, for both in-

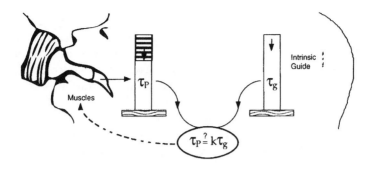

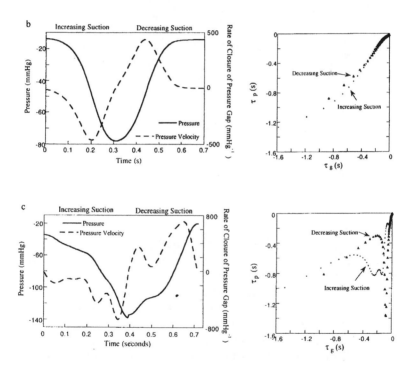

FIG. 1.6.   Tau-G guidance of nutritive sucking in term and pre-term infants. (a) Diagram of the hypothesis; see text for details. (b) Full-term infant. Left: typical plots of intra-oral pressure (solid line) and its time derivative (broken line) during increasing suction (decreasing pressure) followed by decreasing suction (increasing pressure). Right: corresponding plots, for both increasing and decreasing suction, of τ_p (tau of the gap between the intra-oral pressure and its end value) against the hypothesized intrinsic tau-G guide (symbolized as τ_g in the plot). (c) Similar plots as in (b), but for a pre-term infant who showed weak coupling between τ_p and tau-G. See text for more details. From Craig, Grealy, and Lee (2000).

23

creasing and decreasing suction, using the formula: τ_p = (pressure minus end pressure)/(rate of closure of pressure gap). Then τ_p was plotted against τ_g (Fig. 1.6b, right panel) using the formula for τ_G given in Appendix 1, Equation 1. Finally a linear regression analysis was run on the plot to determine the strength of the coupling between τ_p and τ_g (measured by the r^2 value of the regression, which equals the proportion of variance accounted for by the linear model) and to estimate the value of the constant, k, in the coupling equation $\tau_p = k\tau_g$ (measured by the slope of the regression). The mean r^2 values of 12 sucks for each of 12 full-term infants was greater than 0.95 (except for one extraneous value), indicating that the tau of suction was strongly coupled onto a tau-G guide.

Not all babies can suck so well, however. In a further study, the sucking performance of preterm infants born at low gestation and/or birthweight was tau-G analyzed in a similar way over a 4-week period (Craig, Grealy, & Lee, 2000). Figure 1.6c gives an example of the irregular sucking that was symptomatic of poor coupling between tau of suction (τ_p) and tau-G (τ_g). After 4 weeks of feeding experience, only two of the six preterm infants had reached the same strength of coupling between tau of suction and tau-G in the sucking phase as the full-term infants had within 2 days of birth. Furthermore, the preterm infants who showed the most disability in sucking also fared less well in physiotherapy tests conducted (blind) around 7 months corrected age. Thus, tau-G assessment of sucking could be a useful item in the neurological examination of the preterm infant.

Tau-G Guidance of Breathing

Babies also have to coordinate their breathing with their sucking. In another recent study (Craig, Lee, Freer, & Laing, 1999), it was found that term babies breathe regularly during the pauses between sucking, indicating good coordination. However, preterm infants with bronchopulmonary dysplasia, who have difficulty in maintaining adequate levels of oxygenation of the blood during rest, had significantly less regular breathing and shorter duration breaths in the pauses during feeding. This indicates poor control of movement of the respiratory musculature, which may be an important contributing factor in bronchopulmonary dysplasia. It has not been tested whether the normal breathing of term babies is tau-G guided. It seems likely that it is, given the wide range of actions that are. However, the study needs to be done using, for example, an instrumented band around the chest to measure the changes in the circumference of the chest. If it does turn out that healthy infants tau-G guide their breathing, then measuring the degree of tau-G guidance in breathing could be a useful diagnostic tool that could provide useful information for devising therapies.

Tau-G Guidance in Vocalizing

So far the only study of tau-G guidance in vocalizing has been in adults singing a scale and some other musical intervals (Fraenkel, 2001). The singing was legato, and so there was a smooth transition in pitch from one note to the next. Figure 1.7 (top) shows pitch plotted against time for a fe-

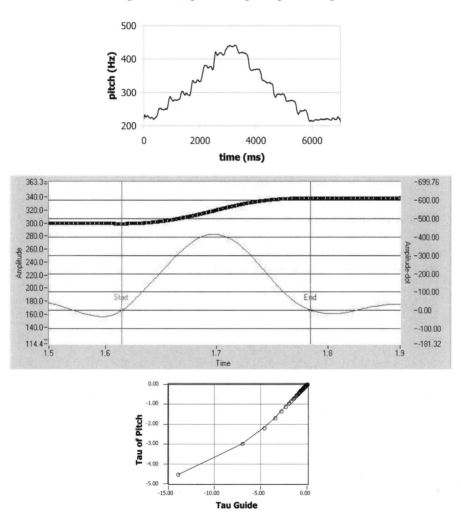

FIG. 1.7. Tau-G guidance in singing a scale legato. Top: How pitch varied with time as a female singer sang a major scale legato. Middle: A pitch-change between two notes: The top line represents pitch, and the lower line represents the rate of change of pitch. The start and endpoints of the movement are indicated. Bottom: An example plot of tau of pitch against a tau-G guide. Data points are 1 ms apart. From Fraenkel (2001).

male singer singing a major scale legato. It looks like a staircase, with the steps corresponding to the notes of the scale. Note that each main step in pitch is usually followed by some vibrato on the goal note. Figure 1.7 (middle) shows an example of how pitch and its time derivative changed as the singer moved from one note to the next. The curves are similar to those for babies sucking (Fig. 1.6). The degree to which a movement in pitch from one note to the next was tau-G guided was determined as follows. First, the main note-to-note movement was demarcated by the times when the rate of change of pitch just exceeded zero. These times are indicated by the start and end lines in Fig. 1.7 (middle). Second, the tau of pitch was calculated as the tau of the gap between pitch and its value at the end of the movement. Third, tau of pitch, τ_p, was plotted against the hypothesized tau-G guide (symbolized as τ_g in Fig. 1.7) for the movement, which was calculated using the formula given in Appendix 1, Equation 1. An example of such a plot is shown in Fig. 1.7 (bottom). Finally, the plot was subjected to a recursive linear regression analysis that removes the leftmost points in the plot one by one until the r^2 of the regression, which measures the percentage of variance accounted for by the hypothesis $\tau_p = K\tau_g$, for constant K, exceeds a criterion level. The criterion was set at 0.98 in the singing study. The number of points remaining, divided by the total number in the movement, measures the percentage of the movement during which intrinsic tau-G guidance is in evidence. The slope of the regression at this point is taken as the measure of K. The mean (SD) of the measures for two singers was: r^2 = 0.983, 0.982; % = 64, 71; K = 0.482, 0.495. Thus, there was strong evidence for intrinsic tau-G guidance of pitch during the last two thirds of the movement in both singers. Furthermore, their K values were similar and such that they landed gently on the next note while keeping mean force and power low.

Do infants tau-G guide the pitch, timbre, or loudness of their voice when crying, cooing, babbling, and so on? Do adults do likewise in speaking? We do not know because the experiments have not yet been run. This whole area needs to be explored. It could help us understand better how vocalizations are produced, and this could be of value in diagnosis and treatment.

GUIDING HEAD, EYE, AND GAZE

This is of vital importance for an animal to pick up accurate information through vision, hearing, and smell about objects and events and about the movement of the animal relative to the environment. Without this ability, perceptual guidance of bodily movement would be severely compromised. In a series of elegant experiments reported in this volume, von

Hofsten and Rosander (1997) showed how an infant develops the ability to coordinate the movements of eyes-in-head and head-on-body to keep gaze on a moving target. Here I would like to develop this theme by taking a general look at head and gaze control.

Let us start with a rural scene. One day as you walk through the woods with your dog, you hear a twig snap behind you in the undergrowth. You both turn around to the source of the sound to see what it is. Out of the corner of your eye, you catch sight of something moving. You swing your gaze after it and see a squirrel bounding away. Your dog, of course, is off like a shot after the squirrel, leaping over branches in hot pursuit, but the squirrel easily avoids capture by running up a tree trunk.

This commonplace scenario illustrates how the head is guided for the purpose of perception. When you hear the snapping twig, you and your dog both turn around to point your heads at the sound source to pick up more information about the event through vision, hearing, and smell (particularly for your dog). You perceive the direction of the sound relative to the head, then use this information, together with online perceptual information about the head when it is rotating, to guide it to point it at the goal. The online information about the rotation of the head relative to the environment is available through vision (by seeing how the head is rotating relative to the environment), through articular proprioception (by feeling how the head is turning relative to the ground), and through the vestibular system (by sensing the acceleration of the head relative to the inertial environment). However, if firm contact with the ground is not maintained while turning (as would apply, e.g., to fish or birds in currents), then vision and the vestibular system would be the only sources of online information for controlling the movement of the head.

While your head and body are still turning, you catch sight of the squirrel. You therefore swivel your eyes in your head to latch your gaze onto it using visual information. You now need to keep you gaze on the squirrel; because it and your head are moving, you have to keep your eyes moving in a controlled way in your head, again using visual information. You may also have to modify your initial planned movement of your head to cope with the emerging situation. Meanwhile your dog has got off to a flying start and you turn your gaze to it. You notice how steadily it moves its head over the ground, keeping it coupled onto the locomotor optic flow field (Fig. 1.4). This is in contrast to the rest of its body, which is engaged in varied vigorous movements to propel it over the rough ground. Also its head is now about to be used as an instrument of action. Before it can close its jaws, the squirrel escapes. (Moving the head with precision as an effector is not, of course, the prerogative of aggressive acts. Birds do it when they are feeding their young, and we do it when eating and kissing.)

Tau-G Guidance of Head, Eye, and Gaze

If we want to explain how the gaze (or head) is guided to a target and kept on the target, we need an answer that is applicable to the general kind of situation just described. This is not only because that is of interest for its own sake, but also because in more circumscribed conditions the same guidance procedures are likely to be used. Otherwise, as conditions changed, the procedure would constantly have to change. To reiterate, the general situation in shifting gaze is when the target object is moving in the world, the eyes are turning in the head, the head is turning on the body, and the body is turning and translating relative to the world.

The presiding motion in this plethora of movement is the closing of the gap between gaze line and the target. The synergic motions of eyes-in-head, head-on-body, and so on are largely incidental, in the sense that they can be executed in a variety of combinations to achieve the same end of guiding gaze to the target and holding it there. However, this does not mean that the synergic motions of eyes-in-head, head-on-body, and so on are not guided. Each has to be guided to stay within body constraints. Earlier in this chapter, I suggested a hypothesis on synergic tau-G guidance of gaze. According to the hypothesis, gaze is tau-G guided to the target, while the synergists are each independently tau-G guided to goal positions within bodily constraints in general over different time intervals. If the hypothesis is correct, the following tau-couplings are predicted: $\tau(X_{G/T},t) = K_{G/T}\tau_G(T_{G_{G/T}},t)$ for gaze/target, $\tau(X_{E/H},t) = K_{E/H}\tau_G(T_{G_{E/H}},t)$ for eye/head, and $\tau(X_{H/B},t) = K_{H/B}\tau_G(T_{G_{H/B}},t)$ for head/body. The durations $T_{G_{G/T}}$, $T_{G_{E/H}}$, and $T_{G_{H/B}}$ may be different.

The hypothesis was tested on adults. The participant started a trial by turning their head and eyes to look at a fixation point over their left or right shoulder. Then at a signal they swung their gaze forward to look at an object that was moving on a horizontal track at head height in their frontoparallel plane (Fig. 1.8, top). The bottom two panels in Fig. 1.8 show typical plots for one participant of the gaze/target, eye/head, and head/world angles and angular velocities. The initial (principal) movements of gaze, eye, and head were taken to start when the velocity exceeded 5% of its peak value on the particular movement and to end just before the velocity dropped to 5% of its peak velocity. The start and endpoints are marked G_0, E_0, H_0, and G_1, E_1, H_1, respectively, in the bottom panel of Fig. 1.8. The three movements were tau-G analyzed for 10 trials in the way described earlier for singing. This gave three measures for each movement: (a) the percentage of the movement that was tau-G guided to the criterion of $r^2 \geq 0.95$, (b) the value of r^2, and (c) the regression slope, $\hat{K}$, which estimates the K value in the tau-coupling equation. The initial (principal) movements of gaze/target, eye/head, and head/world were all strongly tau-G guided (mean % = 99%, mean r^2 = 0.976). The $\hat{K}$ values were quite

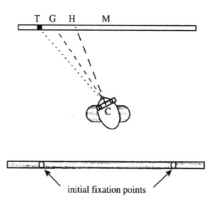

initial fixation points

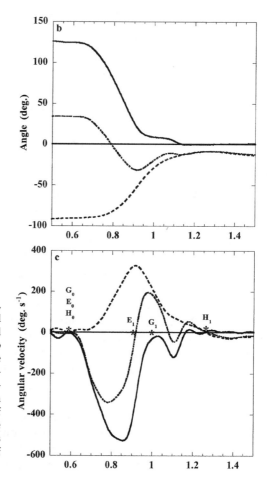

FIG. 1.8. Tau-G guidance of gaze, eye, and head. (a) Experimental setup. (b) Plots, from a typical trial, of gaze direction relative to target direction (solid line), eye direction relative to head direction (dotted line), and head direction relative to world (broken line). (c) The time derivatives of the plots in (b). G_0, E_0, H_0 mark the starts and G_1, E_1, H_1 mark the ends of the principal movements of gaze, eye, and head.

similar: 0.53 ± 0.08, 0.58 ± 0.05, and 0.49 ± 0.11 for gaze/target, eye/head, and head/world, respectively. The values indicate low force and power in the movements. The tau-G guides were not the same, however. They started at slightly different times (the eye/head guide started 7 ± 5ms before the gaze/target guide and 43 ± 21ms before the head/world guide), and their durations were largely different (331 ± 26ms for the gaze/target tau-G guide, 274 ± 22ms for the eye/head guide, and 535 ± 59ms for the head/world guide).

Each initial (principal) movement of gaze/target, eye/head, and head/world was followed by a series of stabilizing movements (Fig. 1.8). The first stabilizing movements were tau-G analyzed in the same way as the principal movements that preceded them. Each stabilizing movement was strongly tau-G guided (mean % = 96%, mean $r^2 = 0.974$). The range of $\hat{K}$ values was slightly broader than for the principal movement—0.602 ± 0.258, 0.400 ± 0.162, and 0.581 ± 0.209 for gaze/target, eye/head, and head/world, respectively—but again all indicate low force and power in the movement. As with the principal movements, the tau-G guides for the stabilizing movements started at different times and were of different durations (89 ± 26ms for the gaze/target, 214 ± 51ms for the eye/head, and 308 ± 150ms for the head/world). These results thus support the hypothesis, described earlier, that tau-G guidance is used in stabilizing on a target.

Development of Tau-G Guidance of Head, Eye, and Gaze

This has not yet been studied. It needs to be. For example, it would be valuable to analyze, in terms of the tau-G guide hypothesis, the movements of gaze, eye, and head when shifting gaze to a moving target, as in the prior experiment, and when tracking (stabilizing on) a moving object (von Hofsten, chap. 2, this volume). This could provide important information about the development of a vital skill. The information gained could be used diagnostically to pinpoint problem areas and suggest possible ways to aid development.

One important aspect of the development of tau-G guidance of gaze is mastering the gaze synergy. Guiding gaze to a target while independently guiding the eye in the head and the head on the body, each with respect to its own movement boundaries, must pose quite a problem for a young baby particularly because the head is relatively so massive. A strategy that babies appear to adopt is stabilizing gaze mainly by moving the head. This would mean that the eyes moved less in the head and so the problem of guiding them with respect to bodily constraints would be reduced. Therefore, the gaze synergy would be simplified. Evidence for the increasing use of head movement comes from a longitudinal study of 11- to 29-week-old infants who (a) visually tracked a toy moving in an arc in front of them, and (b) stabilized gaze on the toy when it was stationary and they were rotated to and fro (Daniel & Lee, 1990). It was found that the proportion of the gaze rotation relative to the body that was due to head movement increased from around 60% to around 90% from 11 to 17 weeks of age and then stayed about constant until 29 weeks of age. By contrast, adults in the same experiment had a head/gaze ratio of about 60%. von Hofsten and Rosander (1997) found a similar developmental trend in increased head movement between 3 and 4 months of age.

GUIDING THE HAND

The hand is a versatile organ and can be guided in numerous ways, some of which are basic and develop naturally, such as reaching and grasping, whereas others are learned, such as writing and playing a musical instrument. Here I concentrate on some basic skills. They contribute to the foundation on which learned movements are built.

Tau-G Guidance of the Hand to an External Goal

I start with an experiment that was designed to test the tau-G guide hypothesis. Adults were asked to perform three reaching tasks that involved moving the tip of a pointer horizontally within a 9 cm zone to a target point on a table at the edge of the zone (Lee, Grealy, et al., 2004). The tasks were designed to test three aspects of the hypothesis: (a) forward and stop—start within the zone, move the tip of the pointer to the target, and stop at it; (b) retreat, forward, and stop—start at the target, move away from it, stop within the zone, immediately reverse direction back to the target, and stop at it; and (c) retreat, forward, and bounce back—as task (b), but bounce back from the target before stopping within the zone. The participants performed each task repetitively for 30 seconds. The motion of the tip of the pointer was recorded at 300 Hz by a Selspot motion-capture system. The participant stood at the side of the table while performing the tasks. Thus, the reaching movements involved movements of joints and muscles throughout the body, as do most everyday reaching movements.

Figure 1.9, rows 1 to 3 (panels a–i), shows how the gap between the pointer tip and its stopping point, $r(t)$, the time derivative of the gap, $\dot{r}(t)$, and the tau of the gap, $\tau(r,t)$ [$= r(t)/\dot{r}(t)$], changed over time during the three types of movement. The data are for one of the six participants. The other participants' results were similar. It can be seen that the graphs in Fig. 1.9 are similar to the latter sections of the theoretical graphs of $x(t)$, $\dot{x}(t)$, and $\tau(x,t)$ in Figs. 1.3a, 1.3d, and 1.3g. Thus, coupling of $\tau(r,t)$ onto a

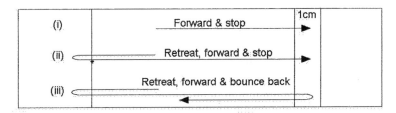

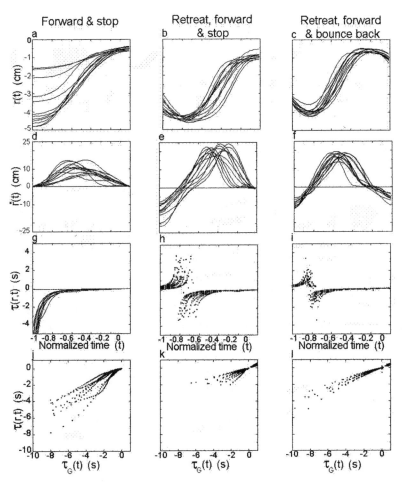

FIG. 1.9. Test of the tau-G guide hypothesis on three reaching tasks with a pointer. The tasks are labeled at the tops of the columns. Results are for one participant over 12 trials. (a–c) Plots of gap between pointer tip and goal position. (d–f) Time derivatives (velocities) of the gaps. (g–i) Taus of the gaps between the pointer tip and its end position. (j–l) Plots of the taus of the gaps against tau-G guides.

tau-G guide is indicated. To test the hypothesis, we plotted each empirical $\tau(r,t)$ against its tau-G guide (computed from Eq. 1, Appendix 1) from the start to the end of the movement. For the movements involving initially retreating from the goal, the start was taken to be when the velocity of retreat reached its peak value. For the bounce-back movement, the end was taken to be when the bounce-back velocity reached its peak. Sample plots are given in Figs. 1.9j, 1.9k, and 1.9l. From the plots we calculated the linear regression coefficients, r^2 and $\hat{K}$. r^2 is the proportion of variance accounted for by the tau-coupling model, $\tau(r,t) = K\tau_G(T_G,t)$, and measures the strength of the tau-coupling. We found the r^2 were high (overall mean 0.97) for all three reaching movements—forward and stop; retreat, forward, and stop; and retreat, forward, and bounce back. This supports the hypothesis that the movements were guided by coupling the tau of the motion-gap to the stopping point at the target onto a tau-G guide through the equation $\tau(r,t) = K\tau_G(T_G,t)$. $\hat{K}$, the regression slope, provides an estimate of the value of the coupling constant, K. $\hat{K}$ was close to 0.5. This meant there was touch contact with the goal, and the peak force and power involved in the movement was low (see Fig. 1.3 and discussion of Fig. 1.3 in the text).

Tau-G Guidance of the Hand to a Bodily Goal

In the preceding experiment, the pointer was tau-G guided to an external goal. This involved using visual information about the tau of the gap between the pointer tip and the external goal. Are movements that use only articular information (derived from sensors in the joints, muscles, and skin) also tau-G guided? The following experiment tested this by requiring adults to move their fingers to a bodily goal with eyes shut. The task was to raise pieces of food from their lap to their mouth (Lee, Craig, & Grealy, 1999). They positioned their head differently on each trial to avoid the possibility of making stereotyped movements and to make sure that they had to perceptually guide their hand through articular information. The movement of the fingers to the mouth was recorded at 312 Hz on a Selspot motion-capture system. Figure 1.10 illustrates the setup and measures computed from the Selspot records. It was found that the gap, $r(t)$, between the hand and mouth was closed by keeping $\tau(r,t) = K\tau_G(T_G,t)$ [in Fig. 1.10, $\tau(r,t)$ is written as τ_r]. The coupling was tight (mean $r^2 > 0.985$ for on average 87% of the movement). Also, the hand had to arrive at the mouth from the right direction to avoid colliding with the nose. This involved controlling the angle α (Fig. 1.10), the steering component of the movement, and was achieved by tau-coupling $\tau(\alpha,t)$ onto $\tau(r,t)$ by keeping $\tau(\alpha,t) = K_{ar}\tau(r,t)$, for a constant, K_{ar}. Again the coupling was tight (mean $r^2 > 0.980$ for, on average, 82% of the movement). Virtually identical results

(a)

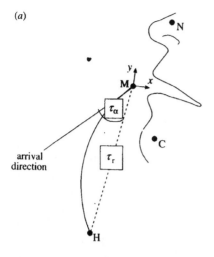

(b)

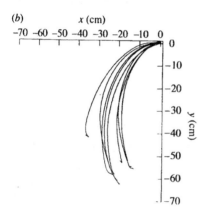

FIG. 1.10. Tau-G guidance of the hand to the mouth. (a) Showing the position of the Selspot LEDs and the taus used in the analysis. (b) Typical paths of the hand to the mouth. From Lee, Craig, and Grealy (1999).

were obtained when the task was performed with eyes open. Thus, the articular information (from sensors in the joints, muscles, and skin) about the movement of the hand to the mouth that was used in guiding it was as precise as when visual information was added.

Development of Tau-G Guidance of the Hand

How does the ability to tau-G guide the hand develop? I consider reaching to external and bodily goals separately because they appear to develop differently. Whereas adults can reach to either with about equal facility, young infants appear to find bodily goals easier. It is a common observation that young infants manage to get their hand to their mouth, but they make a poorer showing of reaching out for toys. In fact infants do not start reaching with any skill for external objects until they are 4 or 5 months old (von Hofsten, 1983). Thus, infants under this age would appear to be not as capable as adults at tau-G guiding their hands to external objects.

Are infants capable of tau-G guiding their hands to bodily goals? Evidence that they are comes from a recent experiment carried out by Hooker (2003) and Perkins (2003). The original purpose of the experiment was to study how young infants move to music. A 10-week-old little girl was supported on a special rest (designed by Colwyn Trevarthen) that simulates being held against the shoulder while allowing free movement of the arms and legs (Fig. 1.11). Selspot LEDs were attached to her hands and feet, and her movements were recorded at 125 Hz as different types of music (jazz, funk, and Indian tabla) were played to her through a loudspeaker. During the concert, which lasted about half an hour and included some quiet periods, she moved her hands up and down and swung her feet sideways. The vertical movements of her right hand and the rightward movements of her right foot (Fig. 1.11) were analyzed in a similar way to that described earlier under tau-G guidance of vocalizing, but using an $r^2 > 0.95$ criterion. The movements were generally found to be strongly tau-G guided. For the rightward movement of her right foot, the mean r^2 across the four conditions was 0.98 for, on average, 97% of the movement. For the vertical movements of her hand, across the four conditions the mean r^2 was 0.97 for, on average, 97% of the movement. There was no significant difference in the degree of tau-G guidance across the four conditions as indexed by the r^2 and the percentage. The mean $\hat{K}$ values for both her foot and hand movements were mainly around 0.6 (range 0.57–0.66), which means that she kept the peak force and power in the movement relatively low and brought the movements to a stop quite gently. An exception to this was that the mean values of $\hat{K}$ for her hand with the funk and tabla music were significantly higher at 0.98 and 0.96. Here she was applying more force and power and bringing her movements to a stop more abruptly. Thus, not only did the experiment provide strong evidence of tau-G guidance of the hand and foot to bodily goals at 10 weeks of age, it also provided evidence suggesting that the baby was modulating the expressive form of her movement by regulating the value of the coupling constant, K, in the tau-G guidance.

If a young baby of 10 weeks of age can tau-G guide her hand and foot to goals within her body space, with or without music, why can she not tau-G guide her limbs to external goals with equal accuracy? She will start reaching for objects only around 16 to 20 weeks of age. Even then her movements will be nowhere near as smooth and well formed as her movements to bodily goals at 10 weeks. Her reaching movements will initially consist of a number of alternations of acceleration and deceleration,

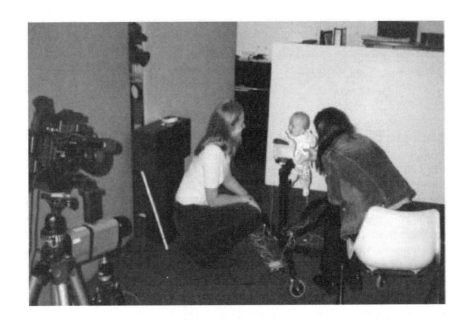

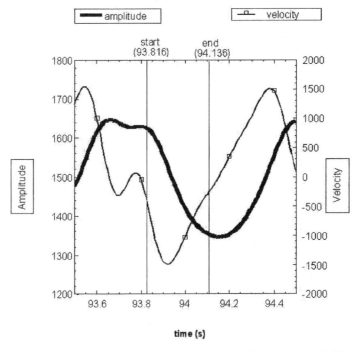

FIG. 1.11. (a) 10-week-old baby girl being settled to hear some music. The Selspot and video cameras in the foreground recorded her limb movements. (b) Typical movement profiles of the 10-week-old infant's right foot. The vertical lines indicate the start and endpoints of the tau-G guidance analysis. From Hooker (2003) and Perkins (2003).

like a driver switching back and forth between the accelerator and brake. As she gets more proficient, the number of switches between acceleration and deceleration will decrease until eventually, by about 31 weeks of age, she is reaching with a single acceleration phase followed by a single deceleration phase—with possibly one or two small acceleration/decelerations added at the end if she needs to zero-in precisely on the object (von Hofsten, 1991). During this period, she will also get increasingly more proficient at catching moving objects (von Hofsten, 1983), and by about 40 weeks she will start using tau in prospectively initiating her catches (Fig. 1.12). Later she will use tau-coupling in hitting a moving ball (Fig. 1.13).

So why can a young baby tau-G guide her hand to a bodily goal so much better than she can to an external goal? When the baby is tau-G guiding her hand to a bodily goal, she is continually sensing the tau of the gap between her hand and the goal through articular sensors in her muscles, joints, and skin (possibly supplemented by vision). She is regulating the force exerted by her muscles so that the tau she is sensing stays in constant ratio with the tau-G she is generating in her nervous system. In the womb, she was able to practice obtaining information through her articular sensors to guide her hands to bodily goals such as her mouth. Therefore, by the time she is born, she is quite adept at guiding her hand to bodily goals. In contrast, when she is guiding her hand to an external goal, she has to use visual information about the tau of the gap between her hand and the goal. Because she cannot use her eyes in the womb, when she is born she has quite a bit of catching up to do with regard to visual guidance. She needs to learn how to pick up tau information visually and put it into action.

A good starting point would be for her to watch her hands moving so that she can both see and feel the same movement and start to get the two senses in registry. Newborns will work to do this, resisting pulls on their hands, even when they can only see their hand in a TV monitor (van der Meer, van der Weel, & Lee, 1996). van der Meer (1997) investigated this further. The newborn baby lay on its back facing sideways (Fig. 1.14, upper). The room was dark except for a narrow beam of light that shone across the baby's chest in the direction she was facing. She could see her hand clearly when she raised it into the beam, but only dimly otherwise. A Selspot LED was attached to the baby's hand to record its movement. Figure 1.14 (lower) shows a typical record of hand movement. The hand moves smoothly into the light beam and stabilizes there. Her movements were not tau-G analyzed and so we do not know to what degree the baby was tau-G guiding them. However, the position and velocity curves in Fig. 1.14 (lower) are similar to the tau-G theoretic gap and gap velocity curves in Figs. 1.3b and 1.3e (apart from the curves being inverted). Therefore, it is likely that a tau-G analysis of the data would reveal that new-

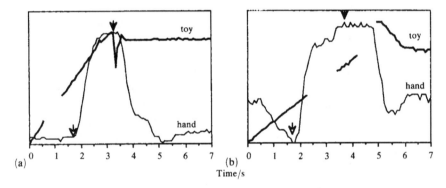

(a)   (b)

Time/s

FIG. 1.12. Visual prospective guidance of catching. Upper: An attractive toy moves on a straight track from the infant's left or right, enticing the infant to reach to catch the toy through the central window, which has occluders either side of it. Lower left: Typical plots for a 20-week-old infant, with the toy moving at 8 cm/s^{-1}, of the y-coordinate of the hand (thin line) and the x-coordinate of the toy (thick line) as recorded by an overhead camera with its optical axis vertical and the x-axis of the image plane parallel to the toy's motion path. Lower right: Typical plots for the same infant at 40 weeks of age, with the toy moving at 6.5 cm/s^{-1}. The open arrows show when the hand begins to move forward, and the closed arrows show when the toy is caught. The first interruptions in the record of the motion of the toy are due to the toy being behind the occluder. By 40 weeks of age, the hand showed prospective control: It started to move before the toy went out of sight behind the occluder and at a time that was more related to the tau of the gap between the toy and the catching place than to the size of the gap. From van der Meer, van der Weel, and Lee (1994).

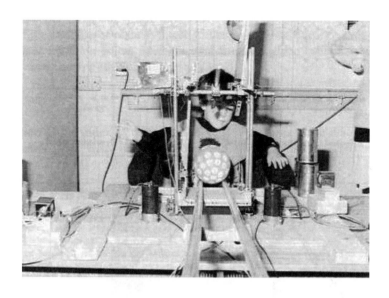

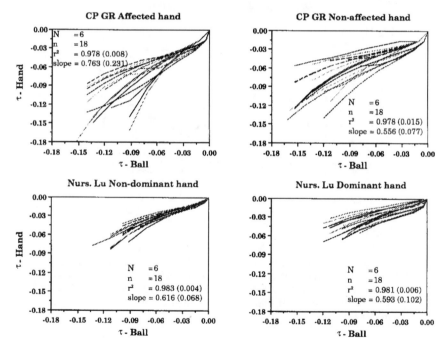

FIG. 1.13. Tau-coupling in hitting. Upper: The ball is rolling down the track toward the nursery school boy. He is going to try to hit a bat hanging to his right of the track just as the ball reaches the bat. If he succeeds, the ball will knock over the cans to his left, causing great glee. Lower: Plots showing the coupling between tau of the gap between the hand and the bat (τ-Hand) and tau of the gap between the ball and the bat (τ-Ball). From van der Weel, van der Meer, and Lee (1996) and Lee, von Hofsten, and Cotton (1997).

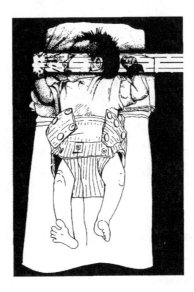

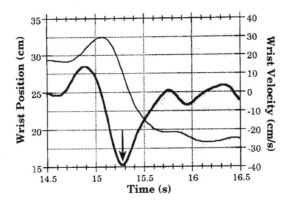

FIG. 1.14.   Upper: A newborn baby moving its hand in a darkened room into a light beam (presumably to see the hand better). Lower: Typical position (thin line) and velocity (thick line) record of the hand measured parallel to the body axis. After time 15.6s the hand was in the light beam. Note how the hand moves smoothly into the light beam and then stays there. From van der Meer (1997).

borns tau-G guide their hands into the light beam. This would imply that young infants are capable of visually tau-G guiding the hand, although they appear not to be when they are presented with an object to reach out for. This apparent disparity could be explained by the different optic flow fields in the two situations. When moving the hand into the beam, the hand moves approximately in a plane perpendicular to the direction in which the infant is facing. Thus, the basic optic geometry is as shown in Fig. 1.4b. In contrast, when reaching forward for an object, the hand moves approximately in the direction in which the infant is facing. In this case, the optic geometry is similar to that for forward locomotion (Fig. 1.4a).

GUIDING THE FEET

As anyone who has traversed uneven ground knows, walking and running are not regular oscillatory processes like those driving a clockwork soldier, despite what some texts assume. Indeed flesh and blood soldiers have to train hard to emulate the regularity of their clockwork counterparts. No, walking and running are far more akin to reaching with the hand than to oscillating. The feet have to be guided to suitable points of contact with the ground from which the body can thrust off to the next point of contact. The optic flow field provides information for this (Fig. 1.4a). Watch a young child at the beach climbing barefoot on rocks and you will see what I mean by reaching with the feet. You will also see toes in a new light—as little fingers gripping the rock.

Tau-G Guiding the Feet When Sprinting

Viewing walking and running in this way naturally leads to this question: Are the feet tau-G guided like the hands are? To answer this question, we recorded (at 250 Hz using Selspot) the limb movements of sprinters running on an indoor track. The first motion-gap we examined was between the toe and the upcoming point of contact with the ground (Fig. 1.15). This motion-gap is clearly important for general running to secure adequate footing. To be sure, running on a track is not the same as running over rough ground. However, it seems highly unlikely that runners will adopt different modes of control depending on the nature of the ground. They

FIG. 1.15.   Tau-G guidance of the foot from one point of contact to the next when sprinting. The motion-gap is between the foot and the upcoming point of contact.

are far more likely to have a single flexible mode of control that they fit to the terrain.

One important thing a runner has to strive for is attaining proper dynamical contact with the ground. The foot not only has to arrive at an adequate place, it has to be moving in an efficient way as it arrives. Suppose, for example, the ground is horizontal like a running track. First, if the foot arrives at the ground while it is still moving forward relative to the ground, this will produce a retarding force on the body. This is, in fact, what runners do if they want to stop, but it is not what a sprinter wants to do when in full flight. Second, if the foot arrives at the ground while it is still moving downward, this will produce a jarring vertical impact with the ground. The vertical impact appears to be minimized in good sprinters. Their footsteps are quiet as they glide over the ground.

A second important thing a runner needs to strive for is moving the limbs efficiently. Taking this point into account, together with the preceding points, we predicted that the toe would be tau-G guided to the ground with a coupling constant, K, which ensured low-impact velocity with the ground while also keeping power consumption low. Mean power consumption is lowest when $0.5 < K < 1$, and it slowly decreases as K increases from 0.5 to 1.0 (Figs. 1.3p and 1.3q). In contrast, for $0.5 < K < 1$, impact velocity increases quite steeply as K increases from 0.5 to 1.0 (Fig. 1.3e). Therefore, keeping power and impact velocity both low should entail a K value at the lower end of the range from 0.5 to 1.0. This is, in fact, what we found. For four sprinters running at speed, the motion-gap between the toe and the ground was tau-G guided, with an $r^2 > 0.95$ during 99% of the movement on average, with mean K values ranging from 0.51 to 0.61.

It would be little use getting your foot accurately placed on the ground if, at contact, it were not also accurately placed horizontally just in front of the hips so that the leg can drive the body forward and upward. Thus, it is also important to control the horizontal movement of the toe relative to the hip. We found this, too, was achieved using tau-G guidance by the sprinters we analyzed. During the backward movement of the toe, the tau of the motion-gap between the toe and its rearmost position (rightmost drawing in Fig. 1.16a) was coupled onto a tau-G, with an $r^2 > 0.95$ during 99% of the movement on average. The mean K values ranged from 0.47 to 0.52. During the forward movement of the toe, the tau of the motion-gap between the toe and its forward-most position (rightmost drawing in Fig. 1.16b) was coupled onto a tau-G, with an $r^2 > 0.95$ during 73% of the movement on average. The mean K values ranged from 0.58 to 0.77. Thus, as with the tau-G guidance of the toe relative to the ground, both power and final velocity were kept low when moving the foot relative to the hip.

FIG. 1.16.   Tau-G guidance of the foot horizontally *relative to the hip* when sprinting. (a) When the foot is moving backward, the relevant motion-gap is the horizontal distance-gap between the current position of the toe and the rearmost position it will reach. (b) When the foot is moving forward, the relevant motion-gap is the horizontal distance-gap between the current position of the toe and the foremost position it will reach. In both (a) and (b), the horizontal distance between the toe and hip are shown as horizontal lines. The length of this line in the rightmost drawings is the goal distance-gap, when the corresponding motion-gap is closed.

Tau-G Guiding the Feet Down a Slope

Running and walking up and down slopes emphasizes the importance of properly guiding the feet relative to the ground and the hips. The steeper the slope, the more precise is the control required. One reason for this is that the horizontal extent of the area of contact with the ground—the base of support—is smaller when walking down a slope compared with horizontal ground. Thus, balance is more difficult (Adolph, 2002; chap. 3, this volume). In a series of elegant naturalistic experiments Adolph (1997) studied how infants develop the ability to perceive which slopes can be safely traversed and which are too steep. In making the perceptual judgment, the infants have to assess the slope in terms of the degree of control they could muster to negotiate it. They have to perceive the affordance of the slope relative to their current action capabilities. The degree of control required to guide the feet to walk safely on a slope could be measured in terms of tau-G guidance of the feet in the following way.

Imagine you are running down a steep slope. You have to keep pushing back on each footfall to stop yourself from tippling forward. To prepare yourself for each push, your foot should be moving forward relative to the ground at contact, but not by too much or else the force on your leg could strain your joints and muscles. The situation is, therefore, different from when sprinting at full speed, when your foot should be stationary relative to the ground at contact. In terms of tau-G guidance of the foot relative to the ground, this means that when you are going down a steep slope your foot needs to be tau-G guided with a K value that is greater than 0.5 so that there is some forward velocity of the foot relative to the ground at contact. The same applies when you are walking down a steep slope. The only difference is that for part of the time both feet are on the ground. Therefore, the trailing foot can also exert some backward force on the body to resist the accelerative force down the slope due to gravity.

With regard to the movement of the foot relative to the hip when going down the slope, this probably has to be such that the foot strikes the ground a little further in advance of the hip (measured horizontally) than it does when sprinting on a horizontal track to be able to develop adequate force backward on the body to balance the gravitational pull.

In summary, running or walking down a slope probably involves modulating the K value for the tau-G guidance of the foot relative to the ground, in particular shifting K away from 0.5 and toward 1.0 to increase the velocity at contact. At the same time, the movement of the foot relative to the hip probably needs to be adjusted to achieve an appropriate position of the foot relative to the hip as it touches down. Both adjustments need to be tuned to the angle of the slope. I say probably because the experimental measurements still need to be made with adults and young children. It would be a most valuable project to undertake—one that should increase our understanding of what is involved in negotiating uneven ground and how the ability develops.

HELPING DEVELOPMENT

Children need help developing movement skills. The need is particularly acute in those who start life in weak physical or neural health. Although there have been great advances in the ability of medical science to save the lives of babies born very prematurely, unfortunately a number of such infants grow up to be disabled. Improving the help given to infants and children in learning to guide their movements is likely to lessen the disabilities. This optimism is justified by a number of cases where severely neurologically damaged infants have nonetheless succeeded in attaining near normal function. The nervous system is apparently able to adjust to damage, providing the child has adequate environmental and human support in developing movement skills.

What is needed to help infants, children, and adults develop movement skills is a set of sensitive measures of movement control that tap into the basic workings of movement control (Lee, von Hofsten, & Cotton, 1997; van der Weel, van der Meer, & Lee, 1996). This is necessary both for accurately diagnosing problems and monitoring progress during therapy or training. Another need, of course, is for therapeutic or training exercises specifically tailored to address the problems that the tests have revealed. General Tau Theory has something to offer here, I believe. First, it provides a precise way to describe a basic component of movement control—the tau-G guidance of closure of motion-gaps. Second, it offers a way to analyze how the closures of different motion-gaps are coordinated together into a single act—as, for example, in sprinting. Third, it provides a precise way to measure how well the different components are executed and how well the coordination is executed. Fourth, it provides a method for analyzing movement skills to reveal unsuspected degrees of coordination, as, for example, was found in infants sucking milk from a bottle. Fifth, it suggests procedures that could be developed to help infants, children, and adults overcome difficulties in executing different components of tasks.

In this chapter, I described a number of studies that indicate the direction in which future research directed toward helping master movement skills might proceed. Further experimental studies need to be carried out to increase our understanding of skill development. In parallel, diagnostic tests need to be developed and tested. Likewise, therapeutic and training procedures need to be devised and evaluated. This is a large undertaking, too large for any single laboratory to carry out, but the outcome could bear much fruit. Readers who are interested in taking up the challenge and would like more information about applying General Tau Theory should visit http://www.perception-in-action.ed.ac.uk/.

ACKNOWLEDGMENTS

The work reported in this chapter was supported by grants from MRC, SERC, ESRC, BBSRC, and University of Minnesota.

REFERENCES

Adolph, K. E. (1997). Learning in the development of infant locomotion. *Monographs of the Society for Research in Child Development, 62*(3, Serial No. 251), pp. 1–162.

Adolph, K. E. (2002). Learning to keep balance. *Advances in Child Development and Behavior, 30*, 1–40.

Bernstein, N. (1967). *The co-ordination and regulation of movement.* Oxford, England: Pergamon.

Bizzi, E., Hogan, N., Mussa-Ivaldi, F. A., & Giszter, S. (1992). Does the nervous system use equilibrium-point control to guide single and multiple joint movements? *Behavioral and Brain Sciences, 15*, 603–613.

Bu'Lock, F., Woolridge, M. W., & Baum, J. D. (1990). Development of coordination of sucking, swallowing and breathing: Ultrasound study of term and preterm infants. *Developmental Medicine and Child Neurology, 32*, 669–678.

Craig, C. M., Delay, D., Grealy, M. A., & Lee, D. N. (2000). Guiding the swing in golf putting. *Nature, 405*, 295–296.

Craig, C. M., Grealy, M. A., & Lee, D. N. (2000). Detecting motor abnormalities in pre-term infants. *Experimental Brain Research, 131*, 359–365.

Craig, C. M., & Lee, D. N. (1999). Neonatal control of nutritive sucking pressure: Evidence for an intrinsic τ-guide. *Experimental Brain Research, 124*, 371–382.

Craig, C. M., Lee, D. N., Freer, Y. N., & Laing, I. A. (1999). Modulations in breathing patterns during intermittent feeding in term infants and preterm infants with bronchopulmonary dysplasia. *Developmental Medicine and Child Neurology, 41*, 616–624.

Daniel, B. M., & Lee, D. N. (1990). Development of looking with head and eyes. *Journal of Experimental Child Psychology, 50*, 200–216.

Feldman, A. G., & Levin, M. F. (1995). The origin and use of positional frames of reference in motor control. *Behavioral and Brain Sciences, 18*, 723–806.

Flanagan, J. R., Ostry, D., & Feldman, A. G. (1993). Control of trajectory modifications in target-directed reaching. *Journal of Motor Behavior, 25*, 140–152.

Flash, T. (1990). The organization of human arm trajectory control. In J. Winters & S. Woo (Eds.), *Multiple muscle systems: Biomechanics of movement organization* (pp. 282–301). Berlin: Springer-Verlag.

Fraenkel, N. (2001). *Singing in tune: A perceptuo-motor problem.* Unpublished undergraduate dissertation in Psychology, Edinburgh University.

Georgopoulos, A. P., Kalaska, J. F., & Massey, J. T. (1981). Spatial trajectories and reaction times of aimed movements: Effects of practice, uncertainty, and change in target location. *Journal of Neurophysiology, 46*, 725–743.

Gibson, J. J. (1966). *The senses considered as perceptual systems.* Boston: Houghton-Mifflin.

Hay, J. C., & Pick, H. L., Jr. (1966). Visual and proprioceptive adaptation to optical displacement of the visual stimulus. *Journal of Experimental Psychology, 71*, 150–158.

Hooker, K. E. (2003). *A study into an infant's perceptuo-motor skills and musical expression through movement.* Unpublished undergraduate dissertation in Psychology, Edinburgh University.

Lee, D. N. (1976). A theory of visual control of braking based on information about time-to-collision. *Perception, 5*, 437–459.

Lee, D. N. (1978). The functions of vision. In H. L. Pick, Jr. & E. Saltzman (Eds.), *Modes of perceiving and processing information* (pp. 159–170). Hillsdale, NJ: Lawrence Erlbaum Associates.

Lee, D. N. (1980). The optic flow-field: The foundation of vision. *Philosophical Transactions of the Royal Society London B, 290*, 169–179.

Lee, D. N. (1998). Guiding movement by coupling taus. *Ecological Psychology, 10*, 221–250.

Lee, D. N., Craig, C. M., & Grealy, M. A. (1999). Sensory and intrinsic coordination of movement. *Proceedings of the Royal Society of London B, 266,* 2029–2035.

Lee, D. N., Georgopoulos, A. P., Clark, M. J., Craig, C. M., & Port, N. L. (2001). Guiding contact by coupling the taus of gaps. *Experimental Brain Research, 139,* 151–159.

Lee, D. N., Grealy, M. A., Pepping, G.-J., & Schögler, B. (2004). *The temporal organization of goal-directed movement.* Submitted for publication.

Lee, D. N., Pepping, G.-J., Lee, T. M., & Georgopoulos, A. P. (2004). *Neural information directing action.* Submitted for publication.

Lee, D. N., Reddish, P. E., & Rand, D. T. (1991). Aerial docking by hummingbirds. *Naturwissenschaften, 78,* 526–527.

Lee, D. N., Simmons, J. A., Saillant, P. A., & Bouffard, F. (1995). Steering by echolocation: A paradigm of ecological acoustics. *Journal of Comparative Physiology A, 176,* 347–354.

Lee, D. N., von Hofsten, C., & Cotton, E. (1997). Perception in action approach to cerebral palsy. In K. Connelly & H. Forrsberg (Eds.), *The neurophysiology and neuropsychology of motor development* (pp. 257–285). London: Mac Keith Press.

Lee, D. N., Young, D. S., & Rewt, D. (1992). How do somersaulters land on their feet? *Journal of Experimental Psychology: Human Perception and Performance, 18,* 1195–1202.

Mathew, O. P. (1991). Breathing patterns of preterm infants during bottle feeding: Role of milk flow. *Journal of Pediatrics, 119,* 960–965.

Péllison, D., Prablanc, C., Goodale, M. A., & Jeannerod, M. (1986). Visual control of reaching movements without vision of the limb: II. Evidence of fast unconscious processes correcting the trajectory of the hand to the final position of a double-step stimulus. *Experimental Brain Research, 62,* 303–311.

Perkins, J. D. (2003). *The need to dance? A study into the effects of music on perceptuo-motor skills in infants.* Unpublished undergraduate dissertation in Psychology, Edinburgh University.

Pick, H. L., Jr., Rieser, J. J., Wagner, D., & Garing, A. E. (1999). The recalibration of rotational locomotion. *Journal of Experimental Psychology: Human Perception and Performance, 25,* 1179–1188.

Rieser, J. J., Pick, H. L., Jr., Ashmead, D. H., & Garing, A. E. (1995). Calibration of human locomotion and models of perceptuo-motor organization. *Journal of Experimental Psychology: Human Perception and Performance, 21,* 480–497.

Soechting, J. F., & Lacquaniti, F. (1983). Modification of trajectory of a pointing movement in response to a change in target location. *Journal of Neurophysiology, 49,* 548–564.

van der Meer, A. L. H. (1997). Keeping the arm in the limelight: Advanced visual control of arm movements in neonates. *European Journal of Paediatric Neurology, 4,* 103–108.

van der Meer, A. L. H., van der Weel, F. R., & Lee, D. N. (1994). Prospective control in catching in infants. *Perception, 23,* 287–302.

van der Meer, A. L. H., van der Weel, F. R., & Lee, D. N. (1996). Lifting weights in neonates: Developing visual control of reaching. *Scandinavian Journal of Psychology, 37,* 424–436.

van der Weel, F. R., van der Meer, A. L. H., & Lee, D. N. (1996). Measuring dysfunction of basic movement control in cerebral palsy. *Human Movement Science, 15,* 253–283.

van Sonderjen, J. F., Gielen, C. C. A. M., & van der Gon, J. J. D. (1989). Motor programs for goal-directed movements are continuously adjusted according to changes in target location. *Experimental Brain Research, 78,* 139–146.

von Hofsten, C. (1983). Catching skills in infancy. *Journal of Experimental Psychology: Human Perception and Performance, 9,* 75–85.

von Hofsten, C. (1991). Structuring of early reaching movements—A longitudinal study. *Journal of Motor Behavior, 23,* 280–292.

von Hofsten, C., & Lee, D. N. (1994). Measuring with the optic sphere. In G. Jannson, S. S. Bergstrom, & W. Epstein (Eds.), *Perceiving events and objects* (pp. 455–467). Hillsdale, NJ: Lawrence Erlbaum Associates.

von Hofsten, C., & Rosander, K. (1997). Development of smooth pursuit tracking in young
    infants. *Vision Research, 37,* 1799–1810.
Woolridge, M., Baum, J. D., & Drewett, R. F. (1980). Does a change in the composition of hu-
    man milk affect sucking patterns and milk intake? *Lancet, 2,* 1292–1294.
Yilmaz, E. H., & Warren, W. H. (1995). Visual control of braking—A test of the tau dot hy-
    pothesis. *Journal of Experimental Psychology: Human Perception and Performance, 21,*
    996–1014.

APPENDIX 1

Derivation of the Equation for the Tau-G Guide, $\tau_G(T_G, t)$

Imagine a ball launched vertically upward from the ground, reaching its
zenith and dropping back to the ground. Suppose u is the velocity at take-
off, g is the gravitational acceleration, and T_G is the flight duration. Ignoring air resistance, $u = gT_G/2$, and the height of the center of gravity of
the ball above the ground at time t (<0) before landing at time $t = 0$ is $y(t) =$
$-ut - gt^2/2$. Eliminating u between these equations, we obtain $y(t) = -(T_G +$
$t)gt/2$. Differentiating this equation with respect to time gives $\dot{y}(t) = -(T_G +$
$2t)g/2$. Hence, $\tau(y,t) = y(t)/\dot{y}(t) = (T_G + t)t/(T_G + 2t)$. By definition, $\tau(y,t)$ is
equal to the tau-G guide, $\tau_G(T_G, t)$. Thus, writing $t_n = t/T_G$,

$$\tau_G(T_G, t) = T_G(1 + t_n)t_n/(1 + 2t_n) \tag{1}$$

for $-T_G = t = 0$, or $-1 = t_n = 0$. (The equation for the special tau-G guide, τ_g, is
the same as Equation [1], the only difference being that τ_g runs over the
time interval $-T_G/2 = t = 0$ rather than $-T_G = t = 0$.)

Suppose that the tau function of a variable x, $\tau(x,t)$, is coupled onto a
tau-G guide, $\tau_G(T_G, t)$, so that $\tau(x,t) = K\tau_G(T_G, t)$ for a constant K. From Eq.
(1),

$$\tau(x,t) = x(t)/\dot{x}(t) = KT_G(1 + t_n)t_n/(1 + 2t_n) \tag{2}$$

We can now derive the motion equations for x. Integrating Eq. (2) with respect to time, t, gives

$$x(t) = x_m 2^{2/K}(-t_n - t_n^2)^{1/K} \tag{3}$$

where x_m (<0) is the minimum value attained by x (when $t_n = -0.5$). Differentiating Eq. (3) successively with respect to time gives

$$\dot{x}(t) = (x_m/T_G)(2^{2/K}/K)(-1 - 2t_n)(-t_n - t_n^2)^{(1/K-1)} \tag{4}$$

$$\ddot{x}(t) = (x_m/T_G^2)(2^{2/K}/K)[(4 - 2K)/K]$$
$$[t_n^2 + t_n + (1 - K)/(4 - 2K)](-t_n - t_n^2)^{(1/K-2)} \tag{5}$$

Next we derive the force, f(x,t), and power, p(x,t), required to move a unit mass in accordance with Eqs. (3), (4), and (5). $f(t) = \ddot{x}(t)$ and so, from Eq. (5),

$$f(x,t) = (x_m/T_G^2)(2^{2/K}/K)[(4 - 2K)/K]$$
$$[t_n^2 + t_n + (1 - K)/(4 - 2K)](-t_n - t_n^2)^{(1/K-2)} \tag{6}$$

$$p(x,t) = \text{rate of change of kinetic energy}$$
$$= d/dt(\dot{x}(t)^2/2) = \dot{x}(t)\ddot{x}(t) \tag{7}$$

where $\dot{x}(t)$ and $\ddot{x}(t)$ are given by Eqs. (4) and (5).

Equations (2), (3), (4), (6) and (7) are plotted in Figs. 1.3a–o for a complete cycle of $\tau_G(T_G,t)$ (i.e., for $-T_G \leq t \leq 0$). Values of $T_G = 1s$, $x_m = -1m$, and mass = 1kg are used in the graphs.

2

▼▼▼▼▼▼▼

The Development of Prospective Control in Tracking a Moving Object

Claes von Hofsten
Uppsala Universitet

THE RELATIONSHIP AMONG ACTION, PERCEPTION, AND COGNITION

Action, perception, and cognition are tightly coupled in development. Not only does action organize perception and cognition, but perception and cognition are also essential for organizing action. Perception is based on online sensory information, whereas cognition is founded on knowledge about rules and regularities in the world. Those two modes of control supplement each other in guiding action. The basic theme of this chapter is that action, perception, and cognition form dynamic systems around which adaptive behavior develops. In such action systems, each part affects and is affected by every other part on equal terms. The development of perception is crucial for developing knowledge about the world, and the child's knowledge about the world guides his or her perception. In the same way, the development of perception and cognition is crucial for the development of action, and the development of action is crucial for the development of perception and cognition. The action systems are associated with strong motives that drive development. According to the present view, the starting point of development is not a set of reflexes triggered by external stimuli, but a set of action systems that are activated by the infant. To begin with, they may be primitive, but as long as there are loops connecting the sensory side and the motor side, a window is open for refining the systems from activity and experience and gearing them to the environment. In this way, the development of perception, cognition, and action and the development of the nervous system mutually influence each other in the process of forming increasingly sophisticated means of solving action problems. With development, the different action systems also become increasingly future oriented and integrated with each other, and ultimately each action will engage multiple coordinated action systems.

A developmental perspective is of crucial importance in understanding how action control comes about. Actions systems do not appear ready-made. Neither are they primarily determined by experience. They are the result of a process with two foci, one in the central nervous system and one in the subject's dynamic interactions with the environment (see Fig. 2.1). It is important to point out that the brain has its own dynamics that makes neurons proliferate in certain ways. However, the emerging action capabilities are also crucially shaped by the subject's interactions with the environment. Without such interaction, there would be no functional brain. Perception, cognition, and motivation develop at the interface between brain processes and actions. Figure 2.1 also includes biomechanics as a special node. It has its own dynamics and is crucially involved in the development of actions. Biomechanics put constraints on actions, and actions modify those constraints over development.

What are the priorities of this developing system? Biology has prepared the infant for action by investing in certain primitives and making

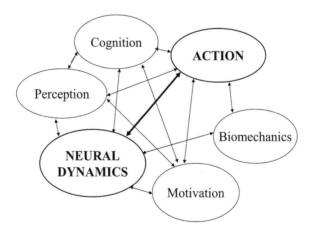

FIG. 2.1.   A schematic description of the dynamic system of development. The system has two focuses: one in the central nervous system and one in the subject's interactions with the environment. Perception, cognition, and motivation develop at the interface between these focuses. Biomechanics is also included as a special node. It has its own dynamics and is crucially involved in the development of actions.

those unfold in specific ways that optimize the developmental process. What are the action capabilities of the newborn child, and how are they transformed during early development? What is the role of learning, and how do action, perception, and cognition mutually sponsor each other in this process?

In the present chapter, I discuss these questions in the context of looking, how it develops in early infancy, and how it comes to organize perception and cognition in development. Looking is of crucial importance for extracting visual information about the world, directing attention, and establishing social communication. Controlled looking involves both head and eye movements and is guided by at least three types of information: visual, vestibular, and proprioceptive. The importance of looking as a window to infants' perception and cognition has long been recognized. The dominating methods in this area either measure looking preference or habituation of looking. Although these methods have proved useful, they do not evaluate looking skills or consider the information required to control gaze. In fact most aspects of looking are not considered at all. Measurements of eye and head movements provide a much richer resource for evaluating perceptual and cognitive development in infancy. For instance, they tell us how coordination problems are solved in development, how perceived motion and change come to be utilized in gaze control, and how infants become increasingly skilled in representing moving objects.

Over the years, we have conducted a large series of studies of the development of looking in infancy. Primarily, two methods for monitoring looking have been used. First, the eye movements have been monitored with EOG combined with opto-electronic recording of head movements. Combining these two measurements gives precise estimation of looking direction in both the time and space domains (von Hofsten & Rosander, 1996, 1997; Rosander & von Hofsten, 2000, 2002, 2003). However, EOG is only optimal for horizontal eye movements. To evaluate the development of vertical eye movements and combinations of vertical and horizontal eye movements, we have used a cornea-reflection technique (ASL; Gredebäck, von Hofsten, & Boudreau, 2002; Gredebäck & von Hofsten, 2004).

THE PROSPECTIVE PROBLEMS TO BE SOLVED

Actions are organized around tasks and defined by goals. Time is irreversible, and the only part of an action that is controllable is the one that has not yet been accomplished. Perceiving one's own movements and predicting how they will unfold in the near future is therefore essential to action control.

Most actions involve movements of more than one body part. In looking, the movements of the head and eyes collaborate in controlling gaze. Actions involving more than one part of the body can only be accomplished if the movements of the different parts are timed and scaled to each other. This is only possible if each body part "knows" what the other parts are going to do ahead of time, which in turn requires the movements of the different parts to be subordinate to one common system or mechanism. Precise timing also requires monitoring the movements of each part of the body prospectively.

In gearing actions to the environment, obstacles have to be avoided and encounters prepared. When walking in a cluttered terrain, a suitable ground support has to be found for each step, and the encounter with the support has to be precisely timed. When reaching for an object, the subject must prepare for the encounter by opening the hand, orienting it appropriately, and closing it relative to the encounter with the object. Actions also have to fit the stream of events in the outside world, and this cannot be done ad hoc because it takes time to perceive the course of events and adjust one's actions to them. For instance, when trying to catch a moving object, the reach has to be directed ahead of where the object is seen, toward a point where the hand and object will meet (von Hofsten, 1980, 1983).

Information for Prospective Control

Access to information about future events is only possible in a world, like ours, that is governed by rules and regularities. In such a world, events project into the future, and what is presently happening informs about what will happen next. Perception is designed to extract such prospective information. For instance, because of inertia, a moving object will only gradually change its acceleration, velocity, and direction of motion. Therefore, sensing those variables gives a good basis for knowing how the object will move next. When an object or a surface is being approached, the inverse of the relative change of sensory magnitudes informs about the time-to-contact with it, and the rate of change of this variable informs whether the encounter is going to be hard or soft (Lee, 1974, 1976, 1992; chap. 1, this volume). Lee and colleagues have shown that humans and animals use this information in situations where timing is crucial to control their approaches to objects and surfaces (Lee, Lishman, & Thompson, 1982; Lee, Reddish, & Rand, 1991; Lee, Davies, Green, & van der Weel, 1993).

Over longer time intervals, it becomes increasingly important to base predictions of what is going to happen next on knowledge of the rules and regularities that govern external events. This knowledge is also useful when information about the task is limited or absent. Such a situation arises, for instance, when one tries to visually track a moving object that gets temporarily occluded by another one. The laws of physics are the most general rules that govern events. Inertia, for instance, makes an object continue to move in the same direction and at the same velocity unless affected by an external force. When affected by an external force, the velocity and direction of motion will change gradually. Gravity constitutes a constant force that affects all object motions in a specific way. Other rules are more task-specific. It helps to know how the motion of a ball depends on different kinds of throws and different winds and how one should position oneself to optimize the chances of catching the ball. Most of this knowledge is tacit and can be expressed in action but not in scripts. However, in certain contexts, explicit descriptions of the movements included in the action can be of great importance. When dancing, the future movements of the partner must be anticipated if coordination is going to be maintained. Although the next step of the partner may be, at least, partly revealed by his or her postural adjustments, and therefore perceived directly, it clearly helps to know the rules of dancing to master it. Finally, when engaging in social communication, verbal utterances and facial gestures must be appropriately timed. It is crucial to know when information is going to be sent by the partner so that the message can be perceived and responded to. It is also important to know when the partner is going to end the pass so that one can prepare a response. Only then can communication flow smoothly. It helps to know something about social rules and the partner's mode of communication, but perception of the partner's intentions is obviously crucial as well.

However, knowledge of the rules that govern events can never replace perceptual guidance of actions. As the prospective time interval increases, the relationship between current changes and future effects may become complex and difficult to penetrate in detail. Indeed as Bernstein (1967) pointed out, the complexity of the active and passive forces acting on a limb during the production of a movement is so huge that it is impossible to totally program a movement in advance even if it is simple. Therefore, the global, long-term planning of actions has to be supplemented with perceptual guidance that gives more precise ongoing information about what is going to happen next.

LOOKING

Looking involves both the eyes and head and includes two tasks: stabilizing gaze and switching gaze. Switching gaze is accomplished with rapid saccadic eye movements followed by adjusting head movements. Such adjustments are controlled by information from the visual periphery or expectations of where the objects of interest are situated in the visual world. Switching gaze with saccadic eye movements is both used to move gaze to new positions and to refixate an object that has slipped away from the point of fixation.

Stabilizing gaze is a more complicated task than switching it. Switching gaze only requires the programming of a new fixation point, whereas stabilizing gaze requires continuous adjustments of gaze direction. It has to compensate for head and body movements that are unrelated to the looking task and smoothly adjust gaze to the change in position of the fixated object when it is moving. There are at least three reasons that stabilizing gaze is of crucial importance for looking. First, without such adjustments, the fixated object will quickly slip out of the foveal region of the visual field. Second, it is of crucial importance to minimize slippages of the retinal projection. Even minor slippages will cause major deterioration of acuity. Third, linear visual flow is informative of the spatial layout of the environment, whereas rotational flow is not. The linear visual flow is inversely proportional to distance—that is, the further away an object is situated, the less its image will move on the retina (motion parallax). In fact, the rotational flow will mask the information conveyed by the linear flow (Warren & Hannon, 1990). Therefore, especially rotational flow needs to be minimized. When turning around, gaze will alternatively stabilize and rapidly switch to new positions.

Compensatory eye movements are controlled by visual as well as vestibular and proprioceptive information. One of the most important functions of the vestibular system is to provide information for such compensations. It is connected to the oculomotor system by an extremely fast loop—the vestibulo-ocular response (VOR). The visual flow that arises when a subject moves also contributes to compensatory eye movements. This is referred to as the oculo-kinetic response (OKR). Information from the neck proprioceptors contributes to the control of compensatory eye movements. This is referred to as the cervico-ocular response (COR; Reisman & Anderson, 1989). Finally, passive movements of the head and body may not only give rise to compensatory eye movements, but also compensatory head movements, the vestibulo-collic response (VCR; Peterson & Richmond, 1988; Keshner & Peterson, 1995). All these mechanisms, except smooth pursuit (SP), have generally been thought of as hard-wired reflexes. There are no doubts that the sensorimotor connections are strong, at least to some degree subcortically linked, and probably prenatally established. However, they are also parts of an action system for stabilizing gaze when the subject is moving. In other words, the various mechanisms have to be subordinated to the goals of this action system.

If both head and eye movements are used to track a moving object, which is most often the case, the head movements involved in the tracking must not elicit compensatory eye movements. If they do, the effects of the head movements will be eliminated. In other words, the gaze stabilizing system must treat head movements differently depending on their functions. Even when the head is involved in the tracking of an object, it may also move for other reasons. It is then of crucial importance that only head movements unrelated to the tracking task are compensated. Solving these problems cannot rely on stereotyped solutions.

To avoid retinal slips of a fixated moving object, the SP must anticipate the future motion of the object. Two such predictive processes have been observed in adult visual tracking (Pavel, 1990). One uses perceived velocity, acceleration, and maybe even higher derivatives of the motion to predict what will happen next through a process of extrapolation. Such predictions are in accordance with inertia, which presumes that an object moving with a certain speed and direction will continue in the same way as before and, when affected by a force, will change its motion gradually. The extrapolation process is important for stabilizing gaze on a continuously moving object, but cannot handle abrupt motion changes because they do not reveal themselves in the just seen motion. For instance, tracking a ball that bounces against another object must rely on knowledge of bouncing rules and object properties.

A further complication is that moving objects are not always visible. In a cluttered terrain, they frequently get occluded by other objects. Tracking an object under such conditions requires the subject to anticipate where and when the object will reappear. Because smooth pursuit requires continuous visual support, it cannot be used for this kind of prospectiveness unless the period of occlusion is short. Instead a saccade is typically made to the point of reappearance. If gaze is moved to the point of reappearance just before the object arrives there and the subject is prepared to continue to track it, the occlusion interferes with the ongoing task in the least possible way.

As indicated earlier, the way we move our eyes and head when perceiving and acting on the world carries information about how this action system is set up and, in addition, crucial information about our perceptual, cognitive capabilities. Infants' gaze direction has long been used to infer their perceptual and cognitive capabilities, but much more information can be extracted if eye and head movements are precisely measured. The research reported on in the present chapter has used two methods for measuring looking. The first one measures horizontal eye and head movements separately; eye movements with EOG and head movements with active (Selspot) or passive (Qualisys, Proreflex) markers. The setup can be seen in Fig. 2.2, which shows the sensors attached and connected to the

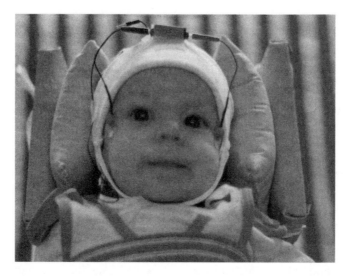

FIG. 2.2.   An infant with the EOG sensors attached to the outer canthi and
with the preamplifier on the head.

preamplifier on the head. The method gives precise evaluation of head
and eye movements over time. The spatial resolution of the eye movements is about 0.4° and of the head movements 0.2°. Data were sampled at
200 to 240 Hz. EOG does not, however, measure vertical eye movements
with the same precision. Therefore, we have used a cornea reflection technique for measuring two-dimensional gaze movements (ASL, Inc). In this
setup, head movements are measured separately with a magnetic tracker
(Flock of Birds, Ascension Inc.), and eye movements are obtained by sub-
tracting the head movements from the gaze movements. Its precision of
the cornea reflection is about 0.5°. This system samples somewhat less frequently (60 Hz).

THE INNATE FOUNDATIONS FOR LOOKING

The looking system is rather well established at birth. Almost immediately after delivery, neonates are ready to look around. They are both able
to use saccadic eye movements to switch gaze between points of interest
and use smooth compensatory movements to stabilize gaze in space. Furthermore, they search for regions that contain significant information like
contours and edges (Haith, 1980), and they focus on faces (Johnson &

Morton, 1991) and moving objects (von Hofsten, 1982). Neonates can also use vision to guide their reaching movements. Neonates like to look at their hands, and they make an effort to continue to view one of their hands when in sight (van der Meer, 1997; van der Meer, van der Weel, & Lee, 1995). For example, van der Meer (1997) showed that neonates move their hands to positions where they are able to see them. She measured spontaneous arm-waving movements while an infant lay supine with its head turned to one side. A narrow beam of light was shown over the baby's face and highlighted the hand when it was within the beam. It was found that the hands were positioned within the light beam significantly more frequently than outside. When the direction of the beam was altered, the distribution of hand movements was moved to the new position of the beam (see Lee, chap. 1, this volume).

Moving gaze to interesting objects constitutes one of the two tasks of looking. The other task is to stabilize gaze on a selected object. How well are neonates able to compensate for their own movements in doing that and pursue the object if it is moving?

Compensatory Eye Movements

The vestibular control of head and eye movements functions well at birth and enables the infant to stabilize gaze direction when they move. According to Finocchio, Preston, and Fuchs (1991), it almost totally compensates for body rotations. Rosander and von Hofsten (2000) found that very young infants use both smooth eye (VOR) and head movements (VCR) to compensate for passive body rotations. They found that neither the head movements nor the eye movements lagged the target, but that the combined head-eye movements did not fully compensate for the body rotations (see Fig. 2.3).

The VOR is traditionally considered to be a reflex. In a situation where the position of the head is suddenly perturbed, it certainly acts as such and results in a small lag of the compensatory eye movements. However, in a situation where the head and eye movements are part of an ongoing compensation for body rotation, then compensations can be prospective. This is even more obvious in the case of active head rotations. von Hofsten and Rosander (1996) found that the eye movements that compensate for active head rotations do not lag the target. One example of such compensatory eye movements is seen in Fig. 2.4. This example shows a 2-month-old infant shaking her head while closing her eyes. The resulting compensatory eye movements led the head rotations with 10 ms. Such a mode of control is possible because the system "knew" about the active head movements ahead of time.

Head movements

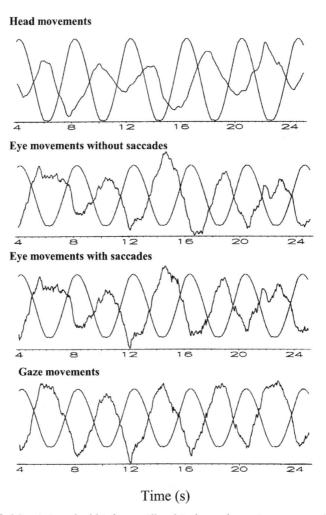

Eye movements without saccades

Eye movements with saccades

Gaze movements

Time (s)

FIG. 2.3. A 4-week-old infant oscillated in front of a stationary target (a happy face). The large eye and head movements completely compensate for the movement of the infant. The eyes are almost exactly counterface to the head rotation.

Tracking Eye Movements

Newborn infants track objects, but the tracking is primarily saccadic—at least for objects of limited size. Dayton and Jones (1964) found that neonates pursued a wide angle visual display with smooth eye movements, but the pursuit became rather jerky for a small target. Other studies have

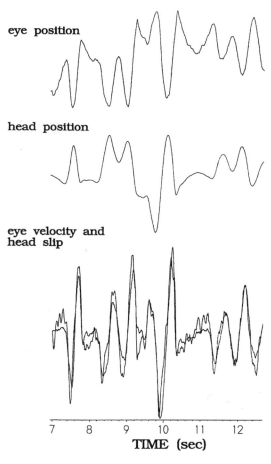

FIG. 2.4.   An example of compensational eye movements in a 2-month-old infant who shook her head while closing her eyes. These eye movements are controlled by the vestibular system. On the average, the eyes lead the head with 10 ms (from von Hofsten, 2003).

supported these findings. Kremenitzer et al. (1979) found that neonates would smoothly track a 12° black circle, however with low gain and only approximately 15% of the time. Roucoux et al. (1983), using a big black circle covering 10° of visual angle, found evidence of smooth pursuit in 1-month-old infants, but only at low velocities and with low gain. Bloch and Carchon (1992) used a red transparent ball covering 4° of visual angle and found only saccadic tracking in neonates. Similar findings were reported by Aslin (1981), who used a black bar 2° wide and 8° high moving sinusoidally in a horizontal path. He found only saccadic following of the target

Eye movements with saccades

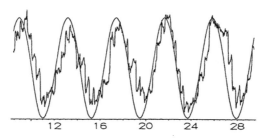

Eye movements without saccades

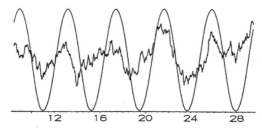

Head movements

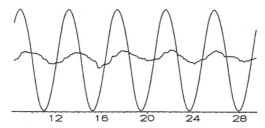

FIG. 2.5.   The same infant at the same occasion as in Fig. 2.3 tracking a target
with mainly saccadic eye movements. The eyes lag the target with 300 ms and
the head with 600 ms. Removing the saccades leaves a small residual of
smooth eye movements that is only moderately geared to the moving target.

up to 6 weeks of age. Our research confirms these findings (Rosander &
von Hofsten, 2000). When eliminating the saccades from the tracking records of infants less than 1 month old, the residual smooth eye adjustments
are small (see Fig. 2.5).

The earliest expressions of visual tracking, however, do not seem to
predict the target motion. von Hofsten and Rosander (1996) found that 1-
month-old infants tracked a wide angle, sinusoidally moving stimulus
with a substantial lag. Figure 2.5 shows an example of a 4-week-old infant
tracking a "happy face" 8° in diameter. As can be seen, both the head and
eye movements lag the target motion.

THE DEVELOPMENT OF VISUAL TRACKING

The proportion of smooth pursuit eye movements reflects the quality of visual tracking. Another indication is the timing of the eye movements. Because visual tracking also involves head movements, their quality and the way they are coordinated with the eye movements is yet another indication of tracking quality. All these measurements have been used in the study of the development of visual tracking.

Smooth Pursuit

From about 6 weeks of age, the smooth part of the tracking improves rapidly. This was first observed by both Dayton and Jones (1964) and Aslin (1981). We (Rosander & von Hofsten, 2000, 2002, 2004; von Hofsten & Rosander, 1997) recorded eye and head movements in unrestrained 1- to 5-month-old infants as they tracked a happy face oscillating sinusoidally in front of them. We found that the improvement in smooth pursuit tracking was dramatic and consistent among individual subjects. Figure 2.6 shows the smooth pursuit gain from 26 infants studied longitudinally; it also shows that individual infants went from almost no smooth pursuit to adultlike performance in just a few weeks. Such rapid emergence indicates that the ability for predictive tracking is a result of new connections being established in the central nervous system rather than something that the infant learns from experience. The onset of SP in infant development parallels closely the emergence of sensitivity to direction of object motion (Atkinson, 2000). Together these facts indicate that the onset of SP is associated with the maturation of the motion-sensitive area of the visual cortex referred to as MT or V5.

As mentioned previously, even newborns track large objects smoothly. This tracking is generally associated with a lag and the gain is low (less than 0.25). It is most probably an expression of OKR, the phylogenetically older visual mode of stabilizing gaze in space. In contrast, the developing smooth pursuit is always predictive. Even when it is insufficient and has to be supplemented with saccades, the smooth part is well timed relative to the head-slip (object motion – head motion). Figure 2.7 depicts the mean lag of a group of nine infants followed from 6.5 to 17 weeks of age. They tracked sinusoidally moving objects of various sizes from 2.5 to 35° of visual angle. It can be seen from Fig. 2.7 that the timing was excellent from the youngest age of the study. The size of the object did not influence performance, and this was also valid for the relative amplitude of the pursuit. The only difference found in the young infants' tracking of the larger and smaller objects was the number of saccades observed. The infants in this study used equal amounts of SP for all target sizes, but they used

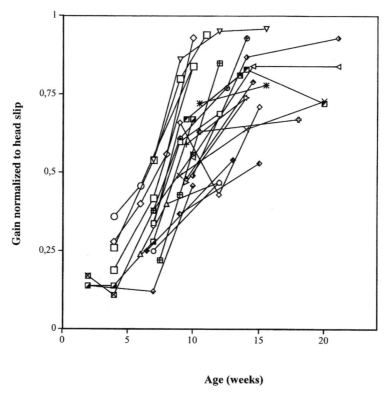

FIG. 2.6.   Records of smooth pursuit development in individuals studied
longitudinally. The measured property of smooth pursuit is the proportion
of eye movement amplitude accounted for by smooth tracking of the moving object (smooth pursuit). Note that most of the development of smooth
pursuit in these subjects occurs between 6 and 12 weeks of age.

more saccades to catch up with the small targets. Thus, the observation
that young infants track larger objects more smoothly than smaller ones
has earlier been taken as evidence that small objects elicit SP while large
objects elicit OKR. This is an illusion.

Circular Visual Tracking

Gredebäck, von Hofsten, and Boudreau (2002) investigated 9-month-old
infants' ability to track a round target moving in a circular trajectory at
0.05, 0.1, 0.2, and 0.4 Hz. A cornea-reflection technique was used (ASL
inc). The results show that horizontal gain had reached mature levels at 9
months. The average vertical gain, however, was still immature, with

large individual differences based on a mixture of over- and underestimations of target amplitude. The timing of gaze was predictive in three of four frequencies for horizontal components, whereas vertical components were only predictive at 0.2 Hz. These effects, together with a larger average distance between target and gaze on vertical compared to horizontal components, indicated that horizontal gaze tracking matured earlier than vertical and that the later had not yet reached adult levels during two-dimensional pursuit at 38 weeks of age.

Type of Prospective Control

To distinguish between extrapolation and logical prediction in the development of SP (see Pavel, 1990), von Hofsten and Rosander (1997) presented two kinds of motions to infants: one sinusoidal and one triangular. The sinusoidal motion changes its velocity gradually and can therefore be extrapolated locally at any part of its trajectory, whereas the triangular one moves with constant speed except at the endpoints of the trajectory where it reverses abruptly. These reversals cannot be extrapolated from the just seen motion. They can only be predicted from knowledge of where or when the motion reverses. von Hofsten and Rosander (1997) found that, in contrast to the tracking of the sinusoidal motion, the tracking of the triangular motion had a distinct lag of 250 ms at 2 and 3 months of age. At every reversal, the gaze lagged behind. At 5 months, this lag was significantly reduced indicating that infants will then begin to learn something about the rules that regulate the abrupt reversals. The results indicate that the infants learned where the object would turn. Two amplitudes were used in this experiment. If a place rule was used, infants would overestimate the lower amplitude and turn later and underestimate the higher amplitude and turn earlier. This is what we found (von Hofsten & Rosander, 1997).

Head Tracking

At around 3 to 4 months of age, there is a dramatic increase in the amount of head movements used to visually track moving objects. This is shown in Fig. 2.7. At 5 months the amplitude of the head tracking was sometimes as large as the amplitude of the object motion. The increase in head movements creates at least two kinds of problems. The first has to do with the timing of the head movements, and the second has to do with the vestibular change they evoke.

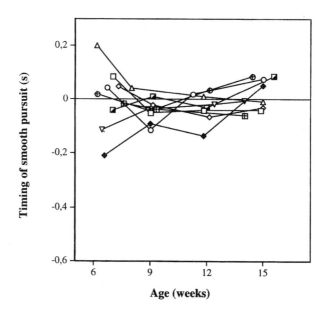

FIG. 2.7. Timing of smooth pursuit in nine individual infants followed from 6.5 to 15 weeks. Note that there is no systematic lag of the pursuit at any age, but the variance is higher at the youngest age level. (From Rosander & von Hofsten, 2002.)

In 5-month-old infants, the head movements lag the horizontally oscillating object quite substantially as shown in Fig. 2.8. We found the mean lag to be 360 ms (von Hofsten & Rosander, 1997).

When compensating for the lagging head, the eyes must lead to stabilize gaze on the target. This creates a problem if the object motion is fast. The eyes might very well have to move more than if the head were kept still. This is because the phase differences between the eye and head tracking can become so large that the two varieties of tracking counteract each other. In other words, instead of contributing to stabilizing gaze on the fixated moving object, head tracking might instead deteriorate gaze stabilization. Figure 2.8 shows such a case. It shows a 5-month-old child tracking an object oscillating at 0.63 Hz. The object covered 40° in 0.8 s and had a maximum velocity of 66°/s. In this condition, the amplitude of the head movement was 73% of the object motion, and it lagged 350 ms, which corresponds to a phase lag of 80°. With this head movement, the eyes had to move 115% of the object motion and lead it by 0.18 s. Instead it moved 67% of the object motion and led by 0.31 s corresponding to 70°. The amplitude of the resulting smooth gaze was 35% of the object motion, and it lagged the object. This is all depicted in Fig. 2.8.

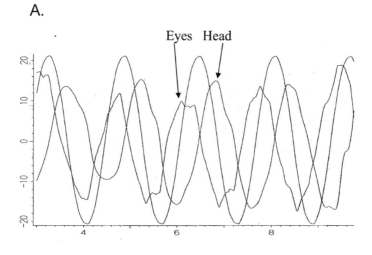

A.

Eyes   Head

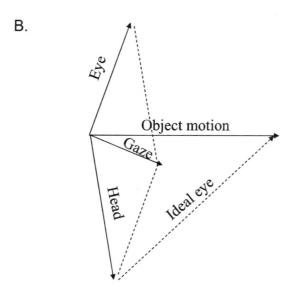

B.

FIG. 2.8.   An example of a 5-month-old infant tracking a fast target with large head movements. The target moved with 0.63 Hz, which means that one cycle was completed in 1.6 sec. (A) The position of the object, the head, and the eyes over time. Note the large phase difference between the head and the eyes. (B) A vector analysis of the different movements involved. The amplitude of the head movement was 73% of the object motion and it lagged the head with 0.35 s (i.e., 80°). To be on target, the amplitude of the eyes had to be 115% of the object motion and lead it by 0.18 s (i.e., 40° [ideal eye]). Instead the amplitude of the eyes was 67% of the head and they led by 0.31 s (70°). The phase difference between the head and eyes made the two movements counteract each other. The amplitude of the gaze was 35% of the object motion and it lagged slightly 0.08 s (17°).

67

The second problem has to do with the fact that a moving head might activate the VOR. An important task of the vestibular system is to maintain a stable gaze direction while the subject is moving around, but this task is incompatible with tracking a target with the head. Therefore, head tracking requires the vestibular responses to be inhibited. In adults, head and eye movements add perfectly to each other in stabilizing gaze on a moving object. This might not always be the case, however, in young infants. Figure 2.9 shows a 6.5-week-old infant for whom compensating eye movements totally eliminated the effects of the head tracking (Rosander & von Hofsten, 2002). The situation was quite paradoxical. The VOR drove the eyes away from the target, and frequent saccades were used to refixate it. Thus, in the end, the head tracking had no effect. All tracking was accomplished with saccades. This was an immaturity effect. When the infant

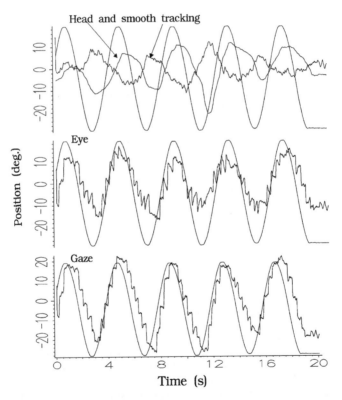

FIG. 2.9.   Head, smooth eye, object, and gaze (vector sum of eye and head) positions in a 6.5-week-old subject who was not able to inhibit the vestibularly induced compensatory eye movements. Note that those compensations totally eliminate the effects of the head movements and all tracking is accomplished with saccades. (From Rosander & von Hofsten, 2002.)

returned for another measurement 3 weeks later, the contributions of head and eye tracking were additive.

In somewhat older infants, head movements do not elicit such a strong VOR, but there are indications that the inhibition is not perfect. Because head movements lag the moving target and the VOR is counterface to the head, the effect of a leaking VOR is to push the smooth eye movements ahead of the target. The larger the head movements, the stronger this effect will be. When analyzing the smooth eye tracking in von Hofsten and Rosander (1997), we found that the eyes were, on the average, significantly ahead of the target (133 ms) for the 5-month-old infants. However, we also found that the amount of lead was rather strongly correlated with gain of head tracking (r = 0.66). The intercept of this linear regression was −32 ms. Therefore, this result supports the leaking VOR hypothesis. Some compensating eye movements are, in general, elicited by head movements at this age.

A special situation where the intrusion of VOR into visual tracking is especially easy to observe is when the visual field rotates with the subject in such a way that the object is always straight ahead. This is a fairly common situation. It occurs every time a subject is positioned inside a moving vehicle like a car. To stabilize gaze on the object, the eyes should remain stationary in this situation. This is not the case. The eyes and head counterrotate and cause the gaze to slip away from the target. This gives rise to a refixating saccade, and the sequence is repeated again and again in a nystagmic way. A typical result from a 4-week-old is illustrated in Fig. 2.10. It can be seen that the magnitude of the counterrotations is less than half compared with the situation where the child is rotated relative to a stationary object. Thus, some inhibition of the vestibular mode of control takes place even though they are insufficient.

The situation where the subject and object move together is different in several respects from the one where subjects actively track an object with the head and eyes. First, it is not only the head that moves, but the whole body. Then the vestibular system not only tries to counterrotate the eyes, but also the head (VCR). Both these counterrotations must be inhibited to stabilize gaze on the object. Second, the body movements are passive. This means that the subject does not know ahead of time exactly how the body is going to move next. Complete inhibition of the vestibular mode of control is then more difficult to attain. As the child develops better control of gaze, the amount of counterrotations of the eyes in this situation decreases as can be seen in Fig. 2.11. However, during the same period, as Fig. 2.11 shows, the head becomes more engaged in the gaze control process, and its counterrotations increase. Thus, although subjects become better able to inhibit the compensatory eye movements, the greater engagement of the head will result in poorer gaze control in this situation at 18 than at 4

VORINHIB condition

a: 4 weeks old   b: 14 weeks old

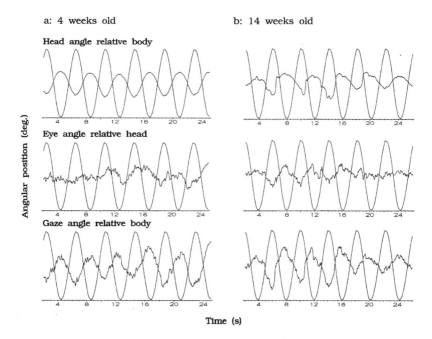

Time (s)

FIG. 2.10.   A situation where the infant and object in front of him or her rotate in synchrony. As the object in this situation is always straight ahead, fix-
ating it requires the eyes to be stationary. The vestibular mode of control,
however, induces counterrotations of the eyes and head. The eyes move in a
nystagmic way. They alternatively drift away from the object and are then
turned back to it by means of a saccade. This is clearly seen in the figure. The
head, smooth eye movements, and gaze movements are depicted together
with the object motion in a 4- and a 14-week-old infant. Note the prominent
counterrotations of the eyes and head. (From Rosander & von Hofsten, 2000.)

weeks of age. It is not necessarily the case that inhibiting two things is
more difficult than inhibiting one. However, if the two factors are relatively independent from each other as the vestibularly controlled eye and
head movements seem to be, then the subject must learn to control each of
them separately.

Thus, engaging the head in visual tracking proves to be a real challenge
for the child. First, skilled tracking requires prospective control of both
eye and head movements. However, to begin with the head lags substantially and makes the task of the eyes more complicated. Often the head
movements do not contribute to the tracking effort. On the contrary, they
make it necessary for the eyes to move more than if the head had been stationary. Second, the already established mode of using vestibular and

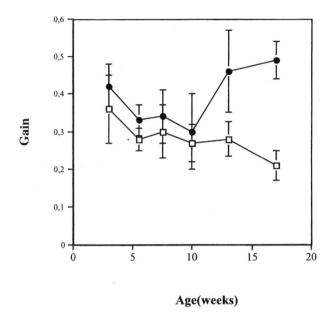

Age(weeks)

FIG. 2.11. The counterrotations of gaze and eyes in a situation where the infant and the object in front rotate together. The data summarize a group of infants followed from 3 to 17 weeks of age. The difference in gain between eyes and gaze corresponds to the contribution of the head. That is, the larger the distance between the two curves, the more head counterrotation there is. It can be seen that the compensatory eye movements become more inhibited with age, but that the amplitude of the head movements increases instead. (From Rosander & von Hofsten, 2000.)

proprioceptive information to maintain gaze direction in space interferes with the effort to track the object with the head. Still at 5 months of age, the child makes some involuntarily compensatory eye movements in response to their own head tracking. The problem is that the vestibular and proprioceptive mode of control cannot be shut off because head and body movements unrelated to the tracking must still be compensated. In adults, the problem is solved by separation of the functional domains of the visual and vestibular systems. At low frequencies (<1 Hz) eye movements are primarily visually controlled, whereas at high frequencies they are primarily vestibularly controlled (Barnes, 1993).

Taking all these problems into account, the task for the child would be much simpler if the head did not move at all. Therefore, the reason that infants persist in engaging the head cannot be because the action outcome is superior. The motivation for doing so must have come from within. It is as if the infants knew that even though the head movements made tracking tasks more difficult, sometime in the future they would be much better off if they could coordinate eye and head movements in the tracking effort. The direct motive is, of course, a different one. I argued earlier that children find it pleasurable to explore their action potentials. When new domains of action possibilities open up as a result of, for instance, the establishment of new neuronal pathways, improved perception, biomechanical changes, or improved mobility in other domains, the child is ready to explore those new possibilities. Such explorations are clearly a necessary part of learning action control. Another example of the pleasure that children find in exploring action space are learning to reach and walk. At a certain stage of development, children can spend hours and hours trying to attain an object in front of them with little or no success. Instead of being discouraged by their repeated failures, they seem ever so happy. The same thing happens when children are ready to learn to walk. At a certain stage, crawling is a much more efficient mode of locomotion. Despite this, children are unstoppable in their urge to explore this new action potential.

THE DEVELOPMENT OF TRACKING
OVER OCCLUSION

Moving objects are not always visible. Objects moving in a cluttered terrain frequently get occluded by other objects. To identify objects across occlusion, their motion must somehow be represented over the occlusion interval. Tracking them under such conditions is even more demanding. To resume tracking without delay after the reappearance of the object, the subject has to direct gaze to the point where the object will reappear when this happens or before. This requires anticipation of the time and position of reappearance and an appreciation of the velocity and direction of motion at that instance. To solve the identity and anticipation problems and preserve spatiotemporal continuity over temporary occlusions, the representations of moving objects must persist over such events.

Because smooth pursuit requires continuous visual support, it cannot be used for this kind of prospectiveness unless the period of occlusion is very short. Instead a saccade is typically made to the point of reappearance. In contrast to smooth pursuit, which is guided by object velocity, saccades are guided by object position. Therefore, saccades made to a moving object have to be based on anticipations of its future position. Rosander and von Hofsten (2002) found that catch-up saccades had this property from about 3 months of age. If a saccade, made in response to object occlusion, is going to be anticipating where and when the object will reappear, the subject has to represent the moving object over the period of occlusion. In other words, such ability reflects significant achievements in object representation.

There are only a few studies investigating the emergence of tracking over occlusion. van der Meer, van der Weel, and Lee (1994) found that 5-month-old infants looked toward the reappearance side in an anticipatory way when observing linearly moving objects that were totally occluded for 0.3 to 0.6 s. Sergienko (1992) observed cases of predictive occluder tracking in 12- to 18-week-old infants. She reported that they made predictive saccades over an occluder twice the size of the occluded object.

Rosander and myself (Rosander & von Hofsten, 2004) studied the timing of occluder tracking in 7- to 21-week-old infants. The object moved back and forth on a horizontal trajectory and was either occluded for 300 ms at the center of its trajectory or for 600 ms at its left turning point. One full cycle of motion was completed in 4 s. The duration of each trial was 20 s and included five cycles of motion. Both eye and head movements were measured at 200 Hz. As in the studies of smooth pursuit reported earlier, both sinusoidal and triangular motions were used. If infants use velocity information when extrapolating object motion, a difference in tracking performance would be seen for the two kinds of motion.

Over the age period studied, Rosander and von Hofsten (2004) found that performance progressed from almost total ignorance of what happened to the object behind the occluder to consistent predictive behavior. Figure 2.12 shows the individual trials from a 7- and a 21-week-old infant. Figure 2.13 shows the mean timing for each cycle in the triangular condition. The results clearly demonstrate that infants below 12 weeks of age did not predictively track objects that were temporarily occluded for 300 ms. For the youngest infants, the occluder edge appeared to become the focus of attention after object disappearance, and this impaired the infants' ability to represent the occluded object and switch gaze to it when it reappeared. It was found that the gaze of 7- and 9-week-old infants remained at the occluder edge of disappearance almost 1 second after the object reappeared on the other side. This means that in many cases the object already reversed direction of motion and was approaching the occluder again before the infants refocused their gaze on the object. This relative incapability to quickly regain tracking had more or less disappeared for the 12-week-olds. At that age level, the infants did not generally track the object in a predictive way, but they moved their gaze promptly to the reappearance point as soon as the object became visible. Initial gaze delay at object reappearance was only about half that of the 9-week-olds. At a group level, the 17-week-old infants predicted the reappearance of the object at the end of the trial where the object moved with triangular motion. The 21-week-olds clearly predicted the reappearance of the occluded objects in both the triangular and sinusoidal conditions after having seen just a couple of oscillation cycles.

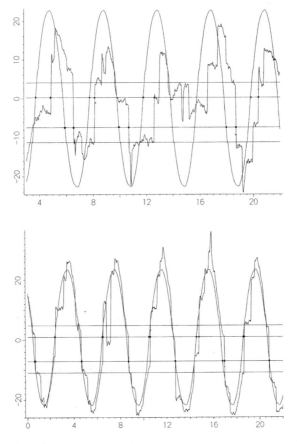

FIG. 2.12.   Gaze movements plotted together with the object motion for single sinusoidal trials with central occlusion. The graph depicts the event over time (horizontal axis) and space (vertical axis). The outer horizontal lines in the figures signify the occluder boundaries. As a centrally placed marker measured the position of the object, only half the object was occluded when the marker passed the occluder boundaries. Therefore, the inner horizontal lines are needed to signify the position of the object marker when the object was totally occluded. Thus, these are positioned half the object width inside the occluder. (From Rosander & von Hofsten, 2004.)

The results obtained by Rosander and von Hofsten (2004) are in general agreement with the numerous habituation studies that have investigated infants' emerging ability to represent temporarily occluded moving objects (Aguiar & Baillargeon, 1999; Baillargeon & Graber, 1987; Baillargeon & deVos, 1991; Johnson et al., 2003; Spelke, Kestenbaum, Simons, & Wein, 1995). In Rosander and von Hofsten (2004), one 12-week-old infant predicted all object reappearances except the first ones in the sinusoidal con-

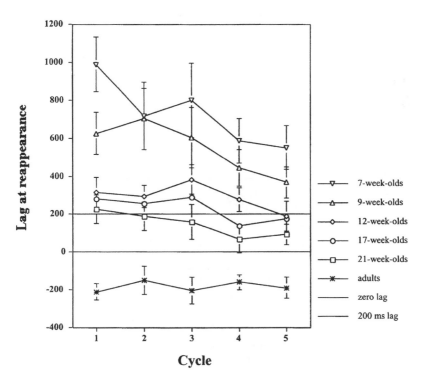

FIG. 2.13.   The average time differences and SE between object and gaze reappearance at each cycle of the centrally occluded trials with triangular motion. Each data point is the average of one occluder passage in each direction
for all subjects in a specific age group. The dotted line corresponds to the
minimum time required for adults to program a saccade to an unexpected
event (200 ms).

dition. Thus, it is not unconceivable that some 2.5-month-old infants
would look longer at a display where a moving object (a tall rabbit) did
not appear in a slit in the occluder as expected (Aguiar & Baillargeon,
1999). The result is also in agreement with the result by Johnson et al.
(2003) indicating that 2-month-olds have problems with temporary occlusion of moving objects. The reason that the present study can be in agreement with both of these studies that seem to generate conflicting results is
because none of them has considered either individual differences or
learning.

   Group-level data only give part of the story. The results demonstrate
the importance of considering individual differences in understanding
development. The individual differences are substantial as depicted in
Fig. 2.14. For instance, while one infant consistently predicted the reappearance of the object at 12 weeks of age, two other infants did not even

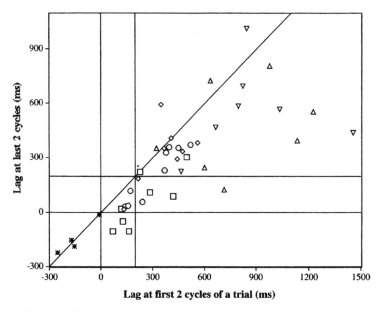

FIG. 2.14. The average timing for the first two cycles of motion in the centrally occluded trials plotted against the average timing for the last two cycles for each of the subjects in Rosander and von Hofsten (2004). The symbols depicting the subjects in the different age groups are the same as in Fig. 2.13 (7-week-old infants = ▽, 9-week-old infants = △, 12-week-old infants = ◇, 17-week-old infants = ○, 21-week-old infants = □). (From Rosander & von Hofsten, 2004.)

show such prediction at 21 weeks of age. In addition to the improvements with age and the individual differences, there were also impressive learning effects. What infants accomplished initially at one age level, they could do after less than 20 s of experience at an earlier age level (see Fig. 2.13). The learning did not become more efficient with age. On the contrary, the improvement in timing was actually more substantial before 12 weeks of age than after. The 9-week-olds almost halved their reaction time to the reappearing object between the first and last cycles of motion in a trial. In fact, the performance of the 9-week-olds at the end of a trial was indistinguishable from that of the 12-week-olds at the beginning of a trial.

Individual differences and the effects of learning in Rosander and von Hofsten (2004) were so great that it is not quite meaningful to discuss the presence or absence of predictive occluder tracking at certain age levels. It all depends on the capability of the specific infant tested and what experience that infant has had immediately prior to the occluder event in question. The learning effects imply that infants' ability to predict the reappearance of a temporarily hidden object changed dramatically over a single 20-s trial. For the triangular motion, the average gaze lag at the first occluder passage at 21 weeks of age was greater than the gaze lag at the last occluder passage at 12 weeks of age. In fact, after 12 weeks of age, most of the improvements in occluder tracking are accounted for in terms of rapid learning over single trials. Even the 21-week-olds, as a group, did not anticipate the reappearance of the object at the beginning of a trial. Only after a couple of encounters of occlusion did they consistently do so.

Another remarkable feature of the learning of occluder tracking was that the representations of the occluded object faded away as rapidly as it was acquired. There was no evidence that the improvement in timing observed over one trial was transferred to the next trial with central occlusion. Both the rapid learning and rapid forgetting have interesting parallels in adults' tracking of temporarily hidden objects. It is a well-known fact that anticipatory smooth pursuit eye movements greater than 4 to 5 deg/s cannot normally be made at will in the absence of a moving target (Kowler & Steinman, 1979). Attempts to perform faster open-loop smooth eye movements invoke saccades (Heywood & Churcher, 1971). In a series of elegant experiments, however, Barnes and associates (Barnes & Asselman, 1991; Barnes, Barnes, & Chakraborti, 2000; Barnes, Grealy, & Collins, 1997; Chakraborti, Barnes, & Collins, 2002; Ohashi & Barnes, 1996; Wells & Barnes, 1998, 1999) found that anticipatory smooth pursuit at the reappearance of the target can be built up with a few prior transient views of the moving stimulus. The smooth pursuit starts just before the object appears and accelerates in such a way that the eyes move with the appropriate speed and in the appropriate direction when it appears. The advantage of such ability is that the eyes can stabilize on the reappearing object without an initial slip that will blur the retinal image. Barnes et al. (1997) suggested that moving stimuli charge a putative internal store of information, but decharge quickly with time. Chakraborti et al. (2002) found that under optimal conditions, no significant decay was observed for gap intervals up to 14 s. It is not a motor memory because it can be built by just viewing rather than pursuing the moving target (Barnes et al., 1997). These ideas of a temporary store for representing object motion fit very well with the graded representation hypothesis (Munakata, 2001; Spelke & von Hofsten, 2001). According to this hypothesis, the ability to represent a temporarily hidden moving target is not something that is either present or absent at a certain age. It builds up with viewing time and decays with time out of view. Instead of asking whether a child at a certain age can represent a moving object over occlusions, one should therefore ask whether the child has the capability to acquire such a representation while viewing the visible object before it disappears behind the occluder.

What are the properties of the persistent representations that allow infants to predict the reappearance of a temporarily occluded moving object? First of all, it is not a question of behavioral inertia. Infants do not track an object over occlusions with smooth eye movements. Instead, the tracking stops at the disappearing edge of the occluder, and one or two saccades are made to the reappearing side. Is this just a question of learning the contingencies of two events, the disappearance and reappearance of an object? Infants are quite clever in picking up such dependencies and use them to predict what is going to happen next (see e.g., Haith, 1994; Kirkham et al., 2002; Saffran et al., 1996). However, the data indicate that this description is too simplified to account for predictive occluder tracking because subjects make precise predictions where and when the object will appear. If contingency were the only factor determining predictive occluder tracking, infants would make a saccade to the other side of the occluder when they see the object disappear behind it. In contrast, Rosander and von Hofsten (2004) clearly showed that the saccades over the occluder were geared to the reappearance of the object, not the disappearance. If they had been geared to the disappearance, gaze should have arrived to the other side much before the object arrived there. That the representations preserve the spatiotemporal properties of object motion behind the occluder is further supported by Gredebäck, von Hofsten, and Boudreau (2002) and Gredebäck and von Hofsten (2004). Gredebäck et al. (2002) found that 9-month-old infants adjusted the latency time of the gaze crossing to the occlusion time of the object. For a 5-s occlusion the infants waited, on the average, 3 s before moving over to the other side of the occluder. For an object occlusion of 2 s infants waited 1 s, and for a 1-s occlusion they waited 0.5 s. Gredebäck and von Hofsten (2004) found the same effect in infants from 6 months of age. Another piece of evidence that the representations of occluded objects preserve the spatiotemporal properties of motion comes from experiments where the object arrives to the other side of the occluder too early. Moore et al. (1978) showed infants magic occlusions where the object started to reappear immediately after they had disappeared. They found that both 5- and 9-month-old infants look back and look away more in this situation than in a control condition with a normal occlusion.

Preserving the spatiotemporal continuity has to do with assumptions of how the motion will proceed behind the occluder. Inertia provides one such basic rule that governs object motion. It states that "objects continue in a state of rest or uniform motion unless acted upon by forces." A simple assumption that no force will act on the temporary occluded object leads to the prediction that the object will continue in the same direction and with the same speed behind the occluder as it had when it disappeared.

von Hofsten, Feng, and Spelke (2000) and Jonsson and von Hofsten (2003) found that 6-month-old infants turned their heads to follow the extension of the initial linear trajectory of an occluded object. Initially, this was a strong tendency. In one condition, the trajectory of the object was perturbed behind the occluder and the object then reappeared at a position perpendicular to its initial trajectory. Even when this was the first occlusion event presented to the infants, they moved to the opposite side of the occluder for several trials. However, they also showed significant learning of the perturbed motion, and after six trials of such motion they consistently moved their head to the place where the object reappeared.

Rosander and von Hofsten (2004) provided more indications that infants act in accordance with the assumption that occluded moving objects continue in the same direction and with the same speed as before. When the occluder was placed at the end of the trajectory, infants moved gaze over to the opposite side. This tendency increased with age. The 21-week-olds made predictive saccades over to the other side of it in almost 50% of such occlusions (see Fig. 2.15). They did this throughout the peripheral trials despite that the object always reappeared on the same side.

The assumption that no forces act on an object while it moves is a special case. It is more common that they move because forces act on them, but forces rarely change abruptly and when they change the effect is gradual. A more reasonable assumption of how objects move behind occluders is therefore that the motion regularities displayed before occlusion continue to be the same during occlusion. Showing infants objects moving in straight paths with constant velocity cannot distinguish between these two alternative explanations because both hypotheses make the same prediction. In sinusoidal motion, however, velocity changes continuously. At the centrally placed occluder, it increases velocity as it disappears and moves faster behind it. Therefore, Rosander and von Hofsten (2004) made the occluder placed at the middle of the trajectory wider for the sinusoidal motion than for the triangular one. The gaze of 12- and 17-week-old infants arrived later for the wider occluder than for the narrow one, indicating that the subjects assumed that the object moved behind the occluder with constant speed. The 21-week-old infants, however, did not arrive later in the sinusoidal than in the triangular condition, indicating that they were able to represent the faster sinusoidal motion behind the occluder. Although the 21-week-olds moved gaze over the peripheral occluder in almost 50% of the cases, they were found to have some sensitivity to velocity change, and this sensitivity biased their behavior at the peripheral occluder. The sinusoidal motion decelerated strongly before disappearance specifying that the object should turn behind the occluder and reappear on the same side, whereas the triangular one moved with constant

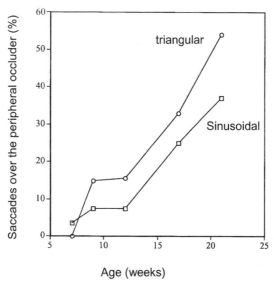

FIG. 2.15.   The proportion of occlusions at the end of the trajectory where the subjects made a saccade over to the other side of the occluder as a function of age. (From Rosander & von Hofsten, 2004.)

speed specifying reappearance on the other side. The 21-week-old infants made significantly fewer false crossings when the motion was sinusoidal than when it was triangular (see Fig. 2.15).

A stronger test of whether infants assume that objects continue to move behind an occluder in the same direction as when they become occluded is to show them a circular motion. If they assume that the motion continues on linear trajectories behind the occluder, they will expect it to reappear on a tangential trajectory from the point of disappearance. However, if the previously seen motion is assumed to continue behind the occluder, infants will look for the moving object along its circular trajectory. Gredebäck, von Hofsten, and Boudreau (2002) presented 9-month-old infants with a target that moved in a circular trajectory at four different frequencies—0.05, 0.1, 0.2, and 0.4 Hz. Gaze was measured with a cornea reflection technique (ASL Inc.). During each cycle, the target disappeared behind an occluder for a duration ranging from 0.25 to 5 s. The results clearly demonstrate that the infants expected the object to continue to move along the previously seen circular trajectory. Although up to a quarter of the circular trajectory was occluded, and consequently the object in such conditions appeared at a position where it moved in a direction perpendicular to the one it had at disappearance, the subjects made precise and correct anticipations of the reappearance of the object in all conditions. This can be seen in Fig. 2.16. Gredebäck and von Hofsten (2004) studied infants'

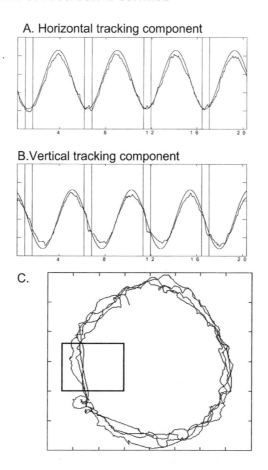

A. Horizontal tracking component

B. Vertical tracking component

C.

FIG. 2.16.   Example of occluder tracking in a 9-month-old infant. The object moves in a circular trajectory and completes a full cycle in 5 s. Ten percent of the circular trajectory is occluded (indicated by the outline rectangle in C). The horizontal and vertical tracking components are shown separately in A and B together with the object motion. The vertical lines indicate the times at which the object disappears and reappears. The timing of the gaze crossings over occluder can be clearly seen in B. (From Gredebäck & von Hofsten, 2004.)

tracking of occluded circular motions longitudinally. The object was al-ways occluded for 20% of their circular trajectory corresponding to 72° of a full circle. The occluder was placed at several different positions, and therefore simple rules of where it would reappear could not be applied. However, the complexity of the task did not seem to degrade perform-ance. At all ages, the anticipatory saccades were precisely directed toward the reappearance position of the target. This fact makes it also possible to exclude explanations of poor performance as expressions of inadequate motor control.

DISCUSSION

For an understanding of the development of perception, action, and cognition, it is of utmost importance to trace their origins in development. I have tried to do that in the present chapter in the context of visual tracking. As described earlier, children come well prepared at birth to use vision to explore their surroundings. They can control their eye movements and switch gaze to interesting locations in their surroundings. This means that the motor commands are mapped onto visual directions (Aslin, 1988). The fact that they turn their eyes to significant stimuli like faces and moving objects is remarkable because patterned vision is not available before birth. The neonate is also able to stabilize gaze in space by compensating for their own body movements. These compensations are rather mature at birth, and they are primarily controlled by the vestibular system and neck proprioception. In contrast, visual control of compensatory eye movements and the smooth movements required to stabilize gaze on a moving object do not function well at birth.

Furthermore, the research presented shows that infants' ability to track visible objects and to keep track of them when they are temporarily nonvisible develops rapidly. Smooth pursuit becomes functional between 6 and 12 weeks of age. In individual infants, the gain doubled or tripled in 2 or 3 weeks. This is depicted in Fig. 2.5. The ability to track objects over occlusion improves in a similarly dramatic way. Although it only results in predictive occluder crossing about 2 or 3 months later, there are improvements in the way infants deal with the occlusion event from the age smooth pursuit begins to develop. Rosander and von Hofsten (2004) found that the development of smooth pursuit eye movements and the timing of the occluder crossings were highly correlated (0.85). This is to be expected if there is an underlying more general development of infants' ability to represent both visible and nonvisible object motion. Just like the persisting representations of object motion during temporary occlusion, smooth pursuit eye movements are stimulated by an "internal signal representing expected target motion, and based on the processing of symbolic cues in the environment" (Kowler, 1990, p. 44). If the gain of smooth pursuit were merely a reflection of how effectively the motion-sensitive structures can drive it when the moving object is visible, there is no reason for a close relationship between the gain of smooth pursuit and timing of saccades over the occluder.

The age range over which smooth pursuit and predictive occluder tracking develop corresponds to a period of rapid increase in interconnectivity of the cerebral cortex (Huttenlocher, 1990). The synaptogenesis seems to reach its peak at around 3 to 4 months in the sensory areas, and it is accompanied by rapid improvements of sensory and sensorimotor skills (Birch, Gwiazda, & Held, 1982; von Hofsten & Rosander, 1997). Stabilizing gaze on moving objects is primarily a question of acquiring prospective control of eye and head movements and integrating these two modes of control into one differentiated mode. A basic prerequisite for this is precise perception of the velocity and acceleration of object motion. In adults, such sophisticated visual motion analysis engages the cerebral cortex and especially area V5 or MT (Tootell et al., 1995; Zeki, Watson, & Frackowiak, 1993). When this area is damaged in adult subjects, subjects cannot see motion and change, and they cannot smoothly pursue moving objects (Zihl, von Cramon, & Mai, 1983). Therefore, most probably, the rapid appearance of well-calibrated and well-timed smooth pursuit from around 2 months of age reflects the synaptogenesis of the motion analyzing parts of the visual cortex. With this resource available, infants can start to learn more about moving objects and to gear their actions to them. This is not only important for looking. In a world of motion and change, all skillful actions must foresee what is going to happen next. For instance, when trying to catch a moving object, the reach must be geared toward a future position where the hand and object will meet (von Hofsten, 1980, 1983).

Prospective action toward moving objects must also be able to handle temporary interruptions in the availability of sensory information about them. Somehow they have to be represented in the brain. They probably reside in the prefrontal areas. Recent evidence shows, for instance, that the Frontal Eye Field (FEF) of rhesus monkeys is involved in the representation of occluded moving objects (Barborica & Ferrera, 2003). Although the prefrontal areas areas continue to develop for many years, recent evidence indicates that they begin to function rather early in development, but somewhat later than in the sensory areas (Huttenlocher & Dabholkar, 1997; Johnson, 1990; Mrzljak et al., 1990). These facts further support the assumption that the emergence of predictive occluder tracking in infants around 3 to 5 months of age reflects the synaptogenesis of the prefrontal parts of the cerebral cortex.

Precise measurement of infants' visual tracking, as in the studies discussed earlier, constitutes a powerful addition to the existing methods of studying infants' emerging perception and cognition. Over the last three decades, habituation and visual preference studies have given important contributions to our understanding of what infants perceive and how they think. However, visual habituation only gives one data point per subject.

In addition, because of the crudeness of measurements, the results from such studies have to rely on group data. The precise measurement of infants' visual tracking allows for estimates of individual infants' ability to represent moving objects at single trials. This opens up a more diversified study of the development of object representation. It makes the method suitable for studying the acquisition of perception and cognition in single subjects over age and how they improve over single experimental sessions. It also makes the method suitable for longitudinal and clinical studies, where the performance of specific individuals and their development are evaluated.

Because visual tracking is the product of a complex action system that involves the eyes, head, and, to a certain extent, the whole body, measuring the performance of the different parts of this system give important insights into how such motor systems develop. In the case of visual tracking, it is interesting to observe how biology has facilitated the solution of certain problems, but this has interfered with the solution of others. In most animals, visual tracking is mainly performed with the head. Developing relative independent functioning of head and eyes is a great leap forward in evolution, but it also creates new difficult problems to solve.

Developmental Processes

Perception and cognition develop at the interface between brain processes and action. They are a function of both and emerge as the result of the dynamic interaction between them. Their expressions reflect both the internal constraints set up by biology and the external constraints of the physical world. For instance, in the process of developing manual control, infants discover new information about objects that differentiate them in more distinct ways from other objects, and they learn rules by which the objects move and relate to other objects. The evolving brain plays a crucial role in timing these developmental processes because the opening of new neural pathways provides new tools for extracting information about the world, for contemplating it, and for acting on it. These tools, however, can only become useful by gearing them to the environment. The increase in specific activities and in their variability as new modes of action are about to emerge is probably the result of a motivation to explore new domains of movement possibilities that have been opened up as a result of, for instance, the establishment of new neuronal pathways, improved perception, biomechanical changes, or improved mobility in other domains. Earlier I used the metaphor of exploring the workspace of one's action systems (von Hofsten, 1997). When the new workspace is known to the child, efficient solutions will be found to specific tasks, and this tends to decrease the variability of the movements produced. When the task space is known, it is always possible to find the smoothest and most economical route through it independently of the previous ones taken. If unexpected problems or obstacles are encountered, a different optimal route will be found that will lead to the goal. The knowledge gathered through systematic exploration of a task is structured into a frame of reference for action that makes planning possible. This is the basis of skill. The importance of practice and repetition is not to stamp in patterns of movement or achieve a immutable program, but rather to encourage the functional organization of action systems (Reed, 1996).

Action systems in early development seem more independent than later. Abilities expressed in one context do not necessarily transfer to another one, and the systems of representations underlying them do not seem to do so either. Just because infants at a certain age can track an object predictively with his or her eyes does not imply that they track predictively with their head (von Hofsten & Rosander, 1997). In other words, infants must discover how action systems are related to each other and how knowledge in one domain can be applied to another one. By exercising their action systems, children develop more generalized skills and more generalized systems of representations emerge.

The Primacy of Perception

Although perception and action are mutually dependent, there is an asymmetry between them. Perception is necessary for controlling actions, and every action requires specific information for its control. Without perception, there is no action. The reverse is only partially true. Action is a necessary part of perceiving, but only in a general sense. Specific actions are not required for producing specific percepts, and action does not tell perception what to perceive. It only provides opportunities for perceiving and guides the perceptual system to where the information is.

This has clear consequences for development. The ability to extract the necessary information must be there before actions can be organized. Only then can infants learn to control the dynamics of their motor system and gear it to the appropriate information. Take, for instance, the speech system where infants' ability to perceive the phonemic and prosodic structure of speech develops much ahead of their ability to produced those sound qualities. The infant is still able to produce sounds and show joy in doing that, but the sounds have a much simpler cyclical structure than suggested by their perceptual abilities.

I can see two processes of perceptual development. The first one is a spontaneous perceptual learning process that has to do with the detection of structure in the sensory flow. As long as there is variability and change in the sensory flow, the perceptual system will spontaneously learn to detect structure and differentiate invariants in that flow that correspond to relatively stable and predictible properties of the world. The second process is one of selecting information relevant for guiding action. This is a question of learning about affordances, and in this process perception and action are mutually dependent on each other. However, before infants can learn about affordances, they must already have detected that structure in the sensory flow. It could not be the reverse.

REFERENCES

Aguiar, A., & Baillargeon, R. (1999). 2.5-month-old infants reasoning about when objects should and should not be occluded. *Cognitive Psychology, 39,* 116–157.

Aslin, R. N. (1981). Development of smooth pursuit in human infants. In D. F. Fisher, R. A. Monty, & J. W. Senders (Eds.), *Eye movements: Cognition and visual perception.* Hillsdale, NJ: Lawrence Erlbaum Associates.

Aslin, R. N. (1988). Anatomical constraints on oculomotor development: Implications for infant perception. In A. Yonas (Ed.), *Perceptual development in infancy. The Minnesota Symposia on Child Psychology* (Vol. 20). Hillsdale, NJ: Lawrence Erlbaum Associates.

Atkinson, J. (2000). *The developing visual brain.* Oxford, UK: Oxford University Press.

Baillargeon, R., & deVos, J. (1991). Object permanence in young infants: Further evidence. *Child Development, 62,* 1227–1246.

Baillargeon, R., & Graber, M. (1987). Where's the rabbit? 5.5-month-old infants' representation of the height of a hidden object. *Cognitive Development, 2,* 375–392.

Barborica, A., & Ferrera, V. P. (2003). Estimating invisible target speed from neuronal activity in monkey frontal eye field. *Nature Neuroscience, 6,* 66–74.

Barnes, G. R. (1993). Visual-vestibular interaction in the control of head and eye movement: The role of visual feedback and predictive mechanisms. *Progress in Neurobiology, 41,* 435–472.

Barnes, G. R., & Asselman, P. T. (1991). The mechanism of prediction in human smooth pursuit eye movements. *Journal of Physiology (London), 439,* 439–461.

Barnes, G. R., Barnes, D. M., & Chakraborti, S. R. (2000). Ocular pursuit responses to repeated, single-cycle sinusoids reveal behavior compatible with predictive pursuit. *Journal of Neurophysiology, 84,* 2340–2355.

Barnes, G. R., Grealy, M. A., & Collins, S. (1997). Volitional control of anticipatory ocular smooth pursuit after viewing, but not pursuing, a moving target: Evidence for a reafferent velocity store. *Experimental Brain Research, 116,* 445–455.

Bernstein, N. (1967). *The coordination and regulation of movements.* Oxford: Pergamon.

Birch, E. E., Gwiazda, J., & Held, R. (1982). Stereoacuity development for crossed and uncrossed disparities in human infants. *Vision Research, 22,* 507–513.

Bloch, H., & Carchon, I. (1992). On the onset of eye-head co-ordination in infants. *Behavioural Brain Research, 49,* 85–90.

Chakraborti, S. R., Barnes, G. R., & Collins, C. J. S. (2002). Factors affecting the longevity of a short-term velocity store for predictive oculomotor tracking. *Experimental Brain Research, 144,* 152–158.

Dayton, G. O., & Jones, M. H. (1964). Analysis of characteristics of fixation reflex in infants by use of direct current electrooculagraphy. *Neurology, 14,* 1152–1156.

Finocchio, D. V., Preston, K. L., & Fuchs, A. (1991). Infant eye movements: Quantification of the vestibulo-ocular reflex and visual-vestibular interactions. *Vision Research, 10,* 1717–1730.

Gredebäck, G., & von Hofsten, C. (2004). Infants' evolving representation of moving objects between 6 and 12 months of age. *Infancy.*

Gredebäck, G., von Hofsten, C., & Boudreau, P. (2002). Infants' tracking of continuous circular motion and circular motion interrupted by occlusion. *Infant Behavior and Development, 144,* 1–21.

Haith, M. (1980). *Rules that babies look by: The organization of newborn visual activity.* Hillsdale, NJ: Lawrence Erlbaum Associates.

Haith, M. M. (1994). Visual expectation as the first step toward the development of future-oriented processes. In M. M. Haith, J. B. Benson, R. J. Roberts, Jr., & B. Pennington (Eds.), *The development of future oriented processes* (pp. 11–39). Chicago: University of Chicago Press.

Heywood, S., & Churcher, J. (1971). Eye movements and the afterimage: 1. Tracking the afterimage. *Vision Research, 11,* 1163–1168.

Huttenlocher, P. R. (1990). Morphometric study of human cerebral cortex development. *Neuropsychologia, 28,* 517–527.

Huttenlocher, P. R., & Dabholkar, A. S. (1997). Regional differences in synaptogenesis in human cerebral cortex. *Journal of Comparative Neurology, 387,* 167–178.

Johnson, M. H. (1990). Cortical maturation and the development of visual attention in early infancy. *Journal of Cognitive Neuroscience, 2,* 81–95.

Johnson, M. H., & Morton, J. (1991). *Biology and cognitive development: The case of face recognition.* Oxford: Blackwell.

Johnson, S. P., Bremner, J. G., Slater, A., Mason, U., Foster, K., & Cheshire, A. (2003). Infants' perception of object trajectories. *Child Development, 74,* 94–108.

Jonsson, B., & von Hofsten, C. (2003). Infants' ability to track and reach for temporarily occluded objects. *Developmental Science, 6,* 88–101.

Keshner, E. A., & Peterson, B. W. (1995). Mechanisms controlling human head stabilization: I. Head-neck dynamics during random rotations in the horizontal planes. *Journal of Neurophysiology, 73,* 2293–2301.

Kirkham, N. Z., Slemmer, J. A., & Johnson, S. P. (2002). Visual statistical learning in infancy: Evidence for a domain general learning mechanism. *Cognition, 83,* B35–B42.

Kowler, E. (1990). The role of visual and cognitive processes in the control of eye movement. In E. Kowler (Ed.), *Eye movements and their role in visual and cognitive processes* (pp. 1–70). Amsterdam: Elsevier.

Kowler, E., & Steinman, R. M. (1979). The effect of expectations on slow oculomotor control: I. Periodic target steps. *Vision Research, 19,* 619–632.

Kremenitzer, J. P., Vaughan, H. G., Kurtzberg, D., & Dowling, K. (1979). Smooth-pursuit eye movements in the newborn infant. *Child Development, 50,* 442–448.

Lee, D. N. (1974). Visual information during locomotion. In R. B. MacLeod & H. Pick (Eds.), *Perception: Essays in honor of James Gibson* (pp. 250–267). Ithaca, NY: Cornell University Press.

Lee, D. N. (1976). A theory of visual control of breaking based on information about time-to-collision. *Perception, 5,* 437–459.

Lee, D. N. (1992). Body-environment coupling. In U. Neisser (Ed.), *Ecological and interpersonal knowledge of the self.* Cambridge: Cambridge University Press.

Lee, D. N., Davies, M. N. O., Green, P. R., & van der Weel, F. R. (1993). Visual control of velocity of approach by pigeons when landing. *Journal of Experimental Biology, 180,* 85–104.

Lee, D. N., Lishman, J. R., & Thompson, J. A. (1982). Visual regulation of gait in long jumping. *Journal of Experimental Psychology: Human Perception and Performance, 8,* 448–459.

Lee, D. N., Reddish, P. E., & Rand, D. T. (1991). Areal docking by hummingbirds. *Naturwissenschaften, 78,* 526–527.

Moore, M. K., Borton, R., & Darby, B. L. (1978). Visual tracking in young infants: Evidence for object identity or object permanence? *Journal of Experimental Child Psychology, 25,* 183–198.

Mrzljak, L., Uylings, H. B., van Eden, C. G., & Judas, M. (1990). Neuronal development in human prefrontal cortex in prenatal and postnatal stages. *Progress in Brain Research, 85,* 185–222.

Munakata, Y. (2001). Graded representations in behavioral dissociations. *Trends in Cognitive Science, 5*(7), 309–315.

Ohashi, N., & Barnes, G. R. (1996). A comparison of predictive and non-predictive ocular pursuit under active and passive stimulation conditions in humans. *Journal of Vestibular Research, 6,* 261–276.

Pavel, M. (1990). Predictive control of eye movement. In E. Kowler (Ed.), *Eye movements and their role in visual and cognitive processes. Reviews of oculomotor research* (Vol. 4, pp. 71–114). Amsterdam: Elsevier.

Peterson, B. W., & Richmond, F. J. (1988). *Control of head movements.* New York: Oxford University Press.

Reed, E. S. (1990). Changing theories of postural development. In M. Woollacott & A. Shumway-Cook (Eds.), *Development of posture and gait across the life span.* Columbia, SC: University of South Carolina Press.

Reed, E. S. (1996). *Encountering the world: Towards an ecological psychology.* New York: Oxford University Press.

Reisman, J. E., & Anderson, J. H. (1989). Compensatory eye movements during head and body rotation in infants. *Brain Research, 484,* 119–129.

Rosander, K., & von Hofsten, C. (2000). Visual-vestibular interaction in early infancy. *Experimental Brain Research, 133,* 321–333.

Rosander, K., & von Hofsten, C. (2002). Development of gaze tracking of small and large objects. *Experimental Brain Research, 146,* 257–264.

Rosander, K., & von Hofsten, C. (2004). Infants' emerging ability to represent object motion. *Cognition, 91,* 1–22.

Roucoux, A., Culee, C., & Roucoux, M. (1983). Development of fixation and pursuit eye movements in human infants. *Behavioural Brain Research, 10,* 133–139.

Saffran, J. R., Aslin, R. N., & Newport, E. L. (1996). Statistical learning by 8-month-old infants. *Science, 274,* 1926–1928.

Sergienko, E. (1992). *The development of anticipation in early human ontogeny* (in Russian). Moscow: Nauka.

Spelke, E. S., Kestenbaum, R., Simons, D. J., & Wein, D. (1995). Spatio-temporal continuity, smoothness of motion and object identity in infancy. *British Journal of Developmental Psychology, 13,* 113–142.

Spelke, E. S., & von Hofsten, C. (2001). Predictive reaching for occluded objects by 6-month-old infants. *Journal of Cognition and Development, 2,* 261–282.

Tootell, R. B. H., Reppas, J. B., Dale, A. M., Look, R. B., Sereno, M. I., Malach, R., Brady, T. J., & Rosen, B. R. (1995). Functional analysis of human MT and related visual cortical areas using magnetic resonance imaging. *Journal of Neuroscience, 15,* 3215–3230.

van der Meer, A. L. H. (1997). Keeping the arm in the limelight. *European Journal of Paediatric Neurology, 4,* 103–108.

van der Meer, A. L. H., van der Weel, F., & Lee, D. N. (1994). Prospective control in catching by infants. *Perception, 23,* 287–302.

van der Meer, A.L. H., van der Weel, F. R., & Lee, D. N. (1995). The functional significance of arm movements in neonates. *Science, 267,* 693–695.

von Hofsten, C. (1980). Predictive reaching for moving objects by human infants. *Journal of Experimental Child Psychology, 30,* 369–382.

von Hofsten, C. (1982). Eye-hand coordination in newborns. *Developmental Psychology, 18,* 450–461.

von Hofsten, C. (1983). Catching skills in infancy. *Journal of Experimental Psychology: Human Perception and Performance, 9,* 75–85.

von Hofsten, C. (1997). On the early development of predictive abilities. In C. Dent & P. Zukow-Goldring (Eds.), *Evolving explanations of development: Ecological approaches to organism-environmental systems* (pp. 163–194). Washington, DC: American Psychological Association.

von Hofsten, C. (2003). On the development of perception and action. In J. Valsiner & K. J. Connolly (Eds.), *Handbook of developmental psychology* (pp. 114–140). London: Sage.

von Hofsten, C., Feng, Q., & Spelke, E. S. (2000). Object representation and predictive action in infancy. *Developmental Science, 3,* 193–205.

von Hofsten, C., & Rosander, K. (1996). The development of gaze control and predictive tracking in young infants. *Vision Research, 36,* 81–96.

von Hofsten, C., & Rosander, K. (1997). Development of smooth pursuit tracking in young infants. *Vision Research, 37,* 1799–1810.

von Hofsten, C., Vishton, P., Spelke, E. S., Feng, Q., & Rosander, K. (1998). Predictive action in infancy: Tracking and reaching for moving objects. *Cognition, 67,* 255–285.

Warren, W. H., & Hannon, D. J. (1990). Eye movements and optical flow. *Journal of the Optical Society of America, A7,* 160–169.

Wells, S. G., & Barnes, G. R. (1998). Fast, anticipatory smooth-pursuit eye movements appear to depend on a short-term store. *Experimental Brain Research, 120,* 129–133.

Well, S. G., & Barnes, G. R. (1999). Predictive smooth pursuit eye movements during identification of moving acuity targets. *Vision Research, 39,* 2767–2775.

Zeki, S., Watson, J. D. G., & Frackowiak, R. S. J. (1993). Going beyond the information given: The relation of illusory visual motion to brain activity. *Proceedings of the Royal Society of London. B. Biological Sciences, 252,* 215–222.

Zihl, J., von Cramon, D., & Mai, N. (1983). Selective disturbance of movement vision after bilateral brain damage. *Brain, 106,* 313–340.

3

▼▼▼▼▼▼▼▼

Learning to Learn in the Development of Action

Karen E. Adolph
New York University

FLEXIBILITY IN SKILLED PERFORMANCE

Fluency and flexibility are the hallmarks of skilled performance (MacKay, 1982; Schmidt & Lee, 1999). Fluency is what makes skills efficient, coordinated, and beautiful to observe. It is the ability to execute skills consistently, accurately, and rapidly, the same way over and over, with little regard to the varying constraints of the current situation. It involves automatization, associative learning, and stimulus generalization. To land free-throws in basketball, for example, players try to run off the same movements in the same patterns as they have practiced thousands of times before, ignoring everything except the rim of the hoop and the ball going through it. Chess masters exhibit fluency when they draw on a well-practiced series of moves in response to a familiar strategy they recognize in the opponent. On a more mundane level, most professors are fluent at typing on their computer keyboards, answering familiar questions about their work, and reading research articles in their field.

Flexibility, in contrast, is what makes skills adaptive and truly functional. It is the ability to alter ongoing behaviors in accordance with changes in local conditions, to muster an appropriate response to completely novel instances of a problem. Flexibility is akin to Harlow's (1949) notion of "learning to learn." As Stevenson (1972) put it:

> The ultimate goal in any type of learning cannot be the retention of large amounts of specific information. For the most part, this information will be

forgotten. What can be retained are techniques for acquiring new information, learning how to attend to relevant cues and ignore irrelevant cues, how to apply hypotheses and strategies and relinquish them when they are unsuccessful. (p. 307)

Rather than repeating old solutions based on associative learning and stimulus generalization, flexibility involves discovering new solutions to novel problems online in response to the demands of the current situation—the NBA superstars who switch from a layup to a slam dunk while hanging in mid-air, the elegant chess masters who beat computers with untried moves, the Iron Chef champions who concoct an entire meal in an hour using a slimy fish as the main ingredient, and so on. Like fluency, flexibility is central to expertise at both professional and everyday skill levels. Flexibility allows backyard jocks to block a jump shot in a pick-up game of basketball, the scruffy chess players in Washington Square Park to separate tourists from their money, and everyday cooks to come home and scrape together a fine meal from remnants in the kitchen without benefit of a recipe.

A recent strike by the Broadway musicians' union highlights the difference between fluency and flexibility. The producers' stance emphasized fluency. They proposed using prerecorded music, arguing that digital "virtual orchestras" provide the same beautiful music reliably (and cheaply) at each performance. The musicians' stance emphasized flexibility. They argued that the essence of live theater is the difference between performances. Because real orchestras can be flexible, performances can be shaped by the immediate eccentricities of the actors and the audience—the way an actor's change in timing sends the musicians scrambling in a new tempo and the unexpected hush of the audience leads the musicians to find new softness of expression.

Traditionally, researchers have focused more on the acquisition of fluency than on flexibility perhaps because the process of attaining fluency is easier to understand, model, and simulate. A machine, after all, such as a chess-playing computer or a mobile robot can capture much of the essence of fluency. In fact replicability is a primary reason for preferring machines over human operators. The acquisition of flexibility is more difficult to understand and model because flexibility requires coping with novelty. It requires creativity and generativity. Flesh-and-blood chess masters can beat a computer because they can create novel solutions to novel problems. Freewheeling robots crash into obstacles that any animal or insect would avoid because the robots cannot find novel solutions to novel problems.

In this chapter, I focus on the acquisition of flexibility. I begin by proposing a simple, general problem-solving framework for understanding behavioral flexibility—whether in basketball, chess, cooking, or my own area of expertise, infant balance control. In the second section of the chapter, I describe the biomechanical problem of keeping balance and explain why balance control requires flexibility. In particular, developmental changes in infants' bodies, skills, and environments, combined with the moment-to-moment flux of everyday movements, create a continual series of novel balance control problems. Using infant balance control as a model system to understand the development of behavioral flexibility, in the third section of the chapter, I report several investigations of infants' responses to novel challenges to balance control that support the utility of the problem-solving framework. In the final section, I report several descriptive studies that begin to constrain theorizing about possible mechanisms for acquiring flexibility in balance control.

PROBLEM-SOLVING FRAMEWORK FOR UNDERSTANDING FLEXIBILITY

My approach to understanding behavioral flexibility is inspired by Harlow and colleagues' (e.g., Harlow, 1949, 1959; Harlow & Kuenne, 1949) studies of "learning to learn" in monkeys and preschool-age children. In the 1940s and 1950s, when most researchers were focused on how animals learn conditioned responses to isolated, single problems, Harlow's group studied how animals learn general strategies and rules for coping efficiently with a class of problems. Monkeys solved discrimination or oddity problems while strapped into a Wisconsin General Test Apparatus. In the discrimination task, monkeys were required to choose the rewarded one of a pair of objects that differed on multiple characteristics and shifted in their left-right positions. After 10 or so repetitions, the experimenter introduced a different pair of objects. The process continued until monkeys could solve new discrimination problems with new pairs of objects after only one trial.

Learning to learn across the class of discrimination problems meant that monkeys had learned to explore both objects and to track the one that covered the raisin or peanut—a sort of win-stay/lose-shift rule. Similarly, in the oddity problems, the experimenter presented the monkeys with three objects: two similar and one different. Learning to learn meant that monkeys could solve new oddity problems with new sets of objects in only one trial; they had learned that the different looking object hid the raisin.

Despite the apparent simplicity of the paradigm, acquisition of flexibility in discrimination and oddity problems was extremely difficult. Adult monkeys required hundreds of pairs of objects—thousands of trials—before they had learned how to learn. Likewise, in the experiments with infant monkeys and preschool-age children, youngsters required thousands of trials to demonstrate flexibility.

In the spirit of Harlow's research endeavors, I propose a general problem-solving framework for understanding behavioral flexibility—whether in discrimination problems or any other type of skill. On the problem-solving framework, the acquisition of flexibility requires learners to do three things: (a) recognize a circumscribed problem space, (b) identify the relevant parameters for operating within the problem space and map their allowable values, and (c) acquire the tools for calibrating or setting the values of the parameters online. For example, in discrimination problems, the problem space is narrowly constricted to new pairs of objects. The relevant parameters are the perceptual qualities of the objects on the WGTA tray. The necessary tools include the sensitivity to visually discriminate the two objects, the exploratory procedure of searching the well beneath one of the objects, and the acquisition of the abstracted win-stay/lose-shift strategy.

The central prediction of this problem-solving framework is that once learners acquire flexibility, they should be able to solve novel problems within the perimeters of the problem space. The corollary prediction is that flexibility should not transfer to problems that reside inside the perimeters of a different problem space. Flexibility in solving discrimination problems means that monkeys could solve endless variations of discrimination problems, but flexibility in the discrimination problem space should not help the monkeys solve oddity problems.

After dozens of studies with human children using variants of discrimination and oddity problem sets (e.g., Stevenson, 1972), the study of learning to learn fizzled. One reason for the loss of interest in studying behavioral flexibility may have been the narrow and artificial nature of the experimental tasks. As a model system, discrimination and oddity problems are elegantly simple and easy to control. However, performance on such simple classes of problems does not map clearly onto the rich potential for flexibility in complex everyday activities such as chess, basketball, cooking, and balance control.

I study balance control in infants as a model system for understanding the development of behavioral flexibility for several reasons. First, balance is perhaps the most important accomplishment in motor skill acquisition. It is the basis of all motor skills involving the head and extremities—moving the head to look and listen, moving the arms to interact with objects, and moving the body for stance and locomotion. Thus, understanding flexibility in the problem space of balance has important implications for motor control. Second, because balance control is implicated in most movements, infants have ample opportunities for learning. Third, in contrast to problem-solving domains where strategies are covert mental processes, in balance control the variables of interest are overt and observable. Fourth, infants' movements are relatively large, slow, and obvious compared with those of adults. As a result, it is relatively easy to observe changes in their movements. Most important, as described later, the need for flexibility is incessant and paramount in balance control. The everyday environment is variable, unpredictable, and full of novel situations. Movements simply cannot be performed in the same way over and over or we will fall. Instead movements must be continually modified to suit the constraints of the current situation.

KEEPING BALANCE

Requirements of Balance Control

For most people, the problem of keeping balance conjures up images of drunken walkers, tightrope walkers, elderly walkers, and infant walkers—situations when balance control seems especially difficult. In fact, the balance control problem is not limited to precarious situations or special populations. Balance is central to all motor skills. Every movement that defies gravity requires balance to stabilize the body and keep it upright. Without balance, we would be like rag dolls, young infants, or some children afflicted with cerebral palsy; we would crumple downward, unable to lift our head, stretch an arm out to reach for a toy, sit up, stand, or locomote.

Figure 3.1A shows a simple physical model of balance control in upright stance. As represented by the dashed lines in the cartoon, the body is always swaying over its base of support (in this case, the body sways around the ankles). The swaying motions are often most noticeable in precarious situations, but are certainly not limited to them. Sophisticated motion analysis techniques reveal subtle back-and-forth swaying motions of the body even in relatively stationary postures such as sitting and standing upright (e.g., Bertenthal & Bai, 1989; Butterworth & Hicks, 1977; Schmuckler, 1997). The body is in subtle motion fighting gravity even when balance is augmented by supporting the body with external structures such as the backrest of a chair, the edge of the kitchen counter or bathroom sink, someone's shoulder, and so on. The forces acting on the body are never perfectly symmetrical, and muscles are never perfectly quiet. Small asymmetries in forces tip the body in one direction, and compensatory swaying responses tip it back in the reverse direction.

To solve the balance control problem, we must keep our bodies within a cone-shaped region of permissible postural sway (Adolph, 2002; McCollum & Leen, 1989; Riccio, 1993; Riccio & Stoffregen, 1988). The narrow bot-

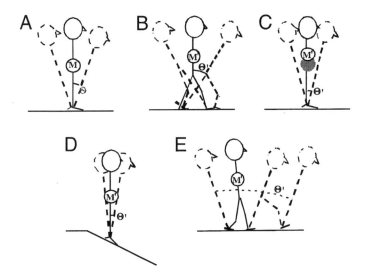

FIG. 3.1. Physical model of balance control (A) in upright stance with sway around the ankles, (B) with widened base of support by splaying the feet apart, (C) under conditions of altered body dimensions (increased mass and upward displacement of the center of mass), (D) under conditions of variable ground surfaces (sloping ground), and (E) in upright locomotion.

tom or point of the cone is the base of support, and the wide top of the cone circumscribes the body's swaying movements. At any given moment, the size of the sway region depends on the size of the available muscle torque—the current level of strength that the body can muster—relative to the size of the destabilizing torque, the forces acting to pull the body over. Angle θ in the figure represents the angular distance the body can move inside the perimeters of the sway region. If the body moves outside the region of permissible postural sway, we fall.

Changing Constraints on Balance

Biomechanical Constraints. Balance control requires flexibility because the biomechanical constraints on balance are continually changing. Figure 3.1 shows several sources of change in the size of the sway region. Figure 3.1B shows that widening the base of support increases the size of the sway region by increasing the size of the angular distance the body can move before falling. With the feet close together, as in Fig. 3.1A, the tip of the cone-shaped sway region is small relative to the size of the body, which is acting like a lever arm. Splaying the feet apart widens the base of support. Figure 3.1C shows that functional changes in body dimensions change the size of the sway region. Increased mass and upward or outward displacement of the center of mass (overall weight gain, pregnancy, wearing a backpack, carrying a sack of groceries, etc.) decreases the size of the sway region by decreasing the angular distance the body can move before falling. Figure 3.1D shows that variations in the ground surface change the size of the sway region. For example, sloping ground decreases the permissible angular sway of the body by decreasing the base of support and requiring additional muscle force to maintain the body's vertical orientation. Figure 3.1E shows that in locomotion, the base of support is dynamic, sort of stretching backward and forward in time and space. When running downhill, for example, the torso can momentarily sway far in front of the feet before the legs move back under the body.

In fact, every variation in the body or ground surface changes the size of the sway region in novel ways. Movements change the size of the sway region by changing the inertial forces acting on the body or by recruiting muscles that would otherwise be used for balance. Even drawing a deep breath, lifting the arms, or bending the knees change the size of the sway region by changing the size of destabilizing torque or the effectiveness of the available muscle torque. Thus, keeping balance is a process of continually solving novel problems within the balance control problem space.

Developmental Constraints.   Changes due to development also change the size of the sway region. Infants' bodies change dramatically over the first 2 years of life. Neonates' top-heavy, spindly legged bodies morph into toddlers' more chunky, cylindrical bodies. Muscle mass to fat ratios increase, head size to body size ratios decrease, and the center of mass lowers relative to the overall height of the body. Growth spurts are dramatic. Rather than growing taller or heavier along smooth, continuous trajectories, infants' growth is episodic: Sudden bursts of growth (e.g., .5–2.5 cm of height in a single day) are interspersed with weeks of inactive plateaus (Lampl, 1983, 1993; Lampl, Veldhuis, & Johnson, 1992).

At the same time that infants' bodies undergo dramatic change, their skill levels also undergo dramatic change. In part due to the increased biomechanical efficiency of their maturing bodies, infants' movements become more proficient (e.g., Thelen, 1984; Thelen & Fisher, 1982; Thelen, Fisher, & Ridley-Johnson, 1984). For example, speed of crawling, a standard measure of crawling proficiency, more than doubles over the first 10 weeks after crawling onset (Adolph, Vereijken, & Denny, 1998; Freedland & Bertenthal, 1994). Step length, a standard measure of walking proficiency, more than doubles in the first 5 months after walking onset (e.g., Adolph, Vereijken, & Shrout, 2003; Bril & Breniere, 1989).

At the same time that infants' bodies and skill levels undergo dramatic change, their environments expand dramatically. As a by-product of looking more mature physically and demonstrating more proficient skill levels, caregivers begin to introduce infants to new aspects of the everyday surrounds (Garling & Garling, 1988); they may remove the safety gates from the household stairs; provide access to the sandbox, wading pool, or playground apparatus; and encourage infants to explore more broadly and strive toward higher levels of proficiency. Infants, in turn, are better able to take advantage of previously unexplored and untested aspects of the environmental layout.

New Postures in Development.   Development changes the sway region in an even more important way. In addition to changing the size of an existing sway region, developmental changes actually create new sway regions. Figure 3.2 shows four postural milestones in infant development. On average, infants sit independently at 6 months, crawl on their hands and knees at 8 months, cruise (walk sideways hanging onto furniture for support) at 10 months, and walk independently at 12 months. The ages and order of acquisition are highly variable (Frankenburg & Dodds, 1967). Some infants cruise before they begin to crawl, sit after they begin to crawl and cruise, or crawl after they begin walking (Adolph et al., 1998; Leo, Chiu, & Adolph, 2000). The normal range in ages spans several months for each milestone. Nonetheless, no infant acquires all four milestones simultaneously. The various postures always appear staggered over several months.

We have argued that each of these postural milestones in development is literally a different balance control system (Adolph, 2002; Adolph & Eppler, 1998, 2002). Each posture involves different relevant parameters with different allowable settings. For example, each posture involves different regions of sway for different key pivots around which the body rotates: the hips for sitting, the wrists for crawling, the shoulders and elbows for cruising, and the ankles for walking. Each posture involves different muscle groups for staying upright and for propelling forward, different vantage points for viewing the ground ahead, different correlations between visual and vestibular input, and so on.

Sitting   Crawling   Cruising   Walking

FIG. 3.2.   Four postural milestones in infant development (sitting, crawling on hands and knees, cruising sideways holding furniture for support, and walking). Reprinted from *Ecological Psychology, 10*(3–4), K. E. Adolph & M. A. Eppler, "Development of Visually Guided Locomotion," p. 314. Copyright 1998 by Elsevier. Adapted with permission.

Learning to Learn in the Development of Balance Control. In summary, developmental changes in infancy contribute to variations in the size of a particular sway region. Similarly, at any age, changes due to practice and the manifold changes due to varying local conditions contribute to variations in the size of a particular sway region. All such changes require behavioral flexibility to cope with novel constraints on balance.

In addition to flux in the size of a sway region, development creates new postural control systems—new sway regions—with a whole set of new parameters. We argue that infant balance control provides an especially informative model system for studying developmental contributions to behavioral flexibility because the creation of new postural control systems is a unique product of infant development. On the problem-solving framework, each new posture in development should be considered as a new problem space. With the acquisition of each postural milestone, infants must discover the boundaries of the new problem space, identify the new set of relevant parameters, estimate the allowable range of values for each, and acquire the tools for calibrating the settings of the various parameters.

On our problem-solving account that infants are "learning to learn" about balance, we make several related predictions. First, the adaptiveness of infants' responses should be predicted by the duration of their experience maintaining balance in each posture, not on their chronological age per se. As shown by the individual curves in Fig. 3.3A, within a particular posture, infants should display higher error rates (fall more often) in their first few weeks of experience compared with lower error rates after several weeks of experience. As shown by the vertical arrows in Fig. 3.3A, across postural milestones, infants should make more errors in less familiar postures compared with more experienced ones. Note that we are agnostic about the order in which postural milestones are attained. The learning curves on the figure could appear in any order. Age alone should not predict the adaptiveness of infants' responses because infants may be highly experienced in sitting, for example, at younger ages and inexperienced in walking at older ages.

A second related prediction of the problem-solving account is that learning to learn about balance should be slow, difficult, and fraught with errors. If adult monkeys required thousands of trials to acquire a learning set to solve novel discrimination or oddity problems in Harlow's (1949) simple model system, human infants might require epochs of trials to acquire sufficient flexibility to cope with the exigencies of balance control in everyday life. The problem space for Harlow's studies was extremely narrow and circumscribed (monkeys were engaged in the discrimination or oddity task only in the context of the WGTA apparatus). In contrast, the problem space for balance control is extremely broad. Infants must ac-

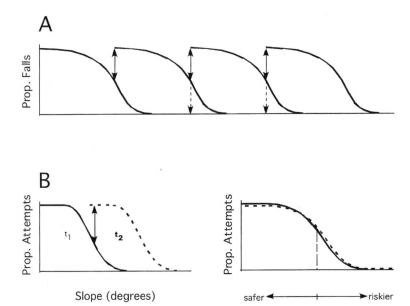

FIG. 3.3.   Learning to learn in the development of balance control. (A) Learning curves for four postural milestones in development. X-axis represents age and experience with each posture. Y-axis represents error rates (falling). Vertical arrows denote differences in error rates due to different durations of experience with each posture with age held constant. (B) Differential responding under different testing conditions (t1 and t2). Curves represent attempts to walk. Left panel shows differential responding plotted against the absolute degree of slope. Right panel shows differential responding plotted against the normalized amount of risk.

tively engage in keeping their bodies in balance during all of their waking hours (even while carried or pushed in a stroller, infants must balance their heads and torsos). Exploratory procedures for searching under the wells in Harlow's studies preexisted in monkeys' repertoires. In contrast, infants must discover and hone many of the exploratory swaying, looking, and touching movements that are required for generating perceptual information about balance control. Most critical, Harlow's monkeys could solve the discrimination and oddity problems by abstracting simple static rules. In contrast, learning to gauge the extent of the current sway region requires infants to abstract dynamic, probabilistic functions.

A third related prediction of the problem-solving framework is that adaptive responding to threats to balance control should be based on the relative amount of risk, rather than on absolute values of the relevant parameters. Learning to learn would mean that infants should disregard particular facts about themselves and the environment (e.g., 20° slopes are risky for walking or "I'm a poor clumsy walker") because static facts are subject to change from moment to moment and week to week. A particular degree of slope, for example, might be perfectly safe when walking unhindered, but impossibly risky when carrying a load. The same slope might be risky last week when walking proficiency was poor, but perfectly safe this week after dramatic improvements in walking proficiency.

As shown in the left panel of Fig. 3.3B, adaptive responding might require infants to respond differently to the same absolute degree of slope (or any other relevant parameter) under different testing conditions (represented by t1 and t2). The curves in Fig. 3.3B represent attempts to walk. Perfectly adaptive responding would be evidenced by matching the probability of attempting to walk with the conditional probability of success. Instead of learning particular facts about absolute values of experimental variables, learning to learn would require infants to figure out the relative amount of risk in the current situation. As shown in the right panel of Fig. 3.3B, infants' level of learning to learn would be reflected by the equivalence of responding at the same relative amount of risk. The curves on the figure are normalized to the same relative risk level.

A fourth related prediction is that learning should be flexible enough to cope with new problems that change the size of a particular sway region. Thus, experienced infants should respond adaptively across changes in their functional body dimensions and skill level due to naturally occurring changes in growth, strength, coordination, and the like and due to experimentally induced changes such as carrying a load or wearing platform shoes. Similarly, experienced infants should respond adaptively across novel variations in the ground surface. Independent navigation of steep slopes, for example, is a novel task for most infants, as is descending from sharp drop-offs, locomoting over gaps in the ground surface, coping with stairs and bridges, and so on. If infants have truly learned how to learn, under conditions of changing bodies, skills, and ground surfaces, infants should be able to use an acquired repertoire of exploratory movements, compensatory sway responses, locomotor methods, and so on to figure out what to do within a common problem space.

Finally, a fifth related prediction is that learning should be specific to each postural milestone in development. Because learning to learn is limited by the boundaries of the particular problem space, infants should show no evidence of transfer (either positive or negative) across developmental changes in posture. We should see four parallel learning curves as illustrated in Fig. 3.3A.

FLEXIBILITY AND SPECIFICITY IN INFANT BALANCE

In this section, I describe several experiments that support our problem-solving approach to the general problem of behavioral flexibility. Our standard research strategy was to pose infants with novel threats to balance under conditions of changing body dimensions, changing skill levels, and changing ground surfaces. As in the classic visual cliff studies (Gibson & Walk, 1960), where infants were encouraged to cross an apparent drop-off covered with safety glass, in our studies, infants' task was to decide whether a surface was safe or risky for balance and locomotion. Caregivers stood at the far side of the surface offering toys, Cheerios, and praise to provide infants with a compelling reason to cross, but they did not advise infants to be careful and did not tell infants how to cross the surface. If infants attempted to cross, we assumed that they perceived the surface to be safe; if they refused to cross or selected an alternative method of locomotion, we assumed that they perceived the surface to be risky.

In contrast to the visual cliff studies, we did not cover our test surfaces with safety glass. Thus, our test surfaces were not only "visually risky," they actually were risky. In the visual cliff studies, infants could feel the safety glass with their hands or feet. Despite viewing the floor far below, most infants reluctantly crossed after one trial (Campos, Hiatt, Ramsay, Henderson, & Svejda, 1978; Eppler, Satterwhite, Wendt, & Bruce, 1997). As a consequence, individual infants could be tested on only one trial, and they could not be tested longitudinally. Results in visual cliff studies can only be reported in terms of the percentage of infants avoiding or crossing.

By removing the safety glass in our studies, we could test individual infants over dozens of trials in multiple conditions in a single session, and we could observe them longitudinally at tightly spaced intervals over several months. In fact, we could collect enough trials for individual infants to use psychophysical procedures so as to plot crude response curves for each baby in each condition.

We capitalized on the fact that infants do not acquire all postural milestones simultaneously so as to compare their responses in more experienced postures versus less familiar ones. We assessed the adaptiveness of their responding by equating the relative amount of risk over changes in the test conditions. To ensure their safety, a highly trained experimenter followed alongside infants and caught them if they began to fall. Because the sensation of falling downward is highly salient, infants tended to display their most accurate judgments, and the need for adaptive responses was paramount.

Sitting and Crawling Over Gaps

Infants' response to the visual cliff has captivated researchers for nearly half a century. Why do some babies blithely crawl over the safety glass while others remain steadfast on the starting platform? The original explanation for avoiding the drop-off was that infants had acquired depth perception (Gibson & Walk, 1960). However, depth perception proves to be only a necessary, not a sufficient, condition for avoidance. Neonates show evidence of sensitivity to depth (Slater & Morison, 1985), and 4-month-olds use depth information to control reaching responses (e.g., Yonas & Hartman, 1993). Subsequent explanations involved fear of heights as a mediator of avoidance (Bertenthal, Campos, & Barrett, 1984; Campos et al., 1978; Campos, Bertenthal, & Kermoian, 1992; Campos, Langer, & Krowitz, 1970), learning associations between the visual information for depth and the consequences of falling (Thelen & Smith, 1994), and learning that balance and locomotion require a floor beneath the body (Gibson & Schmuckler, 1989). On any of these accounts, infants should show adaptive avoidance responses regardless of the posture in which they are tested. A sheer drop-off has, by definition, an abrupt discontinuity in the floor beneath the body, generates a multitude of visual depth cues, and certainly puts infants at a great height above the floor of the precipice.

In contrast to all of these simple fact-based accounts, on the problem-solving approach to balance control, infants should avoid a drop-off when they have learned how to gauge the extent of their current region of permissible postural sway. Learning to learn would predict that infants should show more frequent and accurate avoidance responses in the postures with which they have experience combatting everyday threats to balance.

To test these predictions, we observed infants' responses at the edge of an adjustable gap in the surface of support (Adolph, 2000). As illustrated in Fig. 3.4, trials began with infants perched on a starting platform in a sitting or crawling posture. In both postures, they were urged to lean forward and stretch their arm over the gap toward a lure offered by their parents at the end of the landing platform. By rolling the landing platform along a calibrated track, we could vary the gap size from 0 cm to 90 cm in 2-cm increments. The smallest gaps were perfectly safe. Intermediate sized gaps were sometimes safe and sometimes risky depending on the postural condition and infants' current level of sitting or crawling skill. The largest gaps were impossibly risky. The 90-cm gap was comparable to the size of the standard visual cliff—essentially, a 3 ft long by 3 ft wide by 3 ft deep drop-off.

A   B

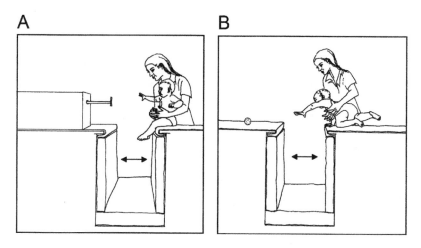

FIG. 3.4. Platform with adjustable gap in the surface of support. (A) sitting condition. (B) crawling condition. Experimenter (shown) followed alongside infants to ensure their safety. Parents (not shown) encouraged infants to span the gap from the far side of the landing platform. Reprinted from *Psychological Science, 11*(4), 292. Copyright 2000 by American Psychological Society. Adapted with permission.

Infants were 9.5 months old (plus/minus 1 week). All babies had more experience sitting (M = 3.4 months) compared with crawling (M = 1.5 months). We reasoned that if infants are learning to learn about balance control, they should respond flexibly and adaptively to novel threats to balance. As one might expect, the infants' parents reported that they had never placed their babies at the edge of a drop-off and encouraged them to lean forward. To the contrary, parents did their best to keep their babies away from the edge of the bed, changing table, kitchen counter, and so on. Most important to the problem-solving framework, if sitting and crawling are different problem spaces, then infants should respond more adaptively in their more experienced sitting posture.

We used an adaptation of a classic psychophysical staircase procedure to estimate the relative amount of risk for each infant in each postural condition (Adolph, 1995). In general, staircase procedures minimize the total number of trials required to estimate a response curve for individual participants. We varied the size of the test increments (in this case, gap size) based on infants' responses on previous trials so as to place most of the test trials along the slope of the response curve, where success ranges from 100% to 0% rather than along the asymptotes, where success is either 100% or 0%. In this way, we could calculate a "motor threshold" or "gap boundary" along the response curve to delineate the difference between safe and risky gaps. We defined the boundary gap as the largest gap infants could manage safely at a $\geq$ 67% criterion. By definition, gap sizes smaller than the gap boundary were increasingly safe, and gap sizes larger than the boundary gap were increasingly risky. We reasoned that if infants respond adaptively to novel threats to balance control, they should attempt safe gaps smaller than their gap boundary and avoid risky gaps larger than their gap boundary.

Two experiments yielded the same result. As predicted by the problem-solving approach, adaptive responding depended on infants' experience with each posture, not their chronological age at testing (they were all the same age). Infants displayed more adaptive responses in their experienced sitting posture compared with their unfamiliar crawling posture at every risky gap size. In their experienced sitting posture, infants attempted safe gaps, but avoided risky ones.

Central to the problem-solving account, infants' responses were based on the relative amount of risk, rather than the absolute size of the gap. They matched the probability of avoiding to the conditional probability of falling (or, equivalently, the probability of attempting to the conditional probability of success). Yet, in their unfamiliar crawling posture, infants leaned too far over the brink and tumbled over the precipice into the experimenter's arms. In the first experiment, 32% of infants accurately avoided falling in the sitting condition, but fell at every risky gap size in the crawling condition. In the second experiment, 47% of infants responded adaptively in sitting, but fell at every risky gap size in the crawling condition. In their crawling posture, these clueless infants pitched forward repeatedly into the 90-cm-wide drop-off.

Results are consistent with the problem-solving approach. Experience with balance control allows infants to respond adaptively to a novel problem type. However, experience with an earlier developing skill does not transfer automatically to a later developing one. Learning is specific to the different problem spaces of sitting and crawling. The dissociation between postures belies previous accounts, suggesting that adaptive responses to disparity in depth of the ground surface depends on factual knowledge or simple associative learning, such as knowledge that the body cannot be supported in empty space, associations between depth information and falling, or the acquisition of fear of heights.

Cruising Over Gaps

Before infants walk independently, they cruise sideways in an upright posture, hanging onto furniture for balance. A long-standing assumption in the literature is that practice cruising teaches infants how to keep balance in walking (Haehl, Vardaxis, & Ulrich, 2000; McGraw, 1935; Metcalfe & Clark, 2000). Assumably, cruisers let go of the coffee table and walk frontward when they have learned to keep balance in an upright posture.

On the problem-solving framework, this assumption can only hold true if cruising and walking represent variants of the same balance control system—that is, if cruising and walking represent different problem types from the same problem space.

However, our casual observations of the infants in our laboratory led us to believe that cruising might be manually controlled. In other words, sideways cruisers appeared to keep balance and steer using their upper extremities rather than their legs. Despite the similarity in upright posture between cruising and walking, the key pivot and critical muscle synergies for maintaining balance in cruising may be in the arms, not the legs. The relevant environmental supports may concern the properties of the furniture ledge, not the properties of the floor. In fact, we hypothesized that infants may not take their legs and floor into account at all for gauging threats to upright balance while cruising.

To test the extent of the cruising problem space, we tested 11-month-old (plus/minus 1 week) cruising infants on our adjustable gap apparatus in two postural conditions (Leo et al., 2000). As illustrated in Fig. 3.5, the handrail condition was relevant for keeping balance with the arms. Infants were encouraged to cruise over a continuous floor with an adjust-

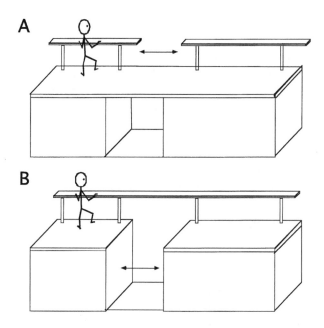

FIG. 3.5.   Platform with continuous floor and adjustable gap in the handrail (top panel) or with adjustable gap in the floor and continuous handrail (bottom panel).

able gap in the handrail (0–90 cm). The floor condition was relevant for keeping balance with the legs. Infants were encouraged to cruise over a continuous handrail with an adjustable gap in the floor (0–90 cm). In both postural conditions, a research assistant showed infants the gap in the floor or the gap in the handrail at the start of each trial to ensure that they saw the size of the obstacle. Parents stood at the far side of the landing platform cheering their infants' efforts while an experimenter followed alongside infants to ensure their safety.

Because more proficient cruisers and infants with longer arms and legs might be able to cruise over larger gaps than less proficient, smaller infants, we used our modified psychophysical staircase procedure (Adolph, 1995) to normalize responses to the relative amount of risk for each baby in each postural condition. Thus, we could compare the adaptiveness of responses across infants and conditions.

Results are very clear. Infants' knowledge about balance control appeared to be limited to manual control of balance. At each risky gap increment, infants displayed more adaptive responses in the handrail condition compared with the floor condition. In the handrail condition, infants matched the probability of attempting to cruise to the conditional probability of success. They cruised over safe gaps in the handrail, but on risky gaps they gripped the starting handrail resolutely and refused to cross or they cruised to the end of the starting handrail and then crawled to the beginning of the ending handrail. The same infants, however, appeared oblivious to the fact that they needed a floor to maintain balance. In the floor condition, despite seeing the gap in the floor, most infants attempted to cruise over every risky gap increment, forcing the experimenter to rescue them as they clung to the handrail with their feet dangling into the precipice.

We serendipitously had the opportunity to observe a handful of infants who were slightly more motorically advanced. Between the time that we had scheduled them to come into the lab as sideways cruisers and the time that they arrived, the infants had begun to take a few independent forward-facing steps. When we tested these brand-new walkers on the adjustable gaps apparatus, they erred in both the handrail and floor conditions. At every risky gap increment, infants fell while attempting to walk from one end of the gap in the handrail to the other and while attempting to walk from one end of the gap in the floor to the other. Not only did new walkers ignore the relevant properties of the floor, they behaved as if they could no longer gauge the usefulness of the handrail for keeping balance.

The evidence suggests that cruising and walking are different balance control systems representing different problem spaces. Practice cruising helps infants gauge threats to balance in a cruising posture based on the parameters that define manual control of balance. However, practice cruising does not lead to flexibility in walking where the problem space and relevant parameters are different.

Walking Over Bridges With Handrails to Augment Balance

In two subsequent experiments, we showed that relatively experienced walking infants can gauge when to use a handrail to augment their balance control (Berger & Adolph, 2003). Using a handrail is mandatory for keeping balance in a cruising posture, but using a handrail is optional in a walking posture. Appropriate use of a handrail in a walking posture would require infants to recognize that under normal walking conditons (e.g., on a flat, wide surface), a handrail is superfluous. However, in a tricky situation, where balance is precarious, manual support via a handrail can extend the region of permissible postural sway.

As illustrated in Fig. 3.6, we tested 16-month-old walking infants on wide and narrow bridges spanning a deep precipice. The precipice was 74 cm long, 76 cm wide, and 76 cm deep to the floor. Its interior was padded with foam to ensure infants' safety. The bridge widths varied from 12 cm to 72 cm wide in 6-cm increments. The narrowest ones were impossibly risky, like walking over a tightrope in a circus act; the intermediate bridge widths were like walking over a plank; and the widest bridge widths were no different from the solid platform. On some trials at each bridge width, a sturdy wooden handrail spanned the precipice along one edge of the bridge, but on other trials we removed the handrail. The experimenter presented each baby with a range of bridge widths and handrail presence in quasi-random orders for 24 trials. Parents stood at the far side of the landing platform to provide incentive for infants to cross, but they did not call infants' attention to the handrail.

Most of the infants in our sample had several months of walking experience. Thus, on the problem-solving framework, the infants should be sensitive to decrease in the size of their sway region on the narrowest bridges and recognize that the narrow bridges posed a threat to balance. Of special interest were the trials when the handrail was available. Infants might discover that they could expand the size of their sway region via the handrail and/or bolster their normal level of muscle strength for generating compensatory sways via manual support on the handrail.

Results are consistent with the problem-solving account. Infants' attempts to walk were scaled to bridge width, indicating that they perceived that the wider bridges were safer and the narrower bridges were riskier. Most important, there was an interaction between bridge width and handrail presence. All of the infants walked over the widest bridges on every trial regardless of whether the handrail was available, but on the narrow bridges infants attempted to walk only when there was a

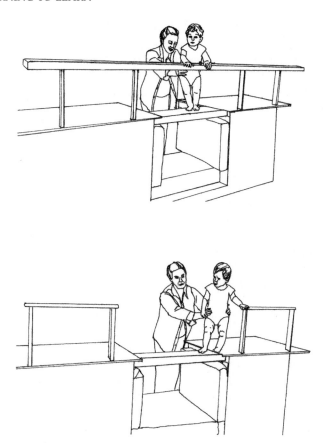

FIG. 3.6. Platform with adjustable bridges spanning a precipice and re-movable handrail. Experimenter (shown) followed alongside infants to ensure their safety. Parents (not shown) encouraged their infants to cross the bridges from the far side of the landing platform. From *Developmental Psychology, 39*(3), S. E. Berger & K. E. Adolph, "Infants Use Handrails as Tools in a Locomotor Task," p. 596. Copyright 2000 by American Psychological Association. Reprinted with permission.

handrail. When the handrail was unavailable, infants refused to leave the starting platform. Most attempts were successful (94%), indicating that infants' decisions were accurate. Although the experimenter vigilantly followed alongside infants, she rarely had to rescue them from falling into the precipice.

Infants' use of the handrail provides corroborating evidence that they viewed the handrail as a potential means to augment balance. On wider bridges, they either ran straight over the bridge to the landing platform without touching the handrail or they tapped the handrail for a few milliseconds as they ran. On intermediate bridges, they held the handrail for

longer durations or slid their hand along the rail as they walked more gin-
gerly. On the narrowest bridges, infants grabbed the handrail before leaving the starting platform and never released it. Many infants tested various
strategies for using the handrail—usually inching along while turned sideways toward the rail, but occasionally facing frontward while holding the
handrail with one hand or even holding the handrail behind their backs.

In a recently completed study with 16-month-old walking infants, we
demonstrated that infants recognize that the handrail must be sturdy
enough to support their weight to be used effectively as a tool to augment
balance (Berger & Lobo, 2003). We varied bridge widths from 12 cm to 48
cm. A handrail was always available along one edge of the bridge, but on
some trials it was made of sturdy wood and on others it was constructed
of a pliant material. As in the earlier experiments, infants ignored the
handrail on the wide bridge, but on the narrower bridges they were more
likely to cross when the handrail was wood than when it was wobbly. Infants were also more likely to mouth the wobbly handrails and push them
down while exploring from the starting platform.

Together these studies suggest that by 16 months infants are exqui-
sitely sensitive to threats to upright balance and clever enough to discover
new ways to protect themselves from falling. Infants used their repertoire
of exploratory procedures (probing the bridges with their feet, taking a
step or two onto the bridge before retreating to the starting platform) to
determine whether bridges were safe for walking. Most striking, by using
their exploratory procedures in the novel bridge/handrail situation
(pushing/pulling the handrail, testing various body positions while holding the handrail, etc.), infants generated visual, tactile, and proprioceptive
information to specify a larger, more stable sway region for crossing the
narrowest bridges.

Crawling and Walking Down Slopes

We used an age-held constant research strategy for testing infants on gaps
and bridges, then tested the adaptiveness of babies' responding in experienced versus unfamiliar postural conditions at the same relative amount
of risk. We used a complementary longitudinal research strategy to test
infants' responses on safe and risky slopes (Adolph, 1997). In the longitudinal research, we held locomotor experience constant at each test session
and allowed age to vary across infants. Thus, we observed the infants repeatedly under fixed testing conditions to compare their responses over
naturally occurring changes in body dimensions and skill levels at the
same relative amounts of risk.

To test infants' responses to the novel problem of descending sloping
ground surfaces, we constructed an adjustable slope apparatus from three

platforms connected by piano hinges (Fig. 3.7). Flat starting and landing platforms flanked a middle sloping section. By pumping a car jack, the slant of the middle section varied from 0° to 36° in 2° increments. The entire surface of the apparatus was covered with plush carpet to provide traction and cushioning if infants fell.

We observed one group of babies every 3 weeks for nearly a year, beginning on their first week of crawling and ending several weeks after they began walking. We observed a second group of babies at matched session times: in their first week of crawling, tenth week of crawling, and first week of walking. To estimate the relative amount of risk, we tested infants with the modified psychophysical procedure to estimate slope boundaries for each infant at each week of crawling and walking to a ≥ 67% criterion (Adolph, 1997). Thus, safe and risky slopes were redefined on a weekly basis relative to each baby's current level of crawling or walking skill. The same absolute degree of slope that was impossibly risky one week when crawling skill was poor might be perfectly safe the next week after crawling proficiency improved. The same degree of slope that was once safe for belly crawling might be risky for hands-knees crawling, a safe slope for hands-knees crawling might be risky for walking, and so on. Immense flexibility—the ability to solve novel problems on the fly— would be required for infants to scale their responses to the relative amount of risk given the dramatic changes incurred in their bodies and skill levels over the course of testing.

As predicted by the problem-solving framework, errors were related to the duration of infants' everyday locomotor experience. In their first

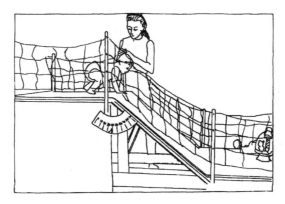

FIG. 3.7.   Walkway with adjustable slope. Experimenter (shown) followed alongside infants to ensure their safety. Parents (not shown) encouraged their infants to descend the slopes from the far side of the landing platform. From *Learning in the Development of Infant Locomotion*, K. E. Adolph, 1997, *Monographs of the Society for Research in Child Development*, *62*(3, Serial No. 251), p. 42. Copyright 1997 by the Society for Research in Child Development, Inc. Reprinted with permission.

weeks of crawling and walking, infants plunged repeatedly over the brink of impossibly steep slopes; average error rates were near to 75%. Gradually, over weeks of crawling and walking, infants' judgments geared in to the limits of their own abilities and error rates decreased. They used alternative sliding methods for descending risky slopes (sitting on their buttocks, backing down feet first, sliding head first prone like Superman) or they avoided descent entirely.

Like Harlow's (1949) monkeys solving discrimination and oddity problems, learning to cope with novel threats to balance was slow, difficult, and fraught with errors. On average, infants required 10 weeks of crawling or walking experience before errors decreased to 50% and 20 weeks or so for errors to decrease below 10%. Note that infants were not simply learning that a helpful adult would rescue them (like a common game of jumping from the kitchen counter into a parents' arms). Although the same experimenter caught infants as they plunged over the brink of risky slopes in their early weeks of crawling and walking, over repeated weeks of testing, infants became more cautious and responded more adaptively, not more reckless and blasé.

Infants' responses represented flexibility of learning, not merely the effects of repeated practice on slopes. Neither infants in the experimental group who were tested every 3 weeks nor the infants in the control group who were tested only at three matched session times had experience descending playground slides or other slopes outside the laboratory. Despite repeated testing involving hundreds of trials on slopes in the experimental group, learning was not dependent on slope experience. The control group of infants who were tested only at three matched session times did not have extensive experience on laboratory slopes. Infants in the control group displayed the same error rates at each matched session time as the infants tested every 3 weeks.

Most dramatic, learning was specific to each postural milestone. The same infants who had refused to crawl down risky slopes as experienced crawlers plunged heedlessly over the brink when they stood up and began walking. There was no evidence that learning about balance control transferred from crawling to walking. Learning was no faster the second time around. Error rates were just as high in infants' first week of walking as they were in their first week of crawling, and the learning curves for crawling and walking were parallel.

In fact, infants showed posture-specific responses from trial to trial. At the end of each walking session, we tested babies in six back-to-back trials on the steepest 36° slope. On the first two trials, we started infants in their unfamiliar upright posture. New walkers attempted to walk over the edge of the precipice. On the next two trials, we started infants in their old, familiar crawling posture. They responded adaptively by sliding down or avoiding descent. Moments later on the last two trials, when we started them in their unfamiliar walking posture, again infants walked over the brink and fell into the experimenter's arms.

Explanations based on simple associate learning, fear of heights, and facts about ground surfaces or infants' bodies cannot account for the results from our longitudinal observations of infants over weeks of crawling and walking. On any of those accounts, infants should have responded the same way to the same absolute degree of slope, and learning should have transferred from crawling to walking. However, we obtained the opposite results. What then do infants learn? On the problem-solving account, infants are learning to learn about balance. They are learning to identify the perimeters of a new problem space, acquire the exploratory procedures for calibrating balance online, and thereby learning to gauge the extent of their current region of permissible postural sway.

Walking Down Slopes Loaded With Weights

Consistent with the problem-solving framework, the longitudinal data suggested that experienced infants can recalibrate the settings of relevant balance control parameters to take into account naturally occurring changes in their functional body dimensions and skills. We put this suggestion to the test by experimentally manipulating infants' bodies and skills (Adolph & Avolio, 2000).

We dressed 14-month-old walking infants in a tight-fitting Velcro-covered vest. Slung over both of the infants' shoulders were a pair of removable Velcro-covered shoulderpacks loaded with feather-weight polyfil or lead-weight pellets (see Fig. 3.8). Both pairs of shoulderpacks could be quickly exchanged by fixing and unsticking the shoulderpacks to the Velcro vest. The weight of the feather-packs was negligible and only made infants larger through the chest. The lead-weighted shoulderpacks increased infants' mass by 25% and raised their center of mass several centimeters above their bellies. With their center of mass displaced upward, destabilizing torque increased. As a consequence, infants' balance was more precarious. On average, we reduced the size of the angle of permissible postural sway by 30%. In effect, we turned relatively maturely proportioned and proficient walking infants into more top-heavy and poorly skilled walkers.

To make infants' task really challenging, we encouraged them to walk down safe and risky slopes. A new adjustable slope apparatus, operated via a drive-screw from a garage door opener, allowed the degree of slant to vary from 0° to 88° in 4° increments. The purpose of testing infants on slopes was to exacerbate the effects of the weights and to allow us to assess how accurately infants could scale their responses to

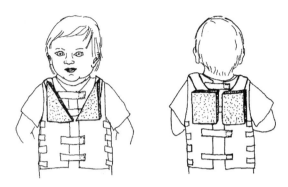

FIG. 3.8. Velcro vest with removable shoulderpacks.

the relative amount of risk. We ran two staircase protocols in tandem, switching from feather to lead packs quasi-randomly from trial to trial. Infants were observed over 58 to 87 trials, with 4 trials placed at each safe and risky increment. We used a 75% success criterion for identifying the slope boundary for each infant in each shoulderpack condition. The study design constituted a strict test of infants' ability to gauge their region of permissible postural sway. Because we switched between staircase protocols in a quasi-random fashion, infants could not know whether their shoulderpacks were loaded with feathers or lead—whether balance was normal or precarious—until the start of the trial when the experimenter put them down on the starting platform and they could feel themselves sway.

Indeed the lead weights affected walking skill. Infants could walk down steeper slopes in their feather-weight packs compared with their lead-weighted packs (4°–16° difference). Thus, very shallow slopes were safe and very steep slopes were risky. Because slope boundaries varied for each baby between shoulderpack conditions, slopes in the intermediate range were sometimes safe and sometimes risky depending on the shoulderpack condition. As illustrated by the vertical arrow in the left panel of Fig. 3.3B, the same absolute degree of slope could mean different things from trial to trial in the two conditions.

Most impressively, infants treated the same absolute degree of slope as safer in their feather packs, but as riskier in their lead packs. Consistent with the problem-solving account, they were more likely to attempt to walk down slopes in the intermediate range when they were wearing their feather-weighted packs than when they were wearing their lead-weighted packs. Recalibration was nearly perfect (approximating the perfectly superimposed curves in the right panel of Fig. 3.3B). Infants displayed only slightly more errors in their novel lead weights compared with their feather weights and only on slightly risky slopes a few degrees steeper than their slope boundaries.

Summary

To summarize, a series of separate experiments supported the predictions of the problem-solving framework for understanding the development of flexibility. Infants' ability to respond adaptively to novel threats to balance depended on the duration of their everyday experience with balance control, not their chronological age. The course of learning was slow and spanned several months of everyday practice. Consistent with learning to learn, but inconsistent with simple associative pairing, adaptive responding was based on relative amount of risk, rather than absolute stimulus increments. Once flexibility was achieved, infants could discover new solutions to novel problems online in the midst of the task. However, adaptive responding to threats to balance was limited to the postures with which infants had extensive experience. Learning did not transfer to new postures in development.

WHAT INFANTS MUST LEARN AND HOW

Flexibility

The central question, of course, in any study of transfer concerns what was learned in the first place that did or did not transfer. I am proposing that learning to learn in infant motor skill acquisition is the same as learning to learn in any task—whether in monkey discrimination problems, chess, basketball, or cooking. To achieve flexibility, learners must define the perimeters of the problem space, identify the relevant parameters for operating within the problem space, and acquire the tools for calibrating the settings of the parameters online.

In this case, infants must map out the limits of each problem space for each new postural milestone in development. They must identify the relevant balance control parameters for each posture that define the problem space, including the key pivots around which their bodies rotate, the relevant parts of their bodies and muscle groups for generating compensatory sway, changing vantage points for viewing the layout of the ground ahead, and various sources of perceptual information. Finally, they must acquire the appropriate exploratory movements—swaying, looking, touching, and testing various strategies—for recalibrating the settings of the appropriate parameters so that they can gauge the size of their current region of permissible postural sway from moment to moment.

How then might learning work? Although the duration of infants' everyday experience with balance and locomotion is a good predictor of adaptive responding in the laboratory tasks, duration of experience tells us nothing about mechanisms. In fact, the actual content of infants' locomotor experience is unknown. To date all theorizing about experience-related mechanisms has been completely unconstrained by empirical facts. Researchers have treated experience like chronological age. Experience is calculated simply as the number of days that have elapsed between the onset date and the test date, just as chronological age is calculated as the number of days elapsed between birth and the test date. Elapsed time, however, is not an explanatory variable without a description of what exactly infants experienced during the passage of time.

Content of Everyday Experience

To redress the deficiency in the literature concerning the nature of infants' everyday experiences with locomotion, my colleagues and I are in the process of conducting a series of diary studies designed to obtain detailed descriptions of infants' everyday experiences with balance control during stance and locomotion (Adolph, 2002). To date the samples include infants living in elevator buildings in an urban setting in New York City and infants living in single-family homes in the suburbs of Pittsburgh. We use a daily checklist diary technique to track the appearance and disappearance of motor skills in infants' repertoires. Each day parents check off whether infants have displayed each of 54 motor skills beginning shortly after infants are born and ending several months after they begin walking (Adolph, Biu, Pethkongathan, & Young, 2002; Biu et al., 2003; Young, Biu, Pethkongkathon, Kanani, & Adolph, 2002). We use a call-in telephone diary procedure to track crawling infants' whereabouts in 15-minute time blocks from the time babies wake up until the time they go to bed over the course of several weeks (Chan, Lu, Marin, & Adolph, 1999; Chan, Biancaniello, Adolph, & Marin, 2000). We have designed several varieties of foot switches to count walking infants' steps as they travel freely around their homes and out of doors (Adolph, 2002). In each study, researchers draw detailed blueprints of infants' homes to obtain information about the places infants visit, the surfaces they travel over, the paths of their locomotor excursions, and the distances they travel between locations.

The diary studies showed vast individual differences on every measure. Infants had different opportunities for learning in their environments, different levels of access to opportunities provided by their caregivers, and different physical abilities and skill levels that might allow them to exploit the various opportunities afforded. For example, infants differed in terms of the available floor space in their homes (New York City infants lived in tiny apartments, whereas suburban infants in Pittsburgh lived in larger, multilevel homes), experience with outdoor surfaces (New York City infants had less experience on grass, but more on concrete), experience with stairs (New York City infants lived in elevator buildings and were delayed in their access to stairs), and so on. Babies began crawling and walking at the wide range of ages that are typical of healthy infants, meaning that infants were subject to any age-related differences in motivation to explore the environment, separate from caregivers, and the like. Infants' bodies and skill levels also spanned the wide ranges typical of healthy infants. Some babies were built like big round Buddhas, and others were slender, small, and wiry.

Despite the range in individual differences, several factors were common across infants. Every baby was exposed to massive amounts of tiny mundane experiences with balance, presented in variable contexts, and distributed widely over time during the course of each day and across days and weeks. These factors—massive doses, equally salient stimulus dimensions and consequences, variable training contexts, and distributed practice schedules—are exactly the factors that facilitate flexibility of learning in laboratory studies of skill acquisition. In short, the diary studies suggest that if researchers could design a practice regimen to promote flexibility in infants' balance control based on what investigators have learned from 100 years of laboratory research on skill acquisition, the training schedule would look much like infants' actual everyday experiences with balance.

For example, we found that crawling infants spent 41% of their waking day (approximately 5 hours), on average, on the floor engaged in active, independent balance control in sitting and crawling postures. In addition, crawlers spent 17% of their waking day (approximately 2.6 hours) in passive locomotion—being carried in caregivers' arms or wheeled around in strollers. They traveled over 6 to 12 different indoor and outdoor surfaces each day at an average speed of 27 to 43 meters/hr. Their total daily crawling distance was between 60 and 188 meters (the length of two football fields). Based on crawlers' average step length, we calculated that babies experienced 1,000 to 3,200 crawling steps each day.

After infants begin walking, opportunities for learning expand dramatically. Our diary studies showed that walking infants spent 50% of their waking day (approximately 6 hours) on the floor maintaining balance in sitting, standing, and walking postures. The step counters showed that babies took approximately 500 to 1,500 steps/hour—9,000 steps/day. Based on infants' average step length, toddlers' maximum total daily distance was 2,700 meters (the length of 29 football fields).

Epochs of Experience. Exposure to balance constraints during infants' everyday life occurs in truly massive doses. For nearly half of their waking day, infants fight gravity unsupported by caregivers or furniture. Each tiny crawling and walking step, each body sway and shift in position, is in a sense like a little training trial of exposure to the challenges of maintaining balance. Compiled over the hours, days, and weeks that characterize infants' protracted periods of experience with each postural milestone, infants' everyday practice regimen is best described in terms of epochs of experience.

In terms of opportunities for learning, our preliminary results provide an astounding contrast compared with earlier research on learning to learn. Recall that Harlow's (1949) learning set studies were a relatively simple preparation. Subjects were posed with discrimination and oddity problems. To acquire flexibility in Harlow's model system, adult monkeys required experience with hundreds of problem types, with 10 blocked trials in each type for thousands of trials. In contrast, in the more complex model system of human infants acquiring balance control, our diary studies show that babies get that many trials before lunch. To put the sheer amount of infants' experience into context, such consistently high levels of exposure are similar to the practice regimens necessary for expert performance in concert pianists and Olympians (Ericsson & Charness, 1994; Ericsson, Krampe, & Tesch-Romer, 1993; Ericsson & Lehmann, 1996).

No One-Trial Learning. Infants' experience is happy and uneventful. We found no evidence of one-trial learning about balance nor any evidence that any particular kind of experience was critical. Despite common-sense intuitions that serious falls might play an important role in learning about balance, most infants sail through their infancy unscathed. Infants in both the crawling and walking diary studies occasionally fell hard enough that they cried and required comforting after a bad spill. However, only 1 of 18 infants tracked longitudinally required medical attention after a fall. Similarly, in earlier studies, where infants were tracked prospectively or parents provided retrospective reports, few infants incurred serious falls during everyday locomotion, and those that had behaved no differently on laboratory tasks compared with those that had not (e.g., Adolph, 1995; Adolph, 1997, 2000; Scarr & Salapatek, 1970). After their accidents, infants dragged their casts and bruises over the brink of steep slopes and cliffs in the same proportions as the rest of the samples.

Variable Practice. Infants' practice with balance control occurs under wildly variable conditions in terms of the surfaces they travel over and stand on, the places in which the surfaces are located, and the events that precipitate the visit. A key to flexibility in balance control is to refrain from forming simple associative pairings so as to identify the critical features that allow online problem solving to occur. Variable contexts may help discourage simple associative pairings. Recall that in Harlow's (1949) studies, the critical factor for learning to learn was practice with varying pairs of shapes that hid the raisin, not the details of any particular problem type. Similarly, laboratory studies of motor skill acquisition in human participants show that learning under a variable practice regimen takes longer compared with blocked practice, but variable practice leads to a broader range of transfer when participants are challenged with novel problems (Gentile, 2000; Schmidt & Lee, 1999). Thus, variable contexts in everyday stance and locomotion may promote flexibility in infants' balance control.

Distributed Practice. Infants' experience with locomotion is not like an enforced march. Rather, babies crawl and walk in bursts of activity—a dozen steps or 100 steps during a quick foray from one place to another—separated by periods of quiet stance when they stop to play, manipulate objects, or interact with a caregiver. Moreover, experience with balance in sitting, crawling, cruising, standing, and walking emerges into infants' repertoires with fits and starts. Infants may sit independently on one day but not on the next or pass criterion for walking for a few days then fail to pass for the next few.

Laboratory studies of skill acquisition suggest that such distributed practice schedules may facilitate learning by providing rest periods to dissipate fatigue and boredom and allow infants to recover their motivation to move. Moreover, distributed practice may provide time to consolidate learning in working memory (Gentile, 2000; Schmidt & Lee, 1999).

SUMMARY

In summary, the diary studies of everyday experiences with balance and locomotion are consistent with a problem-solving framework for understanding the development of behavioral flexibility. The demands for flexibility in balance control are enormous. Changing body dimensions, changing skill levels, and changing environments change the biomechanical constraints on balance from moment to moment. Happily, the opportunities for learning are also enormous. Healthy infants immersed in the rich and varied challenges of everyday life are well prepared to acquire the requisite levels of flexibility (and specificity) that they need to promote adaptive responding under continually changing conditions.

ACKNOWLEDGMENTS

This research was supported by NICHD grant #HD33486. I gratefully acknowledge Marion Eppler, Eleanor Gibson, and Esther Thelen for their help in formulating the ideas in this chapter and Anne and Herb Pick for their inspiration in investigating the relationship between perception and action.

REFERENCES

Adolph, K. E. (1995). A psychophysical assessment of toddlers' ability to cope with slopes. *Journal of Experimental Psychology: Human Perception and Performance, 21*, 734–750.

Adolph, K. E. (1997). Learning in the development of infant locomotion. *Monographs of the Society for Research in Child Development, 62*(3, Serial No. 251).

Adolph, K. E. (2000). Specificity of learning: Why infants fall over a veritable cliff. *Psychological Science, 11*, 290–295.

Adolph, K. E. (2002). Learning to keep balance. In R. Kail (Ed.), *Advances in child development and behavior* (Vol. 30, pp. 1–30). Amsterdam: Elsevier Science.

Adolph, K. E., & Avolio, A. M. (2000). Walking infants adapt locomotion to changing body dimensions. *Journal of Experimental Psychology: Human Perception and Performance, 26*, 1148–1166.

Adolph, K. E., Biu, O., Pethkongathan, S., & Young, J. (2002, April). *Transitions in development: The trajectory of motor skill acquisition*. Paper presented at the meeting of the International Conference on Infant Studies, Toronto, Canada.

Adolph, K. E., & Eppler, M. A. (1998). Development of visually guided locomotion. *Ecological Psychology, 10*, 303–321.

Adolph, K. E., & Eppler, M. A. (2002). Flexibility and specificity in infant motor skill acquisition. In J. Fagen (Ed.), *Progress in infancy research* (Vol. 2, pp. 121–167). Norwood, NJ: Ablex.

Adolph, K. E., Vereijken, B., & Denny, M. A. (1998). Learning to crawl. *Child Development, 69*, 1299–1312.

Adolph, K. E., Vereijken, B., & Shrout, P. E. (2003). What changes in infant walking and why. *Child Development, 74*, 475–497.

Berger, S. E., & Adolph, K. E. (2003). Infants use handrails as tools in a locomotor task. *Developmental Psychology, 39*, 594–605.

Berger, S. E., & Lobo, S. A. (2003, April). *Look ma, both hands; Infants discriminate wooden and wobbly handrails*. Poster presented at the meeting of the Society for Research in Child Development, Tampa, FL.

Bertenthal, B. I., & Bai, D. L. (1989). Infants' sensitivity to optical flow for controlling posture. *Developmental Psychology, 25*, 936–945.

Bertenthal, B. I., Campos, J. J., & Barrett, K. C. (1984). Self-produced locomotion: An organizer of emotional, cognitive, and social development in infancy. In R. N. Emde & R. J. Harmon (Eds.), *Continuities and discontinuities in development* (pp. 175–210). New York: Plenum.

Biu, O., Young, J. W., Pethkongkathon, S. J., Kanani, P. H., Webster, T. M., & Adolph, K. E. (2003, April). *A microgenetic analysis of the trajectory of motor development*. Paper presented at the meeting of the Society for Research in Child Development, Tampa, FL.

Bril, B., & Breniere, Y. (1989). Steady-state velocity and temporal structure of gait during the first six months of autonomous walking. *Human Movement Science, 8*, 99–122.

Butterworth, G., & Hicks, L. (1977). Visual proprioception and postural stability in infancy: A developmental study. *Perception, 6*, 255–262.

Campos, J. J., Bertenthal, B. I., & Kermoian, R. (1992). Early experience and emotional development: The emergence of wariness of heights. *Psychological Science, 3*, 61–64.

Campos, J., Hiatt, S., Ramsay, D., Henderson, C., & Svejda, M. (1978). The emergence of fear on the visual cliff. In M. Lewis & L. Rosenblum (Eds.), *The development of affect* (pp. 149–182). New York: Plenum.

Campos, J. J., Langer, A., & Krowitz, A. (1970). Cardiac responses on the visual cliff. *Science, 170*, 196–197.

Chan, M., Lu, Y., Marin, L., & Adolph, K. E. (1999). A baby's day: Capturing crawling experience. In M. A. Grealy & J. A. Thompson (Eds.), *Studies in perception and action V* (pp. 245–249). Mahwah, NJ: Lawrence Erlbaum Associates.

Chan, M. Y., Biancaniello, R., Adolph, K. E., & Marin, L. (2000, July). *Tracking infants' locomotor experience: The telephone diary.* Paper presented at the meeting of the International Conference on Infant Studies, Brighton, England.

Eppler, M. A., Satterwhite, T., Wendt, J., & Bruce, K. (1997). Infants' responses to a visual cliff and other ground surfaces. In M. A. Schmuckler & J. M. Kennedy (Eds.), *Studies in perception and action IV* (pp. 219–222). Mahwah, NJ: Lawrence Erlbaum Associates.

Ericsson, K. A., & Charness, N. (1994). Expert performance: Its structure and acquisition. *American Psychologist, 49*, 725–747.

Ericsson, K. A., Krampe, R. T., & Tesch-Romer, C. (1993). The role of deliberate practice in the acquisition of expert performance. *Psychological Review, 100*, 363–406.

Ericsson, K. A., & Lehmann, A. C. (1996). Expert and exceptional performance: Evidence on maximal adaptations on task constraints. *Annual Review of Psychology, 47*, 273–305.

Frankenburg, W. K., & Dodds, J. B. (1967). The Denver developmental screening test. *Journal of Pediatrics, 71*, 181–191.

Freedland, R. L., & Bertenthal, B. I. (1994). Developmental changes in interlimb coordination: Transition to hands-and-knees crawling. *Psychological Science, 5*, 26–32.

Garling, T., & Garling, A. (1988). Parents' protection of children from dangers. In J. Valsiner (Ed.), *Child development within culturally structured environments* (Vol. 1, pp. 60–83). Norwood, NJ: Ablex.

Gentile, A. M. (2000). Skill acquisition: Action, movement, and neuromotor processes. In J. Carr & R. Shepard (Eds.), *Movement science: Foundations for physical therapy in rehabilitation* (2nd ed., pp. 111–187). New York: Aspen.

Gibson, E. J., & Schmuckler, M. A. (1989). Going somewhere: An ecological and experimental approach to development of mobility. *Ecological Psychology, 1*, 3–25.

Gibson, E. J., & Walk, R. D. (1960). The "visual cliff." *Scientific American, 202*, 64–71.

Haehl, V., Vardaxis, V., & Ulrich, B. (2000). Learning to cruise: Bernstein's theory applied to skill acquisition during infancy. *Human Movement Science, 19*, 685–715.

Harlow, H. F. (1949). The formation of learning sets. *Psychological Review, 56*, 51–65.

Harlow, H. F. (1959). Learning set and error factor theory. In S. Koch (Ed.), *Psychology: A study of a science* (pp. 492–533). New York: McGraw-Hill.

Harlow, H. F., & Kuenne, M. (1949). Learning to think. *Scientific American*, pp. 3–6.

Lampl, M. (1983). Postnatal infant growth: Leaps and bounds (Abstract). *American Journal of Physical Anthropology, 60*, 215–216.

Lampl, M. (1993). Evidence of saltatory growth in infancy. *American Journal of Human Biology, 5*, 641–652.

Lampl, M., Veldhuis, J. D., & Johnson, M. L. (1992). Saltation and statis: A model of human growth. *Science, 258*(801).

Leo, A. J., Chiu, J., & Adolph, K. E. (2000, July). *Temporal and functional relationships of crawling, cruising, and walking.* Poster presented at the meeting of the International Conference on Infant Studies, Brighton, England.

MacKay, D. G. (1982). The problems of flexibility, fluency, and speed-accuracy trade-off in skilled behavior. *Psychological Review, 89,* 483–506.

McCollum, G., & Leen, T. K. (1989). Form and exploration of mechanical stability limits in erect stance. *Journal of Motor Behavior, 21,* 225–244.

McGraw, M. B. (1935). *Growth: A study of Johnny and Jimmy.* New York: Appleton-Century-Crofts.

Metcalfe, J. S., & Clark, J. E. (2000). Sensory information affords exploration of posture in newly walking infants and toddlers. *Infant Behavior and Development, 23,* 391–405.

Riccio, G. E. (1993). Information in movement variability about the qualitative dynamics of posture and orientation. In K. M. Newell & D. M. Corcos (Eds.), *Variability and motor control* (pp. 317–357). Champaign, IL: Human Kinetics.

Riccio, G. E., & Stoffregen, T. A. (1988). Affordances as constraints on the control of stance. *Human Movement Science, 7,* 265–300.

Scarr, S., & Salapatek, P. (1970). Patterns of fear development during infancy. *Merrill-Palmer Quarterly, 16,* 53–90.

Schmidt, R. A., & Lee, T. D. (1999). *Motor control and learning: A behavioral emphasis* (3rd ed.). Champaign, IL: Human Kinetics.

Schmuckler, M. A. (1997). Children's postural sway in response to low- and high-frequency visual information for oscillation. *Journal of Experimental Psychology: Human Perception and Performance, 23,* 528–545.

Slater, A., & Morison, V. (1985). Shape constancy and slant perception at birth. *Perception, 14,* 337–344.

Stevenson, H. W. (1972). *Children's learning.* New York: Appleton-Century-Crofts.

Thelen, E. (1984). Learning to walk: Ecological demands and phylogenetic constraints. *Advances in Infancy Research, 3,* 213–260.

Thelen, E., & Fisher, D. M. (1982). Newborn stepping: An explanation for a "disappearing reflex." *Developmental Psychology, 18,* 760–775.

Thelen, E., Fisher, D. M., & Ridley-Johnson, R. (1984). The relationship between physical growth and a newborn reflex. *Infant Behavior and Development, 7,* 479–493.

Thelen, E., & Smith, L. B. (1994). *A dynamic systems approach to the development of cognition and action.* Cambridge, MA: MIT Press.

Yonas, A., & Hartman, B. (1993). Perceiving the affordance of contact in four- and five-month-old infants. *Child Development, 64,* 298–308.

Young, J., Biu, O., Pethkongkathon, J., Kanani, P., & Adolph, K. E. (2002, October). *Continuity and discontinuity in motor skill acquisition.* Paper presented at the meeting of the International Society for Developmental Psychobiology, Orlando, FL.

4

▼▼▼▼▼▼▼▼

Information, Representation, and Dynamics: A Discussion of the Chapters by Lee, von Hofsten, and Adolph

William H. Warren
Brown University

Like everyone before me, I would like to thank the organizers of this event for giving me the opportunity to honor Herb and Anne. Both of them provided encouragement and friendship at an early point in my career, as in so many of our careers. Their support was very meaningful to me at the time, and it remains so. What better way to honor them than to come to Minnesota, which I still think of as my second home, and get to spout off my opinions?

It is humbling to be a discussant for three people whose work I admire as much as I do that of David Lee, Claes von Hofsten, and Karen Adolph. I could stand here and happily nod in agreement with 90% of their presentations, but that would make for a fairly boring discussion. So I am going to take the tack of focusing on the other 10% and raise several issues that I hope will stimulate further discussion, but I do so in the spirit of generating more light than heat.

Here are the three issues that I want to pursue. The first is the question of how we should characterize the relationship between information and action, which I think about in terms of control laws. The second is an old one that comes back and bites us all the time: the issue of representation. That is, when should we posit internal representations to explain behavior, as opposed to looking for some other explanation? Finally, a question that I am quite unqualified to raise, not being a developmentalist, is the relationship between development and learning. I would like to offer a bit of my thinking about the first two issues, then make some specific comments on the talks, and finally launch into a more general discussion.

INFORMATION AND ACTION

Let us start with control laws. How is information used to regulate action? We usually think of this very generally as some kind of mapping from informational variables to action variables:

$$a = f(i) \tag{1}$$

Unfortunately, there is little agreement about the form of this function. Such a mapping has been represented in various ways in the literature, and I review a couple of them here (Warren & Fajen, 2004).

First, there is a *kinematic* form for control laws, in which the movement kinematics per se are a function of information:

$$\dot{x} = f(i) \tag{2}$$

That is, the trajectories, velocities, and timing of movements are explicitly determined by the information available to the actor. I think the work that Dave Lee (chap. 1, this volume) describes exemplifies this sort of control law, such as the idea of tau-coupling. In Fig. 1.1, a bat flying to a perch has to coordinate its distance to the landing point and its direction of approach as it comes in for a landing. Lee proposes that the bat couples the tau function for time to arrival at the perch with the tau function for the angle between its current and desired direction of approach, such that these two gaps gradually close to zero at the moment of arrival. Now under this kind of relationship, the bat's trajectory is completely determined by information—that is, by these two tau functions.

The problem I see with such a purely kinematic formulation is that there is no action system in the picture. It assumes that the organization of the action system does not contribute to the form of the behavior, but that behavior is structured solely by information. Thus, it appears to beg the question of how appropriate movements are generated on the basis of that information.

Another form for control laws, which I have been promoting lately, is that information modulates the dynamics of the action system, rather than determining movement kinematics per se.

$$\dot{a} = f(a,i) \tag{3}$$

The observed kinematics are a consequence of the dynamic organization of action—a view reminiscent of the work of Feldman (Asatryan & Feldman, 1965). If we think of the organization of action as being modeled by a dynamical system of some type, then the role of information is to modulate this dynamical system. Specifically, information may influence the location, number, or class of attractors and repellers in the system's dynamics by modulating the state variables or parameters of the system.

One of the first examples of this sort of control law was Gregor Schöner's (1991) model of the visual control of standing posture. He modeled the postural system in a fairly standard fashion as a second-order system, with an added noise term ($\sqrt{Q}\xi_t$):

$$\ddot{x} \quad \dot{x} - \alpha\omega^2 x \quad \sqrt{Q}\xi_t - \frac{c}{\tau} \tag{4}$$

where x is postural position, α is a damping coefficient, and ω^2 is a stiffness coefficient based on the natural frequency of sway. The system is forced by optical information—the inverse of *tau* (c/τ)—which results from body sway or from movement of the surround. The effect of this forcing term is to shift the equilibrium position (or attractor) for standing posture backward and forward, resulting in postural accelerations back and forth with a particular profile determined by the characteristics of the system. Thus, the kinematics of postural sway are not simply a function of information, but result from the way information modulates the action system's dynamics. I want to suggest that incorporating the dynamics of action in conjunction with information is necessary to account for the exhibited behavior.

REPRESENTATIONS AND EXPLANATIONS

Second, let me turn to the hoary chestnut of representation. Note that both Lee and von Hofsten (chap. 2, this volume) invoke internal mental entities of some sort to explain observed behavior: object representations, assumptions about inertia and force, or intrinsic *tau* guides, which I take to be a type of movement representation. I do not think we want to do this lightly. If we are positing representations, they must be well motivated before we make this particular leap. It is incumbent on researchers who introduce such entities to be specific about what they mean by a mental representation and to account for their origins. At one extreme is a formal symbolic representation of the sort promoted in Fodor's (1975) "language of thought" or Newell and Simon's "physical symbol systems" (Newell, 1980). This account has been challenged from a variety of perspectives (Bechtel & Abrahamsen, 1991; Searle, 1980; Shaw, 2003). At the other extreme is a weak form of memory or learning—changes in neural weights that result from experience and influence subsequent behavior, but do not invoke discrete symbol-like entities. Such learning is not problematic as long as its basis in experience can be understood. I want to pursue an intermediate variant that is currently popular, which holds that a mental representation is an internal entity that "stands in" for environmental objects.

Haugeland (1991) and Clark (1997) argued that a representation is an internal state whose functional role is to "stand in" to guide behavior when the environmental features that normally do so are not present. At a minimum, a representation can serve to guide behavior appropriately in the absence of information from the environment. A stronger sense of representation holds that these internal entities can become detached from the environmental conditions that originally produced them and be used to think about the world off-line. Such representations are not bound to a particular behavioral context, but can be used as internal models of the world to perform functions like reasoning, problem solving, or decision making in a kind of cognitive economy.

The problem with representations is that there is a steep philosophical price to pay for them. First, one must confront the question of where the content of internal representations comes from. If you need representations to explain perceptual abilities and the organization of adaptive behavior, you must account for the origin of those representations without appealing to the very abilities they purport to explain or else be doomed to circularity. Second, it is not at all clear how representations are grounded or connected to the world. If our perceptual and mental states are representations, how is it possible for us to know what piece of the world they stand for (Searle, 1980)? This is a deep philosophical problem that does not as yet have an adequate answer. It seems to me that, in order to solve it, one must grant some form of independent nonrepresentational access to the world—a form of direct perception (Gibson, 1966, 1979). But once you have such a nonrepresentational system up and running, it is more parsimonious to push it as far as it will go.

Finally, introducing internal representations into your theory raises the specter of logically regressive explanations. Invoking representations runs the risk of accounting for the organization we observe in behavior by simply attributing it to the properties of the representation. This does not solve any problems, it merely passes the buck to the mentalist realm. Ultimately, you still have to account for the organization of the representation itself.

So the question I raise with the presenters is, what sort of evidence forces us to posit internal representations? Given the deep problems with them, I believe we must be conservative about introducing them into our theories. This is really just an argument from parsimony. At what point does it become necessary to invoke representations to do explanatory work? Do the phenomena of perception and action, oriented behavior in the absence of information, mental imagery, reasoning, or communicative language demand representational entities? Strategically, an appeal to representations should be a last resort—we should first exhaust other explanations that seek to account for behavior on the basis of first principles, such as the available information and dynamics of the system. Even then we must understand how representational entities can emerge from nonrepresentational relations in perception and action because eventually we will be held to account for the structure of the representations too. In science, as in life, there is no free lunch.

Brian Smith (1998) offered a nice thought experiment to probe the nature of representations implicated in the sort of tracking behavior that von Hofsten describes: the case of super-sunflowers. As the sun moves across the sky, ordinary sunflowers in the bud stage actually reorient to track the trajectory of the sun. This sort of tracking system is directly driven by incident light from the sun, with no need for a representation to guide behavior. Smith then imagines a species of super-sunflowers, which continue to track the sun even when it goes behind a tree or cloud. What would make it possible for them to perform this feat? It is apparent that super-sunflowers would have to have some internal process running that keeps them oriented to an absent environmental feature—the missing sun. The question is, at what point are we forced to grant this internal process the status of an internal representation of the sun and its motion?

Let us concoct a story about a tracking mechanism that would keep the super-sunflower oriented to the sun. Suppose that when the sun is shining its motion sets up some sort of pressure differential in the hydrostatic tubules in the stem of the super-sunflower. When the sun goes out of view, hydrostatic pressure continues to move the sunflower in the same direction at the same rate for a period of time. So when the sun appears again, the sunflower is still oriented toward it. Such a mechanism would work by virtue of the fact that the sun moves on a constant trajectory, so a system that matches its visible motion would continue to track the sun when it was hidden.

Should we consider such a process to be a mental representation? Well it certainly is some kind of stand-in that guides the super-sunflower's behavior in the absence of current information. Yet as the example implies, this criterion is too weak. It would lead us to accept any processes that are not stimulus-driven, any "internal states that endure longer than the states in the world that gave rise to them" (Markman & Dietrich, 2000), as full-fledged mental representations. However, the super-sunflower's hydrostatic tubules are just a simple mechanical process that is set into operation by the sun. One might call the process a representation of the sun's motion, but this adds nothing to our understanding of the sunflowers and how they work (van Gelder, 1995). The tubules are plainly not detachable entities that the super-sunflower can use to reason about the world in a cognitive economy. Thus, the definition of a representation as anything that stands in for the environment is too catholic, and hence somewhat empty.

I would argue that a more fruitful way to think about the super-sunflower is as a dynamical system that is entrained by the sun's motion and continues to run in its absence. Information about the sun's trajectory is essential for setting the system going, and the dynamics of the system account for its oriented behavior in the absence of occurrent stimulation without invoking mental representations. This way of thinking may be adequate for sunflowers, but is such a form of explanation sufficient to account for more complex behavior? It has been argued that coupled dynamical systems with multiple time scales can indeed exhibit the sort of complex behavior characteristic of biological systems, including influences of past experience and anticipatory behavior (Keijzer, 1998). The promise of this sort of explanation remains to be cashed in, but people are beginning to work on it. For example, Esther Thelen (chap. 9, this volume) uses a dynamic neural field model to account for certain memory effects, such as perseveration in the "A not B" error. This style of explanation stands in contrast to more cognitivist explanations based on the development of object representations. The transient neural dynamics of this model should probably not be classed as representations because they are bound to a particular behavioral context and are not easily detached and manipulated.

Now Smith suggests that super-sunflowers are actually the first step on the road to full-fledged representations. Once a dynamic tracking process is established, then in some more highly evolved sunflower that process might break off from a specific information-driven behavioral context and be deployed for something else like reasoning or language. At that point, perhaps we have made the leap to internal representations. My point is that we still must account for their origin in perception and action. I am willing to entertain the possibility of such emergent representations, but I am not willing to buy them until we really explore the prospect of a thoroughgoing, nonrepresentational theory of mind (Chemero, 2001; Keijzer, 1998; van Gelder, 1995).

Let me take some of these ideas back to the talks from this session, beginning with von Hofsten's (chap. 2, this volume) work on the development of the control of looking. Admirably, von Hofsten is trying to develop an action-systems approach to looking behavior. He treats the eye, head, and body as systems that an infant has to learn to coordinate by coupling them together in certain ways and modulating them with appropriate vestibular information or neck proprioception. From a developmental point of view, it seems to me that this is more informative than drawing a circuit diagram of the saccadic control system because it reveals the problems that an infant has to solve rather than a purported end-state. Von Hofsten applies concepts of developmental dynamical systems when describing these problems, and eye-head-body coordination may be amenable to dynamical modeling. Yet when it comes to the issue of tracking a target that moves behind an occluder, he willingly goes over to the dark side.

When tracking over occlusions, visual information about the target is not simultaneously available. This leads von Hofsten to invoke a representation of a moving object that guides a saccade to the exit point at the time the object is due to reappear. In my view, this merely relocates the problem. We still have to figure out how the tracking is done. We still have to understand how the infant saccades to the right place at the right time on the basis of information that is available in the object's trajectory, either over single or multiple trials. We are back to the super-sunflower problem: Can we come up with a parsimonious account of tracking behavior that does not presume a representation?

Let us look at tracking over occlusion in a little more detail. Is it possible to account for tracking behavior on the basis of information and a dynamical process of some sort? First, consider the case of the simple linear trajectory. The information available in the trajectory before occlusion actually predicts when and where the object is going to reappear on the other side of the occluder. I am sure Dave Lee could derive a *tau* variable that specifies the exit time, such as

$$\tau = \frac{d}{|v|} \tag{5}$$

where $|v|$ is the target's speed prior to occlusion and d is the width of the occluder. The exit location is specified by the direction of the target's motion prior to occlusion—that is, the linear extrapolation of its trajectory. Thus, the exit time and place are specified by the first-order motion properties of the object before it goes behind the occluder.

However, von Hofsten changes the direction of the object's motion behind the occluder. Over a few exposures, the infant indeed learns to guide the saccade to the new exit location rather than to the linear exit location. Again I think we can account for this based on the available information, this time over repeated trials. The target always appears in the same location, so saccade there. The timing may be governed by a similar tau variable.

But von Hofsten gets even sneakier and uses a sinusoidal or triangular target speed so that the object decelerates behind the occluder, reverses direction, and reappears on the same side. This is really hard for infants to adapt to; they keep saccading to the opposite side, following a linear trajectory. Why might this be so—is it a limitation of their object representations? This is actually not surprising because we know that even adults are rather insensitive to target deceleration, with Weber fractions on the order of 0.5 or more. It may take even longer for infants than adults to learn that the target is slowing down, and to eventually reduce false saccades to the other side of the target. It does not seem to me that such results demand object representations to explain saccadic behavior. Saccades can be guided on the basis of the available trajectory information, whether on a single trial or adapting to new regularities over multiple trials.

Now let me play devil's advocate with myself. What might force us to adopt an object representation here? Suppose the infant had to learn different trajectories for different objects. Imagine you are a rabbit in the cluttered desert and you have to avoid various predators: The coyote runs in a straight path, the fox darts back and forth, and the hawk swoops in on a curved path. To preserve your hide, you have to recognize each predator and anticipate its motion. One could set up an experiment that mimics this situation, in which a blue circle moves on a linear trajectory, a green triangle has a zig-zag trajectory, and a red cross has a curved trajectory. After the infant learns these trajectories, we introduce an occluder. The initial part of the trajectory before occlusion is the same for all objects, and we test whether the infant can anticipate their exits based on the identity of the object and knowledge of its trajectory.

That is a tall order for a 6-month-old saccadic system. Yet even if it learned to track each object successfully, I am not sure I would be convinced. One might propose a dynamical tracking system that is parameterized in a slightly different way based on information about the target object. In fact, that is exactly how we are modeling trajectory formation in locomotor behavior (Fajen & Warren, 2003; Warren & Fajen, 2004). We can model steering toward stationary and moving targets, and avoidance of stationary and moving obstacles, with a dynamical system of similar form having different parameter values, without introducing representations or explicit planning.

Let us now turn to Lee's chapter 1 about the tau guidance of movement. Lee has taken the idea of a tau function and pushed it further than I ever thought possible. Tau was already one of the most ubiquitous informational variables in the study of visually guided behavior. Yet in recent years he has extended the concept from light to sound to movement gaps and force gaps, and he has formulated the idea of tau-coupling to coordinate the closure of two gaps. Most recently, he introduced the idea of an intrinsic tau guide to generate a gap closure in the absence of a coupling to an external gap. Now it seems to me that the intrinsic tau guide is a species of internal representation introduced to explain behavior, with all the attendant baggage mentioned earlier. Essentially, it is a function generator in the central nervous system that can be deployed to create a desired trajectory. The controller thus prescribes the detailed kinematics of the movement.

Is this necessary? Do we need to introduce an internal function generator to account for the organization of behavior, or might we do so in other ways? It may be the case that an intrinsic tau guide can be descriptively fit to a given set of behavioral data, but it does not necessarily follow that a tau guide is being used to generate that behavior. I believe it is more parsimonious to show how such behavior can emerge from the dynamic organization of the action system in conjunction with biomechanical, physical, and informational constraints. In this way, the action system actually has a role in shaping the kinematics of the movement. For example, there are dynamical models of aiming (Mottet & Bootsma, 1999), reaching (Zaal, Bootsma, & van Wieringen, 1999), catching (Peper, Bootsma, Mestre, & Bakker, 1994), and steering and obstacle avoidance (Fajen & Warren, 2003), in which the trajectories emerge from a parameterized dynamical system that is modulated by information, rather than being explicitly specified by an internal pattern generator. More generally, it is important to point out that finding correlations is not enough to justify one particular theory. One has to do the nitty-gritty experiments that compare models by testing conditions that will pry them apart.

LEARNING AND/OR DEVELOPMENT

Third, let us consider Karen Adolph's (chap. 3, this volume) work on the development of balance control in crawling and walking. It seems to me that Adolph is trying to understand perceptual-motor learning in infancy without invoking representations. She describes perception-action systems that have to be parameterized for a given problem space to achieve a certain adaptive behavior. I take her point to be that, as the developing infant acquires new motor abilities and moves from one problem space to another, a new perception-action system has to be assembled. In the case of locomotor development, the infant actually learns different balance control systems for crawling and walking, which must be parameterized for each postural configuration. For a crawling posture, the child must parameterize the system in one way so that it can adapt to variation that is introduced by environmental challenges and body changes and affects the stable region of sway. For a walking posture, the biomechanical degrees of freedom have changed radically, and so has the effect of environmental challenges, so the control relations must be relearned. By exploring their own postural stability in massive practice, the infant maps out this problem space, identifying and setting the values on the parameters that will ensure stability under a range of conditions. Adolph's data are provocative because there is little evidence of transfer from one domain to another. From sitting to crawling or crawling to walking or cruising to walking, infants have to keep relearning balance control all over again. That is an amazing observation.

One question this raises is, how do we define a problem space? Can one be defined independently of the transfer data? At present, if we find no transfer from one task set to another, we call them different problem spaces. Ideally we would like to have some models, probably at a musculoskeletal level, that would allow us to characterize postural stability for different postures. For example, Benoit Bardy has been developing a biomechanical model of standing balance that reproduces the coordination patterns observed in adults, including the transition from inphase to antiphase coordination across the hips and ankles (Bardy, Oullier, Bootsma, & Stoffregen, 2002). If Adolph had such a model for infants, it might allow her to predict stable regions of sway for various environmental challenges (e.g., slopes) and determine the most general parameterization of the model. Similar balance models for sitting, crawling, and walking might allow her to determine the conditions under which a qualitatively different model (with different parameters) or a reparameterization of the same model are needed, and thus the boundaries of a problem space.

I find Adolph's way of thinking about this very congenial. Over the years, I have tried to develop a dynamical account of perception and action, in which learning involves exploring the dynamics and information of a particular task (Warren, 2004). When you learn a new task, you must identify a dynamic organization or "graph" for the action system (Saltzman & Munhall, 1992), its control variables, as well as the relevant information to regulate those control variables. One way to investigate this process is to begin with a model system for which the dynamics are known. We attempted to do just that in an article on learning to bounce in a "jolly jumper" (Goldfield, Kay, & Warren, 1993), and together with Patrick Foo we recently completed a longitudinal study of infant bouncing.

In these studies, we threw 6-month-olds into a novel situation without any instructions, yet over a period of weeks they learned to bounce at a stable frequency. One can model the baby bouncer as a forced mass-spring system. Our data indicate that infants take advantage of the physics of the system: Not only do they drive the system at its natural frequency, they approximately match their leg stiffness to the spring stiffness, getting the highest bounce for the least effort. Somehow infants are exploring the parameter space of leg stiffness and kicking frequency to identify stable values. In our recent study, we measured leg stiffness and ground reaction forces and found that infants explore widely in this parameter space as they learn the task, then abruptly home in on near-optimal values. At the same time, they are learning to use information to appropriately time their kicks. Haptic information from the feet and legs about the bounce cycle would enable an infant to kick at the best phase of the cycle, allowing the system to behave like an autonomous oscillator and transfer to new spring conditions. With appropriate models, there are thus ways to get at the sorts of questions that Adolph is raising: How do children explore the dynamics of a task, parameterize a perception-action system, and achieve stable behavior?

Finally, let me raise the question that goes beyond my expertise. Note that in his chapter on the development of looking, von Hofsten portrays the problem as similar to learning a new skill: How do you learn to coordinate components of your motor system? He suggests that this goes on against a background of innate components (like the VOR and some saccadic control) and maturation of neural perceptual-motor pathways. In her work on the development of balance control, Adolph also portrays the problem as similar to learning a new set of tasks or a new problem space. In this case, learning occurs against a background of changing body size and the emergence of new motor abilities such as crawling or walking. Consequently, the experienced environment is changing, but the problem is basically framed as one of skill learning. The question thus arises: Can perceptual-motor development be reduced to learning in an evolving task space? Or is there something essential about the developmental process that differentiates it from skill learning?

SUMMARY

Let me close by restating the questions that I have posed. First, how should we characterize the relation between information and action? I have argued that information modulates the dynamics of an action system. Thus, the form of behavior is attributable to both perception and action, and we can frame questions about learning in perception-action systems. Second, when should we resort to mental representations to explain behavior? Here I argued that invoking representations is a last resort. We should first try to account for behavior in terms of the available information and multiscaled dynamics and only posit internal mental entities if forced to do so. Finally, is perceptual-motor development just learning in an evolving task space?

OPEN DISCUSSION

Michael Maratsos commented that the argument against representation is essentially a conservative one, which presumes that we know more about the world than we really do. Perhaps one should start conservatively, but it really does not make sense anymore. We have no general grounds to say that one possibility (nonrepresentation) is more likely than the other (representation). Instead we should admit that both are possible and that we do not really know. Another speaker agreed that the best way forward is for some researchers to make conservative assumptions, and others to make less conservative assumptions, and see what surprising ideas arise.

Maratsos emphasized that choosing not to resort to representations risks false negatives, in that it biases us against representations when they may in fact be present. From a developmental perspective, the conservative stance says that we should attribute representations to a child only when he or she starts solving difficult problems. Developmentally, it seems reasonable to suggest that the child develops representations earlier, so they are already available when things get more difficult. Why should representations magically appear when things are difficult rather than develop when they are easier? Maratsos similarly objected to parsimony because there is no reason to believe that biological systems are parsimonious.

Warren responded that our theories should be parsimonious even if nature may not be. Once you throw out parsimony, you have opened Pandora's box, and anything goes as an explanation. We must have good theoretical or empirical reasons to introduce new entities into our theories. Given that X and $X + Y$ are both plausible explanations, we should prefer X until forced to posit something more. Contrary to Maratsos, the field has given the representational zeitgeist a good 50-year shot, and it is now in something of a crisis. Hence, the time has come to take a more parsimonious nonrepresentational approach seriously.

Warren is not opposed to internal representations in principle as long as one can see how to ground them in perception and action. What he is opposed to is invoking representations as an explanation when they do not explain anything, when saying the structure is in the representation just displaces the problem. This applies developmentally as well. For example, it is possible that we may account for the origin of representations as emerging from early perception-action capacities. On such a story, dynamical perceptual-motor processes might become detached developmentally from their original behavioral contexts to form emergent representations, providing the basis for higher cognitive abilities. However, before Warren is willing to accept this easy compromise, he wants to see how far we can push a nonrepresentational theory based in information and dynamics.

Al Yonas said that we may have to look outside the stimulus to account for behavior, and representations provide a heuristic for solving such problems. Claes von Hofsten similarly argued that the purpose of developing the cognitive domain is to expand our perceptual abilities beyond the information given from the environment. He offered the case of mental imagery, such as visualizing oneself walking out the door of one's house, down the path, through the gate, and onto the road. The easiest way to talk about imagery or memory is in terms of representations. Moreover, to communicate with colleagues in cognitive development and other fields, we need to talk about representations. If we talk in terms of dynamics, these fields would not be able to talk to each other. The only problem, and it is a difficult one, is how to define what we mean by representation.

Marty Banks commented that Warren's point about parsimony is really excellent to keep in mind. He argued that the role of representation—or the homunculus—is really as a placeholder for things we have not understood well enough yet. We cannot quite get rid of the homunculus, but we can try to make his job as simple as possible. If we explore enough, it might turn out that representations actually are unnecessary. It might—let's find out.

REFERENCES

Asatryan, D. G., & Feldman, A. G. (1965). Functional tuning of the nervous system with control of movement or maintenance of a steady posture: I. Mechano-graphic analysis of the work of the joints on execution of a postural task. *Biophysics, 10*, 925–935.

Bardy, B., Oullier, O., Bootsma, R. J., & Stoffregen, T. A. (2002). Dynamics of human postural transitions. *Journal of Experimental Psychology: Human Perception and Performance, 28*, 499–514.

Bechtel, W., & Abrahamsen, A. A. (1991). *Connectionism and the mind: An introduction to parallel processing in networks.* Oxford: Basil Blackwell.

Chemero, A. (2001). Dynamical explanations and mental representations. *Trends in Cognitive Sciences, 5*, 141–142.

Clark, A. (1997). The dynamical challenge. *Cognitive Science, 21*, 461–481.

Fajen, B. R., & Warren, W. H. (2003). Behavioral dynamics of steering, obstacle avoidance, and route selection. *Journal of Experimental Psychology: Human Perception and Performance, 29*, 343–362.

Fodor, J. A. (1975). *Language of thought.* New York: Crowell.

Gibson, J. J. (1966). *The senses considered as perceptual systems.* Boston: Houghton-Mifflin.

Gibson, J. J. (1979). *The ecological approach to visual perception.* Boston: Houghton-Mifflin.

Goldfield, E. C., Kay, B. A., & Warren, W. H. (1993). Infant bouncing: The assembly and tuning of action systems. *Child Development, 64*, 1128–1142.

Haugeland, J. (1991). Representational genera. In W. Ramsey, S. P. Stich, & D. E. Rumelhart (Eds.), *Philosophy and connectionist theory* (pp. 61–89). Hillsdale, NJ: Lawrence Erlbaum Associates.

Keijzer, F. (1998). Doing without representations which specify what to do. *Philosophical Psychology, 11,* 269–302.

Markman, A. B., & Dietrich, E. (2000). Extending the classical view of representation. *Trends in Cognitive Sciences, 4,* 470–475.

Mottet, D., & Bootsma, R. J. (1999). The dynamics of goal-directed rhythmical aiming. *Biological Cybernetics, 80,* 235–245.

Newell, A. (1980). Physical symbol systems. *Cognitive Science, 4,* 135–183.

Peper, L., Bootsma, R. J., Mestre, D. R., & Bakker, F. C. (1994). Catching balls: How to get the hand to the right place at the right time. *Journal of Experimental Psychology: Human Perception and Performance, 20,* 591–612.

Saltzman, E. L., & Munhall, K. G. (1992). Skill acquisition and development: The roles of state-, parameter-, and graph-dynamics. *Journal of Motor Behavior, 24,* 49–57.

Schöner, G. (1991). Dynamic theory of action-perception patterns: The "moving room" paradigm. *Biological Cybernetics, 64,* 455–462.

Searle, J. R. (1980). Minds, brains, and programs. *Behavioral and Brain Sciences, 3,* 417–457.

Shaw, R. E. (2003). The agent–environment interface: Simon's indirect or Gibson's direct coupling? *Ecological Psychology, 15,* 37–106.

Smith, B. C. (1998). *On the origin of objects.* Cambridge: MIT Press.

van Gelder, T. (1995). What might cognition be, if not computation? *Journal of Philosophy, 92,* 345–381.

Warren, W. H. (2004). *The dynamics of perception and action.* Manuscript submitted for publication.

Warren, W. H., & Fajen, B. R. (2004). From optic flow to laws of control. In L. M. Vaina, S. K. Rushton, & S. Beardsley (Eds.), *Optic flow and beyond* (pp. 307–337). New York: Kluwer.

Zaal, F. T. J. M., Bootsma, R. J., & van Wieringen, P. C. W. (1999). Dynamics of reaching for stationary and moving objects: Data and model. *Journal of Experimental Psychology: Human Perception and Performance, 25,* 149–161.

II

COMPUTATIONAL COMPLEXITY AND THE INTEGRATION OF INFORMATION

5

▼▼▼▼▼▼▼▼

Object Information, Computational Complexity, and Constraints on Action

Richard N. Aslin
University of Rochester

Any consideration of the role of action in learning and development should begin with the basics: fundamental questions that set the stage for a detailed examination of the mechanisms by which we acquire information and use it to guide behavior. After outlining these questions, I attempt to provide some answers in the research that my colleagues and I have conducted over the past 7 or 8 years.

Organisms behave; that is, they act in and on their environment. Much of this behavior is, at least initially, spontaneous and apparently random. However, on closer inspection, even the earliest behaviors are quite constrained. Some of these constraints arise from physics. For example, a limb of length L can only move so fast when force F is applied to it, and its trajectory of movement is bounded by a small number of degrees of freedom. Other constraints arise from neural systems and their connectivity. For example, sensory and motor pathways are laid down in highly constrained ways during embryogenesis so that, under normal circumstances, neuron A talks to neuron B and not to neuron C. This does not deny the importance of plasticity, which is present in nearly all neural systems, but the most dramatic examples of neural plasticity occur in response to unusual events, such as lesions and sensory deprivation. Finally, many of the constraints on behavior arise from learning; that is, relatively permanent alterations in systems of behavior that result from both general and specific experiences.

Learning, of course, takes many forms—from long-term potentiation mediated by NMDA receptors to predictions about how certain National

Football League teams will perform on a given Sunday. The form of learning that I focus on is at the level of activity. That is, as organisms behave, they engage in a series of movements that we generically call *actions*—things like walking across a surface, catching a ball, or speaking a sentence. In each of these examples, the action involves means–ends behavior; that is, a naive observer would characterize the action as having a goal and an organized set of operations to achieve that goal. Please note that I am not claiming that these goals must be conscious mental states or that the form of the internal representation is what enables these goals to be stored in memory for future use. What I am claiming is twofold. First, the brain has evolved powerful learning mechanisms that extract the informational structure present in the environment; second, activity reveals this structure, which then forms the basis for subsequent actions.

The bulk of this chapter concerns the first claim about what has been termed *statistical learning*. The second claim is perhaps less obvious and deserves elaboration. As organisms behave, they create stimulation, which in turn provides a learning mechanism with the opportunity to acquire stimulus–response, stimulus–stimulus, and response–stimulus correlations (see Campos et al., 2000). For example, walking across a surface creates a dynamic optic flow field across the two retinas and a pattern of vestibular signals. The flow field is modulated by the distance and motion of objects in the visual array as well as by the specific pattern of locomotion and its underlying motor commands. Immediately, one can see that this rich stimulus array, consisting of both external and internal signals, creates a computational problem for any organism with a limited capacity to access, store, and operate on information in real time. What limited set of the infinite number of possible correlations should the organism operate on? One potential way to reduce the computational problem is to posit that actions operate on objects, whether they entail movement of the feet across a surface, movement of the hand to intercept a ball, or movement of the vocal articulators to produce speech. There are a relatively small number of objects on which we operate given the infinite number of correlations that could be objects. A deeper analysis, which I outline later, reveals that operating at the level of objects does not solve the computational problem, but it does reduce it. So how, then, are objects defined?

One way to define an object to which action is applied is by fiat. That is, the organism, through an evolutionary process unique to its species, may have a neural mechanism (e.g., a feature detector, module, or system) that is sensitive to a class of objects and insensitive to all other objects outside that class. Many organisms have such mechanisms, ranging from simple constraints on sensory sensitivity (e.g., wavelengths of light or sound) to more complex categories (e.g., faces or voices). More important, some of these constrained mechanisms do not require any prior exposure to their content, but are fully functional in the absence of such exposure. It may not be politically correct to call these object categories innate, but that is certainly one word that has been used to describe them.

A softer set of constraints takes the form of principles or biases. A classic example is the Gestalt laws of proximity, common fate, and good continuation. All other things being equal, two elements form an object when they are closer together, move together, and look or sound similar to each other. Yet these soft constraints, which presumably arise indirectly from evolution and not directly from a developmental learning mechanism, cannot possibly be sufficient for constraining the actual objects we operate on in the world from the potential objects that we could operate on. The set of actual objects is much smaller than the set of potential objects, yet much larger than the set of objects that is limited by both fiat and Gestalt principles. Thus, most objects must be discovered by exposure to a world that has underlying structure.

Behavior in that world reveals its structure, but only if the organism has a powerful learning mechanism that can extract that structure. Over 100 years of research on learning, with a few brave exceptions, has emphasized that learning (a) is protracted (i.e., it takes repeated exposures), (b) is general purpose (i.e., operates across species and content), and (c) involves a motivating influence (i.e., via reward or punishment). Yet how could such a classic learning mechanism uncover the structure of the world that is potentially revealed by the organism's behavior? The simple answer is that it could not. First, learning must be rapid to move the organism's behavior toward objects on which action can be directed. Second, evolution has likely constrained learning mechanisms to be sensitive to information that has particular relevance to a species, and not all species require the same information. Third, some examples of learning have clear motivational mechanisms, but many others, including the basic ability to learn the objects in the environment, must be based on stimulus correlations that have no immediate positive or negative outcome.

In the next section, I outline evidence from several domains that suggests strongly that all three of these requirements for a nonclassical learning mechanism are present in the human learner, both the adult and infant. Moreover, some properties of statistical learning are shared with other species, whereas others are not.

OBJECTS IN THE AUDITORY MODALITY

The origin of the research summarized here comes from a line of work that was begun in 1995 with Jenny Saffran and Elissa Newport. That work (Aslin, Saffran, & Newport, 1998; Saffran, Aslin, & Newport, 1996; Saffran,

Newport, & Aslin, 1996; Saffran et al., 1997) showed in the domain of speech perception and word segmentation that brief exposure to an uninterrupted sequence of speech syllables was sufficient to enable adults and 8-month-old infants to extract the statistical coherence of syllables from continuous streams of speech even in the absence of any auditory cues to word boundaries. These initial results raise a number of key questions, including whether these statistical learning abilities are language-specific, species-specific, and modality-specific.

In the study by Saffran, Aslin, and Newport (1996), 8-month-old infants were exposed to a continuous stream of speech syllables, with no pauses or other acoustic cues to the segmentation of this stream into coherent groups of syllables. The only source of information for segmentation and grouping was the fact that the 12 unique syllables were constrained to appear in four different triplets (analogous to words), with a fixed order of syllables within a word and a random ordering of words in the continuous stream. These constraints resulted in high relative frequency (RF) and high conditional probability (CP) between syllables within a word and low RF and CP at the boundary between words (see Fig. 5.1A). After 2 to 3 minutes of exposure to a particular stream of syllables, infants' listening times were different for coherent triplets (words) compared with triplets that spanned a word boundary (a part word). A follow-up study (Aslin, Saffran, & Newport, 1998) showed that when the RF of the tested words and part words was equated, infants could rely on CP to discriminate these test items (see Fig. 5.1B).

A key question that arose from these initial demonstrations of statistical learning is whether it is specialized for linguistic materials. We con-

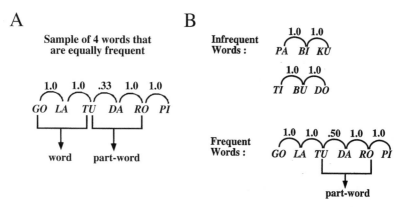

FIG. 5.1. Sample sequences of three-syllable words from (A) Saffran et al. (1996), and (B) Aslin et al. (1998). The average of their statistical structure between adjacent syllables within words and across word boundaries is indexed by relative frequency (RF) and conditional probability (CP).

ducted a number of experiments aimed at the specificity of statistical learning mechanisms for language development. First, we substituted tones for the consonant-vowel syllables and concatenated them into continuous streams containing statistically coherent triplets of tones, as well as tone triplets that were less coherent. Both adults and 8-month-olds performed virtually identically on these tone sequences as they had on syllable sequences (Saffran et al., 1999). These results suggest that a statistical learning mechanism can operate on streams of auditory elements to segment them into coherent subgroups based on their statistical coherence, and these elements do not have to be specifically linguistic.

We then began a series of studies with a nonhuman primate (the cotton top tamarin) to explore whether this statistical learning mechanism is present in a species that does not have a linguistic system, but whose vocalizations have some rudimentary sequential structure. In collaboration with Marc Hauser at Harvard, we used the same streams of speech syllables used by Saffran et al. (1996) and showed that tamarins were sensitive to the statistical coherence of trisyllabic sequences (Hauser, Newport, & Aslin, 2001). Thus, the statistical learning mechanism used by human adults and infants to segment and group sequences of syllables (and tones) in the auditory modality is shared with (at least functionally, if not mediated by the same underlying mechanism) a nonhuman primate.

Our most recent efforts in auditory statistical learning have been directed to higher levels of structure in streams of speech. We have shown that human adults fail to learn the statistical coherence of syllables that are not immediately adjacent in time (Newport & Aslin, 2000; Newport & Aslin, 2004). In contrast, adults can easily learn a similar stream of syllables whose statistical structure is defined by nonadjacent segments (consonants or vowels). Words are not formed by nonadjacent syllables in any natural language, whereas they are formed by nonadjacent segments (consonant frames and vowel harmony) in some natural languages. Interestingly, tamarins show a different pattern of learning on these same test materials, suggesting that different constraints on learning are operating in humans and tamarins (Newport, Hauser, Spaepen, & Aslin, 2004).

Mid-level Gestalt principles could serve as yet another powerful constraint on statistical learning, further reducing the computational complexity of the task. One such demonstration comes from a series of adult experiments by Creel, Newport, and Aslin (2004), in which sequences of tones were constructed with strong statistical dependencies between nonadjacent elements. When these nonadjacent elements came from one pitch range and the intervening elements from another pitch range (which induces a Gestalt process called *pitch proximity* or *stream segregation*; Bregman, 1990), adults performed well in extracting the within-stream statistics. Yet when all the tones came from the same pitch range, which prevents perceptual segregation into two streams, the nonadjacent statistics were not learned.

These results on temporal segmentation and grouping in the auditory modality illustrate that adults, infants, and at least one species of nonhuman primate can employ a powerful learning mechanism to extract from continuous streams of events those elements that cohere solely by their statistical structure. This statistical learning mechanism not only operates rapidly, but does not require reinforcement or overt attention because it functions quite effectively by mere exposure to stimulus streams. Yet what constrains this mechanism so that it does not attempt to compute all possible temporal-order statistics? Take the simple example of the toy language used by Saffran et al. (1996). There are 12 elements (syllables) in this language grouped into four 3-syllable words. There are two general classes of statistics that could be used to characterize the streams of words: frequency-based or n-gram statistics and conditionalized statistics. Frequency-based statistics involve counts of elements and groups of elements. For example, in the Saffran et al. languages, all 12 elements occurred equally often, thereby rendering this first-order statistic ineffective as a grouping cue. However, bigram and trigram frequencies are informative in these languages: Pairs and triplets of syllables occur with higher relative frequency when they form a word than when they span a word boundary (see Fig. 5.1A). There are, of course, an infinite number of n-grams beyond pairs and triplets, so one potential constraint is on the order of the highest n-gram that is computed. Because the number of potential n-grams increases exponentially with a linear increase in the number of elements, it is apparent that the computational complexity of even the simplest string of events quickly becomes intractable. This has been termed the *curse of dimensionality* (Bellman, 1961) or the *combinatorial explosion* problem (von der Malsburg, 1995).

Yet this computational problem is even more serious because frequency-based statistics do not exhaust the information that could be extracted from a string of elements. A variety of conditionalized statistics (e.g., conditional probability, conditional entropy) go beyond simple counts of events by characterizing the likelihood that event Y will occur in some relation to event X. For example, the forward transitional probability of syllable B given syllable A (i.e., B | A) is computed by normalizing the frequency of the syllable-pair AB by the frequency of syllable A. As with frequency-based statistics, there are an infinite number of conditionalized statistics (e.g., E | D, E | CD, E | BCD, E | ABCD, E | B_D, E | A, etc.), which grow exponentially with the size of the set of elements. Thus, an unconstrained statistical learning mechanism simply "blows up" in any real neural system that has limited computational resources. What then are the constraints that enable statistical learning to be tractable and avoid the combinatorial explosion problem?

First, temporal adjacency is a strong constraint: Elements that are closer together in time appear to be much easier to link together as a bigram than elements that are temporally nonadjacent. Second, Gestalt principles operate to constrain element linkages: Elements from the same category are more likely to form a bigram even when other elements intervene between them. Third, and this is rather speculative, there appear to be constraints on how the perceptual space in a given domain is represented. Consider the domain of the sound structure of natural languages. In English there are approximately 40 phonemes: classes of sounds that form the minimal set of elements used to create words. The most efficient code for representing the words of a language would consist of the minimal number of phonemes required to generate all possible words. Yet natural languages do not use such an optimally efficient code. For example, of all possible (and legal) consonant-vowel-consonant syllables in English, only about 13% are actually words. This sparse use of the sound space in a lexicon is an example of inefficient coding. An optimally efficient code could use far fewer phonemes to represent the same number of words. Why is this sparsity common to natural languages? There must be other constraints that outweigh coding efficiency. For example, some sound sequences may be hard to articulate, or some sound sequences may be easily confusable. Thus, there may be a trade-off between coding efficiency and ease of discrimination and/or retrieval from memory. Although at present we cannot assign a weight to each of these three constraints, it seems clear that, perhaps along with other constraints, they enable the human learner to overcome the combinatorial explosion problem and successfully use statistical learning as a mechanism for segmenting and grouping elements in temporal streams.

OBJECTS IN THE VISUAL MODALITY

A question that naturally arises from the foregoing research on statistical learning in the auditory modality is whether the same (or similar) mechanisms operate in the visual modality. Several studies (Fiser & Aslin, 2002b; Fiser, McCrink-Gochal, & Aslin, in preparation; Kirkham, Slemmer, & Johnson, 2002) have shown that temporally ordered visual events are processed by adults and infants in a manner similar to the statistical learning of auditory events. What about the extraction of objects in the visual modality from multiple, static, cluttered scenes? That is, are similar statistical learning mechanisms used in the spatial domain as in the temporal domain? As adults, we take it for granted that the visual world consists of a variety of surfaces and objects lying in different depth planes. Often these surfaces and objects occlude each other, either partially or completely, as the observer or the objects undergo motion through the environment. In addition, objects are typically composed of parts, such as the handle on a cup or the leaves on a tree. Thus, what to an adult seems like a straightforward interpretation of the visual world is, to the naive observer (e.g., an infant), more like the "blooming, buzzing confusion" alluded to by William James.

How might the human infant begin to make sense of an initially complex visual world? One approach is to posit the existence of a set of spatiotemporal basis functions, or receptive field properties, at low levels of the visual pathway. These receptive fields cover the entire retinal image and essentially filter the information received by the visual cortex into a code that can, in principle, represent any image with many fewer elements than would be required if the luminance value of each point (or pixel) was stored. Arguments have been made (e.g., Simoncelli & Olshausen, 2001) that the visual system has evolved an optimal set of basis functions by exposure to a constrained set of images (i.e., the visual world we inhabit as humans). As a result, there is no need for the infant's visual system to learn its basis functions. Rather these basis functions are specified by an epigenetic program that, unless altered by early visual deprivation, matures into the adult set of low-level visual analyzers.

The foregoing approach has been extended beyond simple image properties (e.g., edges and spatial frequency) to the domain of objects and their parts by positing the existence of a hierarchy of basis functions (Biederman, 1987; Marr, 1982). For example, combinations of curved lines and surface texture can be used to represent a cylinder (e.g., a tree trunk), and combinations of curved lines and color can represent a more complex shape (e.g., an apple). This approach has run into two fundamental problems. First, analyses of a large number of diverse objects have not revealed a finite set of mid-level basis functions that is sufficiently small and robust to provide an efficient code. Second, although there is compelling neurophysiological evidence supporting low-level basis functions (Hubel & Wiesel, 1959, 1968), the search for mid-level basis functions has been mixed (Gallant et al., 1996; Opde Beeck et al., 2001; Pasupathy & Connor, 2001). This has led some researchers (Bulthoff, Edelman, & Tarr, 1995) to propose an alternative scheme for object representation: Objects are stored as exemplars (i.e., snapshots) rather than being constructed from a set of object-primitives (e.g., geons). Although such an exemplar model of object perception has some support in the psychological and neurophysiological literatures (Logothetis & Pauls, 1995; Tarr et al., 2001), it has yet to explain how the brain can represent a nearly infinite number of images with high fidelity and ease of access. Thus, there is partial support for both of the foregoing approaches, but neither offers a comprehensive explanation of object perception/recognition, and in particular how the brain (during development or adult learning) forms representations of initially unknown features, objects, and scenes.

Jozsef Fiser and I formulated a new approach to object perception and feature learning that builds on the two approaches described earlier while avoiding their limitations (Fiser & Aslin, 2001). The core of our approach is that once visual information is filtered by low-level analyzers and parsed into a set of base elements, mid-level visual mechanisms extract co-occurrence statistics from these base elements and form new features. In turn, these mid-level features become the basis functions for representing a class of objects. The essential point of our approach is that new features are not defined by arbitrary characteristics (e.g., three-dimensional primitives or two-dimensional snapshots), but rather by the statistical coherence among subfeatures. Interestingly, this approach is one that was articulated 40 years ago by Selfridge (1959) and Barlow (1961) and, more recently, by Barlow (1989, 1990), Atick (1992), and Bialek et al. (2001). The reason this approach was not aggressively pursued in previous empirical research is that it was viewed as logically coherent, but computationally and representationally implausible (i.e., the computational explosion problem).

Consider a simple image consisting of four base elements that have been extracted by low-level analyzers. Those four base elements can be combined to form new features: six unique pairs, four unique triplets, and one quadruplet. If we double the number of base elements from 4 to 8, the number of unique pairs increases from 6 to 28, the unique triplets increase from 4 to 21, and the unique quadruplets increase from 1 to 15. Thus, even without considering new features larger than quadruplets, the total number of possible features made up of 2, 3, or 4 elements increases from 11 to 64, thereby growing exponentially with the number of elements. Of course statistics cannot be extracted from a single image. Rather, the observer must sample many images to determine which co-occurrences are consistently present and which are merely coincidences (i.e., noise). Thus, not only must the learner tally a large number of potentially relevant statistics, but this tally must be applied across multiple exemplars with sufficient fidelity to enable specific features to be learned. This process could be implemented on a computer, which has essentially unlimited computational resources, but it was not viewed as computationally tractable in a human brain.

Despite these arguments against a statistical approach, we recently demonstrated the viability of a visual statistical learning mechanism in adults (Fiser & Aslin, 2001) and infants (Fiser & Aslin, 2002c). The starting point for these experiments was a display that did not confound low-level basis functions with the learning of mid-level features. For example, if we had used simple line segments and two horizontally oriented segments had appeared (by chance) next to each other in the display, they would have formed a local configuration (an extended horizontal line). Yet this new multi-element feature would have emerged from built-in low-level analyzers, not from the effects of a learning mechanism (see Geisler et al., 2001). Therefore, our displays consisted of moderately complex object shapes (filled black on a white background; see Fig. 5.2A) located in a 3 × 3 or 5 × 5 grid so that each shape was clearly defined as a separate element in a multi-element array (see Fig. 5.2B). More important, these displays reduced the likelihood that multi-element features would emerge from low-level analyzers or from the operation of mid-level Gestalt mechanisms (e.g., element similarity or good continuation). This is not to deny the important role of lower level mechanisms in object segregation, but rather serves to focus on the higher level learning mechanisms that could be used to create new multi-element features solely from statistical information.

A set of 12 shapes comprised the elements in our adult studies, and each shape was uniquely paired with another shape, in a particular spatial

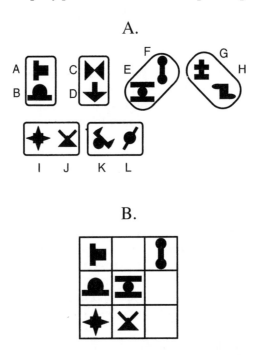

FIG. 5.2. (A) Six base pairs of the inventory of 12 shapes used in Fiser and Aslin (2001), and (B) one of their arrangements in a 3 × 3 grid. (Reproduced with permission from the American Psychological Society.)

configuration, to create six base pairs (see Fig. 5.2A). These base pairs were then randomly distributed within the 3 × 3 or 5 × 5 grid to create scenes consisting of three base pairs (i.e., six elements; see Fig. 5.2B). Subjects were merely asked to watch a series of 144 or 212 scenes presented for 2 seconds each. They were then asked to judge in a two-interval forced-choice (2IFC) posttest the familiarity of pairs of test displays in which a base pair was contrasted with a nonbase pair. A key feature of our experimental design is that we could precisely control the statistics of the base pairs and nonbase pairs.

The statistics of the base pairs was always perfectly coherent (the two shapes had appeared only with each other and in a particular spatial arrangement during the learning phase), whereas the statistics of the nonbase pairs were less coherent. For example, in one experiment all six base pairs occurred with equal frequency during the learning phase. During the test phase, each base pair was contrasted with a part pair consisting of a single element from two different base pairs. As in the case of temporal sequences of auditory elements (see Fig. 5.1), the statistics of these part pairs differed from the statistics of the base pairs in two ways: (a) the relative frequency (RF) of occurrence of a part pair was less than that of a base pair because part pairs were formed from accidental co-occurrences of base pairs, and (b) the conditional probability (CP) of a part pair was less than that of a base pair. After 5 minutes of passive exposure to these multi-element scenes, adults reliably discriminated base pairs from part pairs.

Because CP has been shown in research with animals and humans to be a superior metric of statistical relatedness than RF (Gallistel, 1990; Rescorla & Wagner, 1972), the same frequency balanced design used in Aslin et al. (1998) with speech syllables was used in a follow-up experiment with spatially arranged visual elements. CP is defined as the co-occurrence frequency of the two elements divided by the frequency of occurrence of one of the elements. This CP statistic essentially normalizes the base rate of each element's frequency of occurrence, thereby enabling the predictability of one element vis-à-vis another element to be unaffected by their overall rate of occurrence. Moreover, it has been argued on computational grounds that direct access to CP is the necessary core requirement for efficiently establishing new, complex, visual features based on a statistical learning mechanism (Atick, 1992; Barlow, 1989). Consider why this might be true. If an event occurs very rarely so that its RF is low, but it always co-occurs with another event, then its CP is high. In contrast, if an event occurs very often, but only sometimes in concert with another event (because many other events co-occur with it), it has a high RF but a low CP for that particular co-occurrence. It is clear that high CP between two elements signals a good candidate for a reliable higher order feature, whereas high RF by itself has little value in forming new complex features. Our work with adults showed that after 20 minutes of passive exposure to six-element scenes in which some base pairs occurred with the same RF as some part pairs, but the CP of these base pairs was higher than the CP of these part pairs, subjects reliably chose the more predictable base pairs over the less coherent part pairs. Thus, when RF is held constant, adult learners can extract the greater predictability of element pairs with high CP.

Our work with infants used the visual habituation technique to expose 9-month-olds to simpler versions of the shape displays used with adults. Each scene (see Fig. 5.3) consisted of a single base pair plus a third element that was unrelated to the spatial configuration of the base pair (i.e., a noise element). Twelve shapes were combined into four base pairs, and each base pair was presented with one of four noise elements, thereby forming 16 different three-element scenes. Although the spatial arrangement of each base

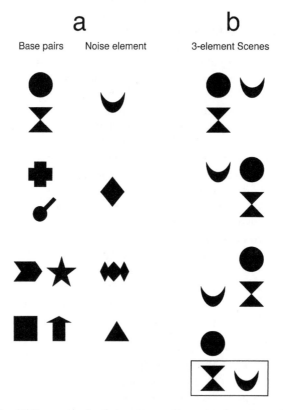

FIG. 5.3.   (A) Base pairs plus their corresponding noise elements used to create 16 different three-element scenes. (B) Sample scenes for one base pair (box indicates a part pair consisting of one base pair element and a noise element). (Reproduced with permission from the American Academy of Sciences.)

pair was fixed across scenes, that base pair's noise element appeared in four different locations with respect to the base pair. Each scene was presented for 1.5 seconds, and the 16 scenes were repeated in random order during habituation until the standard 50% decrement in looking time across trials was met by each infant. Posthabituation test trials presented base pairs or part pairs as in the adult experiments, with a part pair consisting of one element from a base pair plus a noise element (see rectangular box in Fig. 5.3b). In our first experiment, base pairs differed from part pairs in both RF and CP. Infants showed a strong posthabituation looking preference for base pairs over part pairs. In a second experiment, in which the RF of the tested base pairs and part pairs was equated, but their CP differed, infants also showed a strong posthabituation preference for base pairs over part pairs. A third control experiment showed that this preference was not due to the difference in the RF of the single elements.

Follow-up experiments (Aslin & Fiser, 2001; Fiser & Aslin, 2002a) have shown that adults become insensitive to the internal structure of statistically coherent features as the features become learned. The design of these experiments was similar to the previous studies except that some of the 12 shapes were organized into triplets or quadruplets instead of pairs. After the learning phase, a pair from within a triplet or quadruplet was tested against a nonbase pair (two elements with zero CP). This comparison should in principle be an easy task because the embedded pair has a CP of 1. Yet adults were unable to reliably discriminate an embedded pair from a nonbase pair, whereas they could easily discriminate other base pairs that were not part of any larger structure from nonbase pairs. Similarly, infants could discriminate a base pair from a nonbase pair, but they could not discriminate a single element that came from within a base pair from a single element that came from within a nonbase pair, even though the RF of these single elements differed by a factor of two.

In summary, there are four important discoveries we have made in our studies of visual statistical learning in both human adults and infants. First, in the absence of a task (i.e., by mere exposure to multiple exemplars), adults and infants can extract spatial co-occurrence statistics from multi-element arrays. Second, this process of visual statistical learning, at least for simple sets of exemplars (e.g., three- to six-element arrays composed of 12 unique elements) occurs in a matter of 5 to 20 minutes. Third, a variety of statistics are extracted from these arrays, including the most computationally reliable statistic for forming a new visual feature: conditional probability. Fourth, once a statistically coherent spatial structure has been extracted, some of the substructures embedded within it are at least partially deactivated from the underlying representation.

What may not be obvious from our preliminary findings is how a statistically based approach to object perception/recognition overcomes the previously described problem—the exponential growth in the number of features that could be relevant for any given set of exemplars as the number of elements in those exemplars increases (the combinatorial explosion problem). For the statistical approach to be viable beyond the kinds of reduced toy world examples studied in the lab, there must be constraints operating during the extraction of new visual features so that efficient learning can occur unimpeded by the computational and representational limitations of the human brain. Based on our empirical results, we have proposed one solution to this problem: Learners extract the largest coherent structure and retain only that structure as a new feature, rather than also retaining all of the substructures that are redundant with this larger structure. This proposed solution may seem counterintuitive because larger structures must, logically, be built up from substructures. We are not arguing against the logic that wholes are composed of parts. Rather, we are arguing that the simplest description of the largest coherent structure has priority in being represented as a new feature. This whole, once formed from a process of statistical learning, does not require all of its parts (subfeatures) to be stored in the representation of the whole because only a small number of subfeatures is sufficient for a unique representation of the whole. In other words, the representational system for complex objects and scenes rapidly seeks the highest level of statistical structure so that the set of mid-level basis functions can be reduced, thereby circumventing the curse of dimensionality. This does not mean that the subfeatures that are absent from the initial representation can never again be reacquired. Consider the case of face perception. There is compelling evidence (e.g., Maurer, LeGrand, & Mondloch, 2002) that face recognition occurs by the configural processing of facial features that is independent of the processing of the features. Yet when asked to attend to these individual features, subjects can do so, although their processing of these facial features is different from their processing of the configural properties of the face.

Notice that the statistical approach we have outlined shares some of the characteristics of both the universal mid-level (e.g., geon) basis-function approach and the exemplar (e.g., view-based) approach. Like the basis-function approach, complex objects are built up from coherent spatial structures that are defined by their reliable co-occurrences. However, the basis-function approach left unspecified whether these mid-level features are extracted by a learning process during early development or by built-in evolutionary mechanisms (as in the case of low-level analyzers). The statistical approach, like the exemplar approach, proposes that feature extraction requires exposure to multiple exemplars during early development. However, it posits that the representation of objects goes beyond mere storage of raw-image views. The basis-function approach, whose encoding mechanism is shared with the statistical approach, provides a more efficient representation of objects than the exemplar approach because it can construct from a moderate set of mid-level basis functions a large number of object representations, rather than storing a large number of representations as entire objects or viewpoints. What remains unclear is where the basis functions come from and how they are implemented in particular tasks to represent objects and their underlying features. What distinguishes our statistical approach is that we have proposed a specific mechanism—learning co-occurrence statistics by exposure—rather than leaving this mechanism unspecified. Moreover, we have proposed a scheme whereby the combinatorial explosion problem is avoided because biases exist in the human learning mechanism that constrain the types of statistics that are extracted and how they are used to form new features. This latter aspect of our model allows it to be computationally and representationally tractable.

AUDITORY–VISUAL LEARNING

Another potentially important constraint in real-world scenes is the presence of multimodal information. Consider a typical playroom in which dozens of objects are present. How does the infant direct attention to those objects that carry important information? One way to help parse this cluttered scene is to attend to objects that undergo movement in synchrony with a sound. Work by Dodd (1979), Spelke (1979), Walker-Andrews (1982), and Bahrick (1983) has shown that infants are biased to attend to objects that undergo such multimodal temporal synchrony and to discriminate changes in the pairing of particular sounds with particular objects. Gogate and Bahrick (1998) and Bahrick and Lickliter (2000) have shown that infants use this constraint on their attention to facilitate the learning of sound-object pairings and rhythmic information. Yet do infants use this constraint on their attention to learn which objects are most informative in a cluttered scene?

McCrink-Gochal and Aslin (2002) extended these earlier studies by habituating 6-month-olds to an array of three objects undergoing expansion/contraction in size, thereby creating movement discontinuities at their maximum/minimum sizes. Only one of the three objects was paired with a sound that occurred when that object reached its maximum size. During the habituation phase, infants looked significantly longer at the synchronous object than at the other two (nonsynchronous) objects, replicating the earlier preference studies, but with a slightly more complex visual display (three rather than two objects). After meeting a criterion of habituation, each infant viewed a series of test trials with each of the three objects undergoing expansion/contraction, but with no sound present. Infants looked significantly longer to the object that had been presented in synchrony with the sound during the habituation phase. Thus, as in the Fiser and Aslin (2002c) study of infants' extraction of element pairs from multiple scenes based on their statistical coherence, this multimodal study shows that infants also have a preference to attend to objects that have auditory–visual coherence (based on temporal synchrony), and they continue to prefer those objects even when the synchrony is removed after learning.

FROM OBJECTS TO ACTION

The foregoing examples of extracting structure from auditory or visual input does not entail any overt activity on the part of the learner. Such "passive" learning makes the rapid acquisition of statistical information even more impressive than the case of an "active" learner. Yet what happens when statistical learning occurs in the context of ongoing action? Hunt and Aslin (2001) conducted a series of studies using a serial reaction time (SRT) paradigm in which adults were cued sequentially to press one of an array of buttons. On pressing the cued button, another button was cued and a subsequent button press was elicited. Within a continuous stream of such button presses, but unknown to the subject, was a constrained sequential structure. The advantage of this SRT paradigm is that it enables the performance of the learner to be assessed during the course of exposure to the underlying structure, rather than delaying the assessment of learning to the end of the exposure period.

Hunt and Aslin (2001) embedded a triplet or pair-based structure in the SRT paradigm. That is, analogous to the original Saffran et al. (1996) design with speech syllables, sequences of two or three lights were perfectly predictive (CP = 1), whereas the light pair that spanned a pair or triplet boundary had a CP much less than 1 (e.g., 0.17–0.25). After 4 to 6 hours of training with this structure, adults showed RTs that were reliably faster for lights with high CPs (i.e., within a pair or triplet) compared with lights that initiated a pair or triplet. Moreover, when the RF of a pair of lights was held constant, regardless of whether it was within or between a pair or triplet, but the CP of the within pair (or triplet) was greater than the between pair (or triplet), RTs were still faster, indicating that RF differences were not necessary for these faster RTs. These results parallel those obtained by Aslin et al. (1998) with speech syllables and by Fiser and Aslin (2001, 2002b) with spatial and temporal shape displays. Finally, Hunt and Aslin discovered that some adults initially failed to match the underlying pair structure in their RTs. That is, they incorrectly parsed the stream of lights as if it had a triplet or quadruplet structure presumably because they falsely inferred that coincidental between-pair transitions represented consistent underlying structures. Interestingly, these adults eventually settled on the correct pair-based structure as indicated by their RTs. Thus, there must be a self-correction mechanism for learners who did not initially extract the correct underlying structure, and this mechanism did not involve any feedback from a teacher. A similar self-correction mechanism has been hypothesized in child language acquisition.

The visuomotor responses in the SRT paradigm are clearly more demanding than tasks that involve simply watching a set of displays (or listening to a set of tones or syllables). Learning is much more protracted (days rather than minutes), and subjects are generally unaware of the underlying structure. Thus, the act of moving the arm/finger to make an eight-alternative forced-choice button press interferes with the time course of learning the underlying structure, but enables the motor component of learning to be extremely robust.

These results from adults may have implications for the current debate in the infant literature about discrepancies between assessments of cognitive abilities by looking time measures and by motor responses. Take the classic object permanence results from Piaget, in which infants are presented with an object that is quickly covered with a cloth before the infant can reach for it. It is not until 8 to 9 months of age that infants successfully, and apparently effortlessly, lift the cover to retrieve the hidden object. Yet more recent results using looking time measures (e.g., Baillargeon, Spelke, & Wasserman, 1985) suggest that even 5-month-olds understand that a hidden object continues to exist. These drawbridge studies have shown that infants look longer at a display in which a surface appears to pass through a hidden object, suggesting (by one interpretation) that infants find such a display impossible (see the thematic collection of eight articles in Vol. 1, No. 4, 2000 of *Infancy* for extensive discussion and debate of these findings). There are other comparable demonstrations in the literature (see Keen, chap. 11, this volume) that point to clear discrepancies between knowledge as assessed by looking time measures and by motor movements such as object retrieval.

To reiterate, Fiser and Aslin (2002b) showed with 12 simple shapes organized into temporal streams that adults can extract by mere exposure the RF and CP of shape pairs in less than 20 minutes. Yet the Hunt and Aslin (2001) study, with eight button locations organized into temporal streams, required several hours across multiple days for adults to extract these same RFs and CPs. Obviously, the task demands placed on the motor control system were much higher in the Hunt and Aslin study than in the Fiser and Aslin study. The measures were quite different (RTs vs. a 2AFC task). In both studies, we have clear evidence of statistical learning, but of course if we had terminated the Hunt and Aslin study after 20 minutes, there would have been no evidence of learning. However, we would not conclude from such a failure that adults are incapable of extracting statistics from temporal streams because the results of Fiser and Aslin provided clear evidence of such learning. The conundrum in the infant literature is twofold: (a) how much confidence do we have that looking time measures are an accurate reflection of infant knowledge, and (b) is there, in fact, continuity of that "knowledge" across age (and tasks)?

There are no clear answers to this conundrum. It is quite possible that the competence exhibited by infants using looking time measures bears no relation to the analogous competence shown at later ages by motor responses. That is, the knowledge tapped by looking time measures may be different than the knowledge tapped by motor responses, although (logically to researchers who study such phenomena) they involve the same underlying competence. Alternatively, it is possible that the looking time measures of competence used in early infancy are reflective of and form the basis for neural systems used to control motor systems in later infancy.

How might we differentiate between these two possibilities: (a) developmental continuity from perception to action, or (b) independent developmental mechanisms for perception and action? This is reminiscent of the dissociation between explicit and implicit memory (Squire, 1992), which appears to be mediated by independent neural systems. However, in contrast to adult memory, which can be studied in patients with naturally occurring brain lesions or animals with induced lesions, it is not possible to create a situation in which an infant has no access to information about the world except through the stimulation created by its own interactions with that world. Although much of the perceptual information obtained by infants prior to their development of motor control is passive (e.g., by movements carried out by caregivers), once infants gain control over their own locomotion, perceptual information is conflated with self-produced motor responses. Perhaps a paralyzed infant, who has no opportunity to create its own perceptual stimulation via movement, would reveal the role of passive stimulation in the formation of knowledge. However, to determine whether this early knowledge was relevant to (or necessary for) later knowledge as assessed by motor responses, the infant would have to perform motor tasks, requiring removal of the paralysis. In short, it may be impossible to dissociate those aspects of knowledge that are acquired by perceptual systems and those acquired by the interaction between perception and action.

SUMMARY AND CONCLUSION

In the present chapter, I provided a review of recent work on statistical learning in the auditory and visual modalities by adults, infants, and nonhuman primates. I also reviewed how statistical learning is accomplished in a visuomotor task, highlighting the differences in the time course of learning during passive perceptual exposure compared with active perceptual-motor responding. Statistical learning is a remarkably robust and rapid form of learning that does not depend on feedback (reinforcement), but rather operates by mere exposure. Such a powerful learning mechanism must, however, be constrained because of the combinatorial explosion problem—there are simply too many possible statistics that could be extracted for the learner to discover the most important sources of information by trial and error or by computing all possible statistics. A variety of constraints appear to buffer the developing learner from this computational problem, including the presence of low-level feature detectors that are independent of experience, mid-level Gestalt mechanisms that combine features automatically, and a bias to store in memory only the largest coherent feature that has been extracted during the course of statistical learning. The task for future research in this area is to specify in more detail what these constraints on learning are and how they are implemented during the course of development, both in humans and nonhumans. The latter provides an animal model that can be used to reveal the neural mechanisms that support statistical learning in various domains and how action contributes to the acquisition of information about the structure of the perceptual world.

ACKNOWLEDGMENTS

This chapter is based on a talk presented at the 33rd Minnesota Symposium, "Action as an Organizer of Learning and Development," held on October 10 to 12, 2002 to honor the scientific contributions of Herb and Anne Pick. The research described in this chapter was supported by grants from the National Science Foundation (SBR–9873477) and the National Institutes of Health (HD–37082).

REFERENCES

Aslin, R. N., & Fiser, J. (2001, May). *Statistical learning of shape-conjunctions: (Higher) order from chaos.* Sarasota, FL: Visual Sciences Society.

Aslin, R. N., Saffran, J. R., & Newport, E. L. (1998). Computation of conditional probability statistics by 8-month-old infants. *Psychological Science, 9,* 321–324.

Atick, J. J. (1992). Could information theory provide an ecological theory for sensory processing? *Network: Computation in Neural Systems, 3,* 213–251.

Bahrick, L. E. (1983). Infants' perception of substance and temporal synchrony in multimodal events. *Infant Behavior and Development, 6,* 429–451.

Bahrick, L. E., & Lickliter, R. (2000). Intersensory redundancy guides attentional selectivity and perceptual learning in infancy. *Developmental Psychology, 36,* 190–201.

Baillargeon, R., Spelke, E. S., & Wasserman, S. (1985). Object permanence in five-month-old infants. *Cognition, 20,* 191–208.

Barlow, H. B. (1961). Possible principles underlying the transformations of sensory messages. In W. Rosenblith (Ed.), *Sensory communication* (pp. 217–234). Cambridge, MA: MIT Press.

Barlow, H. B. (1989). Unsupervised learning. *Neural Computation, 1,* 295–311.

Barlow, H. B. (1990). Conditions for versatile learning, Helmholtz's unconscious inference, and the task of perception. *Vision Research, 30,* 1561–1571.

Bellman, R. (1961). *Adaptive control processes: A guided tour.* Princeton, NJ: Princeton University Press.

Bialek, W. I., Nemenman, I., & Tishby, N. (2001). Predictability, complexity and learning. *Neural Computation, 13,* 2409–2464.

Biederman, I. (1987). Recognition-by components: A theory of human image understanding. *Psychological Review, 94,* 115–147.

Bregman, A. S. (1990). *Auditory scene analysis.* Cambridge, MA: MIT Press.

Bulthoff, H. H., Edelman, S. Y., & Tarr, M. J. (1995). How are three-dimensional objects represented in the brain? *Cerebral Cortex, 5,* 247–260.

Campos, J. J., Anderson, D. I., Barbu-Roth, M. A., Hubbard, E. M., Hertenstein, M. J., & Witherington, D. (2000). Travel broadens the mind. *Infancy, 1,* 149–219.

Creel, S. C., Newport, E. L., & Aslin, R. N. (2004). Distant melodies: Statistical learning of non-adjacent dependencies in tone sequences. *Journal of Experimental Psychology: Learning, Memory, and Cognition, 30,* 1119–1130.

Dodd, B. (1979). Lip reading in infants: Attention to speech presented in-and-out of synchrony. *Cognitive Psychology, 11,* 478–484.

Fiser, J., & Aslin R. N. (2001). Unsupervised statistical learning of higher-order spatial structures from visual scenes. *Psychological Science, 12,* 499–504.

Fiser, J., & Aslin, R. N. (2002a, May). *Extraction of parts and wholes from multi-element scenes.* Sarasota, FL: Visual Sciences Society.

Fiser, J., & Aslin, R. N. (2002b). Statistical learning of higher order temporal structure from visual shape-sequences. *Journal of Experimental Psychology: Learning, Memory, and Cognition, 28,* 458–467.

Fiser, J., & Aslin, R. N. (2002c). Statistical learning of new visual feature combinations by human infants. *Proceedings of the National Academy of Sciences, 99,* 15822–15826.

Fiser, J., McCrink-Gochal, K., & Aslin, R. N. (in preparation). Extraction of color- and shape-based statistics from sequential events in 9-month-olds.

Gallant, J. L., Connor, C. E., Rakshit, S., Lewis, J. W., & Van Essen, D. C. (1996). Neural responses to polar, hyperbolic, and Cartesian gratings in area V4 of the macaque monkey. *Journal of Neurophysiology, 76,* 2718–2739.

Gallistel, C. R. (1990). *The organization of learning.* Cambridge, MA: MIT Press.

Geisler, W. S., Perry, J. S., Super, B. J., & Gallogly, D. P. (2001). Edge co-occurrence in natural images predicts contour grouping performance. *Vision Research, 41,* 711–724.

Gogate, L. J., & Bahrick, L. E. (1998). Intersensory redundancy facilitates learning of arbitrary relations between vowel sounds and objects in seven-month-old infants. *Journal of Experimental Child Psychology, 69,* 1–17.

Hauser, M. D., Newport, E. L., & Aslin, R. N. (2001). Segmentation of the speech stream in a nonhuman primate: Statistical learning in cotton top tamarins. *Cognition, 78,* B53–B64.

Hubel, D. H., & Wiesel, T. N. (1959). Receptive fields of single neurones in the cat's striate cortex. *Journal of Physiology, 148,* 574–591.

Hubel, D. H., & Wiesel, T. N. (1968). Receptive fields and the functional architecture of monkey striate cortex. *Journal of Physiology, 195,* 215–243.

Hunt, R. H., & Aslin, R. N. (2001). Statistical learning in a serial reaction time task: Simultaneous extraction of multiple statistics. *Journal of Experimental Psychology: General, 130,* 658–680.

Kirkham, N. Z., Slemmer, J. A., & Johnson, S. P. (2002). Visual statistical learning in infancy: Evidence for a domain general learning mechanism. *Cognition, 83,* B35–B43.

Logothetis, N. K., & Pauls, J. (1995). Psychophysical and physiological evidence for viewer-centered representation in the primate. *Cerebral Cortex, 5,* 270–288.

Marr, D. (1982). *Vision.* San Francisco: W. H. Freeman.

Maurer, D., LeGrand, R., & Mondloch, C. J. (2002). The many faces of configural processing. *Trends in Cognitive Sciences, 6,* 255–260.

McCrink-Gochal, K., & Aslin, R. N. (2002, April). *Infant attention to synchrony in a complex visual scene.* Poster presented at the International Conference on Infancy Studies, Toronto, Canada.

Newport, E. L., & Aslin, R. N. (2000). Innately constrained learning: Blending old and new approaches to language acquisition. In S. C. Howell, S. A. Fish, & T. Keith-Lucas (Eds.), *Proceedings of the 24th annual Boston University conference on language development.* Somerville, MA: Cascadilla Press.

Newport, E. L., & Aslin, R. N. (2004). Learning at a distance: I. Statistical learning of non-adjacent dependencies. *Cognitive Psychology, 48,* 127–162.

Newport, E. L., Hauser, M. D., Spaepen, G., & Aslin, R. N. (2004). Learning at a distance: II. Statistical learning of non-adjacent dependencies in cotton-top tamarins. *Cognitive Psychology, 49,* 85–117.

Opde Beeck, H., Wagemans, J., & Vogels, R. (2001). Inferotemporal neurons represent low-dimensional configurations of parameterized shapes. *Nature Neuroscience, 4,* 1244–1252.

Pasupathy, A., & Connor, C. E. (2001). Shape representation in area V4: Position-specific tuning for boundary conformation. *Journal of Neurophysiology, 86,* 2505–2519.

Rescorla, R. A., & Wagner, A. R. (1972). A theory of Pavlovian conditioning: Variations in the effectiveness of reinforcement and nonreinforcement. In A. H. Black & W. F. Prokasy (Eds.), *Classical conditioning II* (pp. 64–99). New York: Appleton-Century-Crofts.

Saffran, J. R., Aslin, R. N., & Newport, E. L. (1996). Statistical learning by 8-month-old infants. *Science, 274,* 1926–1928.

Saffran, J. R., Johnson, E. K., Aslin, R. N., & Newport, E. L. (1999). Statistical learning of tone sequences by human infants and adults. *Cognition, 70,* 27–52.

Saffran, J. R., Newport, E. L., & Aslin, R. N. (1996). Word segmentation: The role of distributional cues. *Journal of Memory and Language, 35,* 606–621.

Saffran, J. R., Newport, E. L., Aslin, R. N., Tunick, R. A., & Barrueco, S. (1997). Incidental language learning: Listening (and learning) out of the corner of your ear. *Psychological Science, 8,* 101–105.

Selfridge, O. G. (1959, November). *Pandemonium: A paradigm for learning.* Paper presented at the symposium on the mechanization of thought processes, London, England.

Simoncelli, E. P., & Olshausen, B. A. (2001). Natural image statistics and neural representation. *Annual Review of Neuroscience, 24,* 1193–1216.

Spelke, E. S. (1979). Perceiving bimodally specified events in infancy. *Developmental Psychology, 15,* 626–636.

Squire, L. R. (1992). Memory and the hippocampus: A synthesis from findings with rats, monkeys, and humans. *Psychological Review, 99,* 195–231.

Tarr, M. J., Williams, P., Hayward, W. G., & Gauthier, I. (2001). Three-dimensional object recognition is viewpoint dependent. *Nature Neuroscience, 1,* 275–277.

von der Malsburg, C. (1995). Binding in models of perception and brain function. *Current Opinion in Neurobiology, 5,* 520–526.

Walker-Andrews, A. S. (1982). Intermodal perception of expressive behaviors by human infants. *Journal of Experimental Child Psychology, 33,* 514–535.

6
▼▼▼▼▼▼▼

The Benefits and Costs
of Combining Information
Between and Within Senses

Martin S. Banks
University of California, Berkeley

There are identifiable benefits and problems associated with intersensory integration. The benefits are manifold, but two come immediately to mind. (a) Complementary information can be gained by using different senses. The hands, for example, can acquire information from the back of an opaque surface that cannot be acquired by the eyes. (b) Using multiple sources of sensory information provides redundancy that can reduce the overall uncertainty of the estimate of an environment property.

The problems associated with intersensory integration are also manifold, but there are three prominent ones. (a) Because each sense acquires information by different means (the eye from the distribution of photons absorbed by retinal receptors and the hand from mechanical forces on the skin and from proprioceptive signals arising from the finger, thumb, and hand), the nervous system must convert the relevant signals into a common representation before integration can occur. (b) All sensory measurements are subject to error, so the method of integration will affect the error in the combined estimate. The best method in terms of minimizing error depends on the type of error, the degree to which the errors are correlated, and so forth. (c) Integrating signals from different senses can be beneficial if differences in the measurements are known to be errors rather than actual signal differences. For example, a visual signal from one object should not be integrated with a haptic signal from another. Hence, there should be rules that determine when integration occurs and when it does not.

In this chapter, I examine, from a theoretical standpoint, the optimal means for intersensory integration in the face of random measurement error. I then compare it to what we know about the intersensory integration in humans.

Rock and Victor (1964) investigated the means by which human observers integrate visual and haptic information for object shape. They had subjects grasp a square while looking at it through a distorting lens that made it appear rectangular. The shape of the unified percept was determined almost completely by vision. It seems that the square felt rectangular because it looked that way. Many investigators have since reported a similar dominance of vision over touch for judgments of size and shape (Festinger et al., 1967; Fishkin, Pishkin, & Stahl, 1975; Gibson, 1933; McDonnell & Duffett, 1972; Miller, 1972; Power & Graham, 1976; Singer & Day, 1969).

Hay, Pick, and Ikeda (1965) investigated visual and proprioceptive contributions to the perception of hand position. They had people view their own hand through a prism that displaced the image horizontally. Perceived hand position was essentially in the visually specified position rather than the proprioceptively specified position. Accordingly, Hay and colleagues called the phenomenon "visual capture." Others have observed similar phenomena (Pick, Warren, & Hay, 1969; Stratton, 1987; Tastevin, 1937; Warren & Pick, 1970; Warren & Rossano, 1991).

The visual dominance observed by Rock and Victor (1964) and Hay et al. (1965) is not necessarily observed with the estimation of all object properties. For instance, when asked to judge the roughness of a textured surface, observers give approximately equal weight to the visually and tactually specified roughnesses (Lederman & Abbott, 1981; see also Heller, 1983; Power, 1980; Welch & Warren, 1980). If visual dominance occurs for some object properties, but not others, is there a more general principle that underlies the integration of vision and touch? I propose that there is such a principle. Specifically, the nervous system attempts to minimize the variance of the final estimate of an object property; in so doing, it gives different weights to sensory signals depending on the object property in question (Ghahramani, Wolpert, & Jordan, 1997). Minimizing the variance is equivalent to reducing the uncertainty in a perceptual estimate.

THEORY

A sensory system's estimate of an environmental property can be represented by:

$$\hat{S}_i = f_i(S) \tag{1}$$

where S is the physical property being estimated and f the operation by which the nervous system does the estimation. The subscripts refer to the modality. Each sensor's estimate, $\hat{S}_i$, is corrupted by noise (i.e., the measurements have random error). The principle of minimizing variance is realized by using maximum-likelihood estimation (MLE; Clark & Yuille, 1990; Ernst & Banks, 2002; Ghahramani et al., 1997; Landy, Maloney, Johnston, & Young, 1995; Yuille & Bülthoff, 1996) to combine the inputs from various sensors. If the noises are statistically independent and Gaussian distributed with variance σ_i^2, MLE of the environmental property[1] is given by:

$$\hat{S} = \sum_i w_i \hat{S}_i \text{ with } w_i = \frac{1/\sigma_i^2}{\sum_j 1/\sigma_j^2}$$

For the case of two inputs—vision ($\hat{S}_V$) and haptics ($\hat{S}_H$)—this becomes:

$$\hat{S} = w_V \hat{S}_V + w_H \hat{S}_H \text{ with } w_V = \frac{1/\sigma_V^2}{1/\sigma_V^2 + 1/\sigma_H^2} \text{ and } w_H = \frac{1/\sigma_H^2}{1/\sigma_V^2 + 1/\sigma_H^2} \quad (2)$$

Thus, the MLE rule states that the optimal means of estimation (in the sense of producing the lowest-variance estimate) is to add the sensor estimates weighted by their normalized reciprocal variances[2] (Clark & Yuille, 1990; Ghahramani et al., 1997; Landy et al., 1995; Oruc, Maloney, & Landy, 2003; Schrater & Kersten, 2000). The variance of the final estimate, $\hat{S}$, is:

$$\sigma_{VH}^2 = \frac{\sigma_V^2 \sigma_H^2}{\sigma_V^2 + \sigma_H^2} \quad (3)$$

Thus, the combined estimate has lower variance than either of the estimates that went into the combination.

Implementation of MLE integration is illustrated for two cases in Fig. 6.1. The stimuli are conflicting visual-haptic stimuli, in which the visually specified size differs from the haptically specified size. The dashed Gaussian functions in the upper panels represent the probability distributions

---

[1]We also have to assume that the Bayesian prior is uniform. A Bayesian prior is the probability distribution that describes the expected values of the environmental property being measured. In the case we examine here—the property of object size—we can safely assume that the distribution of sizes is uniform (no size more likely than others) across the sizes involved in our experimental investigations.

[2]The weights are normalized (meaning that they add to 1) so that the estimate is unbiased.

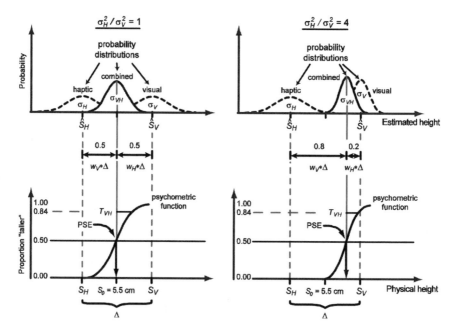

FIG. 6.1.   Implementation of MLE integration. Two situations are depicted. On the left, the variances of the visual and haptic estimates are equal. On the right, the variance of the haptic estimates is four times greater than the variance of the visual estimate. The visually and haptically specified heights differ by Δ. The dashed Gaussian functions in the upper panels represent the probability distributions of estimated height from vision and haptics, and the solid Gaussians represent probability densities for the combined estimate. On the left, the weights given to the visual and haptic estimates are both 0.5, and the mean of the combined probability distribution is equal to the mean of the visual and haptic distributions. The variance of the combined function is half the variance of the visual or haptic distribution. The psychometric function would be the curve in the lower left. With equal visual and haptic variances, the PSE should be equal to the average of the standard's visually and haptically specified heights. On the right, the weight given the visual estimate (w_V) is 0.8 and the weight given the haptic estimate (w_H) is 0.2. Thus, the combined probability density is shifted toward the visual estimate and its variance is 0.8 times the visual variance (Eq. 3). Accordingly, the psychometric function should be shifted toward the visual estimate, so the PSE should be close to the standard's visually specified height.

of estimated size from vision and haptics, and the solid Gaussians represent probability distributions for the combined estimate. On the left, the variances of the visual and haptic estimates are equal: $\sigma_H^2 / \sigma_V^2 = 1$. The weights given to the visual and haptic estimates are both 0.5 (Eq. 2). Therefore, the mean of the combined probability distribution is equal to the mean of the visual and haptic distributions. The variance of the combined function is half the variance of the visual or haptic distribution (Eq. 3). If the observer bases judgments of relative size on the combined probability distribution, the psychometric function would be the cumulative Gaussian in the lower left part of the figure. This function is the proportion of trials in which a no-conflict stimulus ($S_V = S_H$) would be judged as larger than a conflict stimulus (S_V and S_H as shown in the figure) plotted as a function of the no-conflict's size. With equal visual and haptic variances, the point of subjective equality (PSE) should be equal to the average of the conflict's visually and haptically specified sizes. The visual-haptic discrimination threshold—T_{VH}—is defined as the difference between the PSE and the size of the no-conflict stimulus for which it is judged larger than the conflict stimulus on 84% of the trials. On the right side, the variance of the haptic estimate is four times the variance of the visual estimate: $\sigma_H^2 / \sigma_V^2 = 4$. According to Eq. (2), the weight given the visual estimate (w_V) is 0.8, and the weight given the haptic estimate (w_H) is 0.2. Thus, the combined probability distribution is shifted toward the visual estimate, and its variance is 0.8 times the visual variance (Eq. 3). Accordingly, the psychometric function should be shifted toward the visual estimate, so the PSE should be close to the conflict's visually specified size.

AN EXPERIMENT ON VISUAL-HAPTIC ESTIMATION OF SIZE

I described statistically optimal integration, but how does it work in humans? To find out, we examined visual-haptic integration experimentally (Ernst & Banks, 2002). To work out the predictions of the MLE rule, we first determined the variances of the visual and haptic size estimates by conducting within-modality discrimination experiments. That is, we determined the variances of $\hat{S}_V$ and $\hat{S}_H$ (the visual and haptic estimates) by first conducting vision-alone and haptics-alone experiments. Observers viewed a raised bar binocularly or grasped it with the index finger and thumb (Fig. 6.2, bottom). The bar's height varied, but the average was constant. In the haptics-alone experiment, observers indicated which of the two sequentially presented bars was taller from haptic information alone; in the vision-alone experiment, they did so from vision alone. There were four conditions in the visual experiment differing in the amount of noise in the stimulus. By adding noise, we made the visually specified height less reliable.

The haptic stimulus was generated using two PHANToM™ force-feedback devices, one each for the index finger and thumb (Fig. 6.3). The devices compellingly simulate haptic properties such as a bar's size, shape, and stiffness. The apparatus was calibrated to align the visual and

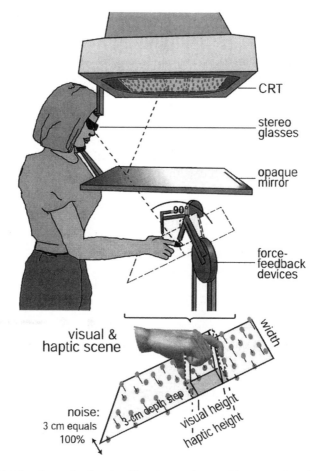

CRT

stereo
glasses

opaque
mirror

force-
feedback
devices

visual &
haptic scene

width

3 cm depth step

visual height

haptic height

noise:
3 cm equals
100%

FIG. 6.2. Apparatus for visual-haptic experiments. Observers viewed the reflection of the visual stimulus presented on a computer monitor (CRT) binocularly in a mirror. CrystalEyes (StereoGraphics) liquid-crystal shutter glasses were used to present binocular disparity. The surfaces of the stimuli were perpendicular to the line of sight. A head and chin rest limited head movements. The right hand was beneath the mirror and could not be seen. The haptic stimulus was presented with two PHANToM force-feedback devices, one each for the index finger and thumb. The visual and haptic stimulus was a horizontal bar raised 3 cm above a background plane. The plane and bar were represented visually by randomly positioned dots that were given appropriate binocular disparity. The plane and bar were represented haptically by the force-feedback device. The visual and haptic stimuli were in the same position in space and had the same dimensions except when the experimental condition required a difference in the visually and haptically specified heights (as shown).

PHANToM™ Force-feedback Device

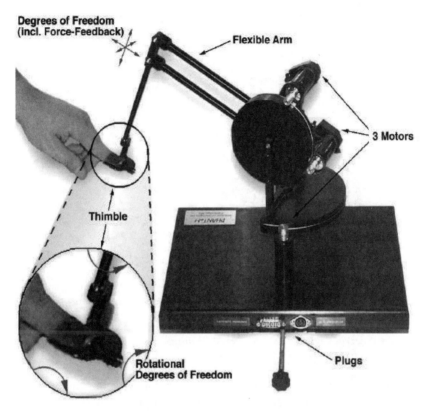

FIG. 6.3.   PHANToM force-feedback device. The three-dimensional position of the finger is monitored in real time. In our setup, there was on PHANToM for the index finger and another for the thumb. When the fingertip or tip of the thumb reached the simulated surface, the device applied an appropriate force (magnitude and direction) on the tip of the digit, creating the compelling sensation of touching a solid object. This model of the PHANToM provides a workspace of 7.5 × 10.5 × 15 inches (19.1 × 26.7 × 38.1 cm).

haptic stimuli spatially. The visual stimulus was a random-dot stereogram simulating the background plane and bar (Fig. 6.4). Noise was added to the visual display to vary its reliability. The noise was a random displacement of the dot depths in the stereogram (direction parallel to line of sight; Fig. 6.4, "with noise").

Within-modality discrimination was measured in a two-interval, forced-choice paradigm. Each trial consisted of two 1-second presentations (visual or haptic) of the bars. In the standard interval, the bar was always 55

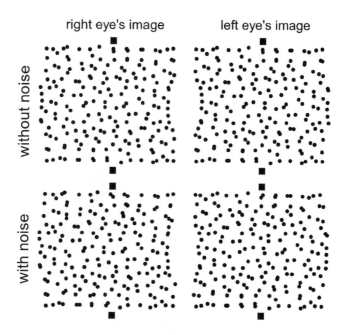

FIG. 6.4.   Stereograms representative of the visual stimuli. View by cross-fusing (directing the left eye toward the right pair of images and the right eye toward the left pair). Top row: Stereogram has no noise, and the horizontal bar is raised above the background. Bottom row: Stereogram of bar and background contains noise (random displacements of dots parallel to the line of sight).

mm tall; in the comparison interval, it was shorter or taller than that. The observer indicated the interval containing the apparently taller stimulus. We plotted the proportion of trials in which the comparison was perceived as taller than the standard against the comparison height. From those functions, we could determine points of subjective equality (PSEs) and just-noticeable differences (JNDs). Figure 6.5a shows the vision-alone and haptics-alone discrimination data. The proportion of trials in which the observer indicated that the comparison stimulus (variable height) appeared taller than the standard stimulus (fixed height of 55 mm) is plotted as a function of the comparison's height. The dashed red line and symbols represent the haptic discrimination data, and the solid blue curves with open symbols represent the visual data for the four noise levels. These psychometric functions were well fit by cumulative Gaussians, so the 84% points—the threshold values—correspond to their standard deviations. The haptic discrimination threshold was approximately 0.085 times the average bar height. As the noise increased from 0% to 200%, the visual discrimination thresholds increased from 0.04 to 0.2 times the average height.

Thus, when the visual noise was 0%, the visual discrimination threshold was roughly half the haptic threshold; when the visual noise was 200%, the visual threshold was more than double the haptic threshold.

From the within-modality measurements, we could specify the optimal integration rule. Specifically, with the measured values of σ_V^2 and σ_H^2, we could specify the model in Eq. 2 with no free parameters.

We then conducted the visual-haptic experiment to compare predicted and observed behavior. Observers simultaneously looked at and felt the raised bar. On each trial, two stimuli were presented sequentially. In one presentation, the visually and haptically specified heights were equal (no-conflict stimulus); in the other, they differed (conflict stimulus). The observer indicated the interval containing the apparently taller stimulus. Fig. 6.5b shows the proportion of trials in which the no-conflict stimulus was chosen as taller as a function of the no-conflict's height. From those psychometric functions, we obtained the PSE—the no-conflict height appearing equal to the conflict height—and the just-discriminable change in height (JND).

As I said earlier, we can predict from the within-modality data what an observer using MLE would do when presented visual and haptic information simultaneously and then compare those predictions to the observed performance in the visual-haptic experiment. I first describe the analysis of the PSE data and predictions for the weights.

The visual weights predicted from the within-modal experiments and the MLE rule are represented by the curve and shaded surround in Fig. 6.5c. The predicted weights vary significantly with the amount of visual noise in the stimulus: The visual weights are higher when the noise level is low and lower when the noise level is high. Now let us compare the predicted weights to the empirical weights (the empirical weights are the ones the observers assigned to vision and haptics while making their judgments in the intermodal experiment). Those empirical weights are represented by the symbols in Fig. 6.5c. The visually and haptically specified heights in the conflict—S_V and S_H—are indicated on the right ordinate. Figure 6.5c shows that as the noise level was increased, the visual weight decreased, and the PSE shifted from S_V toward S_H. The fit between the predicted and observed shifts in weights is very good. Because the noise level varied randomly from trial to trial, the weights must have been set within the 1-second stimulus presentation. Later in this chapter, I suggest a mechanism for such dynamic weight adjustment. In summary, the predicted and observed PSEs are quite similar, suggesting that humans do combine visual and haptic information in a fashion similar to MLE integration.

Of more interest is the analysis of the visual-haptic discrimination thresholds. I say this is more interesting because presumably the purpose of following a certain integration rule is to make the final percept as pre-

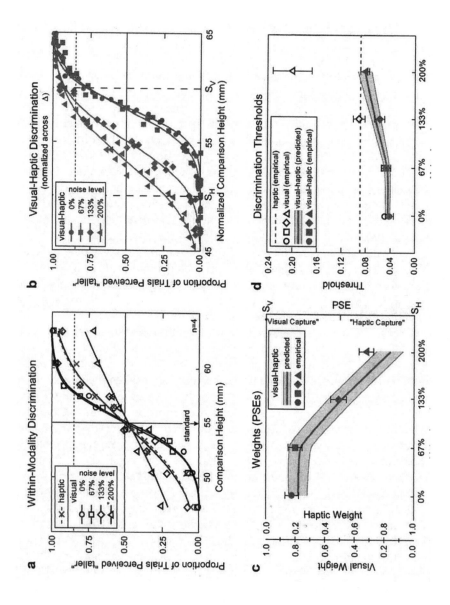

a Within-Modality Discrimination

b Visual-Haptic Discrimination
(normalized across Δ)

c Weights (PSEs)

d Discrimination Thresholds

170

FIG. 6.5. Predictions and data from visual-haptic integration study. (a) Within-modality discrimination data. The proportion of trials in which the comparison stimulus was perceived as taller than the standard is plotted against the comparison's height. Data were averaged across the four observers. Standard's height was always 55 mm (indicated by the arrow). Haptic discrimination data are represented by red xs and the best-fitting cumulative Gaussian by red dashed curve. Visual discrimination data are represented by the four blue curves and sets of symbols, corresponding to different levels of visual noise: circles: 0%, squares: 67%, diamonds: 133%, triangles: 200%. (b) Visual-haptic discrimination data. Proportion of trials in which the no-conflict stimulus was perceived as taller than the conflict is plotted against the no-conflict's height. The conflict's average height was always 55 mm, but the difference between the visually and haptically specified heights. To plot the data on one set of coordinates, we shifted the psychometric functions laterally. The four sets of purple discrimination data correspond with different amounts of visual noise—circles: 0%, squares: 67%, diamonds: 133%, triangles: 200%. (c) Observed and predicted weights (and PSEs). Abscissa represents the visual noise level. Left ordinate is the visual weight (w_V); haptic weight is $1-w_V$. Right ordinate represents PSEs in relation to S_V and S_H (Fig. 6.5b). Purple symbols represent the observed visual weights based on observers' PSEs (Fig. 6.5a). Shaded area represents the weights expected from within-modality discrimination (Fig. 6.5a). Height of shaded area represents expected standard error given standard errors associated with visual and haptic thresholds. (d) Within-modality and visual-haptic discrimination thresholds. Just-noticeable difference in height is plotted against the amount of visual noise. Threshold values are taken from the psychometric functions of (a) and (b). The red dashed horizontal line represents the within-modality, haptic discrimination threshold. Unfilled blue symbols represent the within-modality, visual discrimination thresholds. The visual-haptic discrimination thresholds are represented by purple filled symbols. Shaded area represents the predicted visual-haptic thresholds (Eq. 3). (See Color Panel A.)

cise as possible. According to the MLE rule, the combined estimates should have lower variance, and therefore lower discrimination thresholds, than either the visual or haptic estimate alone (Eq. 3). Said another way, by following this rule, the nervous system will always achieve more precise estimates than from either sensory modality alone (given the earlier-mentioned assumptions). To derive predictions for the visual-haptic discrimination thresholds, we use the within-modal data (Ernst & Banks, 2002). Figure 6.5d shows the predicted and observed thresholds. The unfilled symbols represent the vision-alone thresholds, and the dashed line represents the haptics-alone threshold. The shaded area represents the predicted visual-haptic thresholds; they are always lower than the vision-alone and haptics-alone thresholds at the corresponding noise level. The filled purple points represent the observed visual-haptic discrimination thresholds; as noise level increased, the JND became greater. Most important, the predicted and observed visual-haptic discrimination thresholds are quite similar. As with the PSE data, this suggests that human observers combine visual and haptic information in a fashion similar to MLE integration. By following this rule, humans are taking the best possible advantage of the size information conveyed by the eye and hand.

VISUAL-HAPTIC INTEGRATION WITH NATURALLY OCCURRING CHANGES IN VARIANCE

It is important to know whether the integration rule is applied appropriately with changes in viewing situation—such as changes in viewing distance, lighting, motion, and retinal eccentricity—that affect visual precision. Accordingly, we examined a situation in which the variance of visual estimates changes naturally.

Consider estimating the distance between two parallel planar surfaces. When the surfaces are parallel to the line of sight (Fig. 6.6A), visual estimation is straightforward: measure the retinal angle between the projections of the two surfaces and scale for distance. In this case, error in estimating intersurface distance should increase in proportion to viewing distance. When the surfaces are perpendicular to the line of sight (and transparent; Fig. 6.6B), visual estimation is more difficult: Now one must measure binocular disparity between the surfaces and scale for distance. Because of the geometric relationship between disparity and relative distance, error in estimating intersurface distance should increase in proportion to the square of viewing distance. Thus, we expect visual judgments of intersurface distance to be more precise in the former than in the latter case (McKee, Levi, & Bowne, 1990; van Beers, Wolpert, & Haggard, 2002).

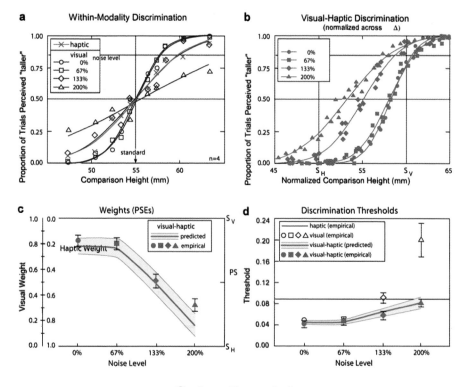

Color Panel A

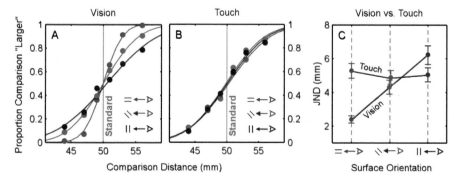

Color Panel B

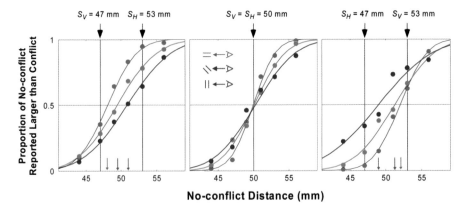

Color Panel C

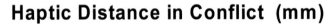

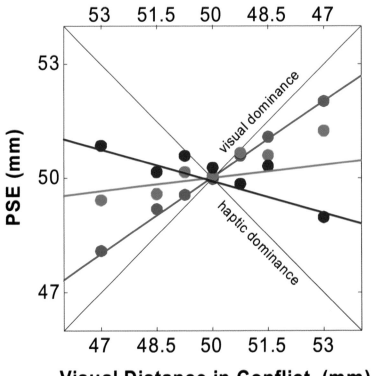

Color Panel D

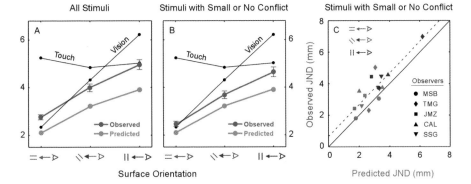

Color Panel E

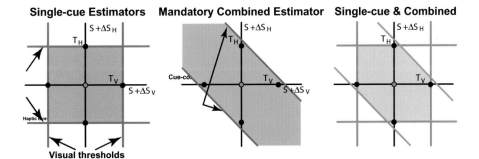

Color Panel F

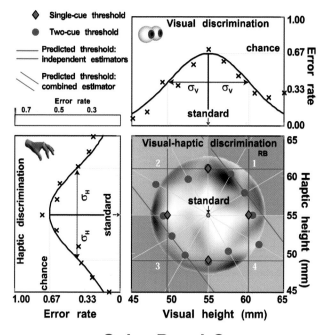

Color Panel G

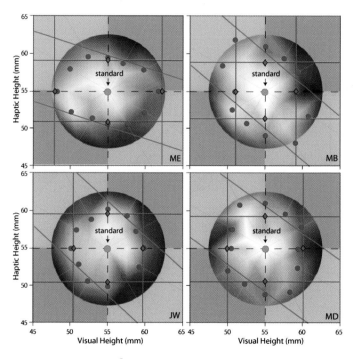

Color Panel H

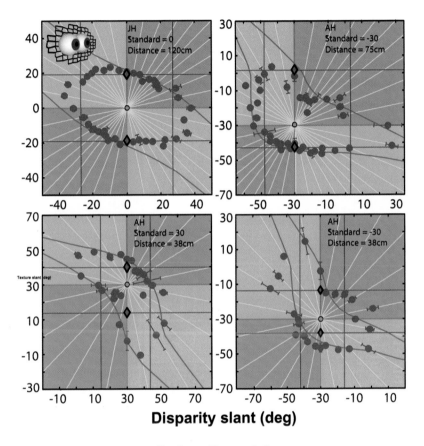

Disparity slant (deg)

Color Panel I

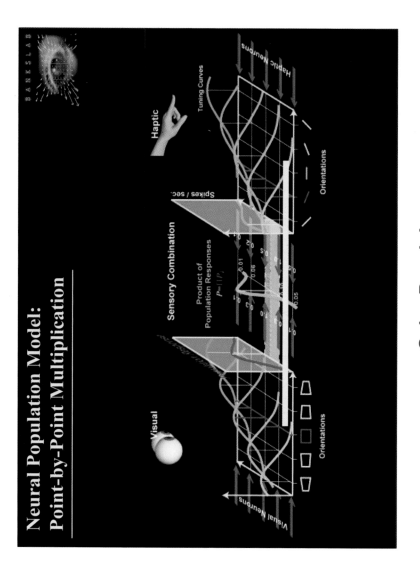

Color Panel J

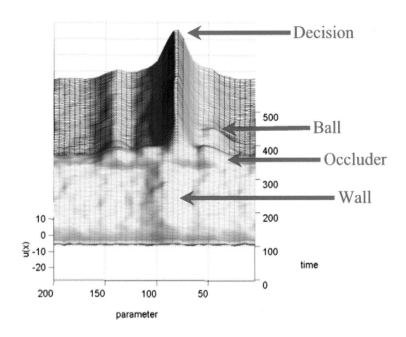

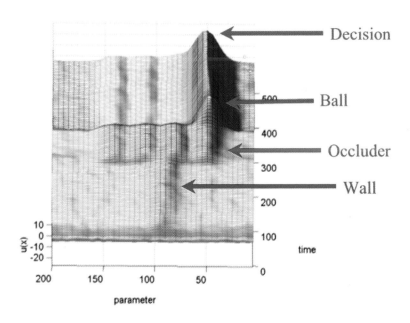

Color Panel K

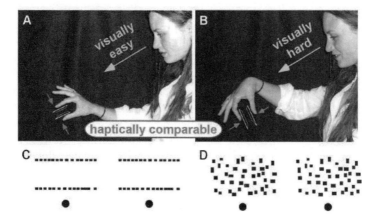

FIG. 6.6. A, B: Estimating the distance between two parallel surfaces. For vision, the task is presumably easier on the left (surfaces parallel to the line of sight) than on the right (perpendicular). For touch, the difficulty is presumably similar in the two cases. C, D: The diagrams below are stereograms depicting the visual stimuli. To view them, converge the eyes (cross-fuse).

If the observer estimates the intersurface distance haptically (active touch), she rotates the wrist to place the finger and thumb in the appropriate orientation. The proprioceptive and efferent signals from the digits are similar in the parallel and perpendicular cases, so in this situation the precision of haptic estimates should not vary with orientation.

Suppose the observer looks at and feels the surfaces simultaneously. Again the MLE integration rule prescribes the strategy for combining visual and haptic estimates that produces the estimate of lowest variance (Clark & Yuille, 1990; Ernst & Banks, 2002; Ghahramani et al., 1997). As stated earlier in this chapter, if the visual and haptic estimates are independent and normally distributed, that strategy is weighted summation of $\hat{S}_V$ and $\hat{S}_H$, and the weights are the normalized inverse variances of the estimates (Eq. 2). The variance of the combined estimate would be lower than the haptic or visual variance (Eq. 3).

We asked observers to judge the distance between two parallel surfaces in two within-modality experiments (vision-alone and haptics-alone) and in an intermodality experiment (vision and haptics together; Gepshtein & Banks, 2003). We expected from the viewing geometry that visual precision would vary with surface orientation and from hand mechanics that haptic precision would not. We also conducted an intersensory, visual-haptic experiment to determine how much weight humans give to vision and haptics as a function of surface orientation and to determine whether combining the two senses yields an improvement in discrimination performance.

The visual stimuli were random-element stereograms of two parallel planes in three orientations relative to the line of sight: parallel, oblique, and perpendicular (Fig. 6.6 shows the parallel and perpendicular cases). The simulated surfaces were textured with sparse rectangular elements and were otherwise transparent. The haptic stimuli were created using the PHANToM™ devices, again one each for the index finger and thumb.

In the within-modality experiments, observers reported which of two stimuli had the larger intersurface distance. The size of the standard stimulus was always 50 mm, and the size of the comparison stimulus varied. In the haptics-alone condition, the observer felt two parallel (invisible) surfaces.

Figure 6.7 shows the results of the within-modality experiment. Figures 6.7A and 6.7B show the proportion of trials for which the comparison was judged as larger than the standard as a function of the comparison distance. As expected, precision with vision-alone was highest when the surfaces were parallel to the line of sight and lowest when they were perpendicular. Also as expected, precision did not vary with orientation in the haptics-alone condition. The just-noticeable differences (JNDs) are plotted in Fig. 6.7C. JNDs for vision-alone increased as orientation changed from parallel to perpendicular; haptic JNDs did not change.

In the intermodality experiment, we presented visual and haptic information specifying intersurface distance. Two brief stimuli were presented in random order: no-conflict ($S_V = S_H$) and conflict ($S_V \neq S_H$). Observers indicated the one containing the larger intersurface distance. Figures 6.8A to 6.8C show the proportion of trials in which the no-conflict stimulus was judged as larger than the conflict stimulus as a function of the no-conflict size. The psychometric functions and PSEs were shifted toward the visual size in the parallel condition and toward the haptic size in the perpendicular condition. These shifts are consistent with the expectation that vision will dominate the judgment when the visual variance is lower than the haptic variance and that the reverse will occur when the visual variance is higher.

We next examined how closely the visual-haptic data conformed to the predictions of MLE integration rule. Using the visual and haptic variances (σ_V^2 and σ_H^2) measured in the within-modality experiments, we calculated the predicted PSEs; these are represented by the colored lines in Fig. 6.9A. If vision completely dominated the visual-haptic percept, the visually specified distances of the conflict and no-conflict stimuli would have to be physically equal to be perceived as equal; the data would have a slope of 1. Similarly, complete haptic dominance would yield data with a slope of −1. If neither vision nor haptics completely dominated, the PSEs would fall between the diagonals. The MLE prediction is closest to visual dominance when surface orientation was parallel to the line of sight because vi-

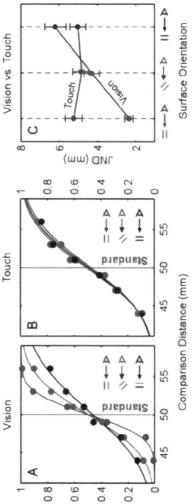

FIG. 6.7. Results of the within-modality experiment. A, B: Proportion of trials in which the comparison was judged as larger than the standard as a function of the comparison's intersurface distance. Red, green, and blue symbols and curves correspond to data from the parallel, oblique, and perpendicular conditions, respectively. A and B show the data from the vision-alone and haptics-alone conditions, respectively. The curves are cumulative normals that best fit the data once averaged across the five observers. C: Observed JNDs (1 standard deviation of the cumulative normals in A and B) as a function of surface orientation. Error bars are ± 1 S.E. (See Color Panel B.)

175

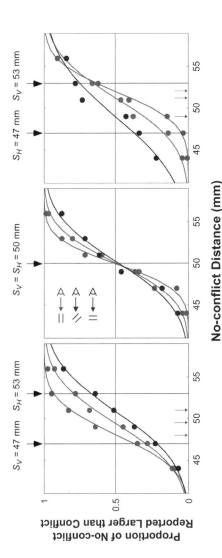

No-conflict Distance (mm)

FIG. 6.8.   A–C: Results of the intermodality (visual-haptic) experiment. The proportion of trials in which the no-conflict stimulus was judged as larger than the conflict stimulus is plotted as a function of the intersurface distance in the no-conflict stimulus. The data have been averaged across the five observers. A, B, and C show the data for conflict pairings (visual-haptic) of {47,53}, {50,50}, and {53,47} mm, respectively (three of the seven conflicts). The red, green, and blue symbols are data from the parallel, oblique, and perpendicular conditions, respectively. The curves are cumulative normals that best fit the averaged data. PSEs are the values of the no-conflict stimulus for which the observer reports that it is larger than the conflict stimulus half the time. Those values are indicated for the parallel, oblique, and perpendicular conditions by the red, green, and blue arrows, respectively. D: Predicted and observed PSEs plotted as a function of the visually specified distance (lower abscissa) or haptically specified distance (upper abscissa) in the conflict stimulus. The diagonal gray lines show the predicted PSEs if vision or haptics completely dominated the combined percept. PSEs predicted by the MLE integration rule (Eq. 2) are represented by the colored lines (derived from the within-modality data averaged across observers). The circles represent the observed PSEs, averaged across observers. (See Color Panel C.)

sual estimates were most precise in that condition. The prediction shifts toward haptic dominance when the stimulus was perpendicular because vision was less precise than haptics in that condition (Fig. 6.8). The data points represent the observed PSEs. The agreement between predicted and observed PSEs is very good.

Figure 6.9B shows the PSE data from individual subjects. The thick lines represent the predicted PSEs, and the data points represent the empirically determined PSEs.

Overall, the PSEs suggest that the brain is nearly optimal statistically in taking varying visual precision into account. However, one cannot determine from average responses (such as PSEs) whether the variability of the

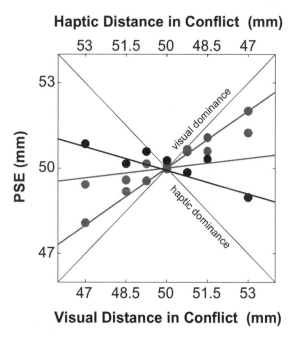

FIG. 6.9. Predicted and observed PSEs in the intermodality experiment. Data averaged across the five observers. Red, green, and blue data points represent the PSEs observed in the intermodality experiment in the parallel, oblique, and perpendicular conditions, respectively. The value of the no-conflict stimulus that was on average perceived as the same height as the conflict stimulus is plotted as a function of different conflicts (visual and haptic heights are shown on the lower and upper abscissae, respectively). The gray diagonal lines represent the predictions for visual dominance and for haptic dominance. Colored lines represent the predictions of the MLE integration rule in each condition. (See Color Panel D.)

combined estimate is reduced relative to the vision-alone and haptics-alone estimates. To examine this, we looked at how discrimination thresholds (JNDs) were affected.

An observer following the MLE rule would make finer discriminations when vision and haptics were both available than when only one was (Eq. 3). Figures 6.10A and 6.10B plot observed within-modality JNDs and predicted and observed intermodality JNDs. Figure 6.10A includes all the data from the intermodality experiment. The observed thresholds were similar to or lower than the visual and haptic thresholds in the within-modality experiments, but the observed thresholds were not quite as low as would be predicted from application of the MLE rule. This may have been caused by occasional awareness of the discrepancy between the visual and haptic stimuli. Perhaps such awareness caused observers to adopt a less-than-optimal strategy (such as switching between only the visual or only the haptic percept when the conflict was noticeable; Ghahramani et al., 1997). To test this, we reanalyzed the data using only trials in which the conflict was 1.5 mm or less. Figure 6.10B shows the result: The observed thresholds were closer to the predictions.

Figure 6.10C shows the predicted and observed JNDs for small or zero conflicts for each observer and each stimulus orientation. The good agreement between predicted and observed shows that individual differences in intermodal discrimination can be largely explained by behavior in the within-modality experiments.

The finding of close correspondence between observed and predicted thresholds shows that humans combine visual and haptic information in a fashion that allows finer discrimination than is possible from either sense alone. Indeed, by the criterion of discrimination capability, the combination approaches statistical optimality.

ARE VISUAL AND HAPTIC ESTIMATES REALLY FUSED?

We have shown how combining information across senses can improve estimation of object properties. Yet if sensory signals really are combined in the manner suggested by the MLE integration rule, it may come at a cost: loss of single-cue information. We investigated whether information from single cues—a visual estimate and a haptic estimate—is lost when visual-haptic integration occurs. To benefit from MLE (in the sense of reducing uncertainty), different cues to the same object property must be well correlated across objects. For example, if an object's size increases, visual and haptic signals both generally indicate the increase, so an organ-

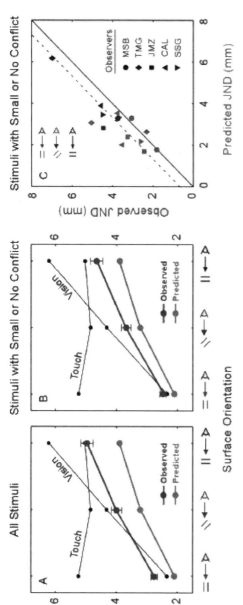

FIG. 6.10. Precision of distance estimates in the intermodality experiment. A, B: Observed and predicted JNDs as a function of surface orientation. Black points and lines represent observed JNDs in the within-modality experiment (see also Fig. 6.7). Cyan points and lines represent predicted JNDs, and purple points and lines represent observed JNDs in the intermodality experiment. A shows the averaged data from all conditions. B shows the averaged data from the smallest conflicts (1.5 mm or less). Error bars are ± 1 S.E. The observed intermodality JNDs are significantly smaller than the smallest within-modality JNDs in the oblique and parallel conditions ($p < 0.05$, z scores of their differences are 2.15 and 2.07). In the parallel condition, however, the observed intermodality JND is indistinguishable from the visual JND (z score of their difference is −0.58). C is observed and predicted JNDs for each observer from the smallest conflicts. The red, green, and blue symbols represent data from the parallel, oblique, and perpendicular conditions for individual observers. The solid diagonal is the line of perfect agreement. The dashed line is a least-squares linear fit to the observed JNDs. It indicates that humans are on average 0.66 mm less precise than ideal. The correlation between the predicted and observed is 0.85. (See Color Panel E.)

179

ism would obtain the benefit of more precise estimates by using MLE. There is, however, a potential cost: Consider the situation in which there are two cues, S_V and S_H. In this case, the MLE is

$$\hat{S}_C = w_V \hat{S}_V + w_H \hat{S}_H. \tag{3}$$

There are combinations of S_V and S_H, producible in the laboratory, for which $\hat{S}_C$ is on average constant. If $S_V = S + \Delta S_V$ and $S_H = S + \Delta S_H$, then $\hat{S}_C$ is constant, on average, for values of ΔS_V and ΔS_H satisfying

$$\Delta S_H = -\frac{w_V}{w_H} \Delta S_V. \tag{4}$$

If the combined estimate (Eq. 2) were the only one available, the nervous system would be unable to discriminate the various stimulus combinations satisfying Eq. 4. In other words, for every increase in S_V, there would be a decrease in S_H, that would yield no change in the combined estimate $\hat{S}_C$. Such physically distinct, but perceptually indiscriminable, stimuli would be metamers[3] (Backus, 2002; Richards, 1979). However, if the nervous system retained the single-cue estimates, $\hat{S}_V$ and $\hat{S}_H$, the various combinations satisfying Eq. 4 would be discriminable from one another. Fortunately, an inability to discriminate stimulus combinations satisfying Eq. 4 would have little practical consequence because such combinations rarely occur in the natural environment. We can, however, generate such combinations in the laboratory and then look for the loss in discrimination capability predicted by MLE. Observing such a loss would mean that the nervous system combines information from different cues to form one estimate of the object property in question (i.e., it would mean that mandatory cue fusion occurs).

In previous studies on cue combination, observers were forced to report perceived size (Ernst & Banks, 2002; Gepshtein & Banks, 2003; Rock & Victor, 1964), position (Hay et al., 1965; van Beers et al., 1999, 2002), distance (Brenner & van Damme, 1999), surface shape (Johnston et al., 1994; Rogers & Bradshaw, 1995; Buckley & Frisby, 1993), surface slant (Backus et al., 1999; Banks, Hooge, & Backus, 2001), or edge location (Landy & Kojima, 2001). These studies tell us that multiple cues are used for the associated judgment, but *not* whether observers lose access to single-cue estimates. To remedy this, we used an oddity task (Hillis, Ernst, Banks, &

---

[3]Metamers are composite stimuli that cannot be discriminated even though their constituents can be. The classic example is the inability to discriminate a yellow light consisting of one wavelength from another yellow light consisting of red added to green.

Landy, 2002). Observers identified, among three stimuli, the stimulus that differed from the other two on *any* dimension. Because observers were free to use any difference, not just the one imposed by the experimenter, the task provided a true test for the existence of cue fusion.

To understand the experimental design, consider Fig. 6.10. The graphs show the visually specified size on the abscissa and the haptically specified size on the ordinate. At the origin (in the background), visually and haptically defined sizes are both zero. The blue diagonal represents other cases in which the visual and haptic sizes are equal. The enlargement in the middle shows one case in which the origin is a stimulus whose visually and haptically specified sizes are both 55 mm (S,S). This is the standard stimulus; an example is shown below in the middle. The standard contained consistent cues, so it was always on the blue diagonal. The abscissa in the enlargement represents changes in S_V and the ordinate changes in S_H. Examples of these comparison stimuli are schematized later; the eye and hand are presented the same heights for the two cases on the left, and the eye is presented a greater height than the hand for the case on the right.

How different must the comparison be from the standard for a person to distinguish the two? By distinguish, we mean the observer can reliably pick out the "odd" stimulus when presented two examples of the standard and one of the comparison. There are at least two strategies. (a) *Single-cue estimators*: Estimates could be made independently of one another (without combination). Once the difference between either estimate, ΔS_V or ΔS_H, reached its own discrimination threshold, $\pm T_V$ or $\pm T_H$, the observer would be able to identify the odd stimulus. The predicted set of thresholds would, therefore, be horizontal and vertical lines (Fig. 6.11, left, red lines) whose distance from the origin was determined by the discrimination threshold of the single-cue estimators. Comparison stimuli within the shaded rectangle would be indistinguishable from the standard. Performance would be no better in one quadrant than in any other. (b) *Mandatory combined estimator*: Only the combined estimate (Eq. 2) is used. Discrimination threshold would be determined only by the difference in the combined estimates for the standard and comparison. Assuming that the variances of the single-cue estimates are equal to the variances used to plot the single-cue-estimation prediction and that the MLE rule is used, the predicted thresholds for the combined-estimation strategy are the green diagonal lines (Fig. 6.11, middle).

To determine how cues are used in discriminating object properties, we conducted an intersensory, size discrimination experiment. We measured single-cue (vision-alone and haptics-alone) and intersensory discrimination (visual-haptic; Hillis et al., 2002). As in the Ernst and Banks (2002)

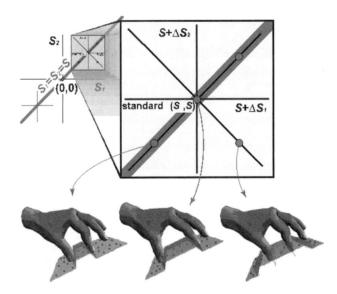

FIG. 6.11. Stimuli and experimental design. The abscissa represents changes in S_V (visually specified height). The ordinate represents changes in S_H (haptically specified height). The icons illustrate the no-conflict and conflict stimuli. The one in the middle schematizes visually and haptically specified heights of 55 mm (which is plotted at the origin). The icon on the left schematizes another no-conflict stimulus in which the visually and haptically specified heights are equal to one another, but smaller than 55 mm. The icon on the right schematizes a conflict stimulus in which the visually specified height is greater than 55 mm and the haptically specified heights is less than 55 mm.

study, the stimulus was a horizontal bar raised above a plane (Figs. 6.2 and 6.10). The visual stimulus was a random-dot stereogram simulating the background plane and bar. On half of the trials, noise was added into the stereogram. The haptic stimulus was again generated using two PHANToM™ force-feedback devices (Fig. 6.3), one each for the index finger and thumb.

Each trial consisted of the sequential presentation of three bars. The standard was presented twice and the comparison once. The observer indicated the one that was different from the other two on any basis. No feedback was given. For both single-cue and intersensory conditions, the standard height was 55 mm and the comparison was selected randomly from a set of predetermined heights. The visual and haptic comparison height was specified by a fixed ratio ($\Delta S_H / \Delta S_V$). Each ratio corresponds to a direction in the stimulus space (Fig. 6.12).

The upper right and lower left panels of Fig. 6.13 show, respectively, error rate (1–proportion correct) for one observer in the vision-alone and

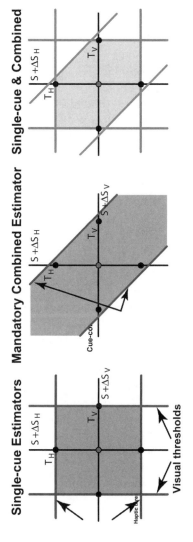

FIG. 6.12. Predicted discrimination thresholds for different combination strategies. Left: Predicted thresholds if observers used independent single-cue estimates. Comparison stimuli within the rectangle would be indistinguishable from the standard (represented by the blue dot at the origin). Middle: predicted thresholds if observers have access to the combined estimate only (Eq. 2). Comparison stimuli between the two lines would be indistinguishable from the standard. Right: predicted discrimination thresholds if observers have access to the single-cue and combined estimates. (See Color Panel F.)

183

haptic-alone conditions. The solid curves are best-fitting Gaussians to the error-rate data. Threshold was defined as one standard deviation from the mean; those values are the red dashed lines. The lower right panel of Fig. 6.13 shows intersensory data for the same observer. These data show that a combined estimator is used in visual-haptic judgments: As expected from use of a combined estimator, thresholds were lower in Quadrants 1 and 3 (where cues are consistent) than in Quadrants 2 and 4 (cues inconsistent). The data also show that single-cue estimators are used: Discrimination thresholds were not significantly higher in Quadrants 2 and 4 than predicted by use of single-cue estimators (Fig. 6.12, left).[4] Figure 6.14 shows the data from the other observers plotted in the same format. All but observer JW exhibited the same pattern of results: elongation in the cues-inconsistent direction relative to the cues-consistent direction.

We concluded that the nervous system has three means to represent object size: vision-alone, haptics-alone, and combined (visual-haptic). It uses the representation that is best suited for the discrimination. This means that we did not observe visual-haptic metamers.

ARE CUES FROM WITHIN ONE SENSE FUSED?

We wondered if cue combination ever involves the loss of single-cue information. It seems more likely that one would observe evidence for mandatory fusion when the cues are combined within one sense. For example, consider two visual cues to surface orientation: binocular disparity and the texture gradient. Disparity and texture cues at the same retinal location almost always come from the same object. Thus, mandatory cue combination would be beneficial if errors in the disparity and texture estimates were a more likely cause of the discrepancy than actual signal differences. For this reason, there would be evolutionary or developmental pressure to rely on the combined estimate instead of the single-cue estimates. The situation is different when integrating signals from the eye and hand. Visual and haptic signals for size do not always come from the same object (e.g., looking at one object while touching another). Mandatory

---

[4]The observers' phenomenology was instructive. They reported using a difference in perceived size when the comparison stimulus was in the cues-consistent quadrants (1 and 3). This percept is well modeled by the equations for combined estimation (Eq. 2). Observers' reports were less consistent with stimuli in the cues-inconsistent quadrants (2 and 4). Sometimes they used a difference in perceived size, but frequently they noticed the conflict between the visually and haptically specified sizes and used the perceived conflict to make the oddity discrimination. The phenomenology is consistent with the hypothesis that observers used three estimators in performing the oddity discrimination: two single-cue estimators and a combined estimator.

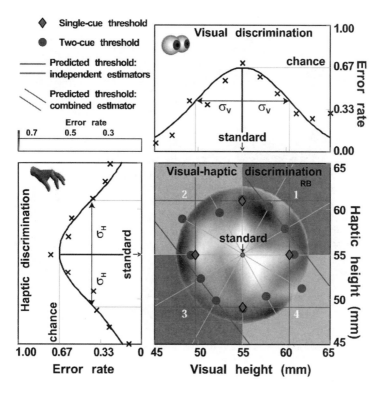

FIG. 6.13. One observer's oddity thresholds in the within-modal and intermodal experiments. The graph in the upper right shows the within-modal, vision-alone thresholds. Error rate (1–proportion correct) is plotted as a function of the comparison's height. The curve is a Gaussian that provides the best fit to the data. The graph in the lower left shows the within-modal, haptics-alone thresholds. The graph in the lower right shows the observed and predicted oddity thresholds in the intermodal (visual-haptic) experiment. The red lines are predicted single-cue estimator thresholds, and the green lines are predicted combined estimator thresholds. The magenta points are the observed oddity thresholds. Lightness within the central gray circle represents the observer's error rate. Quadrants (numbered in white) 1 and 3, where combined estimation predicts improvement relative to single-cue estimation, are highlighted in blue. Quadrants 2 and 4, where combined estimation predicts deterioration relative to single-cue estimation, are highlighted in orange. (See Color Panel G.)

combination of visual and haptic cues would be misleading in such cases. To pursue the idea that mandatory combination is more likely for cues within a sensory modality, we conducted an experiment in which we manipulated two visual cues to slant: disparity S_D and texture S_T.

The stimuli were textured planes slanted about a vertical axis. In most cases, they were viewed binocularly. The textures were Voronoi patterns

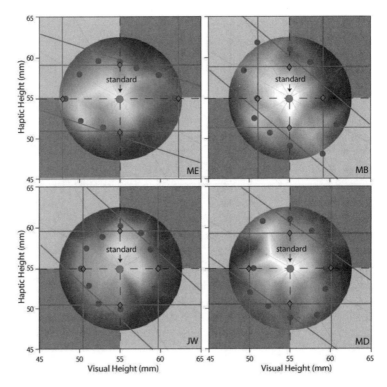

FIG. 6.14. Oddity discrimination thresholds for the four other subjects in
the visual-haptic experiment. As in Fig. 6.13, red lines are predicted single-
cue thresholds. Green lines are predicted discrimination thresholds for combined estimator. Magenta points are the measured visual-haptic discrimination thresholds. (See Color Panel H.)

(de Berg et al., 2000; Knill, 1998) such as those in Fig. 6.15. Each trial consisted of three sequential presentations, and observers indicated the one
that was different on any basis. Various ratios of $\Delta S_T / \Delta S_D$ were presented.
The difference between the standard and comparison along each tested
direction (i.e., each $\Delta S_T / \Delta S_D$) was varied according to an adaptive staircase to find the value that the observer could just reliably discriminate.

Figure 6.16 shows some results for two observers. The red lines represent the predictions for the single-cue estimators and the green curves the
predictions for the combined estimator.[5] Data followed the curves pre-

---

[5]The green curves from the combined estimator are curved because the weights assigned
to an optimal combined estimator vary with texture-specified slant. Specifically, discrimination of one slant from another based on texture cues is much finer for very slanted surfaces
than for surfaces whose slants are close to 0 (Knill, 1998), so the weight assigned to the texture-specified slant should increase with increasing slant (Eq. 2).

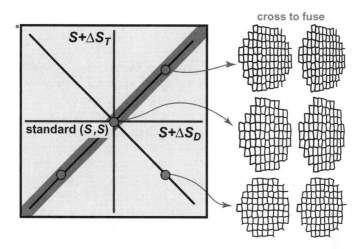

FIG. 6.15. Stimuli and experimental design for disparity and texture gradient experiment. The graph on the left represents the various stimuli in the experiment. Stimuli along the blue diagonal represent no-conflict stimuli in which the disparity- and texture-specified slants are equal to one another. Stimuli in other parts of the graph represent conflict stimuli in which the disparity- and texture-specified slants differ. The stereograms on the right, once cross-fused, allow the reader to see what the stimuli looked like. The stereogram in the middle row is an example of a no-conflict stimulus with the standard slant (S,S). The stereogram in the upper row is another example of a no-conflict stimulus in which the disparity- and texture-specified slants are both larger than the standard. The stereogram in the lower row is an example of a conflict stimulus; the disparity-specified slant greater than the standard's and texture-specified slant is less than the standard's.

dicted from optimal combination, which means that texture and disparity weights are set dynamically trial by trial according to the relative variances of the texture and disparity estimators (Knill, 1998). Remarkably, some thresholds fell outside the rectangle defined by single-cue thresholds (red lines).[6] In those cases, the observer failed to discriminate, on any

---

[6]The observers' phenomenology was informative. In some trials, they perceived a difference in slant (Quadrants 1 and 3). This percept is well modeled by the equations for combined estimation (Eq. 2). In other trials, they perceived a difference in the shape of the surface texture. This occurred in the cues-inconsistent quadrants (particularly in the direction for which S_c is constant, Eq. 4). For example, in the lower right panel of Fig. 6.16, the standard's slant was −30 (i.e., left side far), so the retinal images had smaller and more foreshortened texture on the left. For the four comparison stimuli in Quadrant 2, the disparity- and texture-specified slants differed in opposite directions from the standard stimulus. $\hat{S}_c$ was approximately −30 for these comparison stimuli, but the surface texture was rendered such that the retinal images were nearly equally large (and equally foreshortened) on the left and right. To be consistent with the perceived left-far slant, the surface texture would have to be nonhomogeneous (larger cells on the left and smaller on the right). The odd stimulus was detected

basis, stimuli whose constituents were discriminable: The standard and comparison were metamers (Richards, 1979; Backus, 2002; i.e., we observed mandatory fusion within vision.

Interestingly, we observed different combination strategies in the intersensory (visual-haptic) and intrasensory (vision with disparity and texture as cues) cases. In both cases, we observed the improvement in perceptual precision expected when two consistent cues are combined. We observed different behavior, however, when cues were inconsistent. In the intersensory case, we observed no loss of single-cue information as a consequence of combination: The nervous system retained the single-cue estimates and therefore did not exhibit a large threshold increase when cues were inconsistent. In the intrasensory case, we did observe a loss of single-cue information in that threshold when cues were inconsistent became larger than would have been obtained if observers used single-cue estimates. The absence of large threshold elevations in the inconsistent cues direction for the intersensory case is not surprising. Haptic and visual signals for size do not always come from the same object (e.g., touching one object while looking at another). Mandatory combination of haptic and visual cues would be misleading in such cases. The situation is different in the intrasensory case: Texture and disparity cues at the same retinal location almost always come from the same object. Thus, mandatory cue combination would be beneficial if errors in the texture and disparity estimates were a more likely cause of discrepancy than actual signal differences. For this reason, there would be evolutionary or developmental pressure to rely on the combined estimate instead of the single-cue estimates. This deferral to the combined estimate is evident in the deterioration of performance in the disparity-texture data (Fig. 6.16) in the cues-inconsistent quadrants (2 and 4); observers would have performed better if they used single cues. To highlight this point, we measured thresholds with only one cue present (monocular texture) and with both cues present (texture and disparity) in sequential blocks of trials. For the cues-inconsistent quadrants, thresholds were actually lower in the monocular condition than when both disparity and texture were available. The opposite was true in the cues-consistent quadrants. This result illustrates both the benefits—better discrimination when the cues specify changes in

---

by perceiving this nonhomogeneity. Observers were in this case using shape-constancy mechanisms (which allow one to determine the shape of markings on a slanted surface). We believe, therefore, that observers did not have access to more than one slant percept (e.g., $\hat{S}_C$, $\hat{S}_T$, and $\hat{S}_D$); the slant cues were truly fused. They made the discrimination in the cues-inconsistent quadrants by use of another calculation—shape constancy—that allowed them to perceive the objective shape of the texture on the surface. If this hypothesis is correct, metamers (cases in which discrimination is poorer than predicted by single-cue estimates) occurred when the stimulus made the shape-constancy judgment difficult.

the same direction—and the costs—the loss of single-cue information associated with cue combination.

Our data provide a clear demonstration of depth-cue fusion: Shape information from texture and disparity cues is combined to form a single, fused percept such that some discriminations that could be made from single-cue estimates are not made. We also have evidence for a single fused percept for shape information from haptics and vision, but in this intersensory case, information from single-cue estimates is not lost.

COMPARISON WITH PREVIOUS FINDINGS

There is an enormous literature on intersensory integration, and there has been a large number of observations of visual dominance. In this section, we reexamine the phenomenon of visual dominance (or capture) by looking at work on visual-haptic integration in size and shape perception and visual-proprioceptive integration in the perception of hand and arm position.

In a widely cited experiment, Rock and Victor (1964) examined visual and haptic contributions to the perception of two-dimensional shape. They presented an object that felt like a square but looked like a rectangle. Observers perceived it as a rectangle; in other words, it was perceived like it looked rather than like it felt. A similar dominance of vision over touch has been reported for shape and size judgments (Festinger et al., 1967; Fishkin, Pishkin, & Stahl, 1975; Gibson, 1933; McDonnell & Duffett, 1972; Miller, 1972; Power & Graham, 1976; Singer & Day, 1969). The experiments reported in this chapter, however, show that visual dominance for size judgments is not a general rule. Rather it is the byproduct of a more general principle: The nervous system weights information from the eye and hand according to their statistically reliabilities. Visual dominance probably occurs in size and shape estimation because the eye is better than the hand at those tasks. This argument was made previously by Welch and Warren (1980).

There is also a large literature on the perception of limb position from multiple sensory cues. For example, Hay et al. (1965) found that visually specified rather than proprioceptively specified hand position is the primary determinant of perceived hand position (see also Mon-Williams et al., 1997; Pavani et al., 2000; Pick, Warren, & Hay, 1969; Tastevin, 1937; van Beers, Sittig, & Denier van der Gon, 1996; Warren & Pick, 1970; Welch, Widawski, Harrington, & Warren, 1979). Is this observation of visual dominance also predicted by optimal integration because the eye is simply better at localizing than proprioception is? van Beers, Sittig, and Denier van der Gon (1999) examined the precision of vision-alone and proprioception-alone in the estimation of position in the horizontal plane. They showed that vision is more precise in distinguishing changes in horizontal position (left vs. right), whereas proprioception is more precise in distinguishing changes in depth (near vs. far). (We capitalized on the differing precision of vision in the frontal plane as opposed to in depth in the Gepshtein and Banks study reported earlier in this chapter.) The prisms used by Hay and colleagues (1965) displace the visually specified position horizontally relative to the proprioceptively specified position. Because vision is more precise than arm proprioception for horizontal displacements, MLE integration predicts that the combined percept should be determined primarily by vision. Again visual dominance seems to be a byproduct of the more general principle of weighting sensory information according to its statistical reliability. This idea was put to harder test by van Beers, Wolpert, and Haggard (2002). They introduced horizontal conflicts between vision and arm proprioception as well as in-depth conflicts. Optimal integration would predict greater visual weight in the horizontal case and greater proprioceptive weight in the in-depth case, and this is what they observed experimentally.

There are countless sensory measurements that occur in the nervous system, and we have only begun the investigation of the rules that underlie sensory integration. For the measurements studied thus far (object size, sensed hand position, combination of visual slant cues), it looks like the nervous system combines different sensory cues in a fashion that approaches statistical optimality.

WHEN SHOULD SIGNALS BE INTEGRATED AND WHEN SHOULD THEY NOT?

In intersensory tasks, the MLE integrator described here always uses information from both sensory systems, so the combined percept will always reflect both sources of information. Integration, however, is only appropriate if there is reason to believe that the environmental property in question will be estimated with greater precision from integrated signals. There are at least two cases in which integration is not sensible. The obvious one is the case in which the signals come from different objects in the scene. For example, one certainly does not want to integrate a visual size estimate with a haptic size estimate when the observer is looking at one object while feeling another. What evidence does the nervous system use in such cases to avoid integration or at least avoid usage of an integrated estimate? To our knowledge, there has been little research on this topic, but one can imagine that the estimates must be obtained from roughly the same region in space at roughly the same time to be integrated.

The other case in which it would be unwise to integrate is when the estimate from a sensor may be erroneous. For example, consider the situation in which the eye and hand agree on the location of an object, but the ear reports a very different location. In statistical estimation, an outlier is frequently judged to be misinformative, so it is cast out of the combined estimate. This removal of the effect of a clear outlier is referred to as *robustness*, and there is a large literature on when and how to exclude the influence of outliers (Landy et al., 1995). In robust estimation, the weights associated with different information sources are determined by more than the variances of the sensory estimators; they are also determined by the discrepancy between their estimates. The induced effect provides an example of robustness in human vision. In the induced effect, three cues signal surface slant—eye position, vertical disparity, and perspective—and one is cast out when it becomes quite discrepant from the other two (Banks & Backus, 1998). The perception of surface curvature provides another example of robustness. Three cues signal curvature—disparity, perspective, and accommodation—and again when one becomes quite discrepant from the other two, its influence becomes negligible (Buckley & Frisby, 1993). We found previously that observed JNDs are larger than predicted when the visual-haptic conflict is large, and the observed JNDs are much closer to prediction when the conflict is small. It would be interesting to know what happens as one makes the conflict larger and larger. For example, does robustness occur (meaning that one signal is vetoed) when observers become aware of the conflict between visual and haptic inputs?

NEURAL COMPUTATION OF OPTIMAL WEIGHTS

If the nervous system implements MLE integration, the weights must be proportional to the reciprocal variances of the probability distributions associated with the visual and haptic estimates of the environmental property in question (Eq. 2 and Fig. 6.1). Of course the variances change from one object property to the next (e.g., size, shape, or roughness) and from one situation to another (e.g., visual variance increases as the lighting is degraded). Does the nervous system need to calculate or learn the variances associated with sensory estimators for each property and situation to implement MLE integration? Although explicit calculation or learning might occur (Ernst, Banks, & Bülthoff, 2000; Jacobs & Fine, 1999), there are plausible schemes in which explicit calculation of variances or weights is unnecessary. Here we describe one such scheme. The purpose of presenting the neural scheme is to show that optimal integration could in principle be accomplished with a simple, plausible neural circuit.

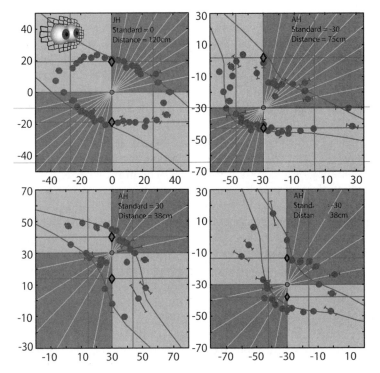

FIG. 6.16.   Oddity discrimination thresholds in the disparity-texture experiment. Data from two observers are shown for different conditions (labeled
in upper right of each panel). The red diamonds represent thresholds for the
texture estimator (separate monocular experiment). The red lines represent
the predicted thresholds from the single-cue estimators. The green curves
represent predicted thresholds from the combined estimator (Eq. 2); they
curve because the weights assigned to an optimal combined estimator vary
with texture-specified slant (Knill, 1998). The magenta points represent
thresholds in the various directions ($\Delta S_t / \Delta S_d$) tested in the oddity discrimination experiment. (See Color Panel I.)

Figure 6.17 depicts the basic scheme. There is a population of visual
and haptic sensors, each sensitive to a range of heights. The visual sensors
are on the left side of the schematic and the haptic on the right. The abscissae on the left and right represent different physical heights. Each sensor
has a tuning function that can be described by the height to which it responds best (the preferred height) and the range of heights to which it responds (the spread of the tuning function). The tuning functions of individual sensors are represented by the blue curves. We first describe the
model with no noise added to the sensor responses.

Consider first the visual sensors and visual stimulus. If a specific height
is presented visually (represented by the brightest bar on the abscissa),

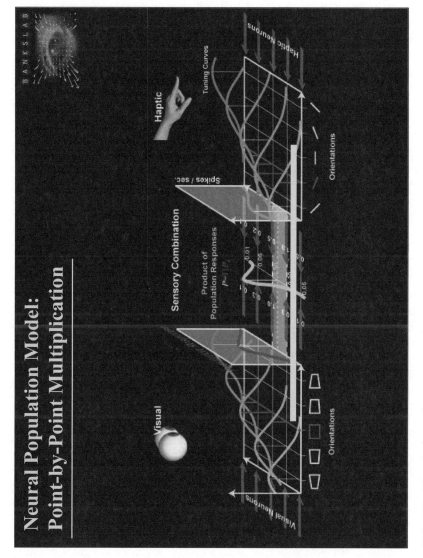

FIG. 6.17.   Neural scheme for integration of two sensory signals. See text for explanation. (See Color Panel J.)

each visual sensor responds according to its tuning function; the responses are represented by the red vertical bars. Obviously, the sensor whose preferred height is closest to the stimulus height will respond most vigorously. We have projected the distribution of responses across the visual sensors onto the vertical gray plane and represented this distribution with a red curve. The projected distribution of responses represents the population response of the visual sensors responsive to stimulus height. Its peak represents the most likely stimulus height according to the visual measurements, and its spread represents the uncertainty associated with the visual height estimate.

Now consider the haptic sensors and haptic stimulus. We assume for the moment that the tuning functions of the haptic sensors are less peaked (greater spread) than their visual counterparts because height is not signaled with the same precision haptically as it is visually. A specific height is presented haptically (represented by the brightest bar on the abscissa), and that height is somewhat less than the height presented visually. We have projected the distribution of responses across the haptic sensors onto the vertical gray plane on the haptic side and represented the distribution with a pink curve. The projected distribution represents the population response of the haptic sensors responsive to stimulus height. Its peak represents the most likely stimulus height according to the haptic measurements, and its spread represents the uncertainty associated with the haptic height estimate. Note that the haptic distribution has greater variance than the visual distribution (because of the assumption about the tuning functions) and its peak occurs at a smaller height than the visual peak (because the haptic stimulus height was less than the visual stimulus height).

The MLE integration rule described by Eq. 2 is a special case of Bayes' Rule:

$$P(S \mid I) \propto P(I \mid S)P(S)$$

where S is the environmental property being estimated and I is the sensory measurement. The right side of Bayes' formula contains the likelihood function (the probability density of measurements given a particular environmental property) and the prior (the probability of a particular environmental property being observed). The left side is the posterior probability; it is the probability of environmental properties given the sensory measurement. In the cases considered in this chapter, one would choose the value of the environmental property at peak of the posterior because it is the most likely value given the sensory measurements.

In the two-cue case shown in Fig. 6.17, Bayes' Rule becomes:

$$P(S \mid I) \propto P(I_V \mid S)P(I_H \mid S)P(S)$$

where I_V and I_H represent the visual and haptic measurements. We assume that the prior $P(S)$ is uniform over the range of environmental properties considered (although it would be straightforward to include nonuniform priors), so $P(S) = 1$. Thus, incorporating the assumption about the prior and the fact that the peak of the posterior is the best guess concerning the value of the environmental property, we simply need to find the maximum of:

$$P(I_V \mid S)P(I_H \mid S).$$

Thus, if we can create distributions like the likelihood functions $P(I_V \mid S)$ and $P(I_H \mid S)$, the product of the two distributions yields the desired outcome. In the neural scheme of Fig. 6.17, we set the widths of the tuning functions such that the peaks and spreads of the population distributions are the same as the means and variances of the likelihood functions. The multiplication of the two sensor distributions is a point-by-point multiplication, where the two populations are in registration according to the stimulus property being estimated. (That is, the visual and haptic sensors are linked such that the visual sensor preferring a given height multiplies its response with the haptic sensor that responds preferring the same height.) The result of the point-by-point multiplication is the yellow distribution in the middle of the figure. This distribution has the same mean and variance as the posterior distribution derived from application of the MLE integration rule. In the neural scheme's final step, the mean of the combined distribution is estimated and that becomes the estimate of the stimulus height. Notice that the neural scheme is entirely feed-forward, and there is no explicit calculation of visual and haptic weights.

The model behaves very much like the MLE integration rule. When the variance associated with the haptic height estimate is greater than the variance associated with the visual estimate, the combined estimate is closer to the visual. When the variances associated with the haptic and visual estimates are equal, the combined estimate is the average of the visual and haptic estimates alone.

Real neurons respond variably to a constant stimulus, so to examine the consequence of response variability, we added noise to the individual sensor neural responses. The response variances of neurons in visual cortex (area V1) are proportional to their firing rates (Peña & Konishi, 2001), and we used this assumption for all the sensors in this model. With added noise, the distribution associated with the combined estimate becomes noisy, so the peak is not necessarily clearly defined. We, therefore, added a step in which a Gaussian distribution is fit to the noisy combined distribution, and the mean of the best-fitting Gaussian becomes the model's estimate of the stimulus property under examination.

Without noise, the neural scheme described here can be made to behave the same as the MLE integration rule. The combined estimate is shifted toward the less variable of the two sensory inputs, and the variance of the combined estimate is generally less than the variance of either sense alone. With added sensor noise, the scheme continues to behave like MLE integration until the conflict between sensor inputs becomes large (i.e., visual height is quite different from haptic height). With large conflicts, the model's combined estimate becomes quite noisy and often quite dissimilar from that given by the MLE rule. In such cases, the sensor distributions (visual and/or haptic) are less noisy. In this case, the better strategy is to use the less variable of the two sensor distributions as the estimate. This behavior is called *robustness* in the statistical literature.

We have shown that one can in principle construct a neural scheme for sensor integration in which the sensor variances (and therefore the weights) do not have to be explicitly calculated: The behavior of an MLE integrator could in principle be achieved through multiplicative interactions among populations of sensors.

ACKNOWLEDGMENTS

Collaborators on various parts of the work described in this chapter include Marc Ernst, Mike Landy, Jamie Hillis, and Sergei Gepshtein. Financial support provided by NIH, AFOSR, NSF, and Silicon Graphics.

REFERENCES

Backus, B. T. (2002). In T. G. Dietterich, S. Becker, & Z. Ghahramani (Eds.), *Neural information processing systems*. Cambridge, MA: MIT Press.

Backus, B. T., Banks, M. S., van Ee, R., & Crowell, J. A. (1999). Horizontal and vertical disparity, eye position, and stereoscopic slant perception. *Vision Research, 39*, 1143–1170.

Banks, M. S., & Backus, B. T. (1998). Extra-retinal and perspective cues cause the small range of the induced effect. *Vision Research, 38*, 187–194.

Banks, M., Hooge, T. C., & Backus, B. (2001). Perceiving slant about a horizontal axis from stereopsis. *Journal of Vision, 1*, 55–79.

Brenner, E., & van Damme, W. J. M. (1999). Perceived distance, shape and size. *Vision Research, 39*, 975–986.

Buckley, D., & Frisby, J. P. (1993). Interaction of stereo, texture and outline cues in the shape perception of three-dimensional ridges. *Vision Research, 33*, 919–933.

Clark, J. J., & Yuille, A. L. (1990). *Data fusion for sensory information processing systems*. Boston: Kluwer Academic Publishers.

de Berg, M., van Kreveld, M., Overmars, M., & Schwarzkopf, O. (2000). *Computational geometry: Algorithms and applications*. New York: Springer-Verlag.

Ernst, M. O., & Banks, M. S. (2002). Humans integrate visual and haptic information in a statistically optimal fashion. *Nature, 415*, 429–433.

Ernst, M. O., Banks, M. S., & Bülthoff, H. H. (2000). Touch can change visual slant perception. *Nature Neuroscience, 3,* 69–73.

Festinger, L., Burnham, C. A., Ono, H., & Bamber, D. (1967). Efference and the conscious experience of perception. *Journal of Experimental Psychology Monograph, 74*(4).

Fishkin, S. M., Pishkin, V., & Stahl, M. L. (1975). Factors involved in visual capture. *Perceptual and Motor Skills, 40,* 427–434.

Gepshtein, S., & Banks, M. S. (2003). Viewing geometry determines how vision and haptics combine in size perception. *Current Biology, 13,* 483–488.

Ghahramani, Z., Wolpert, D. M., & Jordan, M. I. (1997). In P. G. Morasso & V. Sanguineti (Eds.), *Self-organization, computational maps, and motor control* (pp. 117–147). Amsterdam, North-Holland: Elsevier Press.

Gibson, J. J. (1933). Adaptation, after-effect, and contrast in the perception of curved lines. *Journal of Experimental Psychology, 16,* 1–31.

Hay, J. C., Pick, H. L., Jr., & Ikeda, K. (1965). Visual capture produced by prism spectacles. *Psychonomic Science, 2,* 215–216.

Heller, M. A. (1983). Haptic dominance in form perception with blurred vision. *Perception, 12,* 607–613.

Hillis, J. M., Ernst, M. O., Banks, M. S., & Landy, M. S. (2002). Combining sensory information: Mandatory fusion within, but not between, senses. *Science, 298,* 1627–1630.

Jacobs, R. A., & Fine, I. (1999). Experience-dependent integration of texture and motion cues in depth. *Vision Research, 39,* 4062–4075.

Johnston, E. B., Cumming, B. G., & Landy, M. S. (1994). Integration of stereopsis and motion shape cues. *Vision Research, 34,* 2259–2275.

Knill, D. C. (1998). Discrimination of planar surface slant from texture: Human and ideal observers compared. *Vision Research, 38,* 1683–1697.

Landy, M. S., & Kojima, H. (2001). Ideal cue combination for localizing texture-defined edges. *Journal of the Optical Society of America, 18,* 2307–2320.

Landy, M. S., Maloney, L. T., Johnston, E. B., & Young, M. (1995). Measurement and modeling of depth cue combination: In defense of weak fusion. *Vision Research, 35,* 389–412.

Lederman, S. J., & Abbott, S. G. (1981). Texture perception: Studies of intersensory organization using a discrepancy paradigm, and visual versus tactual psychophysics. *Journal of Experimental Psychology.: Human Perception & Performance, 7,* 902–915.

McDonnell, P. M., & Duffett, J. (1972). Vision and touch: A reconsideration of conflict between the two senses. *Canadian Journal of Psychology, 26,* 171–180.

McKee, S. P., Levi, D. M., & Bowne, S. F. (1990). The imprecision of stereopsis. *Vision Research, 30,* 1763–1779.

Miller, E. A. (1972). Interaction of vision and touch in conflict and nonconflict form perception tasks. *Journal of Experimental Psychology, 96,* 114–123.

Mon-Williams, M., Wann, J. P., Jenkinson, M., & Rushton, K. (1997). Synaesthesia in the normal limb. *Proceedings of the Royal Society of London, B264,* 1007–1010.

Oruc, I., Maloney, L. T., & Landy, M. S. (2003). Weighted linear cue combination with possibly correlated error. *Vision Research, 43,* 2451–2468.

Pavani, F., Spence, C., & Driver, J. (2000). Visual capture of touch: Out-of-the-body experiences with rubber gloves. *Psychological Science, 11,* 353–359.

Peña, J. L., & Konishi, M. (2001). Auditory spatial receptive fields created by multiplication. *Science, 292,* 249–252.

Pick, H. L., Warren, D. H., & Hay, J. C. (1969). Sensory conflicts in judgments of spatial direction. *Perception and Psychophysics, 6,* 203–205.

Power, R. P. (1980). The dominance of touch by vision: Sometimes incomplete. *Perception, 9,* 457–466.

Power, R. P., & Graham, A. (1976). Dominance of touch by vision: Generalization of the hypothesis to a tactually experienced population. *Perception, 5,* 161–166.

Richards, W. (1979). Quantifying sensory channels: generalizing colorimetry to orientation and texture, touch and tones. *Sensory Processes, 3*, 207–229.

Rock, I., & Victor, J. (1964). Vision and touch: An experimentally created conflict between the two senses. *Science, 143*, 594–596.

Rogers, B. J., & Bradshaw, M. F. (1995). Disparity scaling and the perception of frontoparallel surfaces. *Perception, 24*, 155–179.

Schrater, P. R., & Kersten, D. (2000). How optimal depth cue integration depends on the task. *International Journal of Computer Vision, 40*, 71–89.

Singer, G., & Day, R. H. (1969). Visual capture of haptically judged depth. *Perception & Psychophysics, 5*, 315–316.

Stratton, G. M. (1987). Vision without inversion of the retinal image. *Psychological Reviews, 4*, 341–360.

Tastevin, J. (1937). En partant de l'experience d'Aristote. *L'Encephale, 1*, 57–84.

van Beers, R. J., Sittig, A. C., & Denier van der Gon, J. J. (1999). Integration of proprioceptive and visual position-information: An experimentally supported model. *Experimental Journal of Neurophysiology, 81*, 1355–1364.

van Beers, R. J., Wolpert, D. M., & Haggard, P. (2002). When feeling is more important than seeing in sensorimotor adaptation. *Current Biology, 12*, 834–837.

Warren, D. H., & Pick, H. L. (1970). Intermodality relations in localization in blind and sighted people. *Perceptions and Psychophysics, 8*, 430–432.

Warren, D. H., & Rossano, M. J. (1991). In M. A. Heller & W. Schiff (Eds.), *The psychology of touch* (pp. 119–137). Hillsdale, NJ: Lawrence Erlbaum Associates.

Welch, R. B., & Warren, D. H. (1980). Immediate perceptual response to intersensory discrepancy. *Psychological Bulletin, 88*, 638–667.

Welch, R. B., Widawski, M. H., Harrington, J., & Warren, D. H. (1979). An examination of the relationship between visual capture and prism adaptation. *Perception and Psychophysics, 25*, 126–132.

Yuille, A. L., & Bülthoff, H. H. (1996). Bayesian decision theory and psychophysics. In D. C. Knill & W. Richards (Eds.), *Perception as Bayesian inference* (pp. 123–161). Cambridge, England: Cambridge University Press.

7

▼ ▼ ▼ ▼ ▼ ▼ ▼

Stats Modules for Babies! Computing Conditional Probabilities and Weighted Variance With Rapid Sampling: A Discussion of the Chapters by Aslin and Banks

Emily W. Bushnell
Tufts University

INTRODUCTION

Although it may be unconventional, I am compelled to start my discussion by noting how delightful and appropriate it is for a Minnesota Symposium to be declared in honor of Herb and Anne Pick. What special people! They are renowned and insightful researchers, demanding and invested teachers, and also caring and sensible individuals. They have served the field generously and the Institute of Child Development enormously, and they have played important roles in shaping the careers of so many currently active figures in perception and developmental psychology. For a lucky subset of these, Herb and Anne have furthermore been like family, providing nurturance, support, and memorably good times. The meeting on which this volume is based was truly a love fest as well as a stimulating and serious scientific meeting.

Among those affected by Herb and Anne are myself (thank you!) and my long-time friends, Dick Aslin and Marty Banks, whose presentations I have been asked to discuss. This is an exciting challenge, as characteristically Aslin and Banks have put forth elegant and impressive ideas, fortified by elegant and impressive data. What each of them has done, in a nutshell, is to identify a computational mechanism that could potentially solve a difficult and long-standing problem in perception or perceptual development. The problem Aslin addresses is no less than that which prompted the whole Gestalt school of psychology—namely, how does a naive perceiver organize the visual scene or other perceptual mélange into meaningful units such as objects or words. His solution is for the perceiver to group elements according to their coherence across multiple instances, and this coherence is revealed by the measure of *conditional probability*— that is, how often does this element occur in the presence of that element, and how often does it occur alone?

The issue Banks addresses has to do with multiple sources of information or "redundant cues," as is often the case in perception. Consider the plethora of cues to depth, for example. To quote Yonas and Granrud (1985a), "God must have loved depth cues, for He made so many of them" (p. 45). There are good reasons to have multiple sources of critical information, of course, but an attendant problem is that they do not always agree with one another. There is random noise (neural and otherwise) within every perceptual source system for one thing, and any two of these may be differentially vulnerable to various biases and environmental degradations for another. Thus, perceivers must have ways to adjudicate instances of conflicting information from redundant cues and decide what source to rely on and to what extent. Bank's solution for this, like Aslin's for the grouping problem, involves a statistical concept. He proposes that perceivers effectively engage in *maximum-likelihood estimation*; they utilize all the different sources of information, but give greater weight to those that are more reliable in the long run, as indicated by their arithmetic variance around the mean.

Both of these computational solutions have immediate appeal in that they are empirically testable and broadly applicable. In the work he presented, Aslin has already shown that the conditional probability mechanism can apply to parsing visual scenes into objects, segmenting sound streams into words, and automatizing response sequences into smooth motor acts. I suppose that using conditional probabilities could furthermore account for children's coming to appreciate occluded objects, causal relations, the distinction between animate and inanimate entities, and other such cognitive achievements. Indeed some of the neural net models designed to simulate the acquisition of these milestones basically amount to conditional probability counters (cf. Mareschal, Plunkett, & Harris, 1995; Munakata, 1998; Munakata, McClelland, Johnson, & Siegler, 1997; Rogers & Griffin, 2002). Maratsos and Chalkley (1981; see also Maratsos, 1988) argued that even abstract grammatical categories such as *noun* and *verb* could conceivably be built up from detecting statistical patterns of words' co-occurrence privileges. Thus, one general "stats module" for computing rates of co-occurrence across multiple instances might be all a baby really needs, in place of all the various domain-specific modules they have been granted lately (cf. Leslie, 1994; Spelke, 1994; Tomasello, 1999, chap. 2; Wynn, 1998).

Banks' solution of weighting information according to its variance is likewise both testable and broadly applicable. In the work he described, Banks verified the mechanism in an instance where the sources of conflicting information are both visual (stereoscopic and texture gradient information for slant) and in another where one source is visual and the other haptic (stereoscopic and hand posture information for size). Obviously, his model could easily be extended to various other visual-visual and visual-haptic conflicts, for example, involving stereoscopic and motion parallax information for slant or visual and haptic information for surface texture. It could also be applied to situations where one cue is visual and the other auditory, as with information for localizing things in space or identifying tempos (e.g., flicker vs. pulse rate). Finally, in keeping with the Symposium's focus on action, Banks' model could be extended to visual-motor situations, too. I think here, for example, of Herb Pick's work with Rieser and others (Rieser, Pick, Ashmead, & Garing, 1995), in which they had subjects walk on a treadmill towed by a garden tractor to decouple their visual flow information for ground speed from kinesthetic feedback information for the same parameter. In fact the variance-weighting mechanism could conceivably work with any pair of perceivable dimensions, provided that each is perceived along a continuum (rather than dichotomously) so that its variance is computable and meaningful.

Given that they can apply across a wide range of phenomena and have received some support in the lab, the next thing to consider is whether Aslin's and Banks' computational mechanisms have any ecological validity. Are these statistical operations feasible under real-world conditions? Is the data they require likely to be available to ordinary perceivers? Do these mechanisms fit with what we already know about perception, development, and perceptual development? In what follows, I address these concerns, first with regard to Aslin's conditional probability scheme and then with regard to Banks' weighted variance. My goal is not so much to critique these ideas as to raise interesting questions about them, place them in a bigger context, and provide some thoughts as to where one could go next with them.

COMMENTS ON ASLIN'S CONDITIONAL PROBABILITY SCHEME

A central feature of Aslin's mechanism is that it requires repeated exposure to the unit in question. For the conditional probability statistic to work, the infant must see a particular configuration of elements or hear a particular sequence of syllables multiple times, and not just multiple times, but multiple times embedded in different contexts. Aslin is explicit about this in laying out his model—"statistics cannot be extracted from a single image; rather, the observer must sample many images to determine which co-occurrences are consistently present and which are merely coincidences." Accordingly, the training trials in both his visual and auditory work involve just this sort of experience.

Its demand for multiple exposures immediately struck me as a potential problem for Aslin's mechanism because human perceivers and even babies are frequently able to learn things with very limited experience. In particular, with both objects and words, infants routinely exhibit what has been called *fast mapping*. For example, researchers have shown novel objects to 9- to 18-month-old infants and either labeled them with a novel word or modeled a novel action with them (cf. Baldwin et al., 1996; Dunham, Dunham, & Curwin, 1993; Meltzoff, 1988a, 1988b; Tomasello, Strosberg, & Akhtar, 1996). The babies were then brought back a few minutes later or sometimes a few days or weeks later, and they remembered what these objects are called and what to do with them. These results not only demonstrate that infants were able to map a word or action to an object after just a few pairings, they also presuppose that the infants successfully segregated the new object from the scene and the new word from the sound stream in just the one training experience. How can we accept Aslin's conditional probability mechanism in the face of this kind of rapid, one-trial learning?

One response to this challenge has been mentioned by Aslin already, and that is the operation of certain biases or soft constraints such as those specified by Gestalt grouping principles. It is possible that these define infants' first guesses as to what are objects in a scene or words in a sentence, and they may often be sufficient to permit rapid and appropriate recognition of new units. Multiple exposures and statistical learning may be needed only when objects or words are inconsistent with these constraints. As an example, in looking at Aslin's four base pairs reproduced in Fig. 7.1, it seems to me that the uppermost one is the most objectlike. This is probably because its two elements are each vertically symmetrical, and furthermore their axes of symmetry are perfectly aligned with one another, thus invoking the Gestalt principles of good form (symmetry) and good continuation. I wonder whether the infants learned this base pair more easily or more robustly than they learned the others, or whether infants would have learned it as readily if the elements were arranged in one of the alternative configurations shown in Fig. 7.2. These are empirical questions, of course, and Aslin's paradigm could easily be adapted to explore them. Thus, somewhat ironically, his method relying on multiple exposures could be used to help identify biases that constrain naive object perception and obviate the demand for multiple exposures.

Another response to the challenge of fast mapping is a matter of statistics itself. Specifically, at least in a closed and stable system, every object or

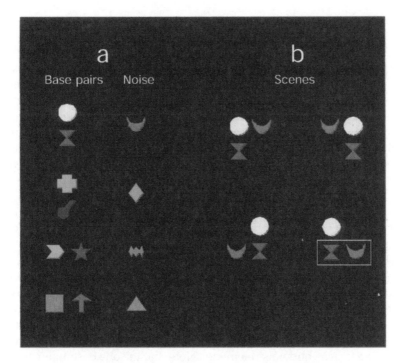

FIG. 7.1.   A reproduction of Fig. 5.3 from Aslin's chapter 5, illustrating the base pairs he used with infants on the left and an assortment of the scenes involving one base pair on the right.

word learned laboriously by the conditional probability mechanism operating over multiple exposures would then reduce the computational load for subsequently learning other new objects or words. For example, given a scene of say 20 or 30 visual elements, it is true that a huge number of pairings, triplets, quadruplets, and so on are mathematically possible. This is the organizational problem Aslin set out to address in the first

FIG. 7.2.   Possible alternative configurations of the components in one of Aslin's base pairs. These are less compatible with Gestalt principles than the configuration Aslin used; would infants have learned them as readily as they learned the one in Aslin's experiment?

place. Yet if an infant already recognizes certain groupings from past experience—sees these few elements here and those few elements there as familiar objects—then the scene becomes far less of a blooming and buzzing confusion. Likewise, if certain parts of a sound stream already stand out as familiar words, the remaining parts become that much easier to parse. In both cases, the number of possible combinations involving just the unknown elements is much smaller than the number involving all of them, and the task of computing conditional probabilities is way more manageable. By this reasoning, statistical learning takes on a sort of "more is less" character over time, and we would expect the acquisition of new object representations and new words to show an accelerating developmental function as the computation load decreases with accruing knowledge. Moreover, fast mapping for a new object or word could occur whenever an infant was already familiar with most of the other objects or words in the situation.

The primary resolution to the problem between Aslin's model and fast mapping, however, is to realize that, in what is typically considered a single trial or exposure, there may actually be many perceptual instances for the conditional probability mechanism to count. This is explicitly the case for scenes that contain many copies of a particular kind of object. For example, consider the scene displayed in Fig. 7.3, which I constructed out of Aslin's base pairs and noise elements. Note that the one base-pair configuration (sphere above hour glass) occurs many times over and in a variety of different immediate contexts. In other words, this single complex image simultaneously contains the same information as Aslin gave his infant subjects across 80 separate smaller scenes presented successively over the course of nearly 3 minutes. Thus, the larger simultaneous scene permits extracting the same structure as the series of smaller ones does—namely, that the sphere and hour glass consistently co-occur and may henceforth be represented as an individual object. This example may seem contrived and unnatural, but just imagine that Fig. 7.3 represents a Wisconsin pasture full of cows, a parking lot full of cars, a room crowded with people, a field of flowers, a shelf stocked with bottles, and so on. Natural and manmade objects alike often come in bunches, and this implies that conditional probabilities pointing to them could sometimes be computed over a single scene.

Moreover, even in the conventional case with a single token of a new object, there may actually be many perceptual instances for the conditional probability mechanism to count. This is because perceivers are not passive; as this volume celebrates, they are usually acting and moving through space while they perceive. Such activities generate shifts in the visual image, which may be important for segregating objects. For example, consider the subset of artificial scenes from Aslin's infant experiments

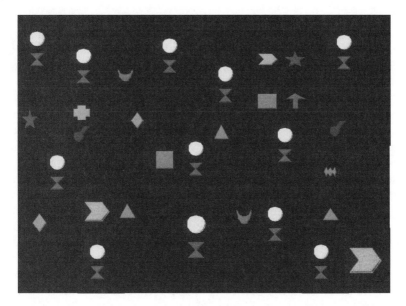

FIG. 7.3. A complex scene containing multiple copies of a particular base pair (the sphere with hour glass) in various local contexts. See text for details.

shown on the right in Fig. 7.1. The top two scenes exhibit just the kind of variation one would experience if she were moving across the scene from right to left while looking at the object—that is, the base pair—against a background that included the noise element. Indeed one could think of these two scenes as freeze frames from the motion parallax or optic flow information a baby might get as she was being rocked back and forth (from left to right) in a stroller or swing. Similarly, the upper right and lower left two scenes could represent freeze frames from the parallax or flow information a baby might get if she were bouncing up and down in a jolly-jumper (cf. Goldfield, Kay, & Warren, 1993) or with a rhythmic stereotypy (cf. Thelen, 1979, 1981). Finally, the four scenes in Fig. 7.1 taken all together could represent freeze frames from the visual information an infant would get if she were holding the object represented by the base pair and looking at it while she waved it around against the background, as babies do. Thus, in brief and commonplace activities—rocking, bouncing, and waving things around—infants effectively are provided or provide themselves with variable stimulus streams just like the ones Aslin showed were sufficient to permit segregating base pairs from noise. During these routine events, the discrete parts of any fixated object maintain their spatial configuration with respect to one another, but their positions with respect to other separate items in the scene are shifting constantly.

The movement-dependent circumstances just portrayed are not much different from descriptions of Gestalt "common fate" or Gibsonian "invariance" in the midst of flux, and certainly both these schools deemed such information vital for object perception. Aslin's model surpasses these earlier concepts with the quantitative precision it offers, but if it is to apply to the same circumstances, we must add the proviso of *rapid sampling*. That is, for the conditional probability mechanism to capture the environmental structure available in an episode of bouncing, say, it would have to register a new instance many times within the episode, with each new perspective on the scene perhaps, rather than wait for a wholesale change of scene. We might imagine that the mechanism snaps a freeze frame and updates its counters accordingly at the end of each movement unit, for example, and not just when the baby is carried to a different venue or wakes up to a new day. The idea of sampling with each movement unit ties perception to action quite neatly, and it yields a sampling rate that actually approximates the rate of stimulus change in Aslin's empirical procedure. Most important, under the conditions of a rapid sampling rate coupled with a moving, behaving observer, multiple exposures in differing contexts would accumulate in minutes, hence meaningful conditional probabilities could be computed within the confines of what we ordinarily think of as a single experience or trial. Thus, Aslin's model is perfectly compatible with fast mapping and one-trial learning, and what initially seemed like a red flag is really just a red herring.

The specter of many samples being taken as an infant bounces in a jumper seat or crawls toward a fixated object raises an additional question regarding the conditional probability mechanism, however, and that is, how much error can it tolerate? In Aslin's experiments with infants, the conditional probability between the two elements of a base pair was perfect (1.0), but in the real world, freeze frames from a perceiver's current viewpoint will sometimes betray the real structure of the environment. For example, certain parts of an object might be occluded by a nearer object or surface, in which case the visible parts would be registered as occurring *without* the occluded parts in a sample taken at that moment. Similarly in speech, the syllables making up a word might occasionally be heard in isolation from one another, as when a speaker is interrupted in mid-stream or when a loud sound drowns out parts of an utterance. A naive mechanism would count these orphans just as it counts any other instances, so over time an object or a word's coherence would be less than perfect. How are objects and words perceived under these circumstances? How close to perfect does co-occurrence have to be for units to be recognized?

Aslin actually explored this issue in some of his studies with adult perceivers. With a word segmentation task, Saffran, Newport, and Aslin

(1996) found that people were able to learn artificial words whose elements had a conditional probability as low as .31, in comparison with conditional probabilities of .1 and .2 for nonword elements. Similarly, with a motor-learning task, Hunt and Aslin (2001) found that people were sensitive to sequences with conditional probabilities of .5 in comparison with conditional probabilities of .17 for the individual elements. Thus, perfect coherence is by no means necessary for a unit to stand out among otherwise random compositions of elements. Indeed in a somewhat related task, Newsome and Pare (1988) found that monkeys were able to detect a direction of motion in random dot displays when the movements of just 2% to 3% of the dots were correlated. It seems that the perceptual system may be responsive to very subtle, graded differences in predictability among elements.

However, although learning can occur with less than perfect predictability, the degree of predictability might very well affect the ease or rate of learning. For example, although performance was above chance in all cases, the participants in the Saffran et al. (1996) research performed better with words whose conditional probabilities were high than with words whose were low. This consideration also might explain why Aslin finds learning motor sequences to be more protracted than recognizing words and objects ("days rather than minutes"). In motor learning, every error or misstep made early on would be duly recorded as a particular succession of elements by the conditional probability mechanism, and this would dilute the distinctiveness of the proper sequence. These issues—how much noncorrelation can the mechanism tolerate, how does this parameter affect ease of learning, are the thresholds for this parameter different for infants versus adults or different for different kinds of information, and so on—are all eminently testable with Aslin's paradigm. We can look forward to learning more from statistical learning in times to come.

COMMENTS ON BANKS' WEIGHTED VARIANCE MODEL

This matter of how the perceptual system responds to error provides a nice segue into my comments on Banks' presentation because the sole purpose of his proposed mechanism is to cope with perceptual imperfection. In particular, the maximum-likelihood estimation (MLE) procedure Banks focuses on is devoted to adjudicating the different values returned by separate sources of information about an object. Such discrepancies are inevitable on account of noise in the nervous system, degradations in the environment, and so forth, which render perceptual assessments never more than just approximations of the distal stimulus' true physical state. Banks starts by showing mathematically that in such multiple-source situations, an estimate combining two sources of information will always be better (less uncertain) than either of the estimates provided by the individual sources, even if one source is routinely more reliable than the other. I do not profess to follow all the equations, but I see this point intuitively. Because each source always provides only an estimate, the value returned by each source will err to either side (too big or too small) of the true value on half of the occasions (assuming normality, no bias, etc.). Hence, on half of the occasions, the estimates from the two sources will both err in the same direction (i.e., both too big or both too small; see Fig. 7.4, short dashed and solid arrows). In such cases, an average of the two values would always be closer to the true value than one of the individual estimates and farther from it than the other. However, on the other half of the occasions, the estimates from the two sources will err in opposite directions from the true value (one too big and the other too small; see Fig. 7.4, long dashed and solid arrows). In these instances, an average of the two will often be closer to the true value than either of the individual estimates, and therein lies the benefit of combining them as a general rule. For any given occasion, the nervous system of course does not know whether the two estimates lie on the same or opposite sides of the true value, but

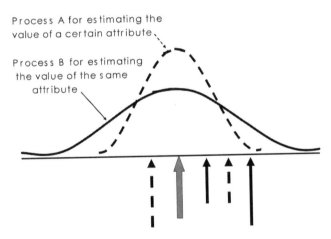

FIG. 7.4.   An illustration of the advantage of using both sources of information about a sensory value even when one source is more reliable (less variable) than the other. The two curves represent the populations of estimates that might be returned by two sensory processes when they are confronted with a stimulus whose true value is represented by the peak of each curve and marked on the abscissa by the stippled arrow. The short arrows indicate an instance such as would occur 50% of the time, where both estimates err in the same direction from the true value. The long arrows indicate an instance such as would occur the other 50% of the time, where the two estimates err in opposite directions from the true value, and hence their average could be closer to the true value than either individual estimate.

where combining them will lead to a more accurate reading on more than half the occasions, that is the way to go.

Banks' next point is that, although it is good to utilize both values in a two-source situation, it is nevertheless optimal to give more weight to the value provided by the more reliable (less variable) source. He establishes this point mathematically, and again it makes sense intuitively. Banks then shows empirically that human perceivers seem to perform exactly according to this strategy. In the first experiment he described, observers' judgments of a conflict stimulus with one size given visually and a different size given haptically were biased toward the visual value, in keeping with the fact that visual discrimination was finer than haptic with these stimuli. However, when visual noise was artificially added to the situation, observers shifted their judgments more toward the value given haptically. Similarly, in the second experiment using the same conflict paradigm, observers' judgments were biased toward the visual value when their viewing angle permitted good visual discrimination and toward the haptic value when it did not. Thus, not only did observers utilize both (conflicting) sources of information in their judgments, as MLE theory would have it, but furthermore their procedure for integrating the two values was fluid, adjusting to give more weight to whichever value was more reliable in a particular experimental condition.

Indeed as Banks also notes, one of the most intriguing aspects of his work is that subjects seemed to weight the different sources of information on a trial-by-trial basis. This is most obvious in the first experiment (i.e., Ernst & Banks, 2002), where the trials with visual noise were randomly interspersed with trials without noise. The results were that subjects weighted the haptic information more heavily on trials with visual noise. However, because subjects never knew what kind of trial was coming next, they must have somehow assessed the reliability (variance) of the visual and haptic estimators online within each individual trial. Yet these trials were only a second long. How can one assess variance from what would appear to be a single sample?

Toward the end of his chapter, Banks outlines a neural scheme that could permit online MLE integration. His scheme does not require any explicit calculation of variance or weights, but it does require specific links between corresponding visual and haptic sensors, which links would have to be explained. I can imagine another neural scheme for online integration, which would not require such cross-sensor links, but which would involve more explicit computation of each sensor's variance. My idea relies on rapid sampling again. I suggested for Aslin's mechanism that a single experience with an object may actually consist of many perceptual samples, and now I suggest for Banks' mechanism that a single perceptual instance (*trial* in his paradigm) may actually consist of many neural samples. As Banks notes, when a particular stimulus is confronted, there is a distribution of responses across a population of neurons tuned to particular values along the dimension in question (e.g., height, slant, size); see Fig. 6.18, the vertical gray plane with a red curve. Typically, the peak of this distribution is taken as a read-out value representing the observer's perception; sensory adaptation experiments verify this notion (cf. Blakemore & Sutton, 1969; Sutherland, 1961).

Now suppose that in the brief time a subject looks at and/or holds a stimulus, a whole succession of read-outs from the relevant population(s) of neurons takes place, say one read-out every 20th or 30th of a second. Neuropsychologists use sampling rates of 100 Hz or more when they record ERPs (e.g., Nelson & Collins, 1991; Nelson, Henschel, & Collins, 1993), so this time frame for brain activity is not preposterous. The peaks of these multiple samples will not be identical even as the person continues to look at or grip the same stimulus on account of spontaneous fluctuations in the nervous system, jitter in the motor system, and, of course, the degree of noise in the stimulus situation as well. That is, contrary to Banks' statement, "the sensor whose preferred height is closest to the stimulus height will" *NOT always* (my addition) "respond most vigorously." Instead the peak responses will fluctuate around the stimulus' true height in something like a normal distribution; this is the issue of perceptual error that Banks introduces in the first place. However, over a short exposure to a stimulus (e.g., a 1-sec trial), the perceiver would get some 20 to 30 different read-outs for the stimulus' height, slant, or whatever—enough to generate a frequency distribution and effectively convey both a mean value and the degree of variance in the perceptual process on that occasion. This dynamic generation of a frequency distribution is illustrated in Fig. 7.5. A similar frequency distribution and neural index of variability would also be generated for a second source of information if one were simultaneously present, as when one looks at and holds an object at the same time. Thus, the proposed rapid neural sampling, at one or two orders of magnitude faster even than the rapid perceptual sampling discussed for Aslin's model, could effectively provide the variances perceivers need to engage in MLE integration of multiple sources, and it could do so on the (experimental) trial-by-trial basis implied by Banks' data.

Either Banks' point-by-point multiplication scheme or the rapid neural sampling idea just discussed could plausibly mediate MLE integration on the per-trial basis that Ernst and Banks' data implicate. However, these data notwithstanding, I do question just how encapsulated the integration process can really be. Widespread perceptual learning and attentional priming phenomena lead one to suspect that there must be some across-trial effects that interact somehow with the basic within-trial variance-weighting mechanism. Consider, for example, the phenomenon of per-

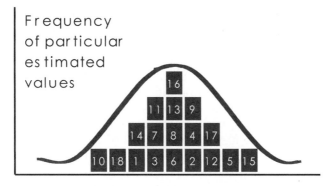

FIG. 7.5. An illustration of how rapid neural sampling could provide an estimate of variance, such as is needed for MLE cue integration. Each black box represents a discrete read-out corresponding to the momentary peak value of the responses of neurons sensitive to the attribute in question (e.g., orientation, brightness, disparity, etc.). During exposure to a particular stimulus, such read-outs are taken every 20th or 30th of a second and are different due to noise of various sorts. The multiple black boxes in the figure indicate the multiple read-outs taken over the course of about 1 second, with the number in each box indicating its order of occurrence. The figure shows that within just a brief exposure, enough read-outs are taken to generate an approximately normal distribution, whose mean would indicate the observer's conscious perception and whose variance would be available for MLE integration with the mean and variance of another process also estimating the same attribute.

ceptual adaptation, such as occurs when observers don prism goggles as in some of Herb Pick's early research. With laterally displacing prisms on, the variance of the visual process for perceiving spatial direction is not affected, but the mean value around which it is centered shifts to one side with respect to the proprioceptive process for perceiving spatial direction. Because the visual sense of direction is more precise than the proprioceptive sense, if the perceiver weighs the two sources of information as Banks proposes, the estimate of a target's location should be pulled toward the manipulated visual value. Indeed this is just what happens— subjects throw at or point to a target and miss by nearly the amount of the prism displacement (Hay, Pick, & Ikeda, 1965). However, this missing happens *only* on the early trials. Over repeated trials, and if the perceiver gets feedback or has some sort of spatial anchor, the two senses of direction slowly re-align and the person's throwing, pointing, and other sensorimotor behaviors ultimately become effective again (Hay & Pick, 1966; Pick, Hay, & Willoughby, 1966). Banks' model of within-trial integration cannot account for this gradual recalibration with instances of constant error between two sources. It seems that the visual and proprioceptive estimates of spatial direction must interact across trials as well as within trials to effect such adaptation. Perhaps the miss itself or the registration of a certain sized discrepancy between the individual estimates of the two sources of information sets some additional adjustment process in motion, as in Banks' discussion of "robustness." In this light, it is noteworthy that perceptual adaptation occurs even when the two sources of information are both visual (e.g., with various pairings of visual cues for depth; cf. Wallach, Frey, & Bode, 1972; Wallach & O'Leary, 1979). Contrary to Banks' conclusion of mandatory intrasensory fusion, this implies that even within vision, single-cue estimates are retained enough to at least assess the scope of their discrepancy and propel recalibration.

Another arena where across-trial effects might become apparent involves the concept of attention. In fact one could construe Banks' weighted equations as complex ways to represent how a perceiver's attention is distributed between the visual information and the haptic, for instance. Yet attention is a malleable thing; it can be shifted, controlled, inhibited, primed, and so forth, as Anne Pick investigated in some of her early research (cf. Pick, Christy, & Frankel, 1972; Pick & Frankel, 1973). Thus, although subjects seemed to derive their weightings on each trial independently when visual noise and no-noise trials were randomly interspersed, I wonder what would happen if the noise trials were blocked so that a whole series of them occurred consecutively and then a no-noise trial was presented. Would subjects' weightings on this critical trial be biased in any way by the preceding consistent emphasis on haptic information, or would their weightings be just the same as on a no-noise trial presented before the block of noise trials? In other words, just how insulated from prior weighting schemes is the weight-setting process on any given next perceptual occasion? This question and others related to it could of course be easily addressed with Banks' conflict paradigm. Thus, as with Aslin's method, we can look forward to learning more from Banks' in the future.

The perceptual adaptation and priming phenomena just discussed naturally lead to the ultimate across-trial issue and the question of interest for most of us connected with the Minnesota Symposium—the question of development. Banks alludes to the adaptiveness of MLE integration with multiple sources, but would it be in place early in life? Would babies weigh redundant information sources optimally, according to their respective variances as mature perceivers do, if they were presented with visual-haptic conflicts such as Banks' subjects were? As it happens, this was exactly the manipulation involved long ago in my dissertation and related research on cross-modal perception (Bushnell, 1982; Bushnell &

Weinberger, 1987). I used a mirror apparatus similar to that employed in Banks' research; with the device, a stimulus hidden up above appeared to be down below where a different stimulus was actually present. Infants sat in front of this arrangement, looked into the mirror, and reached for the object they saw. Behaviors such as manual search, peeking, and surprised or wary facial expressions indicated that preverbal infants were able to detect visual-haptic discrepancies such as between a plastic knobby object and a furry cylindrical one, which was an important new finding at the time. Unfortunately, such gross behaviors showing violated expectancies are about as precise a response as we can get with infants. It is not possible to run hundreds of trials and get ordered size or slant estimates with discrepancies that are small enough to go undetected, as Banks' paradigm requires. Hence, although we can learn that infants are relating two sources of information to one another, we cannot determine whether they are integrating the two sources optimally or establish how the integration process changes over development.

We can, however, engage in some healthy speculation about the integration process and development based on what we know about perceptual development in general. For one thing, we can suppose that as development proceeds, the variance for many sensory estimators reduces as they become more sharply tuned. Thus, acuity improves, stereo acuity improves, auditory localization improves, manual behaviors become more precise, and so forth. For example, referring to Fig. 7.4 again, the solid curve might represent an estimator's performance at an early age, and the dashed curve might represent that same estimator's performance later in development. Furthermore, with any two different estimators, one might increase in precision to a greater extent than the other, so there could actually be reversals over development so far as which of the two estimators has the smaller variance. This is akin to the addition of noise in Banks' experiments, or like the removal of noise really. According to the MLE model, it suggests that where haptic capture, for example, might be the rule at one point in development, vision could dominate at a later point. An example of this shifting reliance due to developmental change may be provided by oral haptic perception and manual haptic perception. Both Ruff (1984; Ruff, Saltarelli, Capozzoli, & Dubiner, 1992) and Rochat (1989) suggested that one of the reasons mouthing and other forms of oral exploration decline over the first year is that manual dexterity and exploration abilities improve so much over the same time period.

Although developmental improvements in precision would alter the weights in MLE equations just as experimental changes in the stimulus situation do, a more dramatic effect related to development involves the addition of whole new terms to some of these equations. That is, the sensory processes for perceiving various attributes are not necessarily all functional at birth. Instead, they emerge one by one as development unfolds. Al Yonas and his students have documented an outstanding example of this with regard to the various sources of information for depth (for reviews, see Yonas & Granrud, 1985a, 1985b; Yonas, Arterberry, & Granrud, 1987). They have established that infants are sensitive to motion parallax information very early—at 2 to 3 months of age if not before—whereas they first show sensitivity to information based on retinal disparity at about 4 to 5 months of age, and they are not responsive to the various "painters' cues" for depth, such as overlap, linear perspective, and texture gradients, until a couple of months after that. Within Banks' model, this kind of staggered development means that young infants are working with a smaller repertoire of sensory estimators compared with an adult in the processes represented by Eq. 1 (chap. 6, this volume). Thus, an adult holding and looking at an object to judge its slant, for example, could bring at least four types of information into the equation—motion parallax, disparity, and texture gradient information from vision and joint receptor information from haptics. However, a young infant in the same situation might have only two estimates to include, from motion parallax and joint receptor information. This consideration could be another reason that infants' perception is not as precise as adults'. Not only is each individual sensory process probably more variable, but in any given instance of perception there may be fewer of them to incorporate into a weighted average.

Instances of staggered development such as with depth perception also raise what may be the *most* interesting developmental question related to MLE integration: When a new source of information emerges developmentally, like when disparity information becomes available at 4 months, how does the baby know which weighted equation to incorporate that term into? For example, how does the baby know that the new neuronal buzz related to retinal disparity specifies the same attribute as the neuronal buzz related to joint receptor information? This problem may be more apparent if I point out that while the baby is holding and looking at an object, not only are the various sensory processes related to slant operating, but information about other attributes is also coming into the system. There would be information about the object's luminance, for instance, about its size specified visually, about its size specified haptically, about its temperature specified haptically, and so on. Given this array of processes all providing neural estimates of some sort, how does the infant know which ones to cluster together and take a weighted average of to compute slant and which ones to keep out of that particular weighted equation?

Some argue that the baby does not know—that in fact the naive infant fuses all of the available information together in one big perceptual equation computing the global intensity of the experience or its arousingness. Lewkowicz and his colleagues have supported this hypothesis by demonstrating certain trade-offs between young infants' perception of visual and auditory stimuli (cf. Gardner, Lewkowicz, Rose, & Karmel, 1986; Lewkowicz, 1991; Lewkowicz & Turkewitz, 1981), and Bushnell (1994) accounted for some of the earliest instances of cross-modal matching, such as the oft-cited Meltzoff and Borton (1979) pacifier study, in terms of this singular dimension of arousal. Others, including Piaget (1952, 1954), suppose just the opposite—that the baby starts out with none or few of the sensory processes linked or coordinated. In this view, the various sensory estimates are initially islands of information unto themselves, and the baby would not realize any gains from MLE integration until the separate estimates became paired or "reciprocally assimilated" through some sort of experience. Along these lines, Bahrick (2000, 2001; Hernandez-Reif & Bahrick, 2001) argued and empirically demonstrated how early sensitivity to certain basic amodal phenomena such as synchrony might lead infants to later discover linkages between more complex and specific sensory qualities.

Whichever of these views is correct—whether an infant's perceptual processes are initially fully (overly) integrated or they are initially fully (overly) isolated—there is a developmental task to be accomplished for the infant to become the optimal perceiver described by Banks. If the various sensory estimations are all fused to begin with, the infant has to sort them out somehow and eliminate many of them from the equation for perceiving slant, for example. If the various sensory estimations are all independent to begin with, the infant has to establish the right pairings somehow and include just a certain subset of processes in the equation for perceiving slant. How does this sorting and pairing, this eliminating and including, happen during development?

CONCLUSION

The astute reader can perhaps see that we have come full circle here. The developmental task arising with Banks' MLE integration scheme is a grouping problem, similar to those that Aslin's conditional probability counters are designed to solve. Which sensory processes are estimates of the same perceptual attribute and should therefore feed into the same MLE equation? Which MLE equation should a newly emergent process be added to? To address these questions, the conditional probability mechanism would need to be adapted to assess co-variation as well as co-occurrence. Thus, over time (e.g., while rotating an object in depth and looking at it), a perceiver could compute that as retinal disparity information increases, for example, texture gradient information does also, but at the same time neither brightness nor temperature information changes systematically. This computation could then instruct the perceiver to include disparity and texture gradient information in the same MLE integration process, but to exclude brightness and temperature information from that same process. So the computational mechanism proposed by Aslin might set the stage during development for the one proposed by Banks to operate effectively. How perfect! I am not sure how this collaboration between the two computational mechanisms would be represented mathematically or instantiated neurally, but I bet Aslin and Banks could work that out.

REFERENCES

Bahrick, L. E. (2000). Increasing specificity in the development of intermodal perception. In D. Muir & A. Slater (Eds.), *Infant development: The essential readings. Essential readings in development psychology* (pp. 117–136). Oxford: Blackwell.

Bahrick, L. E. (2001). Increasing specificity in perceptual development: Infants' detection of nested levels of multimodal stimulation. *Journal of Experimental Child Psychology, 79,* 253–270.

Baldwin, D. A., Markman, E. M., Bill, B., Desjardins, R. N., & Irwin, J. M. (1996). Infants' reliance on a social criterion for establishing word-object relations. *Child Development, 67,* 3135–3153.

Blakemore, C., & Sutton, P. (1969). Size adaptation: A new after effect. *Science, 166,* 245–247.

Bushnell, E. W. (1982). Visual-tactual knowledge in 8-, 9 1/2, and 11-month-old infants. *Infant Behavior and Development, 5,* 63–75.

Bushnell, E. W. (1994). A dual-processing approach to cross-modal matching: Implications for development. In D. J. Lewkowicz & R. Lickliter (Eds.), *The development of intersensory perception: Comparative perspectives* (pp. 19–38). Hillsdale, NJ: Lawrence Erlbaum Associates.

Bushnell, E. W., & Weinberger, N. (1987). Infants' detection of visual-tactual discrepancies: Asymmetries that indicate a directive role of visual information. *Journal of Experimental Psychology: Human Perception and Performance, 13,* 601–608.

Dunham, P. J., Dunham, F., & Curwin, A. (1993). Joint-attentional states and lexical acquisition at 18 months. *Developmental Psychology, 29,* 827–831.

Ernst, M. O., & Banks, M. S. (2002). Humans integrate visual and haptic information in a statistically optimal fashion. *Nature, 415,* 429–433.

Gardner, J. M., Lewkowicz, D. J., Rose, S. A., & Karmel, B. Z. (1986). Effects of visual and auditory stimulation on subsequent visual preferences in neonates. *International Journal of Behavioral Development, 9,* 251–263.

Goldfield, E. C., Kay, B. A., & Warren, W. H. (1993). Infant bouncing: The assembly and tuning of action systems. *Child Development, 64,* 1128–1142.

Hay, J., & Pick, H. L., Jr. (1966). Visual and proprioceptive adaptation to optical displacement of the visual stimulus. *Journal of Experimental Psychology, 71,* 150–158.

Hay, J. C., Pick, H. L., & Ikeda, K. (1965). Visual capture produced by prism spectacles. *Psychonomic Science, 2,* 215–216.

Hernandez-Reif, M., & Bahrick, L. E. (2001). The development of visual-tactual perception of objects: Amodal relations provide the basis for learning arbitrary relations. *Infancy, 2,* 51–72.

Hunt, R. R., & Aslin, R. N. (2001). Statistical learning in a serial reaction time task: Access to separable statistical cues by individual learners. *Journal of Experimental Psychology: General, 130*, 658–680.

Leslie, A. M. (1994). ToMM, ToBy, and Agency: Core architecture and domain specificity. In L. A. Hirschfeld & S. A. Gelman (Eds.), *Mapping the mind: Domain specificity in cognition and culture* (pp. 119–148). New York: Cambridge University Press.

Lewkowicz, D. J. (1991). Development of intersensory functions in human infancy: Auditory/visual interactions. In M. J. S. Weiss & P. R. Zelazo (Eds.), *Newborn attention: Biological constraints and the influence of experience* (pp. 308–338). Norwood, NJ: Ablex.

Lewkowicz, D. J., & Turkewitz, G. (1981). Intersensory interaction in newborns: Modification of visual preferences following exposure to sound. *Child Development, 52*, 827–832.

Maratsos, M. (1988). The acquisition of formal word classes. In Y. Levy, I. M. Schlesinger, & M. S. D. Braine (Eds.), *Categories and processes in language acquisition* (pp. 31–44). Hillsdale, NJ: Lawrence Erlbaum Associates.

Maratsos, M., & Chalkley, M. (1981). The internal language of children's syntax. In K. E. Nelson (Ed.), *Children's language* (Vol. 2). New York: Gardner.

Mareschal, D., Plunkett, K., & Harris, P. (1995). Developing object permanence: A connectionist model. In J. D. Moore & J. F. Lehman (Eds.), *Proceedings of the 17th Annual Conference of the Cognitive Science Society* (pp. 170–175). Mahwah, NJ: Lawrence Erlbaum Associates.

Meltzoff, A. N. (1988a). Infant imitation and memory: Nine-month-olds in immediate and deferred tests. *Child Development, 59*, 217–225.

Meltzoff, A. N. (1988b). Infant imitation after a 1-week delay: Long-term memory for novel acts and multiple stimuli. *Developmental Psychology, 24*, 470–476.

Meltzoff, A. N., & Borton, R. W. (1979). Intermodal matching by human neonates. *Nature, 282*, 403–404.

Munakata, Y. (1998). Infant perseveration and implications for object permanence theories: A PDP model of the AB task. *Developmental Science, 1*, 161–184.

Munakata, Y., McClelland, J. L., Johnson, M. H., & Siegler, R. S. (1997). Rethinking infant knowledge: Toward an adaptive process account of successes and failures in object permanence tasks. *Psychological Review, 104*, 686–713.

Nelson, C. A., & Collins, P. F. (1991). Event-related potential and looking-time analysis of infants' responses to familiar and novel events: Implications for visual recognition memory. *Developmental Psychology, 27*, 50–58.

Nelson, C. A., Henschel, M., & Collins, P. F. (1993). Neural correlates of cross-modal recognition memory by 8-month-old human infants. *Developmental Psychology, 29*, 411–420.

Newsome, W. T., & Pare, E. B. (1988). A selective impairment of motion perception following lesions of the middle temporal visual area (MT). *Journal of Neuroscience, 8*, 2201–2211.

Piaget, J. (1952). *The origins of intelligence in childhood*. New York: International Universities Press.

Piaget, J. (1954). *The construction of reality in the child*. New York: Basic Books.

Pick, A. D., Christy, M. D., & Frankel, G. W. (1972). A developmental study of visual selective attention. *Journal of Experimental Child Psychology, 14*(2), 165–175.

Pick, A. D., & Frankel, G. W. (1973). A study of strategies of visual attention in children. *Developmental Psychology, 9*, 348–357.

Pick, H. L., Jr., Hay, J. C., & Willoughby, R. H. (1966). Interocular transfer of adaptation to prismatic distortion. *Perceptual & Motor Skills, 23*, 131–135.

Rieser, J. J., Pick, H. L., Ashmead, D. H., & Garing, A. E. (1995). Calibration of human locomotion and models of perceptual-motor organization. *Journal of Experimental Psychology: Human Perception & Performance, 21*, 480–497.

Rochat, P. (1989). Object manipulation and exploration in 2- to 5-month-old infants. *Developmental Psychology, 25*, 871–884.

Rogers, T. T., & Griffin, R. (2002, April). *Goal attribution without goal representation: A PDP approach to infants' early understanding of intentional actions.* Poster presented at the International Conference on Infant Studies, Toronto.

Ruff, H. A. (1984). Infants' manipulative exploration of objects: Effects of age and object characteristics. *Developmental Psychology, 20,* 9–20.

Ruff, H. A., Saltarelli, L. M., Capozzoli, M., & Dubiner, K. (1992). The differentiation of activity in infants' exploration of objects. *Developmental Psychology, 28,* 851–861.

Saffran, J. R., Newport, E. L., & Aslin, R. N. (1996). Word segmentation: The role of distributional cues. *Journal of Memory and Language, 35,* 606–621.

Spelke, E. S. (1994). Initial knowledge: Six suggestions. *Cognition, 50,* 431–445.

Sutherland, N. S. (1961). Figural after-effects and apparent size. *Quarterly Journal of Experimental Psychology A, 13,* 222–228.

Thelen, E. (1979). Rhythmical stereotypies in normal human infants. *Animal Behaviour, 27,* 699–715.

Thelen, E. (1981). Rhythmical behavior in infancy: An ethological perspective. *Developmental Psychology, 17,* 237–257.

Tomasello, M. (1999). *The cultural origins of human cognition.* Cambridge, MA: Harvard University Press.

Tomasello, M., Strosberg, R., & Akhtar, N. (1996). Eighteen-month-old children learn words in non-ostensive contexts. *Journal of Child Language, 23,* 157–176.

Wallach, H., Frey, K. J., & Bode, K. A. (1972). The nature of adaptation in distance perception based on oculomotor cues. *Perception & Psychophysics, 11,* 110–116.

Wallach, H., & O'Leary, A. (1979). Adaptation in distance perception with head-movement parallax serving as the veridical cue. *Perception & Psychophysics, 25,* 42–46.

Wynn, K. (1998). An evolved capacity for number. In D. D. Cummins & C. Allen (Eds.), *The evolution of mind* (pp. 107–126). New York: Oxford University Press.

Yonas, A., Arterberry, M. E., & Granrud, C. (1987). Space perception in infancy. In R. Vasta (Ed.), *Annals of child development* (Vol. 4, pp. 1–34). Greenwich, CT: JAI Press.

Yonas, A., & Granrud, C. E. (1985a). Development of visual space perception in infants. In J. Mehler & R. Fox (Eds.), *Neonate cognition: Beyond the blooming buzzing confusion* (pp. 45–67). Hillsdale, NJ: Lawrence Erlbaum Associates.

Yonas, A., & Granrud, C. (1985b). The development of sensitivity to kinetic binocular and pictorial depth information in human infants. In D. Ingle, M. Jeannerod, & D. Lee (Eds.), *Brain mechanisms and spatial vision* (pp. 113–145). Amsterdam: Martinus Nijhoff.

III

ACTIVE LEARNING DURING
EARLY DEVELOPMENT

8

▼▼▼▼▼▼▼

Evidence for and Against a Geometric Module: The Roles of Language and Action

Nora S. Newcombe
Temple University

Studying how people learn about spatial information, and the development of the ability to learn about such information, would seem, on the face of things, to necessitate studying the role of action in such learning. After all spatial knowledge is adaptively important exactly because humans, like all other mobile animals, must know the location of valued objects to move toward them and the location of dangerous objects to move away from them. These valued and dangerous entities are not all within reach or even all within sight. We can only know the world to which we must adapt by traveling within it.

Despite this seemingly obvious point, however, it has taken some time for cognitive and developmental psychology to assimilate the idea that action is important. Spatial representation has often been studied as a static entity—something in the head, which got there somehow, but for which the main task researchers face is to characterize its nature. This view is changing, but we still are not all that clear on how to conceptualize the role of action, and how to study it, even in an inherently action-oriented domain such as spatial cognition.

We do know some things. Humans, like many other animal species, orient using two fundamental kinds of systems. One system is intimately involved with action because it depends on the automatic tracking of movement in the world. From an original vantage point, with respect to which the location of various important entities has been coded, people can keep a running record of both their translatory motion (how far they have gone) and their rotational motion (where and by how much they have changed their direction), and they can adjust the location of important entities with respect to their current position accordingly (e.g., Rieser, Guth, & Hill, 1986; Rieser, Pick, Ashmead, & Garing, 1995). For example, suppose you know the location of the school, the grocery store, and the post office as you stand at your front door. When you leave your house and walk toward the school, moving forward and also turning occasionally, your knowledge of the location of the grocery store and the post office is updated as you move so that you could easily and accurately point to them from any point along your route. This spatial location system has been called *dead reckoning* or *inertial navigation* (Gallistel, 1990). However, although dead reckoning is a useful system, it suffers from some important drawbacks. The most notable problem is that it is subject to drift. Every time you turn, you estimate the amount of the turn with some degree of error. Every time you walk in a straight line, you estimate the distance, but again with some degree of error. These errors concatenate so that at the end of a long and meandering journey, your knowledge of the direction and distance to important locations may be quite inaccurate.

Therefore, it is fortunate (and probably not accidental) that humans and other animals have evolved a second spatial coding system. In this system, information about the distance and direction of important locations from stable landmarks in the environment is used to code location in a way that need not involve the current location of the self. For example, you might encode the location of your house, the school, the grocery store, and the post office with respect to a mountain, a church with a tall spire, and a river that runs through town. Such an environment-centered system does not degenerate as you move. It can be used to recalibrate the dead reckoning system as necessary, following drift of the kind we just discussed, or, more important, as a means to recover from complete disorientation (as might follow a ride on a merry-go-round or a trip on a subway).

An environment-centered system does not seem, when we first think about it, to rely on action except in some relatively trivial ways. Certainly, we build up knowledge of the stable landmarks essential to an environment-centered system by moving through the world. In addition, we use this knowledge about locations relative to landmarks to continue to move through the world. Yet beyond these truisms, are there circumstances in which action (or the possibility of action) engages a form of environment-centered spatial learning that is qualitatively different from that which occurs in learning about the locations of objects in a space that does not afford possibilities for action? In the study of spatial cognition, this contrast has sometimes been referred to as the issue of whether there are crucial differences between large-scale and small-scale spatial thinking (see e.g., Cohen, 1985). However, despite a good deal of discussion, and the conviction that there must be something different about large- and small-scale spatial cognition, the field has never arrived at a consensus as to how to characterize the difference.

In this chapter, I want to consider the possible role of action in large-scale, environment-centered spatial coding in the context of a specific line of work—research concerning a type of environment-centered system that has been termed the *geometric module* (Cheng, 1986; Gallistel, 1990). The work on the geometric module is important because it is not only relevant for understanding spatial representation, but also has ramifications that range beyond the field of spatial cognition. The existence of initial modularity of any kind is an important issue in the field of cognitive development in general. The existence of modularity in infancy and early childhood would be, if empirically validated, one of the most compelling arguments for nativism, in the spatial domain and also in other areas, such as the acquisition of quantitative understanding (Newcombe, 2002). (It is important to note, however, that there is no linkage between modularity in adults and nativism because modularity in adults may be an emergent phenomenon [Karmiloff-Smith, 1992]; it is the existence of initial modularity that is the key question.)

The discussion of the geometric module will begin by covering certain kinds of background information. First, we examine how geometric information has been defined and how it is said to differ from other kinds of environmental information. Second, we outline the kinds of results that have suggested that many animal species, including even young human children, encode geometric information concerning relative distances and angular sizes in their environment. Third, we summarize evidence that such geometric information is encoded in a modular system—specifically, one that is impervious to integration with other kinds of spatial information. Fourth, we look at evidence questioning this claim. Specifically, it appears that children integrate geometric information with other kinds of environment-centered information (and hence geometric information is not modular) in certain circumstances, notably when the containing space is sized in such a way as to allow for comfortable action within it, rather than being small and cramped (Learmonth, Nadel, & Newcombe, 2002). In addition, primates show integration of geometric and nongeometric information (and hence nonmodularity) at least when the nongeometric information involves large rather than small landmarks (Gouteux, Thinus-Blanc, & Vauclair, 2001). Using only large landmarks and ignoring small ones is a sensible enough behavior because large landmarks are much less likely to move than small ones, and hence they have greater cue validity.

A variety of other nonhuman animal species have shown the nonmodularity result as well.

Given this background, we are in a position to consider how geometric information is integrated with nongeometric information, when it is. There are two possibilities. First, in a series of articles, Linda Hermer, Elizabeth Spelke, and their colleagues hypothesized that language (itself often considered a modular ability) can be used as an instrument for bridging the gap between the two kinds of spatial information (Hermer-Vazquez, Moffet, & Munkholm, 2001; Hermer-Vazquez, Spelke, & Katsnelson, 1999; Spelke & Hermer, 1996). They proposed this hypothesis because they observed important developmental transitions around the age of 6 years, when children master the spatial terms to refer to *left* and *right*. They subsequently gathered supportive evidence from correlating production of these linguistic terms with spatial behavior, and also from interference studies conducted with adults. We argue, however, that there are substantial difficulties with this language-as-bridge hypothesis.

If language is not vital to the integration of geometric and nongeometric information, how does such combination take place? A second hypothesis, not involving language, suggests that the integration of landmark and geometric information sources that are initially processed separately takes place routinely in areas of the brain supporting spatial processing. From this point of view, there is no need for language to serve as a bridge between modular information because there is always the potential for combining spatial inputs from a variety of sources to form a unified model of the world. People and nonhuman animals constantly face the issue of integrating spatial information from specialized sensory systems, such as from visual and auditory sources. They do so in a way that is adjusted to capitalize on the cue validities of various kinds of information and to respond adaptively to error feedback (e.g., Gutfreund, Zheng, & Knudsen, 2002). Thus, it would not be surprising if the main determinant of whether potential information sources are integrated is whether each source is judged likely to be relevant and reliable. What information goes into the integration process should be affected by factors such as whether the information is gained in settings that afford action or the possibility of action, and whether the cues offer information likely to be ecologically valid. In addition, the integration process may be affected by whether relevant brain areas are available.

THE GEOMETRIC MODULE

The purpose of this section is to review the theory leading to the hypothesis of a geometric module, as well as the evidence concerning its existence. Some aspects of the data bear additionally on the relevance of language to spatial information integration. However, we defer to the next section a focused look at specific evidence favoring the language-as-bridge hypothesis.

Geometric Versus Landmark Information

Let us consider again the situation in which you remember the location of your home and other locations in your town in relation to an environmental framework that includes a mountain, a church with a tall spire, and a river running through town. The mountain, church, and river are all landmarks, but they differ in some important respects. Some entities are much more extended than others—the spire can almost be treated as a point, although it does of course have some volume, whereas the river defines a boundary rather than a point. Some entities are much more regular than others—the spire may well be completely symmetric, whereas the mountain doubtless is somewhat roughly hewn and appears different from different vantage points. Some entities have distinctive surface features—the spire may have a clock set into it on one side, whereas the river may seem green and smooth wherever one looks at it.

One way to parse environmental information into types is to distinguish geometric and nongeometric information. The spire may be hexagonal, the river may be treated as a curving line, and the mountain can be considered to form an irregular shape, perhaps with a roughly triangular promontory. Such information about extents and angles is geometric. All other information about the landmarks is not geometric—for instance, the color of landmarks (e.g., the green quality of the river) or their surface features (e.g., the clock on the spire) do not enter into a geometric description. Gallistel (1990) speculated that geometric information may be privileged in coding spatial location because it is less likely to change than nongeometric information. For example, the river may become brown several times a year as mud is swept into it upstream, but it may change its course only every few hundred years.

Encoding Geometric Information

In a seminal set of experiments, Cheng (1986) studied how rats use geometric and nongeometric information. The rats were placed in an unmarked rectangular enclosure, with food hidden in one corner (see top left of Fig. 8.1). They were disoriented to eliminate their ability to use the dead reckoning system, and thus to force them to rely only on environment-centered spatial systems, and they were then replaced in the chamber. Cheng found that the rats went to both of the two geometrically identical corners to search for the food, but avoided the two corners in which the relation of the long wall and the short wall was different from that of the

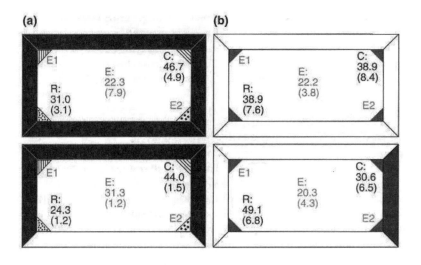

FIG. 8.1. Experimental setups and sample results in experiments on the geometric module involving rats (two left panels) and children (two right panels). From Wang and Spelke (2002).

correct corner. This kind of search pattern shows clearly that there has been coding of the geometric features of the environment: the relative lengths of the walls and the handedness or sense of the relation at the corners (i.e., the fact that the long wall is to the left or the right of the short wall). Similar results have been reported for human children ages 18 to 24 months, as shown at the top right of Fig. 8.1 (Hermer & Spelke, 1994, 1996). Toddlers of this age, following disorientation in an unmarked rectangular room, resemble rats in that they divide their searches equally between the geometrically identical corners, thus showing that they have encoded relative lengths of the walls and handedness relations.

Evidence for Encapsulation

The fact that both rats and human toddlers encode geometric information is an important one. However, taken by itself, this fact does not indicate that there is a geometric module. The evidence reviewed so far might simply indicate that geometric information is one of several kinds of environment-based information that, when integrated with information such as color and surface features, form an environment-centered framework for spatial cognition. Postulating modularity is based on an additional, and very surprising, aspect of the findings in the rectangular room experiments. As shown in the bottom two panels of Fig. 8.1, features of various kinds can be added to the unmarked rectangular enclosure. Given these additions, Cheng (with rats) and Hermer and Spelke (with human toddlers) observed whether these features were used to choose between the two geometrically identical corners. For instance, Cheng colored one wall of the enclosure differently from the other three, put patterned panels over the four corners of his enclosure, and also tried marking the corners with distinctive odors. Hermer and Spelke introduced features such as toys at either end of the room or one wall being covered with a colored cloth. In all cases, the data indicated that landmark information of a nongeometric kind is not used to supplement geometric information even when it would allow for successful choice between geometrically identical locations. Rats and human children continued to divide their searches evenly between the two geometrically correct corners, as they had in unfeatured rooms, ignoring the additional data that would have allowed them to search successfully on all trials. Evidence of this kind points to encapsulation or impenetrability—a crucial attribute of modularity in Fodor's (1983) treatment.

Hermer and Spelke also tested human adults, finding that they did not show the encapsulation phenomenon—adults were able to use a colored wall to disambiguate geometrically identical corners. They proposed that the acquisition of language (specifically, productive control of the terms *left* and *right*) might be a necessary (and sufficient) means to integrate geometric and nongeometric information. This hypothesis was later buttressed with data from correlational studies of children, as well as data from interference studies with adults (Hermer-Vazquez et al., 1999, 2001).

The Cheng results and the Hermer and Spelke results provide impressive evidence of an encapsulated geometric module in rats and children. However, before considering whether language is indeed the mechanism by which human adults might transcend this encapsulation, we should consider other studies that have questioned the existence of such an encapsulated (or impenetrable) module. Although Cheng found that rats show the modularity result, several other species of nonhuman animals apparently do not, including other types of mammals, as well as birds and fish. These findings not only bring the generality and importance of the modularity result into question, they also cast doubt on the language-as-bridge hypothesis because the animals showing integration of geometric and nongeometric information clearly lack a linguistic system.

Evidence Against Encapsulation From Nonhuman Animals

The first set of experiments using nonhuman animals other than rats was done by Vallortigara, Zanforlin, and Pasti (1990), who worked with chickens. The birds searched for food in identical containers located in the four corners of a rectangular enclosure. When the enclosure contained no distinguishing features, the chickens, following disorientation, concentrated their searches in the two corners that are the same from a geometric point of view, thus showing that they can use metric and sense properties for location tasks. When the four containers were marked with distinctive panels, chickens (unlike rats) were able to use the featural information to concentrate their searches almost entirely on the correct corner.[1]

Kelly, Spetch, and Heth (1998) studied another avian species—pigeons. Initially, some birds were trained to search for food in a rectangular environment that had featural information in each corner, and others were trained in an undifferentiated rectangular enclosure. In subsequent testing sessions, pigeons in both groups were found to use geometric information to guide search, showing that geometric information was encoded incidentally during training, even for the pigeons who could succeed simply by concentrating on the salient featural information. Then following initial training and testing, the group of birds that had been trained in the undifferentiated environment received training with featural information in the four corners. Testing sessions followed for both groups of pigeons. In sessions in which featural information could be combined with geometric information to allow choice of the correct corner, both groups were found to use features. In trials in which features were pitted against geometric information by rotating the placement of the panels, pigeons trained with features from the start showed primary reliance on features (although the initial testing showed they had encoded the geometry), whereas pigeons trained initially only with geometry showed a mixture of control by features and geometry. Thus, the history of pigeons' exposure to cues appears to affect the reliance placed on them, which is an interesting finding.

Working with monkeys, Gouteux et al. (2001) found, as have prior studies, that geometric information is used to code location in a rectangular room. They also reported, however, that the monkeys did not show an encapsulation of geometric knowledge; they could in fact use a colored wall to reorient and find a reward. Further experiments showed that monkeys did not use small cues to differentiate the geometry, but that they did use larger cues. This result is quite sensible if one considers that small objects are likely to move, and hence would not often provide a good cue to

---

[1]However, when panels marked only the two corners that were incorrect from a geometric point of view, the chickens were not able to use this indirect (nonlocal) information to distinguish between the correct corner and the rotational equivalent. Human toddlers can use indirect landmarks, however, as shown by Learmonth et al. (2001). More surprisingly perhaps, another avian species (pigeons) can use indirect landmarks as well (Kelly et al., 1998).

spatial location. By contrast, larger objects are much more likely to be stable, and thus to be useful in building a spatial framework.[2]

Perhaps the most dramatic finding of nonmodularity of geometric information is the most recent. Sovrano, Bisazza, and Vallortigara (2002) studied fish, specifically *Xenotoca eiseni*—a species whose natural habitat is shallow, transparent water. Each fish was placed in a rectangular tank that was quite bare, but located within a larger tank that contained food, vegetation, and other fish. They could escape from the inner tank at one of four identical panels located in the corners. When landmarks were unavailable, they concentrated their escape attempts on the geometrically identical corners, demonstrating their ability to use geometric information. When one of the walls of the inner tank was blue in color, they focused their attempts on the correct corner, demonstrating their ability to integrate geometric and nongeometric information. This demonstration of integration is especially striking because it was obtained in a species that would not ordinarily be thought to have any language-like symbolic abilities. Thus, whatever mechanisms support the integration of geometric and nongeometric information, it would seem they could not necessitate the use of language.

Evidence Against Encapsulation From Human Studies

Although the results with various nonhuman animal species are impressive, Hermer-Vazquez et al. (2001) suggested that they could be explained as the product of the extensive training that is typically necessary in working with other species to mold the ability of the animals to participate in the experiments. They argued that only human adults, and children older than 5 years, have been shown to use nongeometric landmarks flexibly and easily, with minimal training. Thus, evaluating the claims of a geometric module requires work with paradigms in which training can be minimal, as is possible in studies of human children. Evidence that there are circumstances in which very young children succeed in using nongeometric landmarks as well as geometric information to reorient would undercut the argument that the animal results showing nonmodularity depend on extensive training.

---

[2]Although research with children has not specifically contrasted small and large landmarks in the same experiment, it is interesting that the encapsulation result has been found with small moveable objects (Hermer & Spelke, 1996), but not with large, stable objects (Learmonth et al., 2001). Contrasts of this kind further support the cue validity approach advocated in this chapter—spatially relevant information is input to an integration system to the extent that past experience gives reason to believe it will maximize search performance.

In fact there is such evidence from young children. Interestingly, coming back to the focus of this volume on action as an organizer of learning and development, whether one gets such evidence or not seems to depend on the size of the enclosure that one uses. Learmonth, Newcombe, and Huttenlocher (2001) noted that Hermer and Spelke used a small rectangular room, more the size of a closet (4 by 6 feet), which lacked ecological validity in that it severely restricted movement. Therefore, we decided to investigate children's use of geometric and nongeometric information in a larger space, although one maintaining the same ratio of length of the small to the large walls as used before—8 by 12 feet as opposed to the 4 by 6 feet used in the earlier studies (see Fig. 8.2). The toddlers in our studies were successful in reorienting using features of various kinds, including a colored wall, in combination with information concerning the geometry of the space. That is, evidence for encapsulation vanished when children were studied in a larger room.

The importance of the size of the enclosure was subsequently demonstrated more conclusively in two randomized experiments. Learmonth et al. (2002) found that children from ages 3 to 5 years, randomly assigned to the small or larger room, showed the encapsulation result in the small room, but the integration result in the larger room. We also found that by 6 years, as also reported by Hermer-Vazquez et al., children begin to integrate geometric and nongeometric information in the small room (as well as continue to show it in the large room).

The findings regarding room size create a problem for the claim of initial modularity and also for the language-as-bridge hypothesis. Very young children can integrate geometric and nongeometric information in the larger room, but not in the small one. If language is required for integration, there is no obvious reason that toddlers should succeed in using landmarks in the larger room—they lack the ability to produce the spatial terms *left* and *right* in it just as they lack them in the small room.

Comparing the available data across the various reports also reveals some interesting patterns that require consideration. Although even very young children do make above-chance use of featural information in large

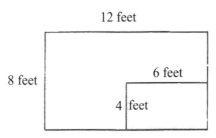

FIG. 8.2. A comparison of the smaller and larger spaces used in experiments with children. From Learmonth et al. (2001).

rooms, which is not true in small rooms, they are not perfect users of such information. Children's performance improves with age in rooms of both sizes. Specifically, the ability to use the colored wall to choose between the geometrically identical corners in the larger space improves at 5 and then again at 6 years of age (i.e., the same age range at which the ability to use the colored wall at all appears in the small room). In addition, performance in the larger room is better than performance in the smaller one even at the older ages. Thus, there are two facts about the data that need to be explained: the consistently greater difficulty of the small room, and the age-related changes that occur in each context. There may well be one factor accounting for the first effect and a different factor accounting for the second effect.

Summary

There is no doubt that a wide variety of animal species, including the young of our own species, encode geometric information. Although the relevant experiments have not been done with all species, it seems likely that geometric information is coded even when it need not be retained to succeed in the task (i.e., when a reward is stably marked with a salient coincident cue). Such findings suggest a powerful spatial learning mechanism that either appeared early in evolutionary history or that has been developed in parallel in a variety of evolutionary lines due to its adaptive significance.

What seems doubtful, however, is whether the encoding of such geometric information is done by a special-purpose geometric module that has little or no interaction with other spatial learning systems. Although evidence of encapsulation has been found with rats and human toddlers (in small rooms), evidence for integration of information has been found in fish, two different species of birds, rhesus monkeys (except with small objects as landmarks), human adults, and human toddlers (in larger rooms). The work with toddlers is particularly important, in that integration was found in situations in which there was no extensive training of how to behave in the situation. The overall pattern of the human data shows two effects in need of explanation: a contrast between use of featural information in small and larger rooms (use of such information is more likely in larger rooms), and an age-related increase in the use of featural information in rooms of both sizes.

THE LANGUAGE-AS-BRIDGE HYPOTHESIS

The preceding review has given reasons to doubt the existence of a geometric module and the idea that language is necessary to integrate information from such a module with other kinds of spatial information. Given these findings, a different way to think about geometric information becomes attractive—the idea that geometric information is one of several kinds of environmental information, along with featural information, that can be integrated to construct an environment-centered spatial coding system, with the circumstances under which each kind of information is used depending on factors such as their cue validity. However, it would be easier to accept this latter approach if one could answer some remaining questions about the existing studies directly supporting the role of language. Specifically, what should we make of the experiments showing that adults seem unable to integrate featural with geometric information when they are engaged in concurrent verbal shadowing (i.e., repeating discourse they hear through headphones while engaged in the task of locating objects following disorientation), although they can use features when asked to do a concurrent rhythmic shadowing task that also engages attention (Hermer-Vazquez et al., 1999). Is the relevant factor the ability to engage in linguistic coding of the spatial information? If not, why do these effects occur? Similarly, why is it that children's ability to integrate featural with geometric information in the small room seems to be related to the acquisition of spatial language as claimed by Hermer-Vazquez et al. (2001)? Is the correlation a real relation or a misleading one caused by some third variable?

Verbal Shadowing

There is a long and venerable history behind the use of interference tasks to identify the processes involved in supporting behavior on a target task. The basic logic is that people cannot do two things at once when both tasks call on the same cognitive processes, at least not at full levels of accuracy and efficiency for each task. Interference experiments generally also use control conditions in which people have to do a different concurrent task—one where there is reason to believe that different processes are involved. Ideally, the two concurrent tasks, one hypothesized to interfere with a target task and the other hypothesized to be noninterfering, have been shown to be equally difficult in a baseline condition. In short, the experiments take advantage of the fact that people are likely to have difficulty chewing gum and whistling at the same time (both involve the mouth and tongue) while most people can easily chew gum and tap their foot at the same time.

Hermer-Vazquez et al. (1999), using this selective-interference design, showed that human adults behaved like young children when asked to reorient in a rectangular room with one colored wall when they are also performing a verbal shadowing task (repeating the words of a taped rendition of reading a newspaper article about politics). The participants retained the ability to use geometric information, concentrating their searches in the geometrically correct corners, but they were at chance in using the blue wall to differentiate the two corners. This result was replicated in subsequent experiments that also showed that a rhythmic shadowing task did not affect the ability of adults to integrate featural with geometric information. Hermer-Vazquez et al. concluded that the ability to conduct linguistic processing was essential to the unfettered ability to utilize featural information, but that linguistic processing was not important for the operation of the geometric module per se.

In interpreting these results, however, it is important to ask whether the only way in which the linguistic shadowing task could create its effect on use of nongeometric features is by interfering with linguistic processing. Is it possible that the task could also act by interfering with a nonlinguistic spatial integration system? Relatedly, we should ask whether the rhythm shadowing task is the best control for verbal shadowing. Is it possible that, although the rhythm shadowing task does not interfere with the operation of a nonlinguistic spatial integration mechanism, other nonlinguistic interference tasks, more spatial in nature, would show such an interference effect?

In exploring these issues, let us return for the moment to consideration of the spatial behavior of chickens—notably, to a fascinating recent study by Tommasi and Vallortigara (2001). Chickens, unlike humans, have a complete decussation at the optic chiasma so that information from the left eye is received almost entirely by the right hemisphere of the bird and information from the right eye goes mostly to the left hemisphere. Experiments in which one or the other eye is patched while the chickens search for hidden food can therefore be used to diagnose what types of information are encoded by the right and left hemispheres during a naturalistic spatial task involving extended visual input and a great deal of physical movement—a methodological luxury compared with the human situation, where the coding of spatial information by the hemispheres can only be coded with strict visual fixation on a midpoint and brief flashed stimuli.

Tommasi and Vallortigara (Experiment 4) trained chickens to find food in the center of a square enclosure, with the center marked by a prominent landmark (see Fig. 8.3). They then tested the birds after shifting the landmark to a corner of the enclosure. They found that chickens allowed to use both eyes and chickens using only their left eye (right hemisphere) both searched in the geometric enter of the enclosure, whereas chickens using only their right eye (left hemisphere) searched almost exclusively around the displaced landmark. These results suggest that the left hemisphere encodes featural information and the right hemisphere encodes geometric information, with integration normally established by hemispheric communication. This communication presumably does not involve verbalization in the chicken.

Could the same process of hemispheric communication be important to the combination of featural and geometric information in humans, providing an alternative mechanism to the language-as-bridge idea for explaining how combination of information occurs? If so, does the hemispheric-integration mechanism provide a clue as to why verbal shadowing might interfere with integration in human adults while rhythm shadowing does not? Let us address these questions in order.

First, there is reason to suspect that hemispheric integration may be important to human spatial functioning as well as to that of chickens. There are several kinds of contrasts between right- and left-hemisphere spatial functioning in humans. In the hippocampus, encoding of relational spatial information seems to occur more on the right side than on the left (Barrash, Damasio, Adolphs, & Tranel, 2000), with left hippocampal areas supporting more categorical coding of objects and features in the spatial layout. In neocortex, human encoding of metric information appears to be a right hemispheric task, whereas encoding of categorical spatial information occurs in the left hemisphere (Hellige & Michimata, 1989; Kosslyn, 1987; Slotnick, Moo, Tesoro, & Hart, 2001). A recent fMRI study has shown that the locus of these effects is, specifically, parietal cortex (Trojano et al., 2002). In addition, studies of children with unilateral brain damage have suggested that the left hemisphere engages in more analytic spatial processing, whereas the right hemisphere is more holistic (e.g., Stiles, Stern, Trauner, & Nass, 1996). Thus, in summary, there is reason to think that human spatial representation, like that of chickens, may also depend on interhemispheric communication.

Proceeding to the next step in the argument, let us consider the idea that verbal shadowing might interfere with integration of nongeometric and geometric information by interfering with a hemispheric integration mechanism rather than by preventing the use of verbal processes. Is there any evidence that verbal shadowing could have such an effect? The question has not been studied specifically, but there are clues in the neuroscience literature that it could work this way. For example, at the hippocampal level, Golby et al. (2001) found in an fMRI study that verbal encoding leads to left-lateralized activation of the medial-temporal lobe, supporting the speculation that verbal shadowing might interfere with categorical coding of features occurring also in these areas, and thus with the use of featural information in spatial processing. As another example, at the neocortical level, working memory for sentences seems to be supported by a large-scale network of brain regions (Haarmann, Cameron, & Ruchkin, 2002), including some areas that may also be vital for spatial information integration. In addition, object memory has been found to require temporal cortex (Abrahams et al., 1999), including some areas that may also be needed in verbal shadowing.

The point of mentioning this evolving work in neuroscience is not that we know at this time where and how interference between a verbal shadowing task and a spatial integration mechanism might occur—rather, the point is that we do not know. Much more needs to be learned about the complex multi-area brain involvements in interference tasks before we can draw what a couple of decades ago would have seemed a safe conclusion—that if a verbal task interferes with some target task, it does so by disrupting verbal coding.

Along the same lines, let us consider what the control task in the Hermer-Vazquez studies controlled for. The rhythm shadowing may have provided an incomplete control condition for verbal shadowing by engaging processes and brain areas that would not be expected to be intimately involved with spatial information integration. Certainly, another task involving rhythm—timed-interval tapping—involves the cerebellum rather than brain areas more relevant for the integration of featural and geometric information (Papka, Ivry, & Woodruff-Pak, 1995; Woodruff-Pak, Papka, & Ivry, 1996). Other concurrent tasks, more spatial and yet still nonverbal in nature, might interfere with integration of features as much as verbal shadowing. For example, consider classic experiments by Brooks (1968, 1970) on the selective effects of spatial and verbal interference. It would be interesting to see whether nonverbal, but definitely spatial, interference tasks would disrupt adults' behavior in the colored wall paradigm. For example, one could ask people to give information on the number of outside and inside angles in block letter Es while also searching for objects following disorientation. Perhaps any task that engages spatial processes, and thus that places demands on areas of the brain needed for spatial integration, would create childlike performance in adults.

Correlations of Spatial Information Integration With Acquisition of Spatial Language

Hermer-Vazquez et al. (2001) gave another reason, in addition to the verbal shadowing results with adults, to suppose that language is vital for allowing the rapid and flexible use of featural information in reorientation. They began by identifying 5 to 6 years as the age range during which children start to use the blue wall to reorient in the small rectangular room, and as also being an age range with sufficient variability in performance to allow for correlation of other aspects of cognitive development with use of features in reorientation. Then working with a new group of children, they gave a variety of cognitive tests, including nonverbal intelligence, digit span, visuospatial span, production of spatial terms (above-below, in front-behind, left-right), and comprehension of these same spatial terms. They reported that the only variable to predict children's ability to reorient was their production of the terms *left* and *right*. Based on these data, they argued that control of such linguistic terms was essential in allowing for rapid and flexible use of features in reorientation.

These findings are intriguing, but there are certain reasons to question the relevance of the data to the question at hand. First, a puzzling aspect of the experiments reported is that children tested for the correlational analysis were not tested in the rectangular room. Instead they were tested in a square room with one red wall. Thus, success on this task did not require the integration of geometric information with sense information because a square provides no informative geometric information. The importance of production of the terms *left* and *right* might be especially pronounced in a situation in which success could be obtained through command of these terms. Children had only to code the correct location as to the left or the right of the red wall.

Another criticism of the developmental argument is that it relies on correlational analysis. The association found might be coincidental rather than causal. Hermer-Vazquez et al. attempted to rebut this criticism by noting that a variety of other plausible correlates, all of which showed statistical properties that would have allowed for detection of a correlation had it been present, did not in fact show significant correlations. Yet it may be that they failed to test the truly causal correlate. Of course such criticisms can always be made of correlational data. However, they acquire more weight if one can specify alternative theories, and there is indeed a candidate for the role of rival causal correlate. As we saw in the previous section, integration of featural and geometric information may require hemispheric connection. It is known that callosal connections develop over childhood and into adolescence (De Bellis et al., 2001; Giedd et al., 1999; Thompson, Giedd, Woods, MacDonald, Evans, & Toga, 2000).[3] Thus, the strengthening of integration of left and right hemispheres could potentially account for the developing ability to use featural and geometric information concurrently. However, we would still need to explain why such integration is easier in larger than in smaller rooms, a matter to which we now turn.

---

[3]If callosal connectivity is important, then children with Williams Syndrome might be impaired at the integration of geometric and nongeometric information because they have reduced and altered callosal structures (Schmitt, Eliez, Bellugi, & Reiss, 2001; Schmitt, Eliez, Warsofsky, Bellugi, & Reiss, 2001).

THE ROLE OF ACTION IN INTEGRATION OF SPATIAL INFORMATION

As mentioned in the introduction, the field of spatial cognition has never really settled the question of what the crucial differences are between large-scale and small-scale spatial cognition. One important distinction contrasts primary spatial representations in which people have actual experience with secondary spatial representations that are symbolic (i.e., maps or models; Presson & Hazelrigg, 1984). By this criterion, the small room and the larger room are not different from each other because children are actually located within each of them.[4] Another distinction contrasts spatial arrays that can be seen at a single glance with those that require gathering of information over time. The small and larger rooms are not different by this second criterion either because seeing all four walls of the rooms requires rotation of the body in both cases.

The major contrast between the small and larger rooms seems, instead, to be a simple one. At 4 by 6 feet, the small room is a cramped space, especially when containing an adult as well as a child. It is difficult to move around it without dodging the other person, and there seems little reason to move around it other than to rotate in place because any corner can be reached in a few steps, even by children with short legs. The 8 by 12 foot room, although it has four times the area of the small room, is not enormous—that is why we labeled it *larger* rather than *large* throughout this chapter. However, a child and an adult in a room that size can feel comfortable in moving and see some reason to do so to reach every side and corner of the room.

Active motion has long been known to be important for focusing spatial attention (e.g., Acredolo, Adams, & Goodwyn, 1984; see summary by Campos et al., 2000). In fact work with animals whose hippocampal cell activity is being monitored shows that spatially related hippocampal activity virtually ceases if the animal is physically restrained, although it can visually inspect the environment (Foster, Castro, & McNaughton, 1989).

---

[4]Gouteux, Vauclair, and Thinus-Blanc (2001) looked at children's use of geometric and featural cues in an experiment in which a table top model rotated on its axis while children hid their eyes. The model was a rectangular box, either unfeatured or with one of its walls a distinctive color. Although the ratio of the long to the short sides of the box was more pronounced than in the room studies (4 to 1 rather than 1.5 to 1), children as old as 5 years of age did not use the geometry of the box to select the corner containing a candy (although adults did). Rather, 4- and 5-year-olds seemed to concentrate on the colored-wall cue, looking for the candy in the two corners that were adjacent to it. This error pattern has never been seen in the room studies and illustrates how different primary and secondary spatial representations may be. However, at a more general level, the data suggest that integrating featural and geometric information is an important developmental challenge, one with differing interim solutions in different kinds of spatial layouts.

More recently, longer term studies in rats where activity in hippocampal cells was being recorded has shown that experience in an enclosure is instrumental in remodeling place fields (Lever, Wills, Cacucci, Burgess, & O'Keefe, 2002). In the context of these data, it is plausible to suggest that the affordance of activity in the larger room allows for more effective spatial learning.

There is also another important contrast between the small and larger rooms—namely, the proportion of the visual field taken up by features in the two cases. Heading information from fixes on landmarks is more useful and ecologically valid when gained from more distal landmarks rather than from proximal ones. Thus, it may be more likely that people would use landmarks in larger rooms because their experience suggests they are valuable. More research is clearly needed to determine whether this factor is important in addition to, or instead of, the role of the affordance of action in larger spaces.

In summary, in this section, we examined the contrast in performance between small and larger rooms. There are at least two possible ways to explain the findings. However, neither of the factors that may create this difference seem likely to explain the progressive developmental change in the ability to use nongeometric cues, seen in rooms of both size. However, the hemispheric cross-talk hypothesis discussed at the end of the last section can explain this aspect of the findings. There are two effects in the data, and there may be two different classes of explanations—one for each.

CONCLUSION

In this chapter, we have seen that there are several reasons to question the existence of an encapsulated geometric module, as well as the importance of language in providing a bridge between geometric and nongeometric information. One powerful line of argument against both propositions is the fact that nonlinguistic animals have shown an ability to integrate the two kinds of information. In addition, the language-as-bridge hypothesis provides no natural way to account for the effect of variables such as the size of the landmark objects and the area of the enclosure. We have also seen that the verbal shadowing studies and the correlations of success on the small room task with acquisition of the terms *right* and *left* do not provide decisive evidence of the existence of a language mechanism that penetrates the impenetrable geometric module.

Moving from the critical to the constructive, we have proposed that spatial information arriving through different sensory-perceptual mechanisms is normally integrated into an environment-centered spatial framework, with the use of information dependent on its cue validity in the situation. Some aspects of development may be accounted for by changes in the neural mechanisms supporting such integration, whereas other aspects of development may be related to the accumulation of experience that determines cue validity. Action facilitates integration by increasing attention and perhaps by being required for neural remodeling.

The arguments in this chapter are relevant to the wider issues of modularity in the study of cognition and cognitive development. Some investigators use the term *module* to apply to the operation of a specialized neural system, in which particular types of information are preferentially processed by certain neural areas, either during sensory input or at higher levels. Such specialization may often or even always be an emergent property of the architecture of the nervous system interacting with the expectable environmental input (Elman et al., 1996). Nothing reviewed in this chapter suggests that such usage of the term is unjustified. Indeed the information integration approach specifically envisions that there are different kinds of spatial information that are in need of integration. It is only the existence of a module in Fodor's (1983) sense that we have questioned and, with that criticism, the idea that development consists largely in the use of innately available modules that are, at some point, linked by language (see also Newcombe, 2002).

ACKNOWLEDGMENT

The writing of this chapter was supported by NSF grant BCS 9905098.

REFERENCES

Abrahams, S., Morris, R. G., Polkey, C. E., Jarosz, J. M., Cox, T. C. S., Graves, M., & Pickering, A. (1999). Hippocampal involvement in spatial and working memory: A structural MRI analysis of patients with unilateral mesial temporal lobe sclerosis. *Brain & Cognition, 41*, 39–65.

Acredolo, L. P., Adams, A., & Goodwyn, S. W. (1984). The role of self-produced movement and visual tracking in infant spatial orientation. *Journal of Experimental Child Psychology, 38*, 312–327.

Barrash, J., Damasio, H., Adolphs, R., & Tranel, D. (2000). The neuroanatomical correlates of rout learning impairments. *Neuropsychologia, 38*, 820–836.

Brooks, L. R. (1968). Spatial and verbal components of the act of recall. *Canadian Journal of Psychology, 22*, 349–368.

Brooks, L. R. (1970). An extension of the conflict between visualization and reading. *Quarterly Journal of Experimental Psychology, 22*, 91–96.

Campos, J. J., Anderson, D. I., Barbu-Roth, M. A., Hubbard, E. M., Hertenstein, M. J., & Witherington, D. (2000). Travel broadens the mind. *Infancy, 1*, 149–219.

Cheng, K. (1986). A purely geometric model in rat's spatial representation. *Cognition, 23,* 149–178.

Cohen, R. (Ed.). (1985). *The development of spatial cognition.* Hillsdale, NJ: Lawrence Erlbaum Associates.

De Bellis, M. D., Keshavan, M. S., Matcheri, S., Beers, S. R., Hall, J., Frustaci, K., Masalehdan, A., Noll, J., & Boring, A. M. (2001). Sex differences in brain maturation during childhood and adolescence. *Cerebral Cortex, 11,* 552–557.

Elman, J. L., Bates, E. A., Johnson, M. H., Karmiloff-Smith, A., Parisi, D., & Plunkett, K. (1996). *Rethinking innateness: A connectionist perspective on development.* Cambridge, MA: MIT Press.

Fodor, J. A. (1983). *Modularity of mind: An essay on faculty psychology.* Cambridge, MA: MIT Press.

Foster, T. C., Castro, C. A., & McNaughton, B. L. (1989). Spatial selectivity of rat hippocampal neurons: Dependence on preparedness for movement. *Science, 244,* 1580–1582.

Gallistel, C. R. (1990). *The organization of learning.* Cambridge, MA: MIT Press.

Giedd, J. N., Blumenthal, J., Jeffries, N. O., Rajapakse, J. E., Vaituzis, A. C., Liu, H., Berry, Y. C., Tobin, M., Nelson, J., & Castellanos, F. X. (1999). The development of the corpus callosum during childhood and adolescence: A longitudinal MRI study. *Progress in Neuro-Psychopharmacology and Biological Psychiatry, 23,* 571–588.

Golby, A. J., Poldrack, R. A., Brewer, J. B., Spencer, D., Desmond, J. E., Aron, A. P., & Gabrieli, J. D. E. (2001). Material-specific lateralization in the medial temporal lobe and prefrontal cortex during memory encoding. *Brain, 124,* 1841–1854.

Gouteux, S., Thinus-Blanc, C., & Vauclair, J. (2001). Rhesus monkeys use geometric and nongeometric information during a reorientation task. *Journal of Experimental Psychology, 130,* 509–519.

Gouteux, S., Vauclair, J., & Thinus-Blanc, C. (2001). Reorientation in a small-scale environment by 3-, 4- and 5-year-old children. *Cognitive Development, 16,* 853–869.

Gutfreund, J., Zheng, W., & Knudsen, E. I. (2002). Gated visual input into the central auditory system. *Science, 297,* 1556–1559.

Haarmann, H. J., Cameron, K. A., & Ruchkin, D. S. (2002, November). *Real time collaborations among brain regions during working memory for sentence meaning.* Poster presented at the annual meeting of the Psychonomic Society, Kansas City, MO.

Hellige, J. B., & Michimata, C. (1989). Categorization versus difference: Hemispheric differences for processing spatial information. *Memory & Cognition, 17,* 770–776.

Hermer, L., & Spelke, E. S. (1994). A geometric process for spatial reorientation in young children. *Nature, 370,* 57–59.

Hermer, L., & Spelke, E. S. (1996). Modularity and development: The case of spatial reorientation. *Cognition, 61,* 195–232.

Hermer-Vazquez, L., Moffet, A., & Munkholm, P. (2001). Language space, and the development of cognitive flexibility in humans: The case of two cognitive memory tasks. *Cognition, 79,* 263–299.

Hermer-Vazquez, L., Spelke, E., & Katsnelson, A. (1999). Sources of flexibility in human cognition: Dual task studies of space and language. *Cognitive Psychology, 39,* 3–36.

Karmiloff-Smith, A. (1992). *Beyond modularity: A developmental perspective on cognitive science.* Cambridge, MA: MIT Press.

Kelly, D. M., Spetch, M. L., & Heth, D. C. (1998). Pigions' (Columba livia) encoding of geometric and featural properties of a spatial environment. *Journal of Comparative Psychology, 112,* 259–269.

Kosslyn, S. M. (1987). Seeing and imagination in the cerebral hemispheres: A computational approach. *Psychological Review, 94,* 148–175.

Learmonth, A. E., Nadel, L., & Newcombe, N. S. (2002). Children's use of landmarks: Implications for modular theory. *Psychological Science, 13,* 337–341.

Learmonth, A. E., Newcombe, N. S., & Huttenlocher, J. (2001). Toddlers' use of metric information and landmarks to reorient. *Journal of Experimental Child Psychology, 80*, 225–244.

Lever, C., Wills, T., Cacucci, F., Burgess, N., & O'Keefe, J. (2002). Long-term plasticity in hippocampal place-cell representation of environmental geometry. *Nature, 416*, 90–94.

Newcombe, N. (2002). The nativist-empiricist controversy in the context of recent research on spatial and quantitative development. *Psychological Science, 13*, 395–401.

Papka, M., Ivry, R. B., & Woodruff-Pak, D. S. (1995). Selective disruption of eyeblink classical conditioning by concurrent tapping. *Neuroreport: An International Journal for the Rapid Communication of Research in Neuroscience, 6*, 1493–1497.

Presson, C. C., & Hazelrigg, M. D., (1984). Building spatial representations through primary and secondary learning. *Journal of Experimental Psychology, 10*, 716–722.

Rieser, J. J., Guth, D. A., & Hill, E. W. (1986). Sensitivity to perspective structure while walking without vision. *Perception, 15*, 173–188.

Rieser, J. J., Pick, H. L., Ashmead, D. H., & Garing, A. E. (1995). Calibration of human locomotion and models of perceptual-motor organization. *Journal of Experimental Psychology: Human Perception and Performance, 21*, 480–497.

Schmitt, J. E., Eliez, S., Bellugi, V., & Reiss, A. L. (2001). Analysis of cerebral shape in Williams syndrome. *Archives of Neurology, 58*, 283–287.

Schmitt, J. E., Eliez, S., Warsofsky, L. S., Bellugi, V., & Reiss, A. L. (2001). Corpus callosum morphology of Williams syndrome: Relation to genetics and behavior. *Developmental Medicine and Child Neurology, 43*, 155–159.

Slotnick, S. D., Moo, L. R., Tesoro, M. A., & Hart, J. (2001). Hemispheric asymmetry in categorical versus coordinate spatial processing revealed by temporary cortical deactivation. *Journal of Cognitive Neuroscience, 13*, 1088–1096.

Sovrano, V. A., Bisazza, A., & Vallortigara, G. (2002). Modularity and spatial reorientation in a simple mind: Encoding of geometric and nongeometric properties of a spatial environment by fish. *Cognition, 85*, B51–B59.

Spelke, E., & Hermer, L. (1996). Early cognitive development: Objects and space. In R. Gelman & T. Kit-Fong (Eds.), *Perceptual and cognitive development. Handbook of perception and cognition* (pp. 71–114). San Diego, CA: Academic Press.

Stiles, J., Stern, C., Trauner, D., & Nass, R. (1996). Developmental change in spatial grouping activity among children with early focal brain injury: Evidence from a modeling task. *Brain and Cognition, 31*, 46–62.

Thompson, P. M., Giedd, J. N., Woods, R. P., MacDonald, D., Evans, A. C., & Toga, A. W. (2000). Growth patterns in the developing brain detected by using continuum mechanical tensor maps. *Nature, 404*, 190–193.

Tommasi, L., & Vallortigara, G. (2001). Encoding of geometric and landmark information in the left and right hemispheres of the avian brain. *Behavioral Neuroscience, 115*, 602–613.

Trojano, L., Grossi, D., Linden, D. E., Formisano, E., Goebel, R., Cirillo, S., Elefante, R., & Di Salle, F. (2002). Coordinate and categorical judgments in spatial imagery. An fMRI study. *Neuropsychologia, 40*, 1666–1674.

Vallortigara, G., Zanforlin, M., & Pasti, G. (1990). Geometric modules in animals' spatial representations: A test with chicks (Gallus gallus domesticus). *Journal of Comparative Psychology, 104*, 248–254.

Wang, R. F., & Spelke, E. S. (2002). Human spatial representation: Insights from animals. *Trends in Cognitive Sciences, 6*, 376–382.

Woodruff-Pak, D. S., Papka, M., & Ivry, R. B. (1996). Cerebellar involvement in eyeblink classical conditioning in humans. *Neuropsychology, 10*, 443–458.

9

▼▼▼▼▼▼▼▼

Using Dynamic Field Theory
to Conceptualize the Interface
of Perception, Cognition, and Action

Esther Thelen
Virgil Whitmyer II
Indiana University

Jean Piaget left a complex legacy for contemporary developmental psychology. His central question—how do children come to know about the world—is still the defining issue in cognitive development. In answering this question, Piaget addressed both the content of human minds and the process by which those minds developed. Thus, Piaget wrote about how the structure of the world—the nature of physical objects, time, causality, number, space—became part of the content of mind—mental structures that exist independent of behavior. He also gave us a theory of the process of development as the gradual assimilation and accommodation of properties of the world through sensorimotor activities.

Since the 1980s, there has been widespread criticism of Piaget. The most serious claim is that Piaget grievously underestimated the conceptual abilities of young infants. Critics claimed that Piaget's tasks were too difficult for uncoordinated infants because he required them to reach for and manipulate objects. In other words, infants lacked the motor skills to demonstrate their true knowledge. When researchers simplified the tasks to require only looking at events, infants of just a few months of age revealed a surprisingly precocial understanding of sophisticated concepts such as the solidity and permanence of objects, inertia, numerosity and causality. If these new claims of early content were true, then Piaget's whole theory of the sensorimotor origins of knowledge must be flawed. Infants appeared to have knowledge before they had the skills to acquire that knowledge by experience (Spelke & Newport, 1998).

If Piaget is indeed wrong, then how could infants have these mental structures so early in life? One alternative has been to claim that such knowledge is innate. Some theorists have proposed that core principles are so important and predictive of the world that they became hard-wired by evolutionary selection. As Piaget has lost favor, this nativist position has become a serious contender for filling the theoretical vacuum (see discussion by Newcombe, 2002).

Yet the nativist position has serious theoretical shortcomings as well. In their 1994 book, Thelen and Smith pointed out the profound dualism of this approach. Nativists must draw a sharp distinction between competence and performance. Competence resides in the abstract, mental structures that are independent, modular, and built in. Performance is everything else: the ongoing perceptual, motor, and emotional processes that are engaged in real-time behavior. Competence is enduring, but performance factors are ephemeral and fragile. The job of the experimenter, in this view, is to choose tasks to reveal the core competence at the earliest ages by minimizing performance demands.

As Thelen and Smith wrote, the nativist agenda has thus emphasized only one aspect of Piaget's question—the content of mind. Yet a list of innate ideas is insufficient for understanding either the complexities of real-time behavior or the longer time processes of change. In reality, the behavior of young children is variable, messy, and idiosyncratic. Efforts to uncover core principles run up against the overwhelming context-sensitivity of tasks that seem quite simple, like watching a display or uncovering a hidden object. What seems like a small change in the task design, instructions, or environment of testing can lead to different outcomes. Innate principles should be more robust, but they are not. It is theoretically vacuous to assign all such variability to performance while competence remains intact because it becomes possible to attribute successes in the task to the presence of core principles and failures to inadequate performance or poor task design.

In 1994, Thelen and Smith called this state of affairs a "crisis in cognitive development." It is nearly a decade since their book, and the crisis in development has not abated and perhaps has become even worse. On the one hand, the list of innate knowledge structures grows longer. On the other hand, so does the counterevidence. The debate is a continuation of an old theme: Is knowledge built in or acquired through experience? Several recent quotes illustrate the dramatic contrasts in views.

For instance, in 1999, the prestigious National Research Council, an arm of the National Academy of Sciences, published a book entitled, *How People Learn: Brain, Mind, Experience and School*. The chapter on early development is a clear reflection of the nativist view.

Research studies have demonstrated that infants as early as 3–4 months of age have the beginnings of useful knowledge. Three examples from many: they understand that objects need support to prevent them from falling; that stationary objects are displaced when they come into contact with moving objects, and that inanimate objects need to be propelled into motion. . . . An ever-increasing body of evidence shows that the human mind is endowed with an implicit mental ability that facilitates attention to and use of representations of the number of items in a visual array, sequence of drumbeats, jumps of a toy bunny, numerical values represented in arrays, etc. (Bransford, Brown, & Cocking, 1999, pp. 84, 89)

Despite the confidence of these highly sanctioned claims, nagging challenges come from many sources. For instance, if infants have innate knowledge about the properties of objects, so should much older children. Yet a headline in a recent edition of the American Psychological Association *Monitor* read, "Toddler's Lack Knowledge of Physical Laws." A subhead proclaimed: "Representation of Objects and Events: Why do Infants Look so Smart and 2-Year Olds Look So Dumb?" Reporting on a talk by Rachel Keen Clifton, the article said: "Unlike young infants, toddlers seem to lack knowledge of certain physical laws. . . . They do not appear to recognize the physical laws of solidity and continuity, knowledge they seemed to have when they were infants" (Ciske, 2002). The evidence that infants can count is also disputed. For example, in a recent review, Mix, Huttenlocher, and Levine (2002) concluded, "Contrary to what has been claimed in current models of early quantification, we failed to find evidence that discrete number is represented in infancy" (p. 293).

OBJECT CONCEPTS IN INFANTS AND TODDLERS

The troubling state of affairs in cognitive development comes from two styles of experiments designed to probe the minds of infants and toddlers who cannot give verbal responses. The first are a large number of experiments called *violation of expectancy*, pioneered by Renée Baillargeon and Elizabeth Spelke (Baillargeon, Spelke, & Wasserman, 1985; Baillargeon, 1987a, 1987b). The logic of these experiments is to minimize performance requirements by asking infants just to look at displays. The displays are based on the idea that infants, like adults, should be surprised when objects in the world defy everyday physics, and that, in infants, this surprise should be manifest by looking longer at the unexpected display.

The classic studies in this domain concern the permanence and solidity of objects. The overall idea is to familiarize infants with a plausible display of some simple physical event until they are bored with it. Then they are tested with two similar events: One is physically possible and the other could only occur by magic. If infants look longer at the impossible event, experimenters infer that they recognize its impossibility and thus must have a concept of the real properties of objects.

Well-known experiments by Baillargeon (Baillargeon et al., 1985; Baillargeon, 1987a, 1987b) and her colleagues using the drawbridge illustrate this paradigm. In the simple version of this task, infants were shown a screen rotating 180 degrees toward them and away from them. For the tests, a block was introduced into the display in the path of the screen. For the possible event, the screen stopped when it encountered the block, rotating only 112 degrees. For the impossible event, the screen continued its path, seemingly passing through the solid block. Infants at 3½ to 5 months looked longer at the impossible display. The researchers inferred that infants understood that the block continued to exist when hidden by the screen and, furthermore, that the babies knew that a screen could not pass through a solid object. This experiment and many others suggested that infants have sophisticated concepts many months before Piaget's account and before they could learn about objects through actions.

If infants have these core concepts about physical events and if their beliefs are continually reinforced by the behavior of objects in their everyday worlds, the concepts should become even stronger as infants get older. Yet efforts to show that much older children use an understanding of simple physics to guide their actions on objects have led to surprising results. For instance, Spelke, Breinlinger, Macomber, and Jacobson (1992) reported that infants as young as 4 months understand that a falling object cannot pass through a solid shelf. Hood, Carey, and Prasada (2000) repeated their experiment as a search task with 2-year-olds. Strikingly, in four different experiments, toddlers failed to search for the toy in accord with the solidity principle. Rather, they consistently reached for the bottom compartment, below the shelf, where they saw the ball fall during the familiarization trials.

A similar experiment by Berthier et al. (2000) gave the same, counterintuitive results. In this important experiment, discussed in Keen (chap. 11, this volume) and to which we return later in this chapter, 2-, 2½-, and 3-year-olds saw a ball rolling down a ramp and behind an occluding screen with four doors. Before experimenters rolled the ball, they placed a wall in the ball's path so the wall would stop the ball behind one of the doors. They claimed there was no memory involved because children always saw part of the wall. Experimenters varied the position of the wall and asked the children to retrieve the ball from behind the correct door. Although children at all three ages could easily retrieve the ball when it was simply placed behind the door, none of the 2-year-olds and few of the

2½-year-olds correctly guessed the correct location when the ball was rolled into position. Most 3-year-olds solved the task. Additional experiments designed to simplify the ball-rolling task did not improve performance in the younger children.

This poses a great theoretical challenge. If core principles like the permanence and solidity of objects are so fundamental to be encoded in the genes and manifest in young infants, they should be powerful enough to guide behavior in older, more skilled children. Why do 2-year-olds fail when 4-month-olds succeed? Hood et al. (2000) suggested four possibilities.

First, perhaps infant looking-time experiments have been misinterpreted and they do not reveal core knowledge. Indeed there has been a great deal of controversy over violation-of-expectancy experiments; they have been criticized for their logic, methods, statistics, and interpretations (Haith, 1998, among others). Although Hood et al. (2000) rejected this possibility, citing the converging evidence from many such studies, we agree with the critics. More on this later.

Second, Hood et al. (2000) considered that the disparate findings are statistical artifacts because looking-time measures compare differences within a child rather than simple measures of success on a retrieval task. Hood et al. rejected this possibility as well because toddler reaching studies have also used multiple trials and measures.

The third explanation by Hood et al. (2000) is that knowledge is not a unitary thing—that there are separable types of mental representations with different developmental time scales. One version of this posits a distinction between the implicit or procedural knowledge tapped by looking tasks versus the explicit, declarative knowledge used for retrieval. According to Bertenthal (1996), knowledge for action is modular and functions "in real time with little or no explicit reference to past experience" (p. 453), whereas "object recognition confirms that even young infants represent defining features and physical constraints that specify the unity and boundedness of objects" (p. 453). Yet this distinction makes the toddlers' behavior even more puzzling. Their everyday behavior shows that they can act in real time and recognize objects simultaneously, and thus act appropriately on objects they recognize.

The version favored by Hood et al. as the best explanation is that the difference lies in knowledge used for prediction and for making sense of what happened after the fact (see also Meltzoff & Moore, 1998). Looking experiments only require that infants notice that the event has violated their expectancies and then match their expected outcomes with the ones presented. Reaching tasks, in contrast, require prediction—a different and more difficult kind of knowledge. This solution is also troublesome. Why would violation of expectancy be easier than predicting where to act?

Without action, there are few consequences for having one's expectancies violated. However, reaching to the wrong place is memorable.

In this chapter, we reconcile the theoretical chasm by elaborating the fourth possible explanation of Hood et al.: that the construct of impermeable and inviolate knowledge principles is wrong and we can understand these tasks perfectly through their real-time dynamics. Our goal in this chapter is to suggest a conceptual framework—dynamic field theory—to unify such disparate results. We demonstrate in one contested domain—object permanence—that infants' and toddlers' behavior can be fully understood by detailed analysis of the tasks used to assess conceptual knowledge and by simulations using dynamic field models. Our take-home message is that knowledge of objects is created by the particular spatial and temporal properties of the task, and that concepts do not exist independently of those tasks. Piaget's notions of the sensorimotor bases of cognition are still likely correct.

NEW KINDS OF QUESTIONS

We contend that researchers—whether nativists or not—are getting conflicting results because they are asking the wrong questions. The accepted way to phrase the question in conventional cognitive development is: What does the (supply age here) child know about (supply the concept here)? The accepted way to answer this question is to design an age-appropriate experimental task by which children can demonstrate their knowledge. If children pass the test and have the concept, then researchers design a task appropriate for younger age children testing the same concepts. This is reiterated until researchers find an age where children do not know (Siegler, 1993). Experimenters choose the task for its conceptual content and assume that infants and toddlers interpret it the same way.

We believe experimenters are asking the wrong questions. We think there is no way to abstractly represent a concept in a task that is not completely tied to the events in the task itself. These include the salience, location, and movement of the objects in the task, the instructions and rewards given to the children, and the timing and repetitions of the events and their components. We demonstrate this in the remainder of the chapter using the dynamic field model to simulate experiments that give conflicting results about what children know about the properties of objects. We show that there is no paradox at all: Both tasks are governed by the same dynamics. Moreover, the nonlinearity of these dynamics means that even small changes in the task events can shift results and create children who both know and do not know.

GENERAL PROPERTIES OF DYNAMIC FIELD MODELS

We use dynamic field models in our simulations (Erlhagen & Schöner, 2002). These models are neurally inspired of the type described and characterized analytically by Amari (1977). The central feature of the models is a one-dimensional activation field, which corresponds to features of the task in a content-neutral way. Each site in the field corresponds to a value of some parameter, and its activation is high when the feature it corresponds to is present (Fig. 9.1).

We call the model content-neutral both because of its potential applications and because of the nature of its states. In the former sense, the model is a general model of perceptual-motor integration. Dynamic field models have been used to account for various phenomena in children and adults (Erlhagen & Schöner, 2002; Kopecz & Schöner, 1995; Spencer, Smith, & Thelen, 2001) and the tasks we describe in this chapter without any significant structural change in the models. In contrast, connectionist models use different structures to simulate different domains (cf. Elman et al., 1996). Dynamic field models differ only in whether we include excitatory or inhibitory memory fields, and these differ only in the signs of their activa-

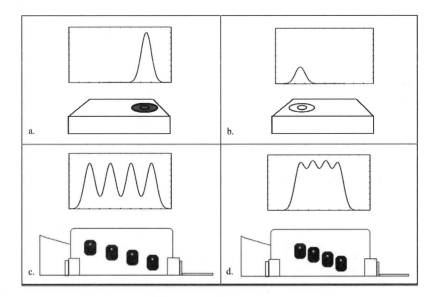

FIG. 9.1. Various stimuli and the corresponding activation in parameter space. (a) A single salient lid of the type used in A-not-B studies; (b) a similar lid, but less salient and in a different location; (c) an occluder of the type used in Berthier et al. with four salient doors; (d) an occluder similar to that in c, but with doors closer together. Note the summation of the Gaussians where they overlap.

tions. They are not special-purpose machines, each designed with the goal of explaining one task, but rather are a precisely and univocally characterized type of system that accounts for the structure of behavior in many different domains.

The models are also content-neutral because they make no appeal to the contents of their states in generating behavior. The only properties of the models that play a causal role in their behavior are parametric properties of the system, such as the activation and distance between sites, which correspond to physical properties of systems that we understand.[1]

By assigning parameters to the field that correspond to the outside world and to the internal state of the person, in a sense we endow it with content. However, dynamic models pose a stark contrast to the content-based explanations found in the developmental literature. Many of these explanations differ in both aspects just outlined. Indeed they are domain specific just *because* they appeal to the contents of infants' beliefs. For example, explanations of infant errors in a search task might appeal to general processes of inference, but they can only be explained if infants fail to have certain beliefs (e.g., contents about the physical structure of the environment). When infants begin to perform the task in the correct way, theorists explain that they have figured out the task—they have acquired the beliefs with the appropriate content to make inferences about the task. This requires that theorists must generate explanations of the acquisition of particular belief sets on a case-by-case basis. A new story about the contents of mental states is necessary for each task in which infants develop cognitive abilities.

Moreover, explanations that rely on "concepts" to motivate behavior face the issue of how the ideas in the head are actually translated into real behavior, which occurs in a rich context, in real time, and in a historical moment. What are the processes by which a belief actually leads to a reach or a look? The dynamic approach does not separate content and process, and thus offers an explanation for behavior without assumptions about beliefs and intentions and their causal roles.

Thus, the activation field is a locus in which information about various aspects of a task—perceptual, motor, and historical components—can be integrated in real time as part of behavior. Information about the perceptual environment as well as the motor history is fed into the field, which in turn generates motor behavior. Accordingly, each site in the activation field must at once correspond to some value of each of these components—it must correspond to some perceptual *and* some motor feature, in both the past and the future. In the most simple model, a site in the activa-

---

[1]Such as systems of neurons, for example, although we do not commit to a straightforward mapping of the model onto brains.

tion field corresponds to a percept at some location x, a memory of a reach to location x, and to a desire to reach to location x. Hence, the content of the field is a sort of abstraction of all these features. The causal effects of a particular state of the field (e.g., whether it will in fact generate a reach) are determined by the context in which the state occurs, both within the field and around the organism.

Beyond the fact that the field must be integrative in this way, we assume as little as possible about the features of the task environment to which the sites in the field correspond: Whether a site represents "button-at-location-x," "pressability-at-location-x," or some other feature is at this point a matter of the modeler's convenience. Presumably there is some fact of the matter that will tightly constrain ultimate theory, but in modeling a small set of task features we are able to choose a dimension that simplifies the model. For example, we can use a one-dimensional field to model a task that might in fact occur in a two-dimensional space. Nevertheless, our choice is constrained by the facts about the systems we are modeling, and we suppose that our ability to successfully model a particular domain tells us something about the nature of the real dimensions of the system.

Each site in the field always has a state of activation, which can be negative or positive. Furthermore, each site tends toward a resting level of activation, h, which is the same for every site in the field. Input can be given to the field simply by adding some value to the activation state of some site or sites. Because of the content-neutrality of the field, activation due to various features of the task, such as an affordance of the task environment, a cue, or a memory trace, is input to the activation field. In the absence of input, the activation level of each site will tend toward h at some rate that is determined by the time scale of evolution of the field τ.

An important feature of these fields is that input to a particular site need not come from sources external to the field. Sites within the field provide input to one another, which allows the field to become self-organizing (Fig. 9.2). Not every site influences every other site at every time, but the influence a site will have on the sites around it is determined by its state of activation in a nonlinear way. A highly activated site will have a strong excitatory effect on nearby sites and an inhibitory effect on sites far from it. A negatively activated site will have no effect on other sites in the field.

This interaction within the field allows peaks to be self-sustaining: Sites near the center of the peak continue to excite one another, which in some circumstances can prevent a peak from settling back to its resting state. Furthermore, this feature allows the field to make decisions between peaks. The inhibition that occurs over large distances will cause a large

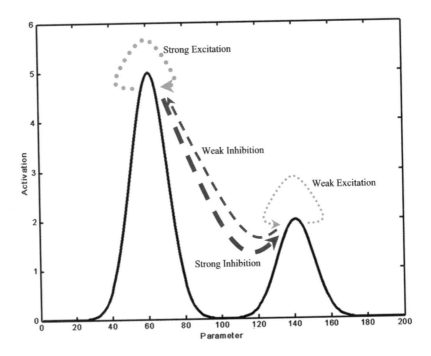

FIG. 9.2.   Self-organization in the field. On the left, the sum of strong excitation and weak inhibition leads to a self-sustaining peak. The sum of strong
inhibition and weak excitation leads to the degradation of the smaller peak
on the right. Larger peaks are likely to be preserved, but noise in the system
means that this is not deterministic.

peak to suppress small peaks at a distance, and local excitation will cause
it to coalesce with nearby peaks.[2]

This decision-making ability is a critical feature of these fields. All human behavior requires integrating and deciding among perceptual
choices. To illustrate how the field generates a decision from multiple inputs, consider the dynamic field model of the A-not-B task (Piaget, 1954;
Thelen, Schöner, Scheier, & Smith, 2001). In the classic A-not-B task, infants must make a decision between two targets, A and B. Recall that the
A-not-B task is a hidden object task in which infants around 9 months of
age will reach to an incorrect target after a number of prior reaches to a
different target. In a canonical version of the task, the infant faces a box
with two lidded wells in which a toy can be hidden. With the box out of
the child's reach, an attractive toy is hidden beneath one lid—"lid A"—

[2]Note that the noise we introduce to the model guarantees that such decisions are not
completely deterministic.

and the child is allowed to retrieve it. After six trials like this, the toy is hidden beneath the other lid—"lid B." After a 3-second pause, the box is again presented to the child. Eighty percent of 9-month-olds will reach back to lid A, although they have seen the toy placed beneath lid B. In fact Smith, Thelen, Titzer, and McLin (1999) demonstrated that the toy is not a necessary feature of the A-not-B task. Infants perseverate at exactly the same rate even if no toy is hidden, but instead the appropriate lid is cued—for example, by waving it. This suggests that the error is a perceptual-motor phenomenon, not a demonstration of false or somehow flawed content about the lids.

The dynamic field model preserves the task and time structure of these events. The activation field maps onto the spatial layout in the abstract way we specified earlier. We make the simplifying supposition that a reach to a location occurs whenever the activation at the corresponding site passes some threshold. We assume that the field begins in its resting state, with every site's activation equal to h. Suppose the experimenter presents a cue at location A, which corresponds to the activation at the top of Fig. 9.3. We input this activation to the field, which causes the field to begin to generate a peak at location A. When the activation at some site in the field passes a predetermined threshold, the baby reaches to the corresponding point.

At this point there are two ways for the field to behave. When the value of the resting activation level, h, is low, the peak cannot excite itself sufficiently to maintain itself, and hence it decays quickly. In this state, the system is purely input-driven—unable to generate behavior in the absence of input. This relation is shown in the middle panels of Fig. 9.3. However, when h is sufficiently high, the field is able to generate self-sustaining peaks (i.e., peaks that continue to exist in the absence of input). Thus, the field can maintain a sort of memory of an input even after the input has been removed (Fig. 9.3, bottom panels). For constant input to the field, there is a level of h below which the field will settle back to its resting state when the input is removed and above which the peak is able to sustain itself in the absence of external input.[3] Hence, h acts as a control parameter for the field. This is the feature we use to model developmental effect in the A-not-B error. When h is high enough for the field to generate self-sustaining peaks, we say that the field is in the *cooperative regime*.

In fact when there is a structured task environment in front of the baby, the infant does not begin with a homogeneous unactivated field. There is always *some* input to the field. We call the input which changes on a rela-

---

[3]Conversely, for constant h there is a value of the input that is sufficiently high to form self-sustaining peaks. Hence, for every value of h there is some input strong enough to generate a self-sustaining peak.

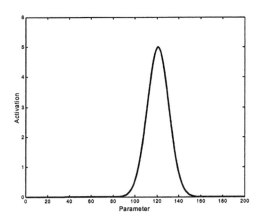

Non-cooperative Regime

input:

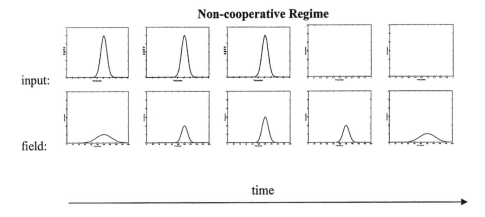

field:

time

Cooperative Regime

input:

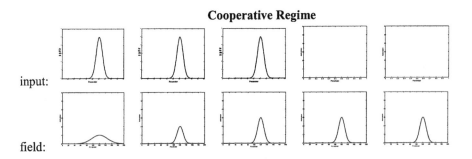

field:

FIG. 9.3. Top: An input to the field (compare to Fig. 9.1a). Middle: The evolution of a field in the noncooperative regime (i.e., with low *h*) when such an input is fed to the field for a period of time and then removed. The field begins in a homogeneous resting state, which moves toward the shape of the input. When the input is removed, the field relaxes to the homogeneous resting state. Bottom: In the cooperative regime, the peak generated by the input is able to maintain itself after the input is removed.

tively slow time scale the *task input*. The faster time scale input, such as the experimenter's cues, we call the *specific input*.

In addition to the activation field, we use a second memory field in the A-not-B model. This field is governed by the same dynamics as the activation field, but without internal interaction and on a slower time scale. The state of this field is then fed back into the activation field, with the effect that this trace of earlier states of the field influences later states to the extent that those earlier states were either long lived or of high activation. This means that there are two types of memory in the field—the memory in the activation field that consists of a self-sustaining peak that continues to exist in the absence of input, and the structure in the second memory field that continues to exist even when the shape of the activation field changes.

In outline form, the model of A-not-B behavior works in the following way. When a 9-month-old, who is likely to make the error, is cued to lid A on the first trial, she generates a peak at the A location in her activation field. The peak results from the two inputs to the field: a symmetrical task input with peaks at the sites corresponding to the locations of the lids, and a single peak at the site corresponding to the cued lid. Her resting h level is not high enough to generate a self-sustaining peak—she is not in the cooperative regime—so the peak at A begins to deteriorate after the cue to A. However, in the absence of competing input, she will likely have an above-threshold peak at A when the box is presented to her, which indicates a reach to A. The state of her activation field is fed into her memory field, which causes a smaller peak to form in memory at the location of her reach—lid A. The peak is small because the memory field evolves on a slower time scale than the activation field, and the reach does not last long enough to generate a large peak.

We assume the activation field to have settled before we start the second A trial, so the second A trial proceeds much in the same way as the first. However, the memory field does not settle back to its resting state between trials. As a result, the small peak at A in the memory field provides further input to the A location in the activation field, which suggests a stronger likelihood that she will reach to the A lid on this trial. If she again reaches to the A lid, then more input is fed into the memory field, and the trace at A becomes even stronger.[4] By the time the infant has seen the target hidden at A six times, she has likely generated a strong peak in her memory field at location A.

---

[4]Note that even the small amount of noise in the system is enough that there is no guarantee that she will always reach to A even on later trials. Also this accumulation of memory to A explains the usefulness of training trials in A-not-B tasks.

On the first B trial, the infant begins with a specific input from the cue to the B location. Her resting h level is still not high enough to allow the resulting peak to sustain itself, so the peak at B grows weaker during the delay period. During the delay period, there is still an input from the memory field, which increases the activation at location A. The result of these conflicting inputs is that infants reach to the B lid when there is no delay, but they reach to the A lid if a delay is imposed before the presentation of the box. Both of these predictions—and a host of others—have been empirically confirmed. Note that the peak in the memory field need not be nearly as strong as the specific input to the activation field to lead to perseveration.

Older infants do not perseverate on B trials, and we model this developmental effect by altering the resting level of the field, h. In the model, older infants have a resting activation level that is high enough that the input generates self-sustaining peaks. In these infants, the first six trials are similar to the first six trials in younger infants. (The exception is that the peak at A can sustain itself in the absence of the cue to A, so older modeled infants reach to A more frequently on the first A trial than do their younger counterparts.) The important difference comes on the B trials. Because peaks in the activation fields of these infants are able to sustain themselves in the absence of inputs, the peak that forms after the cue to B will not fade during the delay. In fact the peak at B will inhibit the input from the memory field at A as a result of the interaction in the field. Accordingly, modeled infants with higher h level do not perseverate on B trials.

Because the contributions to the infants' decisions to go to A or B are expressed in continuous metric dimensions, we can model—and empirically test—the effects of graded changes in the inputs to those decisions. For example, Diedrich et al. (2001) varied the strength and distinctiveness of the B task cue by providing different groups of 9-month-old infants with graded choices. One group received identical targets: red lids on a red box. Three other groups were tested with either orange, yellow, or a colorful striped lid on the red box. As predicted, the red/red group reliably perseverated at A, the orange/red and yellow/red groups responded to A or B at chance levels, and the striped/red group were reliably correct at B. Analyses showed that the contrasting lids worked in two ways: by enticing infants to sometimes reach to B on the A trials and thus diminish the memory built at A, and by increasing their attention to B on the B trials.

Using this relatively simple model, we have generated a rich set of predictions and confirmed them with empirical studies. Because the model simulates general processes that produce decisions to act, it also has wide applicability. In the remainder of the chapter, we use the dynamic field model to resolve the apparent contradiction that has gripped the field: If young infants demonstrate conceptual knowledge with looking tasks, why are older children unable to do so when using manual actions?

RESOLUTION I: HABITUATION

Claims of early infant competence rely on looking experiments. As detailed earlier, experimenters show infants some plausible event and then test them to see whether they detect a violation of that event by looking at it longer. All experiments of this type, whether termed *visual preference* or *violations of expectancy*, are habituation experiments. Habituation, the process of declining interest in a stimulus with repeated presentations, is characteristic of all animals. It is a way for an animal to attend to a novel stimulus, but also to seek new stimuli after a while. The critical question for infant studies is whether infants' looking differences reflect true conceptual understanding of the events or are a result of the process of habituation (Haith, 1998).

Looking at a display or looking away is a perceptual-motor decision completely analogous to making the decision to reach to one location or another. Indeed we show here that a version of the dynamic field model can explain apparent conceptual knowledge through the task dynamics of looking. This raises doubts about the first part of the paradox: Infants may not know very much after all.

There is a large literature on habituation from both humans and other animal studies. Investigators have identified a number of general features of the process that the model must emulate: (a) a decline of response to repeated presentations of a stimulus; (b) more initial response and slower habituation to complex or more arousing stimuli; (c) dishabituation to novel stimuli; (d) re-invigorated interest with a nonspecific boost of activation; (e) preference for the familiar habituating stimulus after a few presentations shifting to a novelty preference after many presentations; (f) in infants, distinct individual differences, with some infants habituating more quickly than others; (g) faster habituation in older infants; (h) habituation and dishabituation a function of the time intervals between stimulus presentations; and (i) dishabituation sometimes depends on the order of the test stimuli (see Sirois & Mareschal, 2002; Thompson & Spencer, 1966).

The principles behind the dynamic field model of habituation are the same as those behind the A-not-B model, although the fields correspond to different features of the task environment (Schöner & Thelen, 2003). The stimuli are again arranged in a one-dimensional activation field, but here each site corresponds to looking-at-a-particular-stimulus. This time the site corresponds to the *identity* of the stimulus, not its location in space.

As with the A-not-B model, habituating and dishabituating stimuli are metrically specified and can be strong or weak, close or far apart. The more similar two stimuli are to one another, the closer they are in the field.[5] In the simple model we present here, we track the activation of two sites in the field, which we assume to be close enough together to have some excitatory effect on one another. If Site 1 is activated above threshold, then the infant looks at Stimulus 1 (if it is present); if Site 2 is activated above threshold, then the infant looks at Stimulus 2.

As with the A-not-B model, we use two coupled dynamic fields. The activation field receives input from the stimulus as well as the second field, and it drives looking. Instead of a memory field, which provides excitatory input to the activation field, the second field is a habituation field, which provides an inhibitory input to the activation field. That is, excitation at Site 1 in the inhibition field is subtracted from the activation at Site 1 in the activation field. Hence, an infant with a peak at Site 1 in her activation field will look at Stimulus 1. The high activation at Site 1 in the activation field will cause her to develop a strong peak in her inhibition field at Site 1. This inhibitory peak provides a negative input to Site 1 in the activation field, which prevents the formation of peaks at Site 1 in the activation field on later trials. Because the peaks have breadth, the more similar Stimuli 1 and 2 are to one another—the closer Sites 1 and 2 are—the more this inhibition will transfer from one site to the other. This explains the greater dishabituation to stimuli that differ greatly from the habituating stimulus than to stimuli that are very similar to the habituating stimulus.

Figure 9.4 demonstrates the course of activation in both fields over a number of trials with a single stimulus. The top portion of the figure plots the input to the activation field, as well as the activation of Site 1 in both the activation and inhibition fields. The activation at Site 1 begins at the resting level, h. When the stimulus is presented (grey line), the activation at Site 1 increases. According to the model, when the activation at Site 1 is greater than 0, the baby looks at the stimulus. On Trial 1, the activation never reaches this threshold, so the baby never looks. Site 1 activation decreases after the stimulus is removed, but it does not relax to the resting level before the next presentation of the stimulus. Accordingly, when the stimulus is presented again the Site 1, activation increases further than on the previous presentation. Only on this second trial does the activation become high enough to cause looking, as indicated in the bottom plot

---

[5]In fact stimuli must be ordered in a higher dimensional space than this, but we begin by modeling the scenario in this simple way. This simplification is further justified by the fact that we only model the activation of two sites in the field. We can consider the distance between these two points in our field to be the Euclidean distance between the two points in whatever higher dimensional space is the right one.

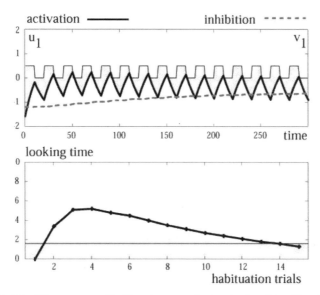

FIG. 9.4. Time course of habituation to a single stimulus. Top: The thin solid line marks the presentations of the stimulus, which is either on or off. This drives the activation of the corresponding sites, u_1 in the activation field and v_1 in the inhibition field. Bottom: Plot of looking time versus number of habituation trials.

("looking time"). Note that the Site 1 activation in the inhibition field tracks the Site 1 activation in the main field, but at a slower rate. Around Trial 4, the Site 1 activation in the inhibition field becomes great enough to counterbalance the input from the stimulus, and the main Site 1 activation reaches a maximum. After this trial, the inhibition is greater than the excitation from the stimulus, and looking time begins to decrease—the infant habituates to Stimulus 1.

These basic dynamics account for all of the phenomena in the habituation literature. For example, there are well-known differences in individual infants' rates of habituation (Bornstein & Benasich, 1986). Without any assumptions about infants' constitutional differences, we can produce fast habituators by simply changing an initial state of the model: raising the initial activation state of the field. Figure 9.5 depicts a simulation in which the initial activation of Site 1 is set at $h + 1.5$. This could occur either when the infant begins the session in a general state of excitement or if the infant happens to look at some display similar in some respect to the training display prior to beginning the sessions. This initial state of excitation leads to increased looking time on early trials, hence to faster habituation. More initial activation may reflect some stable characteristic of the infant, but it may also be due to a more transient level of interest or arousal. The same

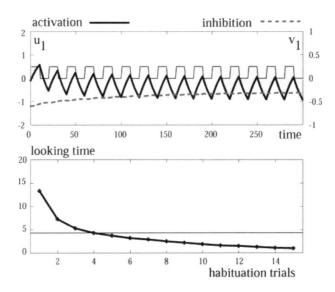

FIG. 9.5. Time course of habituation to a single stimulus in a "fast habituator." Compare with Fig. 9.4. The only difference is the higher initial activation of u_1. Note the drastically different looking time curve.

infant may not be a fast habituator in later tests or with different visual displays.

More important, the model accounts for familiarity and novelty effects as well, and shows how they arise from the same dynamics. Figure 9.6 depicts how the model generates a novelty effect. The top panels represent the activation of Site 1 in each field (u_1 in the activation field, v_1 in the inhibition field), the middle panel represents the activation of Site 2 in each field, and the lower panel represents looking time for both stimuli. The upper panel begins with the same course of habituation modeled in Fig. 9.4. Looking time first increases and then decreases as site v_1 in the inhibition field becomes activated. At about time step 300, the test stimuli are presented. In the left panel, the familiar stimulus is presented first, and in the right panel the novel stimulus is presented first. When the familiar stimulus is presented first, the pattern continues just as before the test, and the infant displays further reduced looking time to the familiar stimulus. However, infants display increased looking time to the novel stimulus relative to the familiar stimulus. There is no absolute increase in looking time to the novel stimulus, but it is preferred relative to the familiar stimulus. In most studies, this is the only aspect of looking time that is reported.

Figure 9.7 depicts the familiarity effect for infants with little exposure to a stimulus. In this case, there are only four habituation trials, which

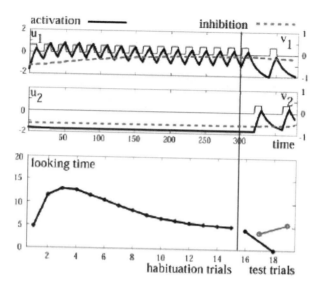

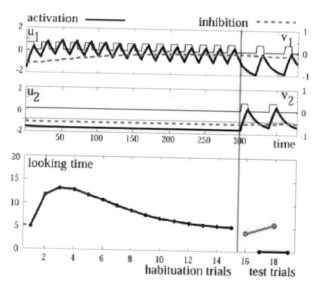

FIG. 9.6. Novelty effect. Simulation of the novelty effect, whereby infants prefer a novel stimulus after many habituation trials. Here we show the time course of activation of two stimulus sites, u_1 and u_2. Also depicted are the activations of the corresponding sites in the inhibition field, v_1 and v_2. The infant is habituated to stimulus u_1 and tested alternatively to u_1 and a second stimulus, u_2. The looking time to u_1 is depicted as a black line and to u_2 as a grey line. Top panel: Familiar stimulus presented first during testing; Bottom panel: Novel stimulus presented first during testing.

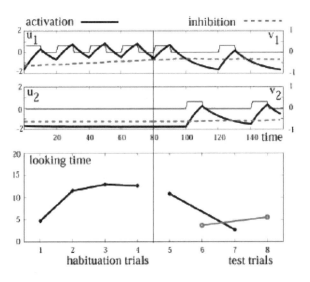

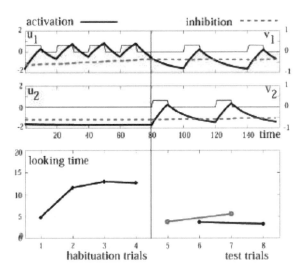

FIG. 9.7. Familiarity effect. Simulation of the familiarity effect, whereby infants prefer the familiar stimulus after few habituation trials. Top panel: Familiar stimulus presented first during testing; Bottom panel: Novel stimulus presented first during testing.

raise the activation of site v_1 somewhat, but do not excite it as much as the many trials in Fig. 9.6. Hence, when the familiar stimulus is presented first at test, the activation at u_1 still outweighs the inhibition at v_1, which causes the infant to look preferentially at the familiar stimulus. When the novel stimulus is presented first at test, the activation at u_1 fades, causing looking time to drop. Hence, both the familiarity effect and the order effect are straightforward consequences of our model. Schöner and Thelen (2003) showed how the dynamics of the model produce the other empirical properties of habituation.

The Drawbridge: Knowledge or Familiarity?

We now turn to Baillargeon's (1987a) famous drawbridge experiment, startling in its claim that infants as young as 4 months understand object properties. (Indeed the article was recently judged to be number 12 in the "20 studies that shook up child psychology"; Dixon, 2003.) Recall that infants are shown a panel—the drawbridge—that rises from the surface before them and rotates through 180 degrees until it contacts the surface again (Fig. 9.8). Once they habituate to this display, they are shown a pair of test stimuli in counterbalanced order. In both test stimuli, a red box is

Simulation of Baillargeon's (1987) "Drawbridge Experiments"

Habituating stimulus	Test 1: "Impossible"	Test 2: "Possible"
	Familiar (?) stimulus, with block boost	Novel (?) stimulus, with block boost

FIG. 9.8.   Baillargeon's (1987a, 1987b) drawbridge experiments. The infant looks at the stimuli from the right of the page. Left: The habituating stimulus consists of a screen that rotates through 180°. In the dishabituating stimuli, a box is introduced. It sits so that it is obscured behind the screen when the screen is around the 90° position. The two stimuli are presented in alternating orders: Middle: The "impossible" stimulus consists of the screen rotating through the same 180° as did the habituating stimulus despite the presence of the box, which should impede such a rotation; Right: In the "possible" stimulus condition the box rotates only as far as the box allows.

added to the display, positioned so that it should inhibit the travel of the drawbridge. In the "possible" test condition, the drawbridge stops when it contacts the (now occluded) box, whereas in the "impossible" test condition, the drawbridge does not stop, but appears to travel right through the space where the box was located when it became occluded. The main result of the study was that 4½-month-olds dishabituated to the "impossible" event, but only when it was presented as the first test stimulus. Baillargeon claimed that this longer looking at the impossible event indicated that the babies noticed something peculiar about it—namely, that it violates physical law.

The experiment is controversial. Some critics have claimed that infants are only looking at the impossible event because there is more interesting motion of the rotating screen (Rivera, Wakeley, & Langer, 1999). Others claim that the effect emerges because infants prefer to look at a stimulus similar to the habituating stimulus, not because it is impossible (Bogartz, Shinskey, & Schilling, 2000; Cashon & Cohen, 2000; Schilling, 2000). Our simulations lend credence to both accounts and indeed demonstrate that habituation dynamics, not any set of beliefs, create looking at the seemingly impossible event.

To simulate Baillargeon's experiment, we assume that the habituating stimulus (180 degrees of screen rotation) shares some activation with the dishabituating stimulus (112 degrees of screen rotation) because the screens share 112 degrees of pathway. Thus, we assume a weak excitatory interaction between Sites 1 and 2, so that looking at Stimulus 1 will cause excitation and habituation at Site 1, as well as some weak excitation and weak habituation at Site 2 and vice versa. Because the 180-degree event is more interesting to infants than the 112, we also give it more input. Finally, when the block is added at the test, we assume that the added interest boosts activation for both possible and impossible test trials. The dynamics of the simulation are similar to those described earlier.

Figure 9.9a illustrates the simulation for the 4½-month-old infants who got the familiar (impossible) stimulus first at the test. The top panel shows the behavior of Site 1, representing the 180-degree rotating screen, and the middle panel, Site 2, the 112-degree event. During habituation, an initially activated site responds to the input by decreasing looking time, reaching criterion in eight trials. Note that because the rotating screens are similar for part of their path, Site 2 shares some activation with Site 1. At test both sites are boosted to represent the influence of the block. Here Site 1, the familiar stimulus, is the first test, alternating with Site 2. The bottom panel gives the looking time.

This simulation shows a strong familiarity effect. The familiar, 180-degree test stimulus—boosted by the block—encounters an already activated Site 1 and together activate a large amount of looking. In contrast,

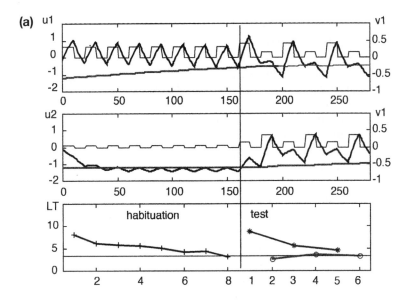

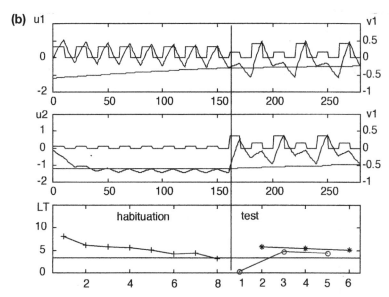

FIG. 9.9. Drawbridge simulations. (a) Familiar ("impossible") stimulus first. The figure shows the time course of activation of two stimulus sites, u_1 and u_2, and the corresponding inhibitory sites, v_1 and v_2. The bottom plot depicts the looking time over the course of the session. (b) Same as (a), but the novel ("possible") stimulus is presented first.

the novel stimulus, coming second, must overcome a highly activated Site 1. It looks as if the infants prefer to look at the impossible (familiar) event.

A different picture emerges when we simply reverse the order of the test stimuli, as shown in Fig. 9.9b. The habituation phase is identical. However, in the interval when infants see the novel display first, activation at the familiar Site 1 declines. Now the familiar stimulus does not provide enough summed activation to provide a large boost in looking, and there is no difference between novel and familiar. Infants do not distinguish between possible and impossible. As in the experiment, the combination of the two test orders gives an overall familiarity effect. Baillargeon (1987a) accepted the main effect, but dismissed the order effect interaction as not important. Our simulations produce both from the same dynamics.

This same model also replicates the results of Baillargeon's (1987a) control condition, in which infants were habituated to the 180-degree rotating ramp and then tested either on the 180- or 112-degree rotation without the block. Baillargeon reported that infants showed no preference. Our simulated infants showed the same results (Fig. 9.10) and showed that the boost given by the box is essential to the recovery of looking seen in the test conditions.

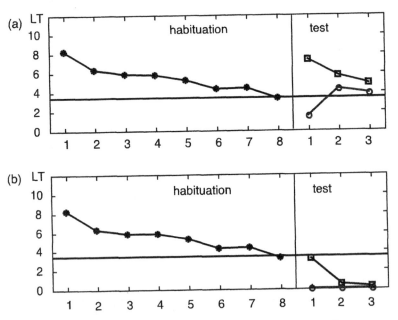

FIG. 9.10. Control and test conditions in drawbridge simulations. Compare with Fig. 9.2 of Baillargeon (1987a). (a) Average looking time of 4½-month-old infants. At test, squares = familiar, circles = novel. Note the overall familiarity effect. (b). Control condition. Reduced familiarity effect over (a).

These simulations produce different outcomes based on a small difference—order of test stimuli—and suggest that habituation and dishabituation depend on the precise nature and timing of the stimulus events. Indeed Schöner and Thelen (2003) successfully modeled all other versions of the drawbridge task with similar small parameter changes, including conditions where infants are younger or older, when there was no block to occlude, using different amounts of screen rotation, when a second block was added, with no habituation phase, when the box was slid back instead of rotated, and when the occluding objects were soft and hard. In none of these simulations did they appeal to infants' beliefs. Habituation dynamics provide a more general and parsimonious process account of infants' looking and not looking.

Because infant precocity rests on a misinterpretation of visual habituation studies, there is no real contradiction between infants' and toddlers' behavior. Moreover, we next explain toddlers' apparent lack of understanding with exactly the same dynamic principles.

RESOLUTION II: HIDDEN OBJECT TASKS

The second horn of the dilemma described at the outset are the hidden object tasks described by Berthier et al. (2000). These investigators have used a series of interesting studies to argue, in contrast to the claims made by Baillargeon and others, that 2- to 3-year-old toddlers do *not* understand basic physical properties of objects. How can it be the case that infants know so much, but toddlers know so little? We show that the same processes of perceptual-motor integration that generate the behavior in the A-not-B and habituation tasks also generate the behavior seen in toddlers in the studies described by Berthier et al. (2000).

The details of this task are critical, and so we recap them before explaining the model. First, the toddlers are familiarized with all the processes involved: seeing the ramp, the placement of the wall that stops the ball, the rolling ball stopped by the wall, and the placement of the occluder.

In the test condition, toddlers begin by looking at the ramp alone. Experimenters place the wall in one of the four locations on the ramp and then position the occluder of the wall and the ramp. They then roll the ball down the ramp behind the occluder and, finally, slide the entire apparatus forward so the toddler can open one of the doors. Children are allowed a second reach if their first one is incorrect. If both reaches are to the wrong door, the experimenter shows the child the ball behind the correct door.

In this task, 2-year-olds perform at chance levels, opening the correct door first on a mere 22% of trials; 2½-year-olds perform slightly better, opening the correct door first on 34% of trials; and by age 3, toddlers do much better, opening the correct door first 74% of the time. Most children have a favorite door. Of the 32 children ages 2 and 2½ years, 27 (84.4%) reached to the same door on over 50% of trials. Furthermore, most children (19/32 children or 59.4%) preferred Door 2. Berthier et al. reported that children perseverate, both to the previously chosen door and to the door that was correct on the previous trial. In the latter case, the toddlers have not opened the door, but they have watched the experimenter retrieve the ball from behind it. Children reach to the previously correct door on 25% to 27% of trials, but 4/32 children perseverated on over 50% of trials. Berthier et al. interpreted these results as deficits in the search strategies of 2-year-olds while the 3-year-old toddlers have figured out the task.

We adapted the basic A-not-B model to simulate all the experimental results of this much more difficult task. As before, the model includes a one-dimensional activation field, which maps onto points in space before the toddler. The model includes a second memory field that develops on a slower time scale than the main activation field. As in the A-not-B model, this field has an excitatory influence on the main activation field. All of the parameters in the model are set to the same values to which they are set in the A-not-B model, except the strengths of the various inputs, which of course vary between task settings.

There are two important differences between this model and the A-not-B model. First, the task is more complex. We treat the ramp task in the same way as the A-not-B task, but with more inputs to the field, distributed with more complexity in time. This does not require a change to the model, but it requires that we change the inputs to the model accordingly. The four doors in the occluder act like four lids in the A-not-B task. Similarly, the wall is part of the task input, and the ball is a specific input at the location at which it moves behind the occluder. These changes are illustrated in Fig. 9.11.

The second difference between our model of the ramp task and our model of A-not-B is how we handle the resting level of excitation of the field, h. As before the value of h determines the field's ability to maintain stable peaks in the absence of input. In the A-not-B model, h was a parameter that we varied with the age of the infant. In contrast, in the Ramp model, we treat h as a variable that depends on the location of the apparatus: When the ramp is in the workspace of the child, the value of h is increased. This is consistent with our interpretation of h as the state of excitation of the child. This is just the sort of thing we see when toddlers behave: Moving a toy close to the child generates a sort of excitation—as if the toddler is suddenly moved to generate a behavior now!

The inputs and the value of h are varied over the course of the simulated trial to model the events that constitute the experiment: Inputs are

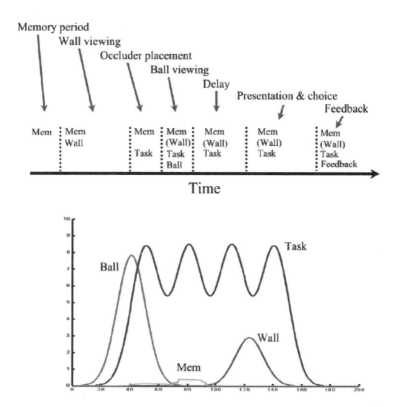

FIG. 9.11. Inputs to the activation field in the simulations of the Berthier et al. "Ramp Study." Top: Time line indicating the inputs to the activation field during various phases of the trial. "Mem" = the state of the memory field, which reflects previous reaches and reinforcement; "Wall" = the wall that stops the ball as it rolls down the ramp. After the occluder is placed, the strength of the wall input is reduced by 80%, indicated as "(wall)"; "Task" corresponds to the doors in the occluder. The delay is the period during which the ball rolls behind the occluder and before the apparatus is within reach of the child. Bottom: The actual inputs used in the simulations that generated the data we report here. The memory curve varies from trial to trial, but we include an example to indicate a typical magnitude of the memory input.

fed into the field with just the temporal structure that corresponds to the experience of a toddler participating in the task. After all of the events take place, the field evolves without input until the activation of any site in the activation field reaches a threshold. We then read the location of this site as the direction in which the child reaches. Despite inputs in various locations that do not correspond to doors, simulated children always reach in the direction of a door.

We simulated four blocks of four trials, which were structured simi-larly to the blocks used in the target paper: The wall was placed behind each door once per block of four trials in pseudorandom order. After each block of four trials there was a pause, during which we allowed the preshaped field to relax (not completely, but more than it does between trials within a block). Then another block followed, with a different door order. Hence, each simulated toddler saw the ball hidden four times be-hind each door for 16 trials. Each order of 16 doors constitutes a condition. We include simulated results from 10 different order conditions, with 20 babies simulated per door order.

We grouped the 2- and 2½-year-olds reported by Berthier et al. (2000) together and modeled the results of this unsuccessful group. (a) Together the real 2- and 2½-year-olds reached to the correct door first on 28% of tri-als; our simulated infants reached to the correct door first on 29% of trials. The top plot in Fig. 9.12 shows the proportion of reaches to the correct door for individual simulated infants. The distribution bears a strong re-semblance to that in Fig. 4 of Berthier et al. (b) Berthier et al. reported that 84.4% of toddlers tested reached to the same door first on more than 50% of trials; simulated infants showed this sort of favoritism on 84.5% of tri-als. The bottom plot in Fig. 9.12 shows the proportion of reaches to the fa-vorite door for individual simulated infants. This distribution is also strik-ingly similar to that in Fig. 4 of Berthier et al. (c) Of the children tested, Berthier et al. reported that 59.4% had Door 2 as their favorite door; of simulated children, 58.0% preferred Door 2 over the other doors. (d) Berthier et al. said that 12.5% of children tested perseverated to the previ-ously correct door on more than 50% of trials; simulated toddlers per-severated to the previously correct door on 15.5% of trials. Berthier et al. did not report the percentages of perseveration in their tests, but our sim-ulated children returned to the door they previously chose on 69% of trials and to the door that was previously correct on 41% of trials.[6] (e) In addi-tion, we have used the same parameter settings to simulate the training condition in which children search for a ball that was hidden through one of the doors. In these simulations, children reach to the correct door 100% of the time, as did the real children tested.

In summary, just as infants' behavior in A-not-B-type tasks can be fully explained by the dynamic field model, so also can we recast this knowl-edge task in toddlers in terms of task dynamics. We demonstrate that per-formance is created from multiple factors, including the background task setup, the salience and location of the events, the timing of the events, and what the child has just done. The nonlinear confluence of these factors can

---

[6]Note that a reach can be in both of these categories if the previously chosen door was the correct one.

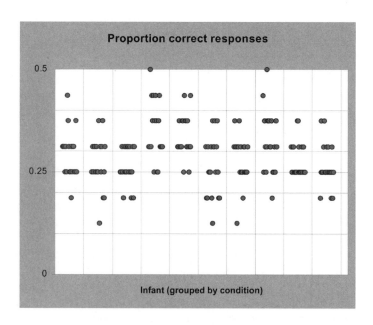

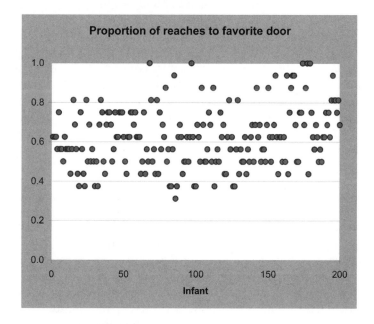

FIG. 9.12. Distributions of responses in ramp simulation. Compare with Figs. 2 & 4 in Berthier et al. (2000). Top: Proportion of reaches to the door with the ball behind it. Individual simulated infants are plotted and grouped by order condition. Performance differs significantly by order. We comment further on the order effect in the next section. Bottom: Proportion of reaches to the infant's favorite door by simulated infant.

make toddlers look dumb or smart. Moreover, we have principled ways to generate and test novel predictions.

Predictions

We can use the dynamic field model to vary the features of the task and generate new predictions. Such simulations have led to surprising results. For example, our simulations show that the order of doors behind which the ball stops makes a difference to the performance of the infants. Simulated toddlers perform significantly better in some order conditions than in others. Butler et al. (2002) looked for an effect of door order in a related study with a sample of about 22 infants.[7] For three blocks of four doors, there are 24^3 possible door orders. So the power of their analysis is quite low, and it is not surprising that they found no effect of order. When we performed an ANOVA (Door Order × Trial) on several groups of 22 randomly selected simulated infants, we found no significant effect of order either. However, when we increased the analysis to include all 200 simulated infants, the door order was highly significant [$F(9, 190) = 5.93; p < .001$].

Furthermore, a toddler's history matters. Simulated toddlers with no history perform quite well on the first trial, but their performance degrades rapidly on subsequent trials. We cannot simply compare our results to the first trials in the Berthier et al. study because once real toddlers undergo training, they already have a history, which influences their performance. The time between trials matters as well. Simulations suggest that longer delays between trials will yield greater success rates and less door favoritism.

Some of the results are even more surprising. For example, the distance between the doors plays an important role in generating door preference. In simulation, moving the doors closer together increases the preference for Door 2. Moving them farther apart decreases this preference. The salience of the doors also matters in an interesting way. Increasing the salience of all the doors improves performance in our simulations. In fact increasing the salience of the apparatus should improve performance. Our simulations also suggest that the ball matters less than we might think! We could replace it with a flashing light at the top of the ramp, and it is likely that we would even see similar results with no ball-like stimulus at all.

The reason the ball may not affect the baby's choice becomes evident when we examine the evolution of the activation field over the course of a single trial (Fig. 9.13a). The effect of the various inputs on the field can be

---

[7]Because this was a preliminary analysis that turned up negative, it is reported briefly. Hence, it is not clear exactly which infants were included.

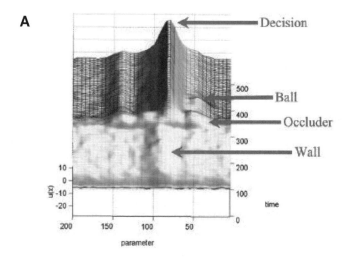

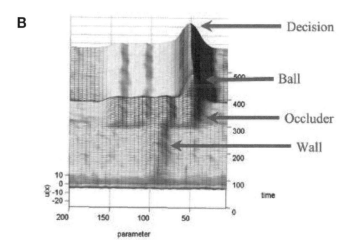

FIG. 9.13. (a) Activation field, early decision. This surface depicts the evolution of the activation field over the course of a single trial. The influence of the various inputs can be seen as they are fed to the field. Here the decision to reach to Door 2 is made early in the trial. Note that the peak has already formed before the ball is presented. This occurs due to the confluence of the wall, the door, and the memory inputs around the Door 2 site. When the peak forms this early, the ball is not strong enough to move it away from Door 2. (b) Activation field, late decision. Here the decision is not made until later in the trial. The early inputs are not strong enough to generate a peak. When the ball is added, a peak forms near the ball at Door 1. (See Color Panel K.)

seen clearly, although in this trial the memory trace to Door 2 blends in with the nearby activation caused by Door 2. The combined effects of these inputs in close proximity to one another is enough to generate a self-sustaining peak before the ball is ever shown to the child. It would take a very strong ball input to move the peak away from its position at Door 2. This sort of evolution is quite common in simulations, and we think it explains the fact that in simulations with no ball at all simulated children's performance is nearly the same in every respect to their performance in the normal simulations. The biggest difference is that they show a stronger preference for Door 2. However, the inputs to the field do not always generate an early peak in this way. The peak in Fig. 9.13b does not form until the ball is presented later in the trial. Hence, the history of the child influences the manner in which the decision to reach is generated. Trial order can be randomized, but not ignored. The door to which a child has recently reached can determine not only the location to which the child decides to reach on the next trial, but also the temporal structure of the decision-making process. Such differences in the dynamics of decision making provide other interesting possibilities for empirical exploration, as well as clear illustration that we must carefully consider every feature of a task.

CONCLUSIONS

These simulations suggest that surprising features of the task can have a profound effect on behavior. Sometimes minor changes in intensities or similarity or timing of the stimuli will have large effects on the experimental outcome. This does not imply, however, that every small change must do so. Some experimental effects are indeed robust, as are some properties of dynamical systems. These nonlinearities, revealed so dramatically in simulation, must also be apparent in the real tasks, but experimenters rarely consider them. When the task is designed to reveal content, the dynamics may not seem relevant, but they are. Experimenters are concentrating on whether infants or toddlers "have" or "do not have" a concept or "know" or "do not know" something about the world. The children, however, are watching interesting visual displays many times over and are behaving according to the perceptual properties of those displays.

For example, in a recent article, Spelke and Hespos (2001) addressed the reaching/looking *decalage* by proposing that infants demonstrate their knowledge of object representations based on the precision of their object representations: "When reaching or preferential looking tasks require a precise representation, then infants' performance will be impaired by occlusion; when reaching or preferential looking tasks demand only an imprecise representation, then occlusion may have little effect on performance" (p. 331).[8] This echoes a suggestion by Munakata et al. (1997) that reaching requires a stronger representation than looking. Moreover, Spelke and Hespos (2001) cited Munakata again that representations of objects are more precise when no other objects compete for attention. Thus, infants are worse at reaching for a hidden object than an object in the dark because the representation of the occluder interferes with the representation of the hidden object, whereas the darkness does not. In this way, Spelke and Hespos (2001) preserved their nativist stance: "We suggest that infants' basic capacities for representing objects are constant over development, but that their object representations increase gradually in precision as they grow" (p. 335).

Although Spelke and Hespos (2001) couched their explanation in terms of "representational precision," we note that they actually opened the door to task dynamics. They predicted, for example, that the duration of interrupted visibility in an occlusion task should matter, as should the nature of the occlusion. Such predictions are perfectly compatible with the dynamic field model.

Yet with the admission that the task dynamics do matter, what is the status of the representational content? We have shown that we can reproduce the seemingly cognitive phenomena without invoking representational states at all—the model makes no explanatory use of the contents of its states. Moreover, the model applies generally, not just to one task. We need not appeal to particular system of beliefs about the world either at 4 months or 2½ years. Studies that purport to reveal infant precocity have not shown that we start out with more than the modest repertoire of sensorimotor abilities that Piaget supposed. Indeed we suggest that we can get much farther than Piaget supposed with just this modest repertoire, but this last claim is a point to be pursued elsewhere, and we are happy here if we have opened the door to pursue it.

ACKNOWLEDGMENTS

We thank Gregor Schöner for his pioneering work on the dynamic field mode and Rachel Keen for kindly sending us videotapes of her experiments. Supported by NIH R01 HD2283017 to E.T.

---

[8]A problem with this formulation is that calling representations *precise* or *imprecise* completely depends on performance. When infants succeed, experimenters infer that they had sufficiently precise representations. When infants fail, their representations were not precise enough for the task.

REFERENCES

Amari, S. (1977). Dynamics of pattern formation in lateral inhibiton type neural fields. *Biological Cybernetics, 27*, 77–87.

Baillargeon, R. (1987a). Object permanence in 3.5 and 4.5 month-old infants. *Developmental Psychology, 23*, 655–664.

Baillargeon, R. (1987b). Young infants' reasoning about the physical and spatial characteristics of a hidden object. *Cognitive Development, 2*, 179–200.

Baillargeon, R., Spelke, E., & Wasserman, S. (1985). Object permanence in 5-month-old infants. *Cognition, 20*, 191–208.

Bertenthal, B. I. (1996). Origins and early development of perception, action, and representation. *Annual Review of Psychology, 47*, 431–459.

Berthier, N. E., DeBlois, S., Poirer, C. R., Novak, M. A., & Clifton, R. K. (2000). Where's the ball? Two-and three-year-olds reason about unseen events. *Developmental Psychology, 36*, 394–401.

Bogartz, R. S., Shinskey, J. L., & Schilling, T. H. (2000). Object permanence in five-and-a half-month-old infants? *Infancy, 1*, 403–428.

Bornstein, M. H., & Benasich, A. A. (1986). Infant habituation: Assessments of individual differences and short-term reliability at five months. *Child Development, 57*, 87–99.

Bransford, J. D., Brown, A. L., & Cocking, R. R. (Eds.). (1999). *How people learn: Brain, mind, experience, and school.* Washington, DC: National Academy Press.

Butler, S. C., Berthier, N. E., & Clifton, R. K. (2002). Two-year-olds' search strategies and visual tracking in a hidden displacement task. *Developmental Psychology, 38*, 581–590.

Cashon, C. H., & Cohen, L. B. (2000). Eight-month-old infants' perception of possible and impossible events. *Infancy, 1*, 429–446.

Ciske, P. (2002, July/August). Toddlers lack knowledge of physical laws. *APS Monitor, 15*.

Diedrich, F. J., Highlands, T., Spahr, K., Thelen, E., & Smith, L. B. (2001). The role of target distinctiveness in infant perseverative reaching errors. *Journal of Experimental Child Psychology, 78*, 263–290.

Dixon, W. E., Jr. (2003). 20 studies that shook up child psychology. *Developments: Newsletter of the Society for Research in Child Development, 46*, 6 & 13.

Elman, J. L., Bates, E. A., Johnson, M. H., Karmiloff-Smith, A., Parisi, D., & Plunkett, K. (1996). *Rethinking innateness: A connectionist perspective on development.* Cambridge MA: MIT Press.

Erlhagen, W., & Schöner, G. (2002). Dynamic field theory of motor programming. *Psychological Review, 109*, 547–572.

Haith, M. M. (1998). Who put the cog in infant cognition? Is rich interpretation too costly? *Infant Behavior and Development, 21*, 167–179.

Hood, B., Carey, S., & Prasada, S. (2000). Predicting the outcomes of physical events: Two-year-olds fail to reveal knowledge of solidity and support. *Child Development, 71*, 1540–1554.

Kopecz, K., & Schöner, G. (1995). Saccadic motor planning by integrating visual information and pre-information on neural dynamic fields. *Biological Cybernetics, 73*, 49–60.

Meltzoff, A. N., & Moore, M. K. (1998). Object representation, identity, and the paradox of early permanence: Steps toward a new framework. *Infant Behavior & Development, 21*, 201–235.

Mix, K. S., Huttenlocher, J., & Levine, S. C. (2002). Multiple cues for quantification in infancy. Is number one of them? *Psychological Bulletin, 128*, 278–294.

Munakata, Y., McClelland, J. L., Johnson, M. H., & Siegler, R. S. (1997). Rethinking infant knowledge: Toward an adaptive process account of successes and failures in object permanence tasks. *Psychological Review, 104*, 686–713.

Newcombe, N. (2002). The nativist-empiricist controversy in the context of recent research on spatial and quantitative development. *Psychological Science, 13*, 395–401.

Piaget, J. (1954). *The construction of reality in the child.* New York: Basic Books.

Rivera, S. M., Wakeley, A., & Langer, J. (1999). The drawbridge phenomenon: Representational reasoning or perceptual preference? *Developmental Psychology, 35*, 427–435.

Schilling, T. H. (2000). Infants' looking at possible and impossible screen rotations: The role of familiarization. *Infancy*, 389–402.

Schöner, G., & Thelen, E. (2003). *Using dynamic field theory to rethink infant habituation.* Manuscript submitted for publication.

Siegler, R. S. (1993). Commentary: Cheers and lamentations. In C. E. Granrud (Ed.), *Visual perception and cognition in infancy* (pp. 333–344). Hillsdale, NJ: Lawrence Erlbaum Associates.

Sirois, S., & Mareschal, D. (2002). Models of habituation in infancy. *Trends in Cognitive Science, 6*, 293–298.

Smith, L. B., Thelen, E., Titzer, R., & McLin, D. (1999). Knowing in the context of acting: The task dynamics of the A-not-B error. *Psychological Review, 106*, 235–260.

Spelke, E. S., Breinlinger, K., Macomber, J., & Jacobson, K. (1992). Origins of knowledge. *Psychological Review, 99*, 605–632.

Spelke, E., & Hespos, S. (2001). Continuity, competence, and the object concept. In E. Dupoux (Ed.), *Language, brain, and cognitive development: Essays in honor of Jacques Mehler* (pp. 325–340). Cambridge, MA: MIT Press.

Spelke, E. S., & Newport, E. L. (1998). Nativism, empiricism, and the development of knowledge. In R. M. Lerner (Ed.), *Theoretical models of human development. Volume 1 of the Handbook of child psychology* (5th ed., pp. 275–340). New York: Wiley.

Spencer, J. P., Smith, L. B., & Thelen, E. (2001). Tests of a dynamic systems account of the A-not-B error: The influence of prior experience on spatial memory abilities of two-year-olds. *Child Development, 72*, 1327–1346.

Thelen, E., Schöner, G., Scheier, C., & Smith, L. B. (2001). The dynamics of embodiment: A field theory of infant perseverative reaching. *Behavioral and Brain Sciences, 24*, 1–34.

Thelen, E., & Smith, L. B. (1994). *A dynamic systems approach to the development of cognition and action.* Cambridge MA: MIT Press.

Thompson, R., & Spencer, W. (1966). Habituation: A model phenomenon for the study of neuronal substrates of behavior. *Psychological Review, 73*, 16–43.

APPENDIX I: THE HABITUATION MODEL

See Shöner and Thelen (2003) for a more thorough discussion of the habituation model. Although the dynamics of the model occur within a continuous field, we simplify the habituation model by tracking only two sites, u_1 and u_2, in the activation field, as well as two corresponding sites, v_1 and v_2, in the inhibition field. Hence, we give the equation for each site:

$$\tau_u \dot{u}_1 = -u_1 + h_u + s_1(t) - c_u \sigma(v_1) + q_u \xi_1(t)$$

$$\tau_v \dot{v}_1 = -v_1 + h_v + c_v \sigma(u_1) + q_v \xi_2(t)$$

$$\tau_u \dot{u}_2 = -u_2 + h_u + s_2(t) - c_u \sigma(v_2) + q_u \xi_3(t)$$

$$\tau_v \dot{v}_2 = -v_2 + h_v + c_v \sigma(u_2) + q_v \xi_4(t)$$

where:

$$\sigma(u) = \frac{1}{1 + exp[-\beta u]}$$

is a nonlinear sigmoidal threshold function, the steepness of which is determined by β. In the simulations reported here, we set $\beta = 5$.

The inputs, s_1 & s_2, represent the stimulation applied to sites u_1 & u_2, respectively. In the drawbridge simulations, the input corresponding to the 180° rotation = 3.24 and to the 112° = 2.40. In these simulations, we assume that the two stimuli are not completely different, so each stimulus also excites the "noncorresponding" site to some degree as well. This is modeled as a common input to both sites = .72. When the block is added, the input is given an additional boost = 1.2. For the control conditions, the boost = .5.

The values t_u and t_v represent the time scales of evolution of the activation and inhibition sites, respectively. In the drawbridge simulations, t_u = 15 and t_v = 600.

The values h_u and h_v are the resting states of activation of the fields, which remain constant throughout the session. Here h_u = −0.6 and h_v = −1.6.

Parameter c_u determines the strength of the inhibitory effect that the habituation variable has on the activation variable. The value of c_v determines the strength of the excitatory effect of the activation variable on the inhibition variable. In the simulations, c_u = 2 and c_v = 2.

The strength of q_u and q_v determine the amount of white, Gaussian noise in the system. In these simulations, both were set to zero.

APPENDIX II: THE RAMP MODEL

The model we have used for the Ramp simulations is a slight variation on the model used in Thelen et al. (2001), where it is described in greater detail:

$$\tau \dot{u}(x,t) = -u(x,t) + S(x,t) + \int w(x - x')f(u(x'))dx' + h + q\xi(x,t)$$

During the early portion of the simulation, we set $h = h_{rest} = -8.3799$. Later, when the apparatus is presented to the child, we increase the value of h to

h_{excite} = −5.4487. The time scale of evolution, τ = 20. The Gaussian white noise strength, q = .1.

For every point x, the input from any other point in the field, x', is determined by the interaction kernel,

$$w(x - x') = -w_i + w_e \exp[-\frac{(x - x')^2}{2\sigma_w^2}]$$

where $w_i > 0$ and $w_e > 0$ are the strengths of the inhibitory and excitatory components and $\sigma_w > 0$ is the size of the excitatory region, which establishes the size of the localized activation patterns. In the simulations reported here, w_i = 1, w_e = 1.6, and σ_w = 10.

The influence of any other point in the field is also mediated by a sigmoidal threshold function, $f(u)$, which allows only sites with sufficiently high activation to enter into the interaction:

$$f(u) = \frac{1}{1 + \exp[-\beta u]}$$

where β determines the sharpness of the sigmoid function. We set β = 1.5.

The inputs, $S(x, t)$, consist of three components (See Fig. 9.11 for the time course of presentation of these inputs):

$$S(x,t) = S_{task}(x,t) + S_{specific}(x,t) + S_{memory}(x,t)$$

There are two types of task input, S_{task}, in the ramp study. The first consists of activation corresponding to the wall, whose location varies from trial to trial:

$$S_{wall}(x,t) = S_{wall,0} \exp[-\frac{(x - x_{wall})^2}{2\sigma_{wall}^2}]$$

In the ramp simulation, we set $S_{wall,0}$ = 2.9 and σ_{wall} = 10, while x_{wall}, the location of the wall, was manipulated over trials. Walls were centered 12.5 units to the right of the door to which they correspond. Furthermore, the strength of the wall input varies over the course of the trial: After the occluder is put in place, the strength of the wall is dropped to 20% of its original value.

The second task input corresponds to the doors in the occluder. It was modeled as the sum of four Gaussians, each centered on one of the four doors:

$$S_{ocl}(x,t) = \sum_{i=1}^{4} S_{ocl,0} \exp[-\frac{(x - x_{ocl}^{i})^2}{2\sigma_{ocl}^2}]$$

In an activation field of 201 sites, $x_{ocl}^{1} = 50$, $x_{ocl \, 1}^{2} = 80$, $x_{ocl}^{3} = 110$, and $x_{ocl}^{4} = 140$. The strength, $S_{ocl,0} = 8.3206$, and $\sigma_{ocl} = 10$. This input is constant across every portion of the trials in which the occluder is in place.

The specific input, $S_{specific}$, corresponds to the ball. It too is a Gaussian centered to the left of the doors, with $x_{ball} = 40$, $\sigma_{ball} = 10$, and strength, $S_{ball,0} = 7.8456$:

$$S_{ball}(x,t) = S_{ball,0} \exp[-\frac{(x - x_{ball})^2}{2\sigma_{ball}^2}]$$

The memory input, S_{memory}, is the state of a separate activation field at the end of the previous trial. This field evolves in a similar way to the activation field, but with neither internal interaction nor noise:

$$\tau_{mem}\dot{u}_{mem}(x,t) = -u_{mem}(x,t) + \Theta(f(u(x,t))),$$

where $f(u)$ is the same sigmoid used above, and Θ is a constant scalar, .7022. The value of the activation field is fed into the memory field only during the reinforcement period after the threshold is pierced. We then allow the memory field to evolve for a period, after which the state of the field remains constant until the next reinforcement period. We set $\tau_{mem} = 200$.

10

▼▼▼▼▼▼▼

Theory, Methods, and Models:
A Discussion of the Chapters
by Newcombe and Thelen & Whitmyer

Bennett I. Bertenthal
University of Chicago

The goals of developmental theory and research are twofold. First, it is necessary to know what develops; second, it is necessary to know how these new developments occur. Both of these questions have long and venerable traditions and are reflected in the major developmental theories of the 20th century. For example, Piaget's (1954) theory of cognitive development described how the child's knowledge of many fundamental categories of knowledge—such as object, space, time, and causality—changed with cognitive development. This theory also attempted to explain these developmental changes in terms of a specific form of equilibration based on the processes of assimilation and accommodation (Piaget, 1952).

By now the equilibration explanation proposed by Piaget has been abandoned by most researchers because it is essentially too abstract and too difficult to know how to apply to specific behaviors. Although the structural components of Piaget's theory relating to the content of the child's mind have fared better, it would be misleading to suggest that his predictions about what develops and when is without controversy. Recent research on the early perceptual and cognitive capacities of human infants challenges many of Piaget's assertions about the more gradual construction of knowledge (e.g., Baillargeon, 1987; Spelke, Breinlinger, Macomber, & Jacobson, 1992; Wynn, 1992). Yet some of this research suggesting precocious knowledge by young infants appears inconsistent with even more recent studies with toddlers who are unable to show the same knowledge presumably shown by infants (Berthier, DeBlois, Poirer, Novak, & Clifton, 2000; Hood, Carey, & Prasada, 2000). These contradictory findings led Thelen and Smith (1994) to suggest a "crisis in cognitive development," but it is not entirely clear whether many of these contradictions are "apparent or real."

In this commentary, I plan to discuss both chapters in the context of how they relate to the complementary issues of "what develops" and "how." First, let me complement the authors for presenting engaging and thought-provoking chapters. In reflecting on the issues discussed in these chapters, I was reminded again of the myriad complexities associated with studying the development of the human mind. One specific goal in writing this commentary is to clarify the evidence necessary for claiming innate capacity. A second goal is to illustrate the strengths and limitations of models of brain development as well as formal models of behavior for explaining human development. The final goal is to highlight some remaining questions about the development of spatial re-orientation and spatial search, and to suggest some of the mechanisms that might contribute to these developmental accomplishments.

One brief note before beginning my commentary. The two preceding chapters present different approaches in supporting the theoretical perspectives of the authors. Newcombe (chap. 8) presents empirical evidence that she claims challenges an innate perspective on a geometric module. By contrast, Thelen and Whitmyer (chap. 9) present findings from a theoretically derived model that simulate previous empirical results without postulating innate concepts, and thus claim that granting innate knowledge to infants is unnecessary and wrong. Both approaches are useful for testing theories, but they necessitate different forms of evaluation, which becomes evident as we proceed with this commentary.

INNATE VERSUS LEARNED BEHAVIORS

The first issue relates to what develops. In essence, much of the controversy according to Newcombe and Thelen/Whitmyer revolves around whether some forms of knowledge are innate or learned. One difficulty with resolving this controversy is that the meaning of innate is rarely defined or specified operationally. In the two preceding chapters, we are presented with two different characterizations of innate knowledge: modularity and competence versus performance. I address both of these constructs in the context of how they are defined, and then I evaluate whether the evidence presented by the authors refutes the claims of the researchers who first reported this evidence.

Before continuing, I digress briefly to illustrate the ambiguities and complexities that accompany debates about innate versus learned behaviors. In developmental science, the differences between innate and learned behaviors are often discussed as if there is an absolute division between these two categories. For example, the instinctual behaviors of lower animals such as insects are assumed innate, whereas the higher level processes of humans are conscious and learned. Research conducted over the past few decades now shows convincingly that a sharp distinction between instinctual or innate behaviors and learned behaviors is untenable (Gottlieb, 1991; Gould & Marler, 1987). Instead the research literature shows that animals are innately prepared to learn some things more readily than others. For example, odor is a more reliable indicator than color for rats (who are nocturnal) when trying to identify dangerous food, and a pigeon is more likely to learn to eat seeds if it experiments with its beak rather than its feet (cf. Gould & Marler, 1987). "The idea that animals are innately programmed to attend to specific cues in specific behavioral contexts and to experiment in particular ways in other contexts suggests a mutually reinforcing relation between learning and instinct" (Gould & Marler, 1987, p. 76). Experimentation involves learning, but this learning is constrained by the natural biases that prepares the animal for adapting to its environment.

This same type of reciprocity between biological preparedness and learning is present in the human species as well. Johnson (1992) presented an excellent example of how young infants learn to recognize faces after showing a bias as newborns to preferentially respond to stimuli resembling faces. This bias helps ensure that young infants are exposed to frequently appearing faces more than less important objects and will quickly learn to recognize familiar faces. In the context of this example, we can ask whether it is appropriate to conclude that face perception is innate or learned. The answer seems to depend on which behavior we define as an index of face perception. Certainly there is some bias in the visual system to fixate and track facelike stimuli from birth, but this bias is not sufficient for recognition or discrimination of faces, although it seems necessary for the development of both behaviors. It thus seems apparent that the distinction between innate and learned behaviors is quite blurry, and thus global characterizations of some behavior as innate or learned do not allow for a very informed assessment of whether the data support or refute the claim. In the following discussion, it is useful to keep these issues in mind in order to evaluate the evidence for and against core concepts or innate behaviors.

Let me now turn to Newcombe's chapter. She has done an admirable job of reviewing the evidence for and against a geometric module. The evidence for a module begins with the report by Cheng (1986) that, following disorientation, rats ignored landmarks and searched for food both at the correct location and at the rotationally equivalent location at the opposite side of the room. According to Newcombe, this finding has been interpreted to suggest that rats reorient to their environment by means of an encapsulated system operating on a geometric description of the surface layout. The reason this system is considered encapsulated or modular is that, following disorientation, rats respond exclusively to geometric information, although nongeometric information is detectable and discriminable under other conditions. Hermer and Spelke (1996) reported analogous findings for young children. Like rats, 18- to 24-month-old children searched reliably and equally at the correct corner and at the geometrically equivalent opposite corner. Their successful use of room geometry showed that they were motivated to perform the task, remembered the object's location, and, like rats, reoriented in accordance with the shape of the surface layout, but not in accordance with non-geometric landmarks, like color of the wall. These findings are some-what reminiscent of the discrimination shift learning literature of the 1960s and 1970s. Recall that young children were reported to perform like rats. They could shift to a new cue within the same dimension, but they could not shift to a new cue from another dimension (e.g., Kendler, Kendler, & Ward, 1972). Subsequent research revealed that this deficit in categorization was more a function of the paradigm than a function of the cognitive limitations of children.

Similarly, the research reviewed by Newcombe suggests that young children's failure to use landmarks could be a function of the paradigm. By simply enlarging the room, young children begin to show more consis-tent use of nongeometric information (Learmonth, Nadel, & Newcombe, 2002; Learmonth, Newcombe, & Huttenlocher, 2001). This evidence is cer-tainly provocative, but is it sufficient to discredit the claims of modularity proposed by Hermer and Spelke? The answer clearly depends on the spe-cific predictions associated with a modular system. Hermer and Spelke (1996) defined a *geometric module* as informationally encapsulated (sub-conscious or automatic use of geometric, but not nongeometric informa-tion to encode location) and task specific (limited to spatial disorientation tasks). As such it is defined as a "core property of geometric knowledge" that emerges early and persists throughout the lifespan.

Strictly speaking, evidence showing that toddlers use spatial land-marks in larger rooms is not inconsistent with the criteria for an innate module because the claim depends only on showing that use of geometric information emerges first. Hermer and Spelke (1996) acknowledged that changes to this reorientation system occur with development, such that the system becomes less modular and more flexible with regard to how lo-calization occurs following disorientation. It is thus not inconsistent with the modularity prediction to report that toddlers use both sources of infor-mation. However, if toddlers used nongeometric information before using geometric information, then the evidence would contradict the prediction that geometric information is privileged because it is associated with an innate module. As far as we know, no such evidence has been reported. An additional test that could prove informative would be to assess younger children in the larger room. If we are endowed with a geometric module, then there should be some age at which infants would use only the geometric information and not the nongeometric information in the larger room. Currently, it seems premature to claim that the evidence reported by Newcombe contradicts the modularity claim. However, this evidence does challenge the developmental claim by Hermer-Vazquez, Moffet, and Munkholm (2001) that nongeometric information is not integrated with geometric information until the development of the relevant spatial language around 5 to 6 years of age.

The evaluation of modularity also raises some important questions about what is meant by a *core concept*. In the case of the research on spatial re-orientation, the youngest children are at least 18 months of age. Thus, there certainly would be ample time for experience to contribute to the development of this module. If this module were primarily a function of experience, it might be possible to show individual differences as a function of rearing environments, but it is difficult to imagine different rearing situations that would differ with regard to the geometric structure of the spatial layout. A more plausible interpretation is to suggest that the infant is biologically prepared to exploit geometric information for the purposes of spatial re-orientation and develops sensitivity to the geometric structure of the environment over the course of the first 18 months. It is currently unclear to me whether Hermer and Spelke would acknowledge the contributions of spatial experience to the development of a geometric module or whether they would claim that this module develops innately without any experience. Once it is acknowledged that some experience contributes to the development of a cognitive system, it becomes a slippery slope to differentiate between a modular knowledge system and knowledge that develops as a function of experience. As previously discussed in the context of Marler and Gould's comments on the relations between instincts and learning, the distinction between biologically prepared and learned behaviors begins to blur as soon as the organism begins to experience environmental stimulation.

In Thelen and Whitmyer's chapter, the authors criticize the nativist perspective on development because it requires a reintroduction of dualism in which competence and performance are distinguished. *Competence* refers to some mental or cognitive model of the knowledge that is endowed to infants, whereas *performance* refers to the various psychological processes—perception, action, attention, memory, motivation, and so on—that are responsible for assessing these competencies. This distinction makes a huge assumption about how knowledge about the world is represented as a rich, independent, internal model. If a putative core concept is not revealed at a young age, it is typically claimed that certain performance factors are responsible for failure to reveal evidence of that concept. Like Thelen and Whitmyer, Matt Longo and I (Bertenthal & Longo, 2002) questioned the utility of this distinction because, as currently operationalized, it grants researchers license to claim innate competence for any skill regardless of whether it is demonstrated in some primitive form at birth or at some later age. At the least, a principled set of criteria is needed to claim what skills constitute core or innate competencies and what skills are associated with the performance of these competencies. As discussed by Thelen and Whitmyer, a more constructive approach is to view the infants' developing sensitivity toward perceptual and cognitive capacities in terms of both stimulus and response variables that contribute to performance. In so doing, the researcher can examine how multiple cognitive, perceptual, and motor variables interact with the stimulus and its context and produce different levels of performance at different ages.

It is not surprising that Thelen and Whitmyer would object to a competence–performance distinction to study the mind because it is diametrically opposed to the view of embodied cognition that Thelen (see Thelen & Smith, 1994) advocates. Personally, I share a similar view that cognition is spread across brain, body, and environmental artifacts. For example, it is not necessary for an infant to develop a representation of the path of a ball to show predictive tracking because the visuomotor system includes a feedforward mechanism with a short-term memory store to ensure smooth tracking (Bertenthal, 2002). There is, however, an important distinction between my view of embodied cognition and the radical view articulated by Thelen and Whitmyer. In their view, "there is no way to abstractly represent a concept in a task that is not completely tied to the events in the task itself." If this view is taken literally, then it requires that we give equal weight to all variables associated with a task, but experience shows that some variables are extremely important and others are inconsequential. Moreover, infants begin to generalize their responses across multiple conditions as they gain greater experience with the specific concept being tested. For example, 4-month-old infants show evidence of object unity when a partially hidden rod is translated back and forth, but 6-month-old infants generalize this response to rotations as well (Eizenman & Bertenthal, 1998). Eventually, infants are able to symbolically represent some concepts so they can be generalized to new situations without first learning about them through actions. This new skill is especially apparent with the development of language and the generalizability of specific labels to new objects, people, and events (Waxman & Markow, 1995).

Given the preceding considerations, it is not only possible, but often preferable, to study cognitive development without measuring a large number of variables. If the goal is to study concept development or knowledge of physics, for example, then a time-honored tradition is to hold all extraneous variables constant, manipulate the stimulus information at different ages, and assess how performance changes. Ideally, it would be useful to then assess the generalizability of these findings by changing the task or stimulus. Regrettably, most of the research on early cognitive development is conducted in a fragmented and piecemeal way, so we rarely have the opportunity to evaluate performance across a range of ages and stimuli.

MODELS AND METHODS

The second topic for comment is concerned with how new knowledge develops. It is commonly acknowledged that the field of developmental science has not been successful in developing models and methods for studying change, and thus progress on this issue has been at best marginal (Bertenthal & Longo, 2002; Siegler, 1994). The previous two chapters offer some rare insights into the challenges and opportunities associated with studying developmental change. Newcombe presents some novel speculations on the mechanism responsible for developmental changes in spatial re-orientation based on recent research on hemispheric integration in animals. Thelen and Whitmyer devote much of their chapter to describing a formal model based on dynamic field theory to show how habituation and dishabituation in infants changes as a function of the cooperation of different variables, and similarly how toddlers' spatial search for a hidden rolling ball changes as a function of the parameterization of the child and task. Both chapters are discussed in turn.

One of the most surprising findings in the research on spatial disorientation is that children do not begin to consistently use nongeometric information to code the location of the correct container until 5 to 6 years of age. Hermer-Vazquez, Spelke, and Katsnelson (1999) used a verbal shadowing task with adults to show that this task interfered with their ability to use nongeometric information in a search task, but it did not interfere with their ability to use geometric information. By contrast, a rhythmic shadowing task did not affect adults' ability to use nongeometric information in the same search task. In a subsequent study, Hermer-Vazquez et al. (2001) reported that children's ability to re-orient was correlated with their production of the linguistic terms *left* and *right*. Based on these findings with children and adults, Hermer-Vazquez et al. concluded that the development of spatial language served as a bridge for integrating geometric and nongeometric information. Although this convergent evidence is suggestive, Newcombe does a commendable job showing that the current evidence is insufficient to draw any firm conclusions. Of course this does not necessarily mean that the hypothesis posed by Hermer-Vazquez et al. (2001) is wrong, but it does mean that more conclusive evidence is required.

Although Newcombe's criticisms are not sufficient to completely refute the hypothesis of Hermer-Vazquez et al., she also challenges their hypothesis by proposing a different explanation for the developmental shift in spatial reorientation. Newcombe reports several differences between the right and left hemispheres in spatial functioning in humans. In the hippocampus, the right side encodes relational spatial information, and the left side encodes categorical information about spatial layout. In neocortex, the right side encodes metric information, whereas the left side encodes categorical spatial information. Newcombe hypothesizes that verbal shadowing could disrupt hemispheric integration because the results from different studies show that verbal processing may interfere with categorical coding of spatial features. Moreover, this evidence suggests that the development of hemispheric integration is necessary before children consistently use nongeometric as well as geometric cues in spatial reorientation tasks.

This explanation is incomplete and quite speculative, but its explanatory value lies with attempting to show a convergence between brain and behavioral development. This strategy is becoming increasingly common in developmental science. For example, Berthier, Bertenthal, Seaks, Sylvia, Johnson, and Clifton (2001) tested the proposal by Bertenthal (1996) that dorsal and ventral pathways in the developing brain are integrated gradually to explain why 9-month-old infants could not inhibit predictive reaching for a rolling ball, whereas the same age infants could inhibit predictive tracking. Presumably, the integration of visual information and the control of visual tracking develop earlier than the integration of visual information and reaching. The problem with both the interpretation by Berthier et al. as well as the hypothesis proposed by Newcombe is that brain–behavior relations are still primarily correlational, and thus the evidence for explaining behavioral development in terms of brain changes is more suggestive than definitive.

Nevertheless, the modeling of behavioral development in terms of brain development is at the least heuristic for suggesting how knowledge is organized. Also recent progress in neuroimaging and neuropsychology is beginning to offer opportunities for testing the relations between brain and behavior more directly. For example, my colleagues and I (Grezes, Fonlupt, Bertenthal, Delon-Martin, Mazoyer, & Decety, 2001) recently showed with fMRI that adults' perception of biological and nonbiological motions are mediated by spatially dissociable regions in the occipital-ventral region of the cortex, and that biological motions but not non-biological motions were also mediated in the parietal cortex. These results provide compelling evidence that biological and nonbiological motions are represented separately in the brain.

Whereas the previous models were fairly limited in scope, the attempt by Thelen and Whitmyer to explain behavioral development in terms of a dynamic field model is extremely ambitious. In essence, they describe a content-neutral model that they claim could apply to any task or at least those that involve some choice between responses. The model is derived from dynamic field theory, which assumes that actions are the dynamic function of both the immediate stimuli in the environment and the recent and longer term history of the system in similar situations. Models based on this theory have now been developed to explain infants' performance on the A-not-B error (Thelen, Schöner, Scheier, & Smith, 2001), infants' performance on habituation tasks (Schöner & Thelen, 2003), and toddlers' performance on a search task in which correct performance requires an appreciation of the solidity of a partially hidden barrier (Thelen & Whitmyer, chap. 9, this volume).

Let us consider how this model explains habituation, which is typically a decision to look at or away from a stimulus. This decision evolves in two interacting fields that are a function of the perceptual information. (a) The activation field consists of two or more sites defined by the activation strength of each stimulus. The similarities of the stimuli determine the distance between sites, and thus the degree of reciprocal activation or inhibition between sites. This field receives input from the stimulus as well as from the second (habituation) field, and collectively this input drives looking. (b) The habituation field receives input from the activation field and controls the level of inhibition at the different sites. When these fields are combined in the model and the different variables are parameterized correctly, simulations reveal many commonly reported findings associated with habituation studies.

One of the most interesting findings is that the model offers an explanation for why infants with little exposure to a stimulus tend to prefer the familiar to the novel test stimulus. Although the empirical evidence supporting this finding is fairly sparse, further support would have important implications for interpreting many studies testing the content of the infant's mind with a preferential looking paradigm. In particular, it may be necessary to reevaluate the interpretation for some of the recent studies claiming that infants look longer at an "impossible event" when that stimulus is at least superficially similar to the familiarization stimulus. According to the results of the model, longer looking is not a function of infants' detecting an impossible event, but rather a function of the familiar stimulus generating a stronger looking preference. A similar point was made recently by Sirois and Mareschal (2002).

The more general claim by Thelen and Whitmyer is that " 'knowledge' of objects is created by the particular space and time properties of the task itself, and that concepts do not exist independently of those tasks." Presumably, the dynamic field model succeeds where other models do not because this model encompasses all the relevant variables, such as object salience, location, instructions and rewards, timing, and repetition of events, whereas other models are typically limited to the contents of the mind. Although Thelen and Whitmyer offer some impressive evidence showing the success of their model, it is not clear that this success is sufficient to demonstrate the superiority of the new model relative to previous accounts of the phenomena discussed.

In evaluating this model, we follow the recommendations of Popper (1959, 1963) and apply four steps for assessing its truthfulness or validity. The first step is formal and involves the testing of the internal consistency of the theoretical system to evaluate whether it contains any contradictions. If the model contained contradictions, it would not successfully predict observed behaviors. Given that this model predicts the empirical evidence, we submit it passes this first step.

The second step is semiformal and involves the axiomatizing of the theory to distinguish between its empirical and logical elements. This step makes the logical form of the theory explicit; failure to do so can lead to asking the wrong questions and searching for empirical data where none is available. Indeed this is the point made by Thelen and Whitmyer about many current theories, and their model tries to avoid this problem by making the logical assumptions explicit and specifying all the relevant behaviors or empirical elements. This is no easy feat, and each test of the model requires a comprehensive analysis of the task. Regardless of the final disposition of the model, Thelen and Whitmyer should be commended for their thorough and highly informative analyses of the habituation and object search tasks.

The third step involves comparing the new theory with existing ones to determine whether it constitutes an advance on them. This comparison can take two forms—qualitative or quantitative. Thelen and Whitmyer offer a qualitative comparison of their model to other models or explanations for habituation or object search. In essence, they claim that their model is superior because it appeals to fewer logical elements or theoretical constructs, such as mental concepts, and explains behavior in terms of the empirical elements or behaviors that are specifiable. The problem with this claim is that all models include logical or theoretical constructs, and the dynamic field model is no exception. This model does not posit any specific concepts, but it does posit a memory that is necessary to explain developmental differences in performance. The nature of this memory is left unspecified, which makes it difficult to evaluate its logical similarity to the construct of stored knowledge, which the authors eschew as unnecessary. In the final analysis, it is difficult to truly evaluate how similar or different the new model is from previous models because the evaluation is highly subjective.

One possible solution to the previous problem is to quantitatively compare the predictions of the dynamic field model relative to the predictions of other models and empirically demonstrate that the new model is more successful in predicting the data. In essence, this is the standard approach used by mathematical modelers when testing the explanatory value of one model relative to others. Currently, it may be difficult to satisfy this criterion because there are few phenomena in early cognitive development that have been explicitly modeled. One relevant exception involves competing habituation models, which are summarized by Sirois and Mareschal (2002). If the dynamic field model is indeed superior to these other models, it should be possible to show this advantage quantitatively.

The final step in the evaluation of a theory is the most critical and involves the ability of the theory to predict new results. If such predictions are shown to be true, the theory is corroborated (but never verified). If the prediction is shown to be false, the theory cannot be completely true, and the quest for improving the current theory or finding a new theory begins. The lynchpin for meeting this criterion is to show that the theory can be falsified. In the case of dynamic field theory applied to habituation and object search, the evaluation on meeting this criterion is mixed. On the one hand, the authors report that the model leads to some novel predictions when applied to the object search paradigm used to test toddlers. If the predictions are wrong, then the model and, ultimately, the theory are falsified. On the other hand, predictions for current as well as new findings are based on unspecified procedures for assigning specific values to the parameters of the model. As far as I can tell, these assignments are not determined by some principled procedure, but rather by the trial-and-error efforts of the model builder.

Thus, it is difficult to falsify the model. If one version of the model fails to simulate the empirical results, it is not necessary to assume that the model is incorrect because the parameters can continue to be modified until the model simulates the results. Thus, it is conceivable that a whole class of phenomena can be demonstrated by simply tweaking one or two parameters. The arbitrary setting of parameters appears to represent a major gloss of the model, and it calls into question the possibility of relating these parameters to true psychological variables, which systematically vary along one or more dimensions.

As a case in point, consider the problems associated with defining the salience and discriminability of the stimulus. This is a problem that still confronts researchers studying adult perception, and the difficulty of the problem is only increased when studying human infants. I have spent a great deal of time and effort dealing with this problem in trying to assess what infants perceive when presented with moving point-light displays of biological motions (see Fig. 10.1). It is possible to parse this display at multiple levels of analysis, and adults perceive different information depending on the task. Based on empirical research, we know that depending on the task adults can perceive everything from the trajectories of the individual point lights to the configural structure and dispositional characteristics of the depicted person (Bertenthal, 1993). It is much less clear what infants perceive, but we know that their percepts change with age and experience. We also know that by 5 months of age infants not only perceive the configural structure of these displays, but they recognize them as depicting a familiar object. When the stimulus is presented upside down or reconfigured as a quadruped, it is no longer recognized and variations of this stimulus are not discriminated (Bertenthal, 1993). Surprisingly, 3-month-old infants discriminate all of these displays because they are responding to a different and more local form of information (i.e., pairwise relations or triads comprising limbs) in the point-light displays (Booth, Pinto, & Bertenthal, 2002).

What are the implications of these findings? The so-called *salience* of these displays cannot be determined arbitrarily if the modeled parameters are going to have any psychological reality. As I just reported, 3-month-

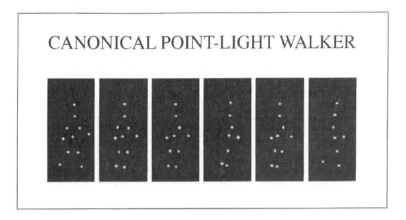

FIG. 10.1. A series of six sampled frames from a computer animation depicting a point-light walker display. These displays consist of 11 points of light moving as if attached to the head, shoulder, hip, elbows, wrists, knees, and ankles of a person walking.

old infants discriminate variations in biological motions not discriminated by 5-month-old infants. This finding is counterintuitive and would not be predicted a priori. Contrary to the assumptions of Thelen and Whitmyer, parameterizing salience or discrimination does not depend only on the stimulus information. It depends also on what is in the head of the infant, which includes stored knowledge. Thus, it is not even sufficient to provide a formal metric for parameterizing the stimulus because infants may or may not respond in accordance with this metric.

In summary, the theory tested by the dynamic field model does not fully satisfy the criteria established by Popper, but this is meant less as a criticism than as a challenge. Relative to current conceptualizations in the field of cognitive development, this theoretically derived model is extremely unusual in its specificity and breadth. Most important, we view this model as an existence proof for demonstrating the enormous difficulty in specifying the process of development, but also for suggesting that the explanations of developmental phenomena are tractable.

REMAINING QUESTIONS

Let me now turn to the last point of my commentary and address some remaining questions about the development of spatial re-orientation and spatial search. As previously discussed, Newcombe reports that toddlers do not rely exclusively on geometric cues when a larger room is used, and this finding plays a prominent role in challenging the argument for a geometric module. This difference in performance as a function of room size may at first seem anomalous, but on further consideration some intriguing explanations emerge.

Newcombe suggests that the differences between using landmarks in the small and large rooms may be attributable to the affordance of more activity in the larger room. It is suggested that the opportunity for more movement will focus greater attention on the landmarks in the room. This is certainly possible, although it has not been tested directly. A somewhat different possibility is that the path integration system, involving the continuous updating of the relation between self and each object during self-movement (Wang & Spelke, 2002), is sufficient to maintain spatial orientation in the small room, but not the large room; thus, spatial landmarks are not encoded as relevant to spatial orientation in the small room. Accordingly, children are limited to the continuously updated path integration information, which includes distances and directions of surfaces (i.e., geometric information) following their disorientation in the small room. They have not encoded the landmark information because it was unnecessary, and thus they are unable to use this information to re-orient. This interpretation is consistent with the evidence that rats re-orient in accordance with landmark features when they are tested in a familiar environment because additional experience allows them to develop some representation of the unique features or landmarks of the environment (Biegler & Morris, 1996). Analogously, adults tested in this same situation, without the benefit of any specific instructions, might also show a failure to integrate landmark information on the first trial because they do not yet know what additional information is relevant to the task.

Regardless of whether this interpretation is correct, the discrepancy concerning performance as a function of room size is intriguing. This type of discrepancy in assessing children's competence is becoming increasingly common as we develop more and more tasks for assessing what is presumed to be the same skill. It is especially common in research assessing young children's concepts. For example, Kalina Michalska and I recently conducted a study testing numerical identity in 5- and 9-month-old infants. Previous research by Xu and Carey (1996) suggested that infants are incapable of responding to the featural identity of objects for judging numerical identity until 12 months of age. We designed an experiment involving more meaningful and attractive stimuli to challenge this assertion. As can be seen in Fig. 10.2, infants were familiarized to a face that translated across the screen and was occluded briefly. Test trials consisted

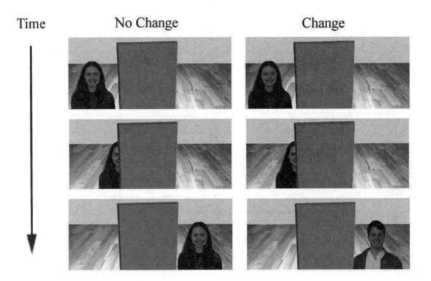

FIG. 10.2. Three sampled frames from a computer animated stimulus in which the identity of the person remains the same after reappearing from behind the occluding screen (left panel) or the identity changes after reappearing from behind the occluding screen (right panel).

of the same face or a different face reappearing to the right of the screen. In essence, this study could be construed as nothing more than a face discrimination experiment. We know from a considerable number of earlier studies that infants can readily discriminate faces by 4 to 5 months of age (Gauthier & Nelson, 2001). If infants were simply discriminating these two faces, they should have looked longer at the event involving the novel face. This is exactly what we found at 9 months of age, but not at 5 months of age. Apparently, these younger infants were encoding the path of the moving face, but not the features of the moving face. The path was identical in both familiar and novel conditions, and thus 5-month-old infants showed a form of change blindness (e.g., Levin, Simons, Angelone, & Chabris, 2002) and perceived both events as equivalent. One implication of this finding is that competencies assessed with one task are not always revealed when assessed by another task.

Finally, some of the results presented by Thelen and Whitmyer are intriguing, but the explanations are elusive because the dynamic field model cannot explain how the parametric changes occur. For example, the model explains developmental transitions in the search for hidden objects by proposing that, after a certain amount of experience, the input generates self-sustaining peaks because of a higher resting activation level. In contrast to a less developed system, these self-sustaining peaks do not decay. If the attention or memory for the correct site does decay, then the other site activated by the memory for the previously found object becomes dominant and drives reaching.

At an abstract level, this account for developmental change seems fine, but it seems to beg the question as to what really changes that enables infants' search to become successful. What is the psychological analogue to an increase in resting activation level? Does this increase represent greater attention or short-term memory, or does it primarily represent an increase in the inhibitory response toward a previously successful search location? The strength of the model is that it constrains the possible interpretations, but a definitive answer to this question must await experimental tests of the different interpretations.

FINAL COMMENTS

Research on the what and how of early development is extremely difficult because the available repertoire of responses by infants is fairly limited, and verbal responses, which constitute the most informative source of information in the psychologists' toolkit, are completely unavailable. Moreover, the behaviors that are measured are continuously changing, and these changes must be considered relevant to assessment even if they seem incidental to the concept or skill being tested. For developmental science to continue to make progress, it is essential to be as clear as possible about the theoretical constructs that motivate the research and, in turn, to conduct studies and develop models that will inform these theories. The preceding two chapters offer some excellent insights into how to go about such a program of research. In my commentary, I tried to show where the authors were most successful and where they may have overstated their conclusions. If this commentary is successful, then it may motivate the authors to pursue some of the issues that remain underspecified or unresolved.

ACKNOWLEDGMENT

I'd like to express my appreciation to Matthew Longo and Katharina Rohlfing for their comments on this chapter.

REFERENCES

Baillargeon, R. (1987). Object permanence in 3.5 and 4.5 month-old infants. *Developmental Psychology, 23,* 655–664.

Bertenthal, B. I. (1993). Perception of biomechanical motions by infants: Intrinsic image and knowledge-based constraints. In C. Granrud (Ed.), *Carnegie symposium on cognition: Visual perception and cognition in infancy* (pp. 175–214). Hillsdale, NJ: Lawrence Erlbaum Associates.

Bertenthal, B. I. (1996). Origins and early development of perception, action, and representation. *Annual Review of Psychology, 47,* 431–459.

Bertenthal, B. I. (2002). Visual occlusion and infants' predictive tracking. *Investigative Ophthalmology and Visual Science, 39*(Suppl.), S29.

Bertenthal, B. I., & Longo, M. R. (2002). Advancing our understanding of early perceptual and cognitive development. *Human Development, 45,* 434–440.

Berthier, N. E., Bertenthal, B. I., Seaks, J. D., Sylvia, M. R., Johnson, R. L., & Clifton, R. (2001). Using object knowledge in visual tracking and reaching. *Infancy, 2,* 257–284.

Berthier, N. E., DeBlois, S., Poirer, C. R., Novak, M. A., & Clifton, R. K. (2000). Where's the ball? Two- and three-year-olds reason about unseen events. *Developmental Psychology, 36,* 394–401.

Biegler, R., & Morris, R. G. M. (1996). Landmark stability: Studies exploring whether the perceived stability of the environment influences spatial representation. *Journal of Experimental Biology, 199,* 187–193.

Booth, A., Pinto, J., & Bertenthal, B. I. (2002). Perception of the symmetrical patterning of human gait by infants. *Developmental Psychology, 38,* 554–563.

Cheng, K. (1986). A purely geometric model in rat's spatial representation. *Cognition, 23,* 149–178.

Eizenman, D., & Bertenthal, B. I. (1998). Infants' perception of partially occluded objects during rotation and translation. *Developmental Psychology, 34,* 426–434.

Gauthier, I., & Nelson, C. (2001). The development of face expertise. *Current Opinion in Neurobiology, 11,* 219–224.

Gottlieb, G. (1991). Experimental canalization of behavioral development: Theory. *Developmental Psychology, 27,* 4–13.

Gould, J. L., & Marler, P. (1987). Learning by instinct. *Scientific American, 256,* 74–85.

Grezes, J., Fonlupt, P., Bertenthal, B., Delon-Martin, C., Mazoyer, P., & Decety, J. (2001). Does perception of biological motions rely on specific brain regions? *NeuroImage, 13,* 775–785.

Hermer, L., & Spelke, E. S. (1996). Modularity and development: The case of spatial reorientation. *Cognition, 61,* 195–232.

Hermer-Vazquez, L., Moffet, A., & Munkholm, P. (2001). Language space, and the development of cognitive flexibility in humans: The case of two cognitive memory tasks. *Cognition, 79,* 263–299.

Hermer-Vazquez, L., Spelke, E., & Katsnelson, A. (1999). Sources of flexibility in human cognition: Dual task studies of space and language. *Cognitive Psychology, 39,* 3–36.

Hood, B., Carey, S., & Prasada, S. (2000). Predicting the outcomes of physical events: Two-year-olds fail to reveal knowledge of solidity and support. *Child Development, 71,* 1540–1554.

Johnson, M. H. (1992). Imprinting and the development of face recognition: From chick to man. *Current Directions in Psychological Science, 1,* 52–55.

Kendler, H. H., Kendler, T. S., & Ward, J. W. (1972). An ontogenetic analysis of optional intradimensional and extradimensional shifts. *Journal of Experimental Psychology, 95,* 102–109.

Learmonth, A. E., Nadel, L., & Newcombe, N. S. (2002). Children's use of landmarks: Implications for modular theory. *Psychological Science, 13,* 337–341.

Learmonth, A. E., Newcombe, N. S., & Huttenlocher, J. (2001). Toddlers' use of metric information and landmarks to reorient. *Journal of Experimental Child Psychology, 80,* 225–244.

Levin, D. T., Simons, D. J., Angelone, B. L., & Chabris, C. F. (2002). Memory for centrally attended changing objects in an incidental real-world change detection paradigm. *British Journal of Psychology, 93,* 289–302.

Piaget, J. (1952). *The origins of intelligence in children* (M. Cook, Trans.). New York: International Universities Press. (Original work published 1936)

Piaget, J. (1954). *The construction of reality in the child* (M. Cook, Trans.). New York: Basic Books. (Original work published 1937)

Popper, K. R. (1959). *The logic of scientific discovery.* (Translation of *Logik der Forschung.*) New York: Basic Books. (Original work published 1935)

Popper, K. R. (1963). *Conjectures and refutations: The growth of scientific knowledge.* London: Routledge.

Schöner, G., & Thelen, E. (2003). *Using dynamic field theory to rethink infant habituation.* Manuscript submitted for publication.

Siegler, R. S. (1994). Cognitive variability: A key to understanding cognitive development. *Current Directions in Psychological Science, 3,* 1–5.

Sirois, S., & Mareschal, D. (2002). Models of habituation in infancy. *Trends in Cognitive Science, 6,* 293–298.

Spelke, E. S., Breinlinger, K., Macomber, J., & Jacobson, K. (1992). Origins of knowledge. *Psychological Review, 99,* 605–632.

Thelen, E., Schöner, G., Scheier, C., & Smith, L. B. (2001). The dynamics of embodiment: A field theory of infant perseverative reaching. *Behavioral and Brain Sciences, 24,* 1–34.

Thelen, E., & Smith, L. B. (1994). *A dynamic systems approach to the development of cognition and action.* Cambridge, MA: MIT Press.

Xu, F., & Carey, S. (1996). Infants' metaphysics: The case of numerical identity. *Cognitive Psychology, 30,* 111–153.

Wang, R. F., & Spelke, E. S. (2002). Human spatial representation: Insights from animals. *Trends in Cognitive Science, 6,* 376–381.

Waxman, S., & Markow, D. (1995). Words as invitations to form categories. *Cognitive Development, 29,* 257–302.

Wynn, K. (1992). Addition and subtraction by human infants. *Nature, 358,* 749–750.

IV

USING REPRESENTATIONS
TO GUIDE ACTION

11

▼▼▼▼▼▼▼

Using Perceptual Representations
to Guide Reaching and Looking

Rachel Keen
University of Massachusetts–Amherst

In the mid-1980s, the method of preferential looking, long a stand-by for studying infants' visual behavior, was adapted to answer questions about very young infants' conceptions of objects and events. A landmark study by Baillargeon, Spelke, and Wasserman (1985) challenged the long-held Piagetian notion that infants did not have object permanence until around 8 to 10 months of age. In contrast to Piaget's hidden object task, which involved removing a cloth and reaching for the object, the new procedure used looking longer to events inconsistent with physical laws. The new paradigm, dubbed "violation of expectation," was a welcome change in procedures because it could test infants before they began to reach. The authors reasoned that very young infants who are unable to search for objects because of motoric immaturity might have knowledge of hidden objects, but be unable to show it in a search task. In a series of studies following the original (for reviews, see Baillargeon, 1993; Spelke, 1991), the new looking-time task featured objects either stationary or undergoing motion out of sight behind a screen. When the screen was raised, the object was either in a position one would expect from physical constraints on the motion or another position that was inconsistent with physical constraints. By presenting infants with perceptual events that appeared to be possible (within the laws of physics) and impossible (violating physical laws), their data revealed that very young infants looked longer at impossible events.

    I describe a prototype experiment, selected because our experiments with toddlers described later in this chapter were modeled after it. In Experiment 3 of a *Psychological Review* article by Spelke and colleagues (Spelke, Breinlinger, Macomber, & Jacobson, 1992), the Experimental group saw a ball rolling left to right going behind a screen. When the screen was lifted, infants saw the ball resting against a bright blue wall; this event was repeated for several habituation trials. The Control group saw a hand lower a ball beside the wall; when the screen was raised, they too saw the ball resting against the wall during habituation. The purpose of this habituation phase was to decrease the infant's looking time at the event so that a recovery could be observed during test trials; otherwise there would a ceiling effect with looking time high at all events during test trials. (Not all experiments feature habituation trials, but many do.) For test trials, a second wall was introduced in front of the original wall. The consistent event showed the ball resting against the near wall (novel position, but consistent with physical laws), whereas the inconsistent test event was the ball resting against the far wall (old position, but violating physical laws). In this study, 3-month-olds in the Experimental group looked longer at the ball resting in a position that implied it had passed through the first barrier on the track. Control infants looked equally at both test events.

   Through a long series of studies conducted independently by Spelke and colleagues and Baillargeon and colleagues, these investigators concluded that infants between 2 and 5 months of age had knowledge about solidity of objects occupying space, and that two objects could not occupy the same space at the same time. Spelke's theory of infant cognition has a key concept termed *core knowledge* (Spelke et al., 1992). Two aspects of core knowledge that have been well researched in infancy are the principles of continuity and solidity. The continuity principle states that objects exist continuously and move on connected paths over space and time. The solidity principle states that objects occupy space such that two objects cannot occupy the same space at the same time. Other aspects of core knowledge involve gravity, inertia, and so on, but the experiments with toddlers to be presented here concern only continuity and solidity.

STUDIES OF TODDLERS' KNOWLEDGE
OF PHYSICAL LAWS

After almost two decades of dozens of studies, psychologists have arrived at a new view of infants' conception of the world—that is, a world in which objects are bounded, solid, and move on continuous paths following physical laws. This view upset the classic Piagetian conception of the young infant, who lacked object permanence until 8 to 10 months of age and did not achieve full knowledge of invisible displacement until 18 months (Piaget, 1954). Just when we were becoming comfortable with this modern view of infant cognition, several studies with children of 2 to 3 years of age indicated that toddlers appeared to not have knowledge of solidity or continuity. From the start, it is important to note that all of the seemingly disconfirming evidence came from studies in which children had to search for objects, in contrast to the infant looking-time data. Initially Bruce Hood startled us with intriguing data that showed 2-year-olds made interesting errors that he termed a *gravity bias* (Hood, 1995). Children watched balls dropped through one of three holes, each connected to an opaque tube. The three tubes criss-crossed so that the ball fell into a cup not directly below where it was dropped. Surprisingly, children searched directly beneath the hole where they saw the ball dropped rather than following the law of continuity, which would lead them to search where the connecting tube ended.

Our first contribution to the troubling toddler data indicated that children under 3 years appeared not to have knowledge of solidity (Berthier, DeBlois, Poirier, Novak, & Clifton, 2000). Our task, with an event modeled after Experiment 3 in Spelke et al. (1992) described earlier, was an action task where infants had to predict where the ball would be to search correctly. To help children become familiar with the event, they were thoroughly familiarized with the apparatus before test trials began. First, we wanted to make sure that children could find the ball if we simply opened a door, placed a toy inside, and closed the door. As expected, children were able to find the toy immediately on these trials that involved a simple hiding procedure (see Fig. 11.1 for view of child finding a toy in the apparatus). Next, with the screen removed to reveal the entire track, the experimenter demonstrated how a barrier could be placed in various positions. Children watched as the experimenter placed a barrier on a track, followed by lowering a screen with four doors, so that the track and bottom part of the barrier were concealed. The top of the barrier protruded several centimeters above the screen. At the beginning of each test trial, the experimenter drew the child's attention to the ball and released it at the top of the track, which was always in full view. The apparatus was pushed forward, and the child was invited to open a door to find the ball. The barrier could be placed at any door, and trials proceeded with each door being correct an equal number of times. Children liked this game and readily opened doors several times—between 8 and 12 trials.

The task required that children use their knowledge of barriers to predict where the ball would be. Thus, we turned the looking task into one where the child must do something—that is, find the ball. To do this, the child must reason about and predict the ball's location, then make an active selection of the right response. We fully expected this task to be easy in that knowledge of solidity would lead to the correct choice of door.

FIG. 11.1.   View of the apparatus used in Berthier, DeBlois, Poirier, Novak, and Clifton (2000). The child has opened Door 3 and found the ball resting against the barrier. Copyright 2000 by the American Psychological Association. Reprinted with permission.

Children at 2 and 2½ years of age, however, found this task to be difficult. Not until 3 years were the majority of children able to perform above chance. Their knowledge appeared to be much less sophisticated compared with data from the infant looking-time studies.

A scatterplot of data for the three age groups is displayed in Fig. 11.2. Each dot in the scatterplot represents one child's proportion correct over all trials. We used the binomial distribution to test whether each child's performance was above chance (.25). A one-tailed test for each child yielded: at 2 years, 0/16 were above chance; at 2½ years, 3/16; at 3 years, 13/16. The box on the distribution encloses data between the 25th and 75th quartiles; the middle line is the median for the group. Interestingly, their errors were not random. Some children selected a "favorite door" and chose it more than 50% of trials, whereas some perseverated, going back to the previously correct door. (One child chose wrongly on 100% of the trials because he always opened the previously correct door and our procedure was never to repeat the same door.) Some chose a door adjacent to the wall, but the wrong side, suggesting they made a connection between wall and ball, but without taking into account direction of the ball's movement.

Our findings with toddlers were independently confirmed by Hood, Carey, and Prasada (2000). In Experiments 1 and 2, their task differed from ours in two ways: The response was between two choices not four, and the movement was vertical in that a toy was dropped from above and landed on an upper or lower shelf. In Experiment 3, the motion was horizontal, and children pointed to the location where they thought the object

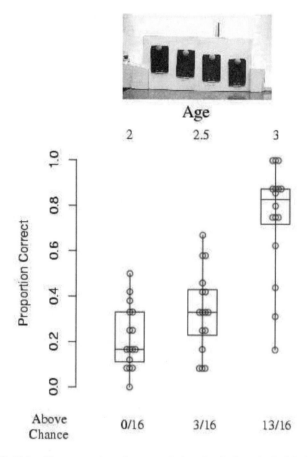

FIG. 11.2. The proportion of correct choices for finding the ball behind a door placed in an opaque screen. Each dot represents one one child's performance, and the number of children in each age group choosing the correct door more than chance is shown at the bottom of the figure. Horizontal lines show the median, and boxes enclose data between the 25th and 75th percentiles. The data in this figure are from Berthier, DeBlois, Poirier, Novak, and Clifton (2000). Copyright 2000 by the American Psychological Association. Reprinted with permission.

was hidden rather searching. As in Berthier et al. (2000), 2-year-olds were at chance in choosing the correct location of the toy despite variations in task and mode of responding. However, 2½-year-olds took into account the effect of a barrier on the toy's movement behind the screen and performed above chance with both variations. It may be that simplifying the task to two choices aided the older children's achievement.

MORE VISUAL INFORMATION AND GAZE BEHAVIOR

We conducted two experiments in which we gave the child more visual information—one that offered additional information during the ball's movement and one that eliminated hidden movement altogether. In Butler, Berthier, and Clifton (2002), we substituted a tinted Plexiglas screen for the wooden opaque screen, leaving only the four doors opaque (see Fig. 11.3 for view of apparatus). In addition to sight of the top of the barrier, this manipulation provided two new cues: sight of the ball rolling between doors and failure to emerge from behind the door with the barrier. We also videotaped the child's looking behavior to see whether tracking the ball correctly would be related to correct door choice.

The additional visual information did not seem to help most 2-year-olds (only 6 out of 20 children were above chance), but it did help the 2½-year-olds substantially (10 out of 12 children were above chance). For the younger children, just having visual information about the ball's movement did not translate into the necessary action to find the ball. Note that in this task it was not essential that the top of the barrier be used as a cue for the ball's location; either noticing where the ball disappeared or using nonemergence was sufficient to solve the problem.

Was visual scanning associated with selecting the correct door? Does scanning to the correct door mean that the child will then open it? Not necessarily. On the left side of Fig. 11.4, bars show correct tracking on about 50% of trials for both age groups. On the right side of Fig. 11.4, we show the proportion of trials when a child opened the correct door, given that he or she had scanned correctly. There was a striking age difference.

FIG. 11.3. View of the apparatus used in Butler, Berthier, and Clifton (2002). The ball can be seen rolling between Doors 2 and 3. Copyright 2002 by the American Psychological Association. Reprinted with permission.

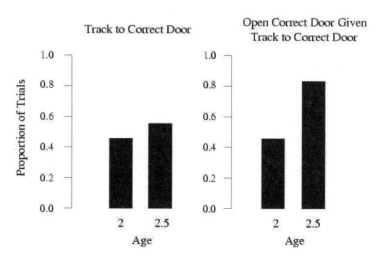

FIG. 11.4. The bar graph on the left shows the proportion of trials on which children tracked the ball to the correct door; the bar graph on the right shows the proportion of trials that children opened the correct door after they had tracked correctly. Data are from 2-year-olds' search strategies and visual tracking in a hidden displacement task. By S. C. Butler, N. E. Berthier, and R. K. Clifton, 2002, *Developmental Psychology, 38*, 581–590. Copyright 2002 by the American Psychological Association. Reprinted with permission.

At 2 years of age, children chose the correct door on only 46% of trials when they had tracked the ball to where it disappeared behind the correct door. By 2½ years, if they scanned to the correct door and stopped, this pattern was strongly associated with opening that door (about 83% of the time).

The clue to the 2-year-olds' difficulty lies in what they did after tracking the ball correctly. If 2-year-olds broke their gaze away from the correct door after tracking the ball, they chose correctly only 31% of the time, compared with 47% with no gaze break. Although both age groups were equally likely to look away at some point while tracking the ball (about 40% of trials for both groups), this behavior was unrelated to correct choice for the older children. Only the 2-year olds needed the visual *crutch* of watching the ball disappear and then locking their gaze on that door until they made a response. A break in attention was fatal to their making the correct choice.

The pattern of failures in this task by the 2-year-olds suggested that not only did they apparently fail to understand solidity, but they also appeared not to understand continuity. They often opened doors beyond where the ball had stopped (e.g., the ball stopped behind Door 2, but the child opened Door 3) and occasionally opened doors they had seen the ball roll past. These data stand in contrast to those from infants. Spelke and Kestenbaum (1986; described in Spelke, 1988) tested the continuity principle using a looking task with 4-month-old infants. They found that they appeared to recognize that objects move on spatiotemporally continuous paths. In this task, infants were habituated to an object moving back and forth behind two screens with a space between. If the object's trajectory carried it behind one screen, across the space, and out the far side of the other screen, infants looked longer on a test trial when screens were removed and revealed two objects rather than one. Just like adults, infants appeared to interpret this event as a single object moving continuously behind two screens. Another group of infants saw discontinuous movement in which objects moved back and forth behind the outer edge of each screen, but were never seen in the space between. This type of movement led to this group looking longer on a test trial display revealing only one object rather than two. The sophisticated understanding of object movement revealed by looking behavior was not found when toddlers had to use this knowledge to search for a hidden object. This may be a striking example of Bremner's injunction that we distinguish between perceiving and using that perceptual information to guide action (Bremner, 1997), a point we come back to in the discussion.

The second manipulation of visual information eliminated hidden movement of the ball altogether (Mash, Keen, & Berthier, 2003). We wondered whether the toddlers' problem was representing the path of a moving object after it disappeared behind a screen. What if we rolled the ball in full view and then brought down the occluder over a stationary ball resting by the wall? Note that this manipulation not only removes hidden movement, but also eliminates any requirement of reasoning about solidity of objects. When the screen is pulled over the ball, no reasoning about solid barriers stopping solid balls is necessary because the ball has already stopped. The top of the barrier can still be used as a marker for the ball's position because of its proximity, but knowledge of the solidity principle is irrelevant.

We tested eighteen 2-year-olds and eighteen 2½-year-olds in this condition. We used the same apparatus as in Berthier et al. (2000) and same familiarization procedures, but just reversed the sequence of when we rolled the ball and brought down the occluder. We termed the trials on which the ball was rolled and stopped in full view stationary ball trials. All children had stationary ball trials first, followed by moving ball trials exactly as in the original study (Berthier et al., 2000; see Fig. 11.5 for examples of these two types of trials).

We hypothesized that the stationary ball would be much easier to find because it did not move when out of sight and was fairly similar to the hiding event in our familiarization trials. Recall that during familiarization children were able to find a toy when a door was opened, a toy placed inside, and the door closed. In both cases, the toy did not move after being hidden, but on stationary ball trials the entire screen descended over the ball rather than a single door being closed. Furthermore, and this may have been most critical, the child saw movement of the correct door when the experimenter opened and closed it to hide the toy on familiarization trials, but saw no indication of the correct door on stationary ball trials.

There was, to our surprise, virtually no improvement in performance of the 2-year-olds; 2 out of 18 children performed above chance, very similar

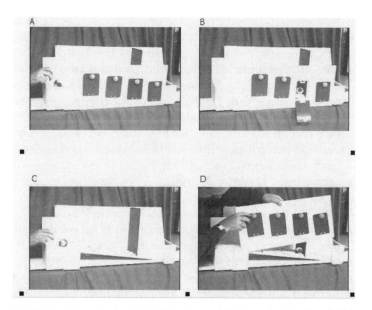

FIG. 11.5. View of two trial types used in Mash, Keen, and Berthier (2003). The top panel shows the apparatus and event that were presented to children called moving ball trials, in which the ball rolled behind an opaque screen and continued moving out of sight. The bottom panel shows the apparatus and event that were presented to children called stationary ball trials, in which the balled rolled down the track and came to rest against the barrier before the screen was lowered. This figure was adapted with permission from Mash, Keen, and Berthier (2003). Copyright by Lawrence Erlbaum Associates. Reprinted with permission.

to 0 out of 16 children in the original study. The 2½-year-olds fared a bit better; 7 out of 18 were above chance compared with 3 out of 16 in the original study. Performance on the moving ball trials was almost identical to that in the original study. Only one out of eighteen 2-year-olds and four out of eighteen 2½-year-olds were above chance. These results replicate those of Berthier et al. (2000). In summary, the data from Mash et al. (2003) indicate that hidden movement of the ball was not the major obstacle in determining the ball's location behind the screen, and, second, that receiving numerous trials with the stationary ball did not facilitate performance on the moving ball trials.

Once again, as in Butler et al. (2002), looking behavior proved to offer valuable insight into the toddlers' thinking processes beyond their search behavior. In both age groups, gaze behavior was related to whether they reached correctly. We scored looking time while the ball rolled, and the occluder was brought down over the stationary ball. Most children watched during these events, but performance appeared to be unrelated to fixations during the ball's occlusion. We also scored looking time as to whether children maintained their gaze on the correct location throughout the entire trial or whether they broke their gaze between watching the ball as the occluder was lowered and selecting a door to open. This measure was related to performance. When children fixated the ball during its occlusion and maintained fixation until they opened a door, they were almost certain to be successful. Taking a sample of children from both age groups (n = 19 out of 36) who fixated the position of the ball continuously on some trials and on some trials broke their gaze, we examined how correct they were following these different visual behaviors. When these children did fixate continuously throughout the entire event, they were correct 94% of the time (40 out of 43 trials). When they broke their gaze at some point, they were correct on 41% of trials (45 out of 109). One reason that so few children performed above chance was their failure to use consistently the successful strategy of maintaining gaze where the ball disappeared. Most often gaze was broken, and this appeared to degrade any knowledge of where the ball was.

To facilitate our comparison of the three studies presented thus far, Table 11.1 summarizes these findings in terms of children exceeding chance in each condition, given in proportions because different numbers of children participated in various studies. The two conditions featuring the moving ball behind an opaque screen were most difficult, followed by the stationary ball in which performance improved slightly. The most dramatic improvement was seen in the 2½-year-olds in the transparent screen condition. They appeared to use partial trajectory information and non-emergence of the ball to determine its location. Although giving more visual information did not boost performance of 2-year-olds as expected,

TABLE 11.1
Mean Proportion of Children Performing above Chance

	2 years old	2½ years old
Opaque screen (Berthier et al., 2000)	0.0 (0/16)	.19 (3/16)
Clear screen (Butler et al., 2002)	.30 (6/20)	.83 (10/12)
Stationary ball (Mash et al., 2003)	.11 (2/18)	.39 (7/18)

Note. Number of children above chance over total number tested is shown in parentheses.

close examination of visual behavior brought some insight to the toddlers' problems with this situation. Along with the transparent screen study (Butler et al., 2002), the stationary ball data provided strong evidence that 2-year-old children are extremely dependent on gaze behavior in figuring out where to search for the ball. The visual crutch of maintaining fixation on point of disappearance was effective when used. Finally, what may be most striking about the stationary ball data is that removing the requirement of reasoning about solidity of objects did not improve performance. The results from the original study (Berthier et al., 2000) and that of Hood et al. (2000) were interpreted to mean that toddlers had little or no knowledge of continuity or solidity, yet removing the necessity for this knowledge did not help performance. Other explanations must be sought.

EQUATING TASK REQUIREMENTS
BETWEEN INFANTS AND TODDLERS

Clifton (2001) speculated that differences in task requirements might underlie the apparent discrepancies between infant data and toddler data. When infants are tested with events that violate physical laws of solidity and continuity, they react to visual displays of object movements. They do not have to predict where an object might be, nor do they have to know in advance the object's exact location. To plan and execute a search that would yield the ball in our door task, toddlers must know in advance the exact location, not merely before or after the barrier. Because the search task requires both prediction and more complex motor planning, it is obviously more difficult than the looking-time task. We needed to turn the door task into a looking-time task to see whether toddlers would succeed under similar circumstances given to infants (Frank Keil first suggested this idea to me in a lab visit in 2000).

To put the child into an observer role, we had a puppet, Ricky the rac-
coon, open the door to find the ball in the same apparatus used in previous door studies (Mash, Clifton, & Berthier, 2002). The standard event was
that Ricky opened a door and found a ball. On the two "possible" or consistent test trials, Ricky opened the wrong door and found no ball. On the
two "impossible" or inconsistent test trials, Ricky opened the correct door
and found no ball. After each test trial, the screen was lifted so the child
could see the ball in the correct spot for possible trials and in the incorrect
spot (beyond the wall) for the impossible trials. There were two looking
measures: (a) one when Ricky opened a door and found no ball (a discrimination here would require prediction that the ball be at a certain door),
and (b) another when the screen was lifted (this discrimination would
only require recognition that the ball seemed to be in the wrong place on
inconsistent trials).

Two-year-olds looked longer on inconsistent trials when the screen
was lifted and they saw the ball in the wrong place. This looking-time
measure is analogous to that used by Spelke et al. (1992) when infants
looked longer when the screen was lifted and the ball had apparently
rolled through a solid barrier. Our looking measure that required prediction missed significance; toddlers looked longer, but not significantly longer ($p < .07$) when Ricky first opened the correct door and found no ball.
Hood, Cole-Davies, and Dias (2003) also ran a looking-time task using a
replica of our door apparatus. In their task, the experimenter opened two
doors simultaneously, one on either side of the barrier. Two-year-olds
looked longer when the ball was on the wrong side of the barrier. In both
studies, when task requirements put the child in the role of passive observer, children appeared to recognize incongruous event outcomes, just
like infants.

IS PREDICTION THE PROBLEM?

To the adult, the problem of finding the ball appears patently simple. Yet
as we saw 2-year-olds fail time and again in variations of this task, we began to ask ourselves what component processes were involved. First, in
both the looking-time and search tasks, the child needs to understand the
role of the barrier in stopping the ball. There is evidence for this understanding in the looking-time task with both infants and toddlers, but the
test is one of responding to a discordant perceptual array. No prediction
concerning the ball's whereabouts is involved. The door task requires prediction supported by additional abilities. To make an accurate prediction,
the child must integrate the spatial relations of wall/ball/door when the
critical elements are out of sight. We designed a study that required pre-

diction and understanding of the barrier's role, but we reduced the number of elements involved and gave full visual access to the display when the prediction was being made (Kloos & Keen, in press).

We presented 2-year-olds with a variation of the door task that required understanding of the role of the barrier to make a correct prediction, but with no search and no occluder. In this task, the experimenter presented the bare track and demonstrated how the barrier could be moved to different positions on the track. A small doll called Lorie was introduced, and the experimenter explained that Lorie liked to catch a ball that was rolled on the track. The experimenter demonstrated that to be successful Lorie had to stand just in front of the barrier on the side from which the ball was rolled. The E demonstrated that if Lorie stood in front of the wall with a space between her and the wall, she would be knocked over by the ball when it rolled down the track. Then the E demonstrated that if Lorie stood behind the wall, the ball would stop at the wall and Lorie would not be able to catch it. The correct place for Lorie to stand was again demonstrated; the ball was rolled and came to rest just at Lorie. Training proceeded in which the barrier was moved around, and each time the child was asked to place Lorie where she would catch the ball. After six familiarization trials of rolling the ball from one direction, the experimenter reversed the slope of the track. The barrier was again placed on the track and the ball was rolled to show the new direction of movement, but no demonstration with Lorie was given. Test trials proceeded with the ramp in the new slope position.

Children were scored as correct if they placed Lorie within 4 cm of the barrier on the correct side. Placements greater than 4 cm in front of the barrier and anywhere behind it were scored as incorrect. The children seemed to understand the task because they placed Lorie correctly on 87% of the familiarization trials, but this could have been imitation of the experimenter's placement in part. On test trials, the group proportion correct was .49, but this conceals the wide variation among individuals. Nine of the 17 children were correct on .40 or fewer test trials. The most frequent error was putting Lorie back in the previously correct position—a finding readily explained by Thelen and colleagues' analysis of perseverative errors (Thelen, Schoner, Scheier, & Smith, 2001). Eight children were above .50 and four were above .75 correct. Two children achieved perfect performance, immediately switching Lorie to the correct side of the barrier when the slope changed. The spread of these data indicates a transition period around 2 years of age. Some children are able to predict the ball's motion with regard to the barrier if the physical elements are fully displayed, but the majority of 2-year-olds still have trouble extrapolating this movement and using it to base their action with Lorie on. It would be interesting to see whether children would learn from their mistakes over multiple sessions and come to adjust their behavior in the face of any slope change.

USE OF CUES, DIRECT AND INDIRECT

Throughout the series of door studies, no evidence emerged that the children ever used the top of the barrier as a visual cue for which door to open. Performance only improved, and then primarily for 2.5-year-olds, when additional information was provided about the ball's trajectory (Butler et al., 2002). Why was this blatant visual marker ignored? One possibility is the difficulty that children may have in using indirect cues. The top of the wall is adjacent to the door and not physically connected to it. This spatial separation makes it an indirect cue, unlike sight of the ball's movement and disappearance, which are cues directly connected to the ball. Similarly, Hood's (1995) twisted opaque tubes are indirect cues to the falling ball's destination.

DeLoache (1986) did an interesting study that speaks to this issue. Using children around 2 years of age (21–28 months), she had them search for an object hidden in one of four visually distinct containers. They were successful, but when these same distinct containers were mounted on top of four identical boxes and the object was hidden in one of the boxes, performance dropped. DeLoache concluded that 2-year-olds have trouble integrating visual cues that are adjacent but not actually part of the hiding place. In a study with 12-month-olds, Bushnell, McKenzie, Lawrence, and Connell (1995) hid a toy under 1 of 58 cushions spread out in a large plastic wading pool. The target cushion was a different color, and infants had no problem crawling to and uncovering the toy. When the task changed so that the target cushion was similar to all the rest but its location was marked by an adjacent colored cushion, infants failed with this spatially indirect cue. In retrospect, we would predict that the top of the barrier would not serve as a good cue to the ball's location. It is behind the door to be opened and not directly part of the hiding place. This indirect cue requires the child to engage in an if-then chain of reasoning: if the barrier is here, then the ball is behind the door in front of the barrier. Following DeLoache, we would also predict that making the doors distinct rather than identical might aid performance.

HAVING KNOWLEDGE VERSUS USING KNOWLEDGE

Very young infants—3 to 4 months of age—are able to discriminate between two perceptual events, one of which appears to violate physical laws of solidity and continuity. Toddlers, 2-year-old children, also make these perceptual discriminations and, like infants, look longer at the discrepant event outcome. They fail, however, when these same events form the basis for a search task in which they must predict an object's location in advance. Although the infant data are striking, we need to examine what kind of knowledge the infant must have to express discrimination through looking behavior. If the 3-month-old could reach, would he or she know where to reach to find the object? Based on our data with toddlers, I would guess "No," they would probably not know where to search for the hidden object. The basis of their looking longer on inconsistent trials may be closer to Adele Diamond's characterization of infants' detecting that "something is amiss" without knowing exactly what is amiss (Diamond, 1998). We can still be impressed, however, that 3-month-olds have some knowledge of out-of-sight events, including permanence of objects and their solidity; otherwise they would not respond differentially to the two test events. In a thoughtful analysis of the conflicting evidence from early infant data and object search data like the A not B error, Bremner (2001) stressed that having object knowledge is different from using that knowledge to solve problems. He also pointed out that procedures used in violation of expectations studies cannot tell us whether the infant can use such knowledge to achieve some action. Making a similar point, Willatts (1997) described the precocious infant in these studies as a "couch potato," who looks but does not have to take any action. The theme from both of these authors is that detection of perceptual differences is not the same as using information to guide action.

In noting that infants and young children appear to be limited to recognizing after-the-fact incongruous perceptual events, I proposed that when such an ability is available early in development, it aids the construction of future knowledge about the world, serving as a building block for eventual prediction and more complex thinking about objects (Keen, 2003). At every age, perception frequently outruns action and is often insufficient for action. If the necessary cognitive and motor skills that underlie the desired action are not present (either through immaturity or lack of learning), the ability to act may not accompany perception. An example of perceptual discrimination outstripping use of this information can be found in Stager and Werker (1997). They found that 14-month-old infants were unable to use two highly similar phonetic sounds in a word-learning task, yet they easily distinguished those same sounds in a perceptual discrimination task. As adults, we can perceive the correctness of others' actions or physical events involving action, but may not be able to act ourselves necessarily. Spectator sports are based on taking pleasure in observing the athletic skills of others, although we are incapable of such actions ourselves. We can perceive, understand, appreciate, and even be able to perceive mistakes without being able to make the play ourselves. Let me give a personal example. As an amateur pianist, I make many mistakes when playing the piano. To facilitate my learning, my teacher will play the passage both wrongly (as I played it) and correctly. She then asks if I can hear the difference because she knows that if I cannot hear a difference, I cannot even begin to correct my fingers to perform the right actions. Perception must precede performance, but even so, it is not sufficient for implementation. I hear the difference, but must work hard to be able to play the passage correctly. In a similar manner, in Baillargeon, Graber, DeVos, and Black (1990), babies perceived the difference between correct and incorrect actions that an adult performed long before they could perform such an action. In the A not B task, in Hood's gravity task, and in our door tasks, the children are not merely detecting a violation of some physical law or rule. Instead they are solving a search problem, and the knowledge requirements are more precise and more difficult than a perceptual discrimination.

REACHING VERSUS LOOKING

It is tempting to take the foregoing arguments and data and use them to claim that the problem is not having knowledge versus using knowledge, but is more simply a matter of response mode. There is a wealth of data in which looking performance is superior to reaching in a variety of tasks (e.g., Ahmed & Ruffman, 1998; Baillargeon & Graber, 1988; Berthier, Bertenthal, Seaks, Sylvia, Johnson, & Clifton, 2001; Hofstadter & Reznick, 1996). The source of this dissociation has been interpreted as due to characteristics of the reaching response, rather than cognitive problems. Zelazo, Reznick, and Spinazzola (1998) presented several experiments showing that perseverative errors in A not B tasks seem to heavily depend on active responding before postswitch trials. Thelen and colleagues (chap. 9, this volume; Thelen, Schoner, Scheier, & Smith, 2001) developed a dynamic systems model that emphasizes motor effects from prior reaches as a major contributor to reaching errors. According to this view, perseveration of motor responses is inherent in the response system, which limits flexibility of responding (in our case, choice of door). I agree that repetition has a powerful effect on motor behavior at every age—we have all experienced motor perseveration when attempting to change old habits. It undoubtedly contributes, to some degree, to the toddlers' difficulty in these search tasks, but I do not consider it to be a root cause of their failure to open the correct door.

With regard to our "door" task, my view is that incorrect strategies do not obstruct the solution, but rather emerge when children cannot solve the problem. That is, rather than responding randomly in the absence of knowing the solution, children adopt a strategy such as going back to the same door or to a previously correct door. When 3-year-olds solve the problem, the incorrect strategies fade, appearing infrequently. The contrast between 2- and 3-year-olds is also found in their willingness to play the game. Two-year-olds appear to be delighted (and I think they are also surprised) when they open a door and find the ball. They seem to regard the apparatus like a slot machine that "pays off" now and then, but who knows when. They are willing to go for 10, 12, or more trials in this situation. In contrast, it was much harder to get 3-year-olds who can solve the problem to keep playing for more than six or eight trials (see Berthier et al., 2000). If a child can solve the door problem, it quickly becomes boring because the expected outcome is met on every trial.

There is additional evidence that questions whether reliance on motor aspects to explain reaching errors is warranted, and whether reaching performance is actually inferior to looking. For example, in the A not B task (Bell & Adams, 1999) and recognition memory tasks (Diamond, 1995), infants showed comparable performance when looking and reaching. In a series of studies that spanned more than a decade, our lab investigated reaching for hidden objects by 6-month-old infants. In our task, infants reached for sounding objects hidden by darkness rather than by occlusion with covers, as is typical in Piaget-type object search tasks. Infants displayed sensitivity to both location and object properties of unseen objects. Infants reached differentially to an object's spatial location in the azimuth (Perris & Clifton, 1988) and with regard to its distance from the body (Clifton, Perris, & Bullinger, 1991). They were able to orient their hand appropriately to a horizontal or vertical rod that was visible (rod was lit from within) when beyond reach, but invisible (light in rod was extinguished) when it was moved to within reach (McCarty, Ashmead, Lee, Goubet, & Clifton, 2001). Infants reached differentially to small versus large objects (Clifton, Rochat, Litovsky, & Perris, 1991) when size was signaled by attaching different sounds to the two objects. Although all of the studies described earlier had ongoing sound during the reach, Goubet and Clifton (1998) devised a task in which sound was present at the start of a trial that signaled direction of a ball's movement, but the final destination had to be remembered with no auditory cue. Six-month-olds reached in the appropriate direction under these circumstances, executing a reach with no visual or auditory support. Finally, several studies argue against a practice effect from reaching in the light. Infants reached for sounding objects in the dark when given no prior trials in the light (Clifton, Perris, & McCall, 1999), and they made appropriate lateral reaches in the dark when all reaches to objects in the light were executed at midline (Clifton et al., 1991; Goubet & Clifton, 1998). In these studies, infants were not repeating in the dark motor movements they had made in the light.

Infants look extremely competent when reaching in the dark, showing similar kinematic parameters, including hand deceleration when approaching the object, just as in the light (Clifton, Rochat, Robin, & Berthier, 1994). Rather than asking why reaching performance is deficient compared with looking, I would claim that the real difference to be explained is why reaching for objects hidden by darkness is so much easier than lifting a cover off an object in the light. Initially authors (Baillargeon et al., 1990; Diamond, 1995) proposed that the covered object is hard for the infant because it is a means–end task: first remove the cover, then find the object. This two-part sequence is difficult for infants under 8 to 9 months of age, and the direct reach in the dark eliminates means–end action. Several studies indicate that means–end action cannot be solely responsible for the difference, although it undoubtedly adds to the difficulty of reaching for covered objects in the light.

Spelke and von Hofsten (2001) put up an occluder to block a portion of a moving object's trajectory in a predictive reaching study. The occluder was a barrier to vision but not reaching because it was offset so as to obscure sight of the object just before the contact space. Because a successful reach had to begin when the object was out of sight, this manipulation hid the object at a critical moment. Infants' predictive reaching plummeted in the occluder's presence, so eliminating means–end action did not help reaching for a hidden object in the light. Munakata, McClelland, Johnson, and Siegler (1997) devised a means–end task in the light with the object visible or not visible. Infants performed successfully in the first case, but not in the second. In a subsequent study Shinskey and Munakata (2003) instituted an important control of comparing toy versus no-toy trials in both light and dark. In the light a means–end action was necessary, but in the dark a direct reach could obtain the toy. They found that 6-month-olds reached more often in the dark on toy versus no-toy trials, but found a reverse effect when the toy (or no-toy) was under a cloth in the light. They supported previous research that claimed infants were sensitive to hidden objects in the dark, and showed that this sensitivity was greater in the dark than the light.

McCall and Clifton (1999) made a direct comparison of the same means–end action task in the light and in the dark. In both light and dark 8-month-olds were presented with an object encased in a box whose lid had to be opened before a toy could be removed. A small speaker that emitted tape-recorded sound was also mounted inside the box. The purpose of the sound was to specify the location of the box in the dark, as its position varied from trial to trial. The sound turned off when the lid was opened. This made little difference in the light because infants could see the toy and reach for it, but if a second reach directed toward the toy was made in the dark, this would imply that infants remembered the toy and its location inside the box. Infants performed this sequenced action in the dark, even though the second reach was made without visual or auditory support.

Why should a means–end task be accomplished in the dark, but not when the object is hidden in the light, as in Munakata's task? I propose that when the object is hidden in the light, the infant gets distracted by all the remaining things still in view—other objects, the experimenter, even the infant's own body and clothing. In the dark, there is no distraction, so attention gets focused on the task at hand. There is no visual surround to draw attention away. The sophisticated manual behavior in the dark is counterintuitive and demands explanation. The power of distraction can be investigated in studies run in both light and dark. For the former, one could have the room be in semidarkness with a spotlight on the covered objects. This should focus the infant's attention similarly to how an audience in a theater is drawn to action taking place on a lighted stage. Experimental situations in the dark could explore how perception (or rather the memory of previous perception) supports and directs action with variations of ways that have been tried previously, including the addition of visual distracters in the dark. The hypothesis is that adding distraction in either illumination condition will diminish performance, whereas reducing it will promote performance. If this hypothesis proves valid, this would strongly support theorizing about infants' representational capacities.

CONCLUSIONS

The apparent discrepancy between infants' and young children's ability to understand laws of the physical world concerning solidity and continuity lies in the task requirements. Search tasks used with older infants and toddlers require prediction, use of indirect cues, and the incorporation of perceptual knowledge into solving a problem with appropriate action. As long as infants and toddlers can be passive observers, they do not have to use perceptual information to develop an action plan. In this situation, they express knowledge about the barrier's role in stopping the ball and constraining its final position by looking longer at displays when physical laws appear to have been broken. When the situation demands search for a hidden object, the multiple difficulties associated with achieving the goal may prevent expression of the infant's understanding of some basic components of the problem. The remaining tasks for us are to delineate in greater detail what perceptual knowledge consists of, including ways it might be used, and to understand more fully how the process of implementing appropriate action plans develops in early childhood.

ACKNOWLEDGMENTS

The research reported here was supported by grant HD27714 from the National Institutes of Health and a Research Scientist Award MH00332 from the National Institute of Mental Health to Rachel K. Clifton (now Rachel Keen). I am very grateful to all of my collaborators, especially my colleague, Neil Berthier, and to Samantha Butler, Clay Mash, and Heidi Kloos, postdoctoral fellows who contributed invaluably to the work presented here.

REFERENCES

Ahmed, A., & Ruffman, T. (1998). Why do infants make A not B errors in a search task, yet show memory for the location of hidden objects in a nonsearch task? *Developmental Psychology, 34*, 441–453.

Baillargeon, R. (1993). The object concept revisited: New directions in the investigation of infants' physical knowledge. In C. E. Granrud (Ed.), *Visual perception and cognition in infancy* (pp. 265–315). Hillsdale, NJ: Lawrence Erlbaum Associates.

Baillargeon, R., & Graber, M. (1988). Evidence of location memory in 8-month-old infants in a nonsearch AB task. *Developmental Psychology, 24*, 21–41.

Baillargeon, R., Graber, M., DeVos, J., & Black, J. (1990). Why do infants fail to search for hidden objects? *Cognition, 36*, 225–284.

Baillargeon, R., Spelke, E., & Wasserman, S. (1985). Object permanence in five-month-old infants. *Cognition, 20*, 191–208.

Bell, M. A., & Adams, S. E. (1999). Comparable performance on looking and reaching versions of the A-not-B task at 8 months of age. *Infant Behavior & Development, 22*, 221–235.

Berthier, N. E., Bertenthal, B. I., Seaks, J. D., Sylvia, M. R., Johnson, R. K., & Clifton, R. K. (2001). Using object knowledge in visual tracking and reaching. *Infancy, 2*, 257–284.

Berthier, N. E., DeBlois, S., Poirier, C. R., Novak, J. A., & Clifton, R. K. (2000). Where's the ball? Two- and three-year-olds reason about unseen events. *Developmental Psychology, 36*, 394–401.

Bremner, J. G. (1997). From perception to cognition. In G. Bremner, A. Slater, & G. Butterworth (Eds.), *Infant development: Recent advances* (pp. 55–74). Hove, UK: Psychology Press.

Bremner, J. G. (2001). Cognitive development: Knowledge of the physical world. In G. Bremner & A. Fogel (Eds.), *Blackwell handbook of infant development* (pp. 99–138). Oxford, UK: Blackwell.

Bushnell, E. W., McKenzie, B. E., Lawrence, D. A., & Connell, S. (1995). The spatial coding strategies of one-year-old infants in a locomotor search task. *Child Development, 66*, 937–958.

Butler, S. C., Berthier, N. E., & Clifton, R. K. (2002). Two-year-olds' search strategies and visual tracking in a hidden displacement task. *Developmental Psychology, 38*, 581–590.

Clifton, R. K. (2001). Lessons from infants: 1960–2000. *Infancy, 2*, 285–309.

Clifton, R. K., Perris, E. E., & Bullinger, A. (1991). Infants' perception of auditory space. *Developmental Psychology, 27*, 187–197.

Clifton, R. K., Perris, E. E., & McCall, D. M. (1999). Does reaching in the dark for unseen objects reflect representation in infants? *Infant Behavior & Development, 22*, 297–302.

Clifton, R. K., Rochat, P., Litovsky, R., & Perris, E. (1991). Object representation guides infants' reaching in the dark. *Journal of Experimental Psychology: Human Perception and Performance, 17*, 323–329.

Clifton, R. K., Rochat, P., Robin, D., & Berthier, N. E. (1994). Multimodal perception in human infants. *Journal of Experimental Psychology: Human Perception & Performance, 20*, 876–886.

DeLoache, J. S. (1986). Memory in very young children: Exploitation of cues to the location of a hidden object. *Cognitive Development, 1*, 123–137.

Diamond, A. (1995). Evidence of robust recognition memory early in life even when assessed by reaching behavior. *Journal of Experimental Child Psychology, 59*, 419–456.

Diamond, A. (1998). Understanding the A-not-B error: Working memory vs. reinforced response, or active trace vs. latent trace. *Developmental Science, 1*, 185–189.

Goubet, N., & Clifton, R. K. (1998). Object and event representation in 6½-month-old infants. *Developmental Psychology, 34*, 63–76.

Hofstadter, M., & Reznick, J. S. (1996). Response modality affects human infant delayed-response performance. *Child Development, 67*, 646–658.

Hood, B. M. (1995). Gravity rules for 2- to 4-year-olds? *Cognitive Development, 10*, 577–598.

Hood, B. M., Carey, S., & Prasada, S. (2000). Predicting the outcomes of physical events: Two-year-olds fail to reveal knowledge of solidity and support. *Child Development, 71*, 1540–1554.

Hood, B. M., Cole-Davies, V., & Dias, M. (2003). Looking and search measures of object knowledge in pre-school children. *Developmental Psychology, 39*, 61–70.

Keen, R. (2003). Representation of objects and events: Why do infants look so smart and toddlers look so dumb? *Current Directions in Psychological Science, 12*, 79–83.

Kloos, H., & Keen, R. (in press). An exploration of toddlers' problems in a search task. *Infancy*.

Mash, C., Clifton, R., & Berthier, N. E. (2002). *Two-year-olds' understanding of event outcomes when reaching and looking*. Symposium presentation at the International Conference on Infant Studies, Toronto, Canada.

Mash, C., Keen, R., & Berthier, N. E. (2003). Visual access and attention in two-year-olds' event reasoning and object search. *Infancy, 4*, 371–388.

McCall, D. M., & Clifton, R. K. (1999). Infants' means-end search for hidden objects in the absence of visual feedback. *Infant Behavior & Development, 22*, 179–195.

McCarty, M. E., Clifton, R. K., Ashmead, D. H., Lee, P., & Goubet, N. (2001). How infants use vision for grasping objects. *Child Development, 72*, 973–987.

Munakata, Y., McClelland, J. L., Johnson, M. H., & Siegler, R. S. (1997). Rethinking infant knowledge: Toward an adaptive process account of successes and failures in object permanence tasks. *Psychological Review, 104*, 686–713.

Perris, E. E., & Clifton, R. K. (1988). Reaching in the dark toward sound as a measure of auditory localization in infants. *Infant Behavior & Development, 11*, 473–491.

Piaget, J. (1954). *The construction of reality in the child*. New York: Basic Books.

Shinskey, J., & Munakata, Y. (2003). Are infants in the dark about hidden objects? *Developmental Science, 6*, 273–282.

Spelke, E. S. (1988). Where perceiving ends and thinking begins: The apprehension of objects in infancy. In A. Yonas (Ed.), *Perceptual development in infancy: The Minnesota symposia on child psychology* (Vol. 20, pp. 197–234). Hillsdale, NJ: Lawrence Erlbaum Associates.

Spelke, E. S. (1991). Physical knowledge in infancy: Reflections on Piaget's theory. In S. Carey & R. Gelman (Eds.), *The epigenesis of mind: Essays on biology and cognition* (pp. 133–169). Hillsdale, NJ: Lawrence Erlbaum Associates.

Spelke, E. S., Breinlinger, K., Macomber, J., & Jacobson, K. (1992). Origins of knowledge. *Psychological Review, 99*, 605–632.

Spelke, E. S., & von Hofsten, C. (2001). Predictive reaching for occluded objects by 6-month-old infants. *Journal of Cognition and Development, 2*, 261–281.

Spelke, E. S., & Kestenbaum, R. (1986). Les origines du concept d'objet. *Psychologie Francais, 31*, 67–72.

Stager, C. L., & Werker, J. E. (1997). Infants listen for more phonetic detail in speech perception than in word-learning tasks. *Nature, 388*, 381–382.

Thelen, E., Schoner, G., Scheier, C., & Smith, L. B. (2001). The dynamics of embodiment: A field theory of infant perseverative reaching. *Behavioral and Brain Sciences, 24*, 1–86.

Willatts, P. (1997). Beyond the "couch potato" infants: How infants use their knowledge to regulate action, solve problems, and achieve goals. In G. Bremner, A. Slater, & G. Butterworth (Eds.), *Infant development: Recent advances* (pp. 109–135). Hove, England: Psychology Press.

Zelazo, P. D., Reznick, J. S., & Spinazzola, J. (1998). Representational flexibility and response control in a multistep multilocation search task. *Developmental Psychology, 34*, 203–214.

12

▼▼▼▼▼▼▼

The Role of Action in Understanding and Using Environmental Place Representations

Lynn S. Liben
The Pennsylvania State University

As readers of this volume will know well by the time they reach this sentence, the current chapter is part of a collection designed to honor Anne D. Pick and Herbert L. Pick, Jr. Most contributors owe personal debts to Anne and Herb, and all owe intellectual debts, often evident in their shared commitment to the ecological theories of J. J. and E. J. Gibson. At first glance, my own place in this context may seem surprising. Despite my interactions with both Gibsons during my undergraduate days at Cornell, my theoretical identification is unquestionably more Piagetian than Gibsonian. Furthermore, much of my empirical work (and the focus of this chapter) concerns *representations*, a construct commonly greeted with suspicion by ecological psychologists. I believe, however, that the seeming discord between these traditions is in many ways only illusory. Thus, I begin this chapter by highlighting some of the core compatibilities between the work of the Picks and the Gibsons, on the one hand, and aspects of Piagetian theory and of my own conceptual and empirical work on representations, on the other (*Identifying an Ecological Niche for Constructivists and for Representations*).

Following the presentation of this general theoretical context, I briefly consider some of the ways in which action may be involved in representational understanding (*Linking Actions and Representations*). The bulk of the chapter is dedicated to reviewing empirical work that my colleagues and I have done to investigate individuals' understanding of place representations (*Understanding Representations: Empirical Illustrations*). I close by arguing that this research is important not only for what it suggests about the ways that everyday action may facilitate individuals' developing understanding of representations, but also for what it suggests about the possible *limitations* of these naturally occurring developmental processes. I argue that as educators, we should also explore ways to design and implement interventions to facilitate representational understanding more richly and more universally (*Conclusions and a Call to Action*).

IDENTIFYING AN ECOLOGICAL NICHE FOR CONSTRUCTIVISTS AND FOR REPRESENTATIONS

At the core of the clash between scholars working within a Piagetian or constructivist tradition and those working within a Gibsonian or ecological tradition is a difference of opinion about the source of environmental information. Ecological psychologists hold that all information is in the environment, not constructed by the perceiver. More important, however, what any given environment affords to any given organism depends on the organism as well as the environment. "An affordance . . . is equally a fact of the environment and a fact of behavior. It is both physical and psychological, yet neither" (J. J. Gibson, 1979, p. 129). The affordance of a water surface as a support for locomotion, for example, differs depending on whether the organism encountering it is a water spider (*gerris remigis*) or a human being (at least for those among us who cannot walk on water). To take a simple but compelling illustration from color perception, what is an entirely white primrose to a human perceiver has a deep purple center to the bee. In short, environmental affordances differ depending on who or what is there to perceive it. In this sense, the organism has an essential role in shaping the Gibsonian child just as it does in shaping the Piagetian child.

Cognitive constructivists hold that information is forged by the organism. However, the constructivist organism (e.g., the human child) does not forge that knowledge in isolation. It is neither the product of a Kantian conceptual inheritance nor of a lifetime of passively recorded environmental experiences. Instead, at least as I would argue the case, the constructed knowledge is the outcome of a profound interplay between a prepared organism and a real, physical world that offers the opportunity to build certain kinds of information but not others. Thus, individuals' constructed knowledge is affected not only by organismic constraints, but also by environmental constraints. In this sense, what is in the environment has an essential role in shaping the Piagetian child just as it does in shaping the Gibsonian child.

The preceding use of the phrase "at least as I would argue the case" is not simply rhetorical. Rather it is meant to acknowledge that even the way one depicts relations among alternative theoretical views is open to interpretation. Thus, for example, when E. J. Gibson and A. D. Pick (2000) offered a diagram to highlight relations among theories, the Piagetian approach was placed on one side (under the "enrichment" family) and the ecological approach was placed on the other (under the "differentiation" family). However, irrespective of whether one accepts or rejects the characterization of Piagetian and Gibsonian approaches as falling on distinct familial lines of descent, the two approaches share a core commitment to something that undergirds this entire volume—namely, the essential role of *action* for learning and development. Indeed, even having placed Piagetian and Gibsonian approaches on two distinct familial lines, E. J. Gibson and A. D. Pick (2000) acknowledged the compatibility of the two traditions with respect to this dimension:

> A further distinction between construction theories and the ecological approach is that neither information-processing nor rationalist approaches link perception with action. *Except for Piaget*, construction theories do not hypothesize a role for action in perceptual development. The ecological approach, on the other hand, emphasizes the fundamental reciprocity of perception and action. (p. 12; italics added)

It is a simple matter to find illustrations of the importance of action in both theories. In Piagetian theory, perhaps the most obvious is that all of development—including higher level cognition—is said to be grounded in sensorimotor activity (e.g., Piaget, 1952, 1954). Contemporary scholars offer Piagetian theory as an embodied view of mind that avoids the Cartesian mind–body split (Overton & Müller, 2002). In ecological theory, action is at the center of perception. J. J. Gibson (1979) railed against methods that fixed eyes, heads, or bodies in research laboratories, arguing that movement is at the core of human perception, which takes place in real environments.

Just as organismic qualities affect the affordances of water surfaces and colors of primroses, they affect more molar aspects of the experienced environment as well. Thus, human biology constrains what information is afforded by (or constructed via interactions with) the worldly environment in which we move. Thus, for example, we can walk but not fly. We can swim, but not live, mate, and raise our young under water. Within some modest variation across the life span (as humans grow and later shrink), across history (as human stature increases), and across individuals (from jockeys to basketball players), we are all of roughly the same size (at least when contrasted to, say, ants or bacteria at one end and, say, elephants or dinosaurs on the other), and we all have roughly the same means of locomotion. Thus, we generally experience vistas from an upright position—from a certain viewing height and at a certain distance.

Again within a range of variation, we are able to experience—first hand—only a tiny portion of our planet. Those first-hand experiences provide information about that environment while providing information about our own place *in* that environment (J. J. Gibson, 1979).

Of course just as prosthetics or perceptual amplifiers can open up visual information that would otherwise be unavailable to the human perceiver (as in developing the technology to record and then display information contained in portions of the electromagnetic spectrum that lie outside visible light—e.g., infrared, ultraviolet, or x-ray photography), so, too, humans have developed prosthetics and amplifiers that expand their access to the large-scale spatial environment.

One kind of expansion comes from developing ways to travel through and thus experience the world in ways that go well beyond what our physical biological endowment would otherwise allow. Thus, to name only a few, we have cars, trains, hot air balloons, submarines, airplanes, space ships, skis, bicycles, and all-terrain vehicles. The distance, speed, angle, and sheer quantity of the spatial environment that we can experience using these amplifiers of human locomotion present challenges to our processing capacities.

A second means of expansion, and the one on which the current chapter focuses, are representational amplifiers that allow us to experience the world without directly traveling through it. Having introduced the suspect term *representations*, I would hasten to note that the term carries many different meanings, only some of which may be distasteful to ecological psychologists. A taxonomy suggested roughly a quarter of a century ago (Liben, 1981; reproduced in Fig. 12.1) provides one model for organizing

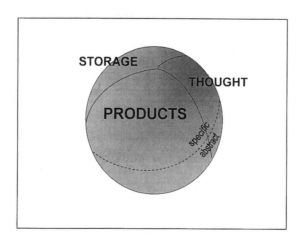

FIG. 12.1. Types and contents of spatial representations based on Liben (1981).

alternative meanings by distinguishing among the two *contents* (specific and abstract) and three *types* of spatial representations (spatial storage, thought, and products).

Representations of *specific content* concern information about particular objects or places, as in one's knowledge about the relations among buildings in downtown Minneapolis. Representations with *abstract content* provide general systems—for example, a Cartesian coordinate system. Although in theory it is useful to distinguish between the two contents, in practice it may be difficult or perhaps even impossible to separate them completely. First, they are theoretically interconnected. For example, one's environmental knowledge of downtown Minneapolis may be expected to differ depending on whether one does or does not organize locations using a Cartesian grid. Second, an identical task may draw on both abstract and specific contents. For example, success on the Piagetian water-level task taps knowledge of how gravity affects the behavior of liquid in the physical world as well as the ability to use an abstract coordinate axis system (see Liben, 1981, 1991).

Intersecting these two contents are three *types* of representations. One type—*spatial storage*—refers to spatial representations that are recorded in some way in the brain, including traces that are not normally accessible to consciousness. The second—*spatial thought*—is the kind of spatial representation to which we have conscious access, illustrated by the images of street intersections that people envision as they attempt to given someone directions to their house. Finally, the third—*spatial products*—refers to any kind of *external* spatial representation illustrated by a road map of Minneapolis or a weather map of the United States.

In my original presentation of this figure (Liben, 1981), I noted that a spherical representation was used intentionally for several reasons. Most important here is the reason that a sphere—by implying rotation—avoided privileging a single type of representation. Although I originally oriented the sphere so that spatial thought was at the center (in keeping with the emphasis of my work at the time), I also noted that the sphere could just as legitimately be oriented with another type at the center. Indeed it is the orientation used in Fig. 12.1 that best reflects my own current program of research and that, happily for the current context, is perfectly compatible with an ecological approach. That is, what is rejected in the ecological view is the idea that mental representations (spatial thoughts) are the driving force behind the acquisition of knowledge as the organism explores and moves through the actual environment. What is *not* rejected is the idea that concrete representations (spatial products) are a source of environmental information.

The contrast may be clarified by considering the following comments by E. J. Gibson and A. D. Pick (2000):

On the one hand, there is the assumption common to both the information-processing and rationalist approaches, with their roots in enrichment theories and in earlier empiricist and nativist views, that the information available to sensory systems is impoverished, ambiguous, and otherwise insufficient to support perception. Consequently, these theories assume construction of representations or inferences to supplement the information. On the other hand, the assumption of the ecological approach, rooted in functionalism, holds that information is normally ample and structured, and that it fully specifies the layout, surfaces, objects, and events of the world. Consequently, this theory emphasizes activities of exploration and processes of detection, selection, and abstraction for obtaining information about the world and about oneself. (p. 11)

These statements clearly refer to "information available to sensory systems" and the "activities of exploration and processes," which are involved during exploration in the actual organism-ecology niche. Yet an ecological perspective recognizes that there are constraints on what activities of exploration are available to a given organism (e.g., see earlier discussion of human size and locomotion), and thus it is compatible with the idea that there is much that is inaccessible to human processes of detection, selection, and abstraction. Given that humans need to move in and communicate about environments in ways that go beyond action-based, direct perception in the environment itself, as a species we have developed concrete, spatial representations (or spatial products) to help us do so. The distinction between mental representations used as guides to direct perception and surface representations used as social mediators was explicitly acknowledged by J. J. Gibson (1966) when he distinguished between "perceptual cognition, or knowledge of the environment, and symbolic cognition, or knowledge *about* the environment. The former is a direct response to things based on stimulus information, the latter is an indirect response to things based on stimulus sources produced by another human individual" (p. 91). It is representations in the latter sense—that is, *spatial products*—that are the focus of the remainder of this chapter.

My claim is *not* that representations like maps, aerial photographs, and scale models are re-presentations (as in "to present again") or simulations of what would be available to the perceiver in the ecology. Spatial products do *not* afford the same kinds of information that the natural environment affords, nor do they afford the same kinds of actions. In fact we (Downs & Liben, 1988, 1993; Liben, 2000, 2001; Liben & Downs, 1989, 1992) have taken exactly the opposite position by arguing that these are representations that are symbolic, creative, communicative statements about the referential world and, as such, offer bases for knowledge and insights that would not otherwise have been detected directly. Furthermore, and again, in sympathy with an ecological perspective, we have noted that external representations like maps are *not* artificial laboratory research devices invented by psychologists (Liben & Downs, 1989). Instead they are part of human ecology and have been for millennia (e.g., Downs & Liben, 1993; Gibson, 1966, 1979; Harley & Woodward, 1987; Stea, Blaut, & Stephens, 1996; Tversky, 2001). As a real part of our human ecology, these representations are themselves objects to be explored, manipulated, and acted on. External representations like maps are humankind's way of allowing us to take the very real ecology in which we live, record our understanding of it, communicate about it to others, and—most important—amplify it in ways that go beyond what we would be able to see and process in the here and now of our perceptual capacities.

One kind of evidence that place representations provide a different kind of information than that provided by the actual environment derives from the observation that many kinds of representations look little like their referents. Illustrative are shell and stick charts from the Marshall islands, which bear no physical resemblance to the islands and sea currents for which they stand (see Downs & Liben, 1993). A second kind of evidence that place representations are independent sources of information about the world is the observation that people harbor beliefs that have no other obvious origin. Illustrative is the finding that people commonly overestimate the size of Greenland (Nelson, 1994)—a misconception presumed to result from repeated exposure to maps in the Mercator projection, which exaggerate distances toward the poles. Another illustration of the representational source of knowledge comes from anecdotal observations of people's responses to seeing the map of Europe shown in Fig. 12.2.

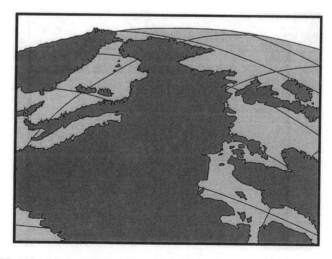

FIG. 12.2.   Map of Europe as seen from the east. From Liben (2001), based on Harrison (1944).

Viewers encountering this map for the first time typically begin with confusion (e.g., "What is this map *of*?"), proceed to skepticism ("This map is
wrong!"), and end with some insight (e.g., "Oh, I hadn't realized that the
path between Russia and Spain was so direct!"). Just as what is "known"
about the size of Greenland appears to come from repeated exposure to
Mercator projection maps, what is "known" about spatial relations among
European countries appears to come from repeated exposure to north-at-
the-top maps. Maps in orientations that are atypical for one's culture and
era (as in the map of Europe seen from the east shown in Fig. 12.2) allow
new insights to emerge.

Having argued that maps are different from the real world and are responsible for supplementing knowledge gained directly from it, I would
not want to argue that the kinds of actions that people have with spatial
products are identical to the kinds of actions they have with the actual environment. However, I do want to argue that some of the same kinds of
theoretical and empirical approaches that are useful for understanding direct perception, cognition, and action can also be useful for understanding
how people interact with and learn from external spatial representations
like maps. I develop this point briefly in the next section of this chapter, after which I turn to some of the empirical work that my colleagues and I
conducted to study individuals' developing understanding and use of external place representations.

LINKING ACTIONS AND REPRESENTATIONS

To say that processing the actual world and processing representations of
the world are not identical is not the same as proposing that no similarities
exist. Nor is it to suggest that there is no articulation between action and
understanding of representational artifacts. On the contrary, there are various actions both with respect to the referential environment and with respect to the representations that may affect understanding.

First, to the degree that understanding place representations in part
draws on understanding the referent world that those representations depict, all person–environment actions become relevant. There have been
many ways to conceptualize these actions, including with respect to the
kinds of spaces being acted within and on. For example, there are the relational actions involved in the space of the body and with the immediately
manipulable space that surrounds it (e.g., actions relating body-body,
body-object, and object-object; see H. L. Pick & Lockman, 1981); actions
between the body and more distant, but still visible places (e.g., keeping
track of target locations despite self-movement in a space; see Acredolo,

1978; Rieser, 1979); and actions involved in pointing or navigating to spaces that are currently out of sight (as in pointing from self toward known locations in a familiar building; see Hardwick, McIntyre, & Pick, 1976). To the degree that a given place representation provides information that is similar to (albeit neither identical to nor as rich as) that provided in the real world (see Gibson, 1971, 1979; Kennedy, 1974), a user is likely to draw on similar kinds of actions. Indeed a suggestion made in the later discussion of empirical data is that individuals find it easier to interpret place representations that present information similar to that available from moving around in the actual environment. Consider the ease with which we can interpret the photographs of vacation trips shown to us by family and friends, or the photographs that typically adorn postcards or travel books. When images show landscapes from angles and distances at which the referent landscapes might be viewed given the perceptual and locomotor capacities of our species, they are usually simple to interpret. In contrast, when images provide views that fall beyond human visual experience, they typically prove to be more difficult to understand. To illustrate, consider the difficulty of interpreting the image shown in Fig. 12.3, which provides a vertical (straight-down) and distant (aerial) view unlike any that would be possible with unaided human capacities.

A second class of actions concerns discriminating representational surfaces from referential meanings. Under most circumstances, adults make this discrimination automatically. The classic exception is the response to *trompe l'oeil* (or "fool the eye") art, in which viewers are tricked into "seeing" a real, three-dimensional object when in reality there is only a two-dimensional representational surface. It is action—head or body movement—that quickly makes the representational surface (and hence trick) apparent (see Kubovy, 1986). For young children, the identification of representational surfaces appears to require more exploratory action. There have been reports of infants grasping at patterns drawn on fabric or paper, light patterns on the floor, or photographs in books, although whether these actions reflect confusion or surface exploration remains uncertain (see Liben, 1999, for a review).

Third are actions aimed at bringing the representation into a matched orientation with respect to the viewer. The orientation may be defined intrinsically with respect to the physical upright of the referential object. For example, a house rests on its foundation, not its roof, and thus one would expect to align the vertical axis of a depicted house with the vertical axis of the viewer. There is evidence that this understanding, too, must develop. For example, toddlers (18 and 24 months) do not re-orient books handed to them upside down and seem to be undisturbed when adults read to them from an inverted book (DeLoache, Uttal, & Pierroutsakos, 2000).

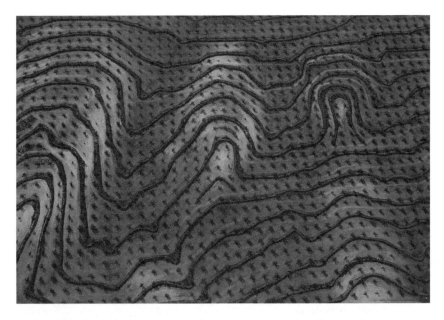

FIG. 12.3. Earth from an unfamiliar vantage point. © Yann Arthus-Bertrand from *Earth from Above*. Reproduced by permission of the photographer. The original photo is in color. Full descriptions of the photograph and the Earth from Above project are found in the Endnotes.

Orientation of a referent may also be defined by convention, such as the contemporary tendency to favor orienting maps with north at the top. When representations break these conventions, viewers often act to reinstate them. For example, when the map shown in Fig. 12.2 is given to viewers, they often re-orient it so that Italy is at the bottom "where it belongs" despite the distorted nature of the resulting image. If it is displayed on a screen, viewers commonly turn their heads.

Finally, a viewer's current position with respect to a perceptually available environment may temporarily create a privileged orientation of the referent. Again viewers may create a match by re-orienting the representation, as when users re-orient maps to bring them into alignment with the surrounding environment. Orientation may also be defined with respect to the representation (rather than the referent). Representational orientations may be defined in a number of ways. At the surface level, a particular viewing position may be privileged by the way that the representation is framed. Rectangular representational surfaces (e.g., rectangular pieces of paper, wall screens, or computer monitors) privilege viewing positions in which edges are parallel or orthogonal to the horizon. A user may thus "straighten out" a representational surface that is askew. Orientation may also be fixed for components of a representation even above and beyond any inherent orientation of the objects represented. Illustrative are maps in which buildings or the topography are drawn using an oblique perspective view. Such representations not only specify the inherent vertical axis of buildings, but also privilege a particular viewing direction or azimuth that is not inherent in the buildings. That is, the representation—but not the real building—specifies a single direction of approach. Unless one orients such maps in their intended directions, buildings or topography may be confusing or even uninterpretable.

It is not only the *components* of a representation that may privilege a particular viewing position. Perspective representations define a particular station point. Considerable research has been directed to seeing whether viewers are sensitive to these station points and the conditions under which perspective views remain robust even when there is a mismatch between the representational station point and the physical vantage point of the viewer (see Hagen, 1986; Kulbovy, 1986, for thorough discussions of relevant perceptual and artistic issues). In addition, there are some kinds of images in which a "matched" vantage point is essential, as in anamorphic art (i.e., when the image is completely distorted unless the surface is viewed from an oblique angle; see Gombrich, 1961).

Although brief, the preceding comments illustrate the general point that action is relevant not only for the ways that we learn about the world, but also for the ways in which we interact with representations of that world. These general points are instantiated in a range of empirical work discussed next.

UNDERSTANDING REPRESENTATIONS: EMPIRICAL ILLUSTRATIONS

Overview

Having argued that research focused on place representations is fully compatible with an ecological approach, and having mentioned briefly some of the ways in which action may be relevant for processing these representations, I turn now to some of the empirical work that we have conducted since the model of spatial representations shown in Fig. 12.1 first appeared. Here again my choice of phrase is not simply rhetorical: I use the term *we* because most of the research described here is collaborative. Particularly central have been a long-standing collaboration with Roger Downs and a more recent collaboration with Kim Kastens, both of whom work in disciplines in which place representations are central—geography and marine geology, respectively.

Our empirical work has addressed children's and adults' understanding of the links among the three constructs shown in Fig. 12.4—the self, the referent space, and the representation. One goal of our research has been to explore individuals' understanding of the relation between themselves and some space (i.e., the relation depicted by the solid line in Fig. 12.4). For example, if I were to ask you—wherever you may be reading these words—to point to the Washington Monument, I would be asking about a self-space relation. Work on this link is omitted from the present chapter because it does not involve external place representations.

Another goal of our research has been to study people's understanding of the relations between an external representation and its referent space, apart from the individual's own place in that space (i.e., the relation shown by the dashed line in Fig. 12.4). An illustrative task would be one in which a respondent, seated in Minneapolis, is asked to interpret a portion of an aerial photograph of downtown Chicago. Work of this kind is reviewed in the following section entitled "Interpreting Representations From Beyond the Depicted Space." A third goal of our work has been to study individuals' understanding of the simultaneous relations among the three constructs—that is, the relations that are implied once the third link (shown by a dotted line in Fig. 12.4) is added. Illustrative are tasks in which people are asked to consult an actual map (not a cognitive map) to figure out where they are in an actual environment or to make a decision

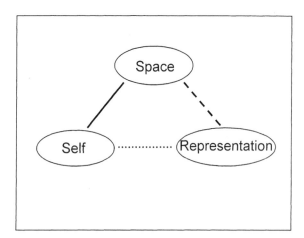

FIG. 12.4.   Central constructs in the study of understanding place representations.

about which way to turn next. Work addressed to these issues is discussed in the second section entitled "Understanding Self-Space-Representation Relations From Within the Depicted Space."

Finally, given that our work has revealed significant variability among individuals within any given age, our research has been addressed to identifying and explaining group and individual differences in performance. In addition to conducting correlational research, we have also conducted experimental work designed to test whether particular experiences have an impact on performance on self-space-representational understanding. Illustrative work is described in the final section entitled "Group and Individual Differences in Understanding Place Representations."

Interpreting Representations From Beyond the Depicted Space

Overview. As explained earlier, one focus of our research has been on individuals' success in interpreting the referential meaning of place representations in general, irrespective of their own position in the represented place. This kind of understanding is essentially reading or decoding the meaning of the representation in a way that is akin to reading or decoding the meaning of prose. Understanding can occur at the level of interpreting individual, isolated pieces of the representation (words in the case of prose; individual graphic components in the case of graphic place representations) as well as at the level of interpreting the representation as a whole (e.g., the thrust of the paragraph or story in the case of prose; the patterns of hills and valleys or distributions of agricultural land in the case of graphic place representations). For this kind of understanding, individuals need not concern themselves with their own location with respect to either the representation or with respect to the referential space (although as noted later, some individuals may spontaneously attempt to do so nevertheless).

Using a taxonomy developed earlier (Liben, 1997), this aspect of our work has used one of two methods. The first, *representational-correspondence* methods, are those in which participants are asked to relate information from one representational form to another. For example, shown a location on an aerial photograph, the participant is asked to find the isomorphic location on a line map of the same area, perhaps in a different scale or orientation. Or, shown a component of a map such as a particular symbol, the participant is asked to describe it using another representational medium such as language. The second, *meta-representational* methods, are those in which participants are asked to reflect on or analyze some aspect of representations apart from their denotative meaning. For example, shown two different maps of the same city, the participant is asked to describe how they differ and how each might offer different uses or insights.

Sampled next are data from two studies in which children were asked to identify the meaning of place representations at both the molar and componential levels. The first is an interview study designed to provide a relatively open-ended format for children to offer their interpretations of a variety of place representations; the second is a more highly controlled investigation designed to examine the degree to which understanding varies systematically in relation to the scale and viewing angle of aerial photographs. I close the section with a brief discussion of the difficulty of distinguishing cleanly between cases in which respondents are "in" versus "beyond" the depicted space.

Interview Data.   In an initial study of representational understanding in very young children, we interviewed preschool children (ages 3–6 years) using a variety of representations of large-scale environments (Liben & Downs, 1989, 1991). For example, we showed children a standard road map of Pennsylvania and an aerial photograph of downtown Chicago, and we recorded children's spontaneous identifications and their responses to general questions such as, "What do you think this shows?" In addition, we examined children's responses to structured questions ranging from those that merely asked about a portion of the representation to those that asked about the viability of a specific interpretation. Illustrative of the former were questions like: "What do you think this [pointing] is?" or "Do you think you could find something that shows a road?" Illustrative of the latter were questions like: "Hmm . . . I think maybe this is a road . . . do you think it could be that?" We used the latter kind of question because our pilot work had shown that when the interviewer offered interpretations in a hesitant manner, children were perfectly willing to reject them, often vehemently.

We found that children were quite good at understanding that overall, the map or photograph showed a place of some kind, albeit not always with an appropriate degree of specificity. For example, the road map of Pennsylvania was identified, variously, as "States and stuff," "Indiana, Pennsylvania," "Part of Africa," and, by one child, as "California, Canada, the West, and the North Coast." The aerial photograph of Chicago was identified as, "It's a city . . . because there's so much stuff in there— houses, roads, building," "Part of all of town," "Big state . . . lots of states," and even "That's the United States. Because the United States has a lot of people and a lot of cars and a lot of roads" (see Liben & Downs, 1989,

1991). Children's identifications of more specific components of these representations, however, revealed more dramatic category errors, including some that might be linked to an action-based analysis of understanding representations. That is, errors were consistent with the idea that it is particularly difficult to understand place representations when the environment is depicted from distances or angles that fall outside of embodied experiences that humans have in real spatial environments.

For example, children were often confused in interpreting the scale of representations. On the map of Pennsylvania, illustrative were children's rejections of the interviewer's interpretation that a line might show a road, as in one 4-year-old child who protested that it could not be a road "because it's too skinny for two cars to fit on." On a plastic relief map, another child rejected the possibility that the raised parts could show mountains because "they aren't high enough." Similar responses were found to aerial photographs, including one of an unfamiliar location taken from a large distance (a 1:12,000 aerial view of downtown Chicago) on which children commonly made viewing distance-related errors such as identifying boats on Lake Michigan as "fish," roads as "ropes," and the Chicago River as "a snake." Even when we used a somewhat larger scale representation of a familiar environment, we saw scale errors. For example, we showed a 1:9,600 aerial photograph of the local community to a 4-year-old child and pointed to the building in which his father worked. Asked whether he thought it might be his dad's building, the child reacted with a vehement "no" because "his building is *huge*! It's as big as this whole map!"

Other misinterpretations on the aerial photographs may be understood as reflecting the unfamiliar nature of the photograph's straight down, vertical (or nadir) viewing angle. On the aerial photograph of Chicago, for example, a triangular parking area was identified as a "hill" and tennis courts as "doors" (Liben & Downs, 1989, 1991; see also Spencer, Harrison, & Darvizeh, 1980, for similar findings). We interpret these as angle errors because the interpretations would be sensible if, instead of viewing the environment from straight down, it were being viewed from the front.

Children's and Adults' Interpretations of Oblique and Nadir Aerial Photographs.   As in any clinical interview, the specific questions or their order varied considerably across participants in the study just described. In a more controlled design, we have investigated the apparent importance of viewing distance and viewing angle for participants' success in interpreting components of aerial photographs (Liben, Dunphy-Lelli, & Szechter, in preparation).

We asked both preschool and adult participants to identify a number of components of aerial photographs that varied with respect to viewing distance and viewing angle. Specifically, the aerial photographs were taken either from a relatively near or far viewing distance (both still well beyond the scale of normal human–environment perceptual experience) and were either from directly overhead (nadir view) or from an angle (oblique views similar to those seen when looking at a landscape from a mountain top). By crossing these two variables, photographs were thus far nadir, near nadir, far oblique, and near oblique views. We selected photographs so that exemplars of particular referents (e.g., baseball fields, railroad depots) would appear on at least one of each type of photograph.

When shown the near nadir photograph shown in Fig. 12.5 and asked what the circled section showed, all 33 adults answered correctly, saying either that it was a "baseball diamond," "field," or "sporting field." Not surprisingly, the 4½- to 5½-year-old children had more difficulty, with only 4 of 32 giving one of these answers. Among the remaining responses, some could be considered correct, although vague (e.g., "ground," "grass"), others incorrect but perhaps reasonable (e.g., "building," "parking lot"), and still others dramatically incorrect (e.g., "eyeball," "mushroom," "spider web," "thermometer," "parachute," and "seashell"). An analysis of variance (ANOVA) on the number of correct identifications revealed an interaction of age and angle: Adults were performing virtually at ceiling on all kinds of photographs, but children performed signifi-

FIG. 12.5. Near nadir photograph used in aerial identification task with baseball field circled.

cantly better on the oblique view (irrespective of viewing distance). Far more research will be needed to go beyond these descriptive data to identify what factors account for these age-linked and stimulus differences (e.g., an increased opportunity to see the environment from other perspectives as in airplane travel, more experience in using graphic representations, or more advanced understanding of projective spatial concepts). What the data already demonstrate, however, is that children have relatively greater difficulty when asked to interpret representations that depict the referent world in ways that are less like their embodied encounters with that referent world.

Are Respondents Really "Beyond" the Depicted Space?   In closing this section of the empirical review and providing a transition to the next, I must acknowledge that the distinction between someone being "beyond" versus "in" a depicted space is not entirely a clean one. When asked to interpret concrete representations (spatial products), respondents may draw on stored (i.e., mental) representations of experienced environments. Indeed the argument that viewers find it easier to interpret place representations that reflect experiences like those derived from human action in space than those that do not (e.g., oblique rather than vertical perspective views) implies at least some role for other kinds of spatial representations (in the taxonomy offered earlier, spatial storage or spatial thought). In addition, insofar as the place representations used are of real, known, and identifiable environments (such as downtown Chicago), there is always the possibility that respondents relate themselves to the depicted environment, although we, as investigators, had not intended them to do so.

Anecdotal evidence from our research suggests that these links are indeed made by some respondents. In one investigation, we asked college students to complete a correspondences task in which the challenge was to find analogous locations and directions in two images of the same referent space (see Liben, 2001). For example, shown an arrow pointing at a particular location on an east-facing aerial photograph of Boston, the respondent was asked to place an arrow on a north-facing plan map of Boston so that the arrow would point at the same location in Boston and approach it from the same direction. In informal conversation following data collection, several respondents—despite completing the task in a windowless room in a campus building in Pennsylvania—mentioned that they had been thinking about their current location in relation to Boston as they worked. Thus, as with many distinctions, there are some fuzzy boundaries between the research described earlier in which respondents are said to be "beyond" the depicted space and the research discussed next in which respondents are undeniably "within" it.

Understanding Self-Space-Representation Relations
From Within the Depicted Space

Overview. The tasks discussed previously, in which the environment depicted in the place representations was not perceptually available to the respondent, reflect a major way that place representations are commonly used in daily life. Illustrative are cases in which we encounter maps or photographs of other nations (or even celestial bodies) in the daily newspaper, consult an atlas to learn about the relations among countries or about their topographic features, or view photographs and maps in a travel magazine to select our next vacation site. In the tasks described next, the respondent is actually "in" the environment depicted by the representation. This condition also characterizes a way in which place representations are commonly used in the real world—that is, linking some perceptually experienced location to a represented location.

In some cases, the experienced location of interest is a self-location. This is, of course, the situation encountered when an individual uses a map as a navigation tool. Here the challenge is to figure out not only where one is "on the map," but also where (on the map) one wishes to go next, what route (on the map) may be used to reach that target location, and then, in turn, to figure out how to implement that route in the actual space. To do so successfully, one must identify initial location and orientation on the map and in the space, and then continually update correspondences between the two by linking how far one has traveled "on the map" and "in the space" and by coordinating turns "on the map" with turns "in the space." These requirements may be particularly challenging to meet when the map and self are unaligned. For example, it may be particularly difficult to understand the self-space-representation correspondences when the map is oriented with north at the top and the traveler is facing south (so that a turn "to the left" on the map corresponds to a turn "to the right" in the environment).

In other cases, the experienced location of interest is not self, but rather some other perceived object or event. This situation, too, is a common one, particularly for those working in disciplines for which georeferencing of data is essential (e.g., geology, geography, urban planning, architecture). If the user is located exactly at the to-be-mapped referent (as when, say, one is in a park and recording locations of patches of poison ivy as they are found directly underfoot), the demands are equivalent to those described earlier for self, except that orientation information and route planning are generally irrelevant. However, if the user is not actually standing at the to-be-mapped location (as when, say, one is recording the locations of types of geological formations viewed from a distance), the task of identifying correspondences between the environment and map also draws on the user's ability to judge location information within the space. Such judgments might be made directly by relying on human perceptual capacities (e.g., as in judging the incline of a hill one is facing; see Proffitt, Creem, & Zosh, 2001; judging the distance to or some object in view; see Loomis, Da Silva, Fujita, & Fukusima, 1992) or employing some tool (e.g., as in surveying land by using—in earlier eras—a Theodolite or a Gunter's chain—or, in contemporary times—an electronic laser-based instrument equipped with a Global Positioning System [GPS]).

The empirical illustrations given in this section thus draw from studies in which respondents are asked to indicate, on a map, the location (and perhaps orientation) of either themselves or some other object or person. Of interest is whether success on such tasks varies in relation to representation variables (as in the contrast between plan and oblique perspective maps); alignment variables (as in the contrast between conditions in which map-referenced and body-referenced "left" and "right" are or are not matched); and vantage-point variables (as in whether the space is viewed from ground level or from an oblique angle). Because the individual is *in* the space depicted by the representation, participants in these tasks thus may draw from the full set of self-space-representation relations shown in Fig. 12.4.

Preschoolers' Performance With Classroom Maps. In one illustrative study (Liben & Yekel, 1996), we asked preschool children (4–5 years) to use maps of their own highly familiar classroom to indicate the locations of objects in the room. Before the child arrived for the session, we placed some new objects in the room (e.g., a teddy bear and a lunch box). The session began with a brief discussion of maps and with instructions that helped the child align the map with the room and identify some correspondences (e.g., those between the hallway and playground doors on the map and in the room). The child was then asked to find one target object at a time, point to it in the actual space, and then place a sticker on a map to show the object's location.

Particularly relevant for the present discussion was the manipulation of the type of map. Children completed tasks (in counterbalanced order) with a plan map (as if one were looking straight down on the room from directly overhead) and an oblique perspective map (depicting the room from a raised angle). Some of the children's comments showed that the vertical view was indeed difficult to interpret. For example, during the instructions that oriented the children to the map, three children spontaneously misinterpreted the double sink as a "door." Similar to the tennis court example described earlier, interpreting the double sink as a door is consistent with the possibility that the child is interpreting the pattern of lines as if they represented something approached from face on (i.e., in an "elevation" view of door panels), rather than from directly overhead.

The patterns of success and failure on the plan and oblique maps were also consistent with the notion that a plan view would be especially hard to interpret. To illustrate, Fig. 12.6 shows data from one target location. Children's sticker placements that fell within the correct area are omitted from the figure. Thus, each black dot shows an *incorrect* placement of a sticker. Given that only errors are shown (20 maximum per map), what is immediately apparent from the high number of black dots on the plan map is that performance was quite poor on this representation. In contrast, the relative dearth of dots on the oblique perspective map shows that performance was generally quite good. The types of errors also contrast between the two maps. The errors on the plan map tended to be relatively dramatic. Many were far from the correct region, and many stickers were placed on furniture symbols rather than on the representational floor. In contrast, errors on the oblique map tended to be more minor. Three were very near the correct location; three were in a nearby, similar region (an open floor area); and only two were placed on the entirely wrong category of symbol (i.e., on furniture).

An ANOVA on the total number of correct responses to all items showed that overall performance was better on the oblique than on the plan map, and there was a significant interaction between map type and map order. When children were asked to work with the oblique map first, their later performance on the plan map was significantly better than if they had been asked to begin with the plan map. Interestingly, the advantage that accrued from the oblique perspective map appeared to come

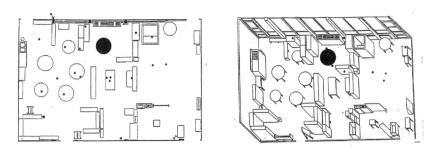

FIG. 12.6.   Composite maps of children's sticker responses on plan (left) and oblique perspective (right) maps. Large black circles indicate where the target object was located in the room, including a margin of allowed error to be counted as a "correct" response. Small black circles show locations of erroneous responses. (Thus, the smaller number of circles on the oblique map indicates that most responses were correct.) Data from Liben and Yekel (1996).

from the depicted vantage point of the representation, rather than from the perceptual vantage point of the viewer. That is, there was no effect of manipulating the actual vantage point from which the child viewed the room while completing the sticker task (seated at a desk in the room vs. seated at a desk in an elevated observation booth at one side of the room; see Liben & Yekel, 1996). It appears that children found it easier to identify the representational meaning of symbols when they depict information in ways that are similar to what is seen through action in the environment. Having cracked the code in distinguishing between furniture and floor representations, they could extend their understanding to the more abstract geometric symbols of the plan map.

A final indication that children expect the representation to mimic experiences obtained as they move through the environment is derived from the debriefing conversations. At the end of the sticker location tasks, we gave each child a fresh copy of the plan map and asked if there was anything that could have made the maps better or easier to understand. Over half the children suggested that a way to improve the plan map would be to have legs on the tables—an improvement actually implemented by one participant, as shown in Fig. 12.7.

Elementary School Children's Performance With Classroom Maps.   In a second illustrative study, we (Liben & Downs, 1993) used plan maps and tasks similar to those of the study described earlier, except that the tasks

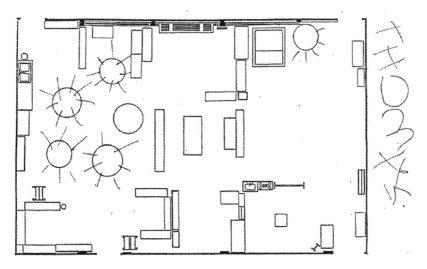

FIG. 12.7.   Map as amended by one 4-year-old child when asked if there was a way to make the map of his classroom better. Data from Liben and Yekel (1996).

required children to represent orientation as well as location information on their maps. We manipulated the relation between the map and space by asking children to complete the tasks once when the map was facing in the same direction as the room (i.e., aligned) and once when the map had been rotated by 180° (i.e., unaligned). In addition to the task manipulations, we also tested a broader age range of children (who were in kindergarten and Grades 1, 2, and 4/5) and included various individual difference measures of spatial skills (discussed later). Children were again tested in their own familiar classrooms, and had previously been introduced to the maps, and had been guided to notice some correspondences between the map and room (e.g., the relation between the real and representational doors and windows). One of the investigators then went to various predetermined locations and pointed straight ahead. Children were asked to put arrows on their maps to show where he was standing and which direction he was pointing.

Figure 12.8 (left) provides a composite map of all responses in one first-grade classroom under the aligned condition. The pattern of responses suggests that there is some difficulty in identifying both location and direction on the plan map with high precision. However, most responses are in the right general area, most are on the floor as they should be, and most

FIG. 12.8. Map showing composite of children's arrow placements to show location and pointing direction of person in the classroom under aligned (left) and unaligned (right) conditions. Correct answers are shown by open arrows. Reproduced from Liben and Downs (1993).

are aiming in roughly the right direction. Figure 12.8 (right) presents the comparable data for the unaligned condition. At the group level, it is clear that this version of the task was challenging. Especially interesting are the arrows in the lower right quadrant of the map oriented toward the upper left corner of the map. These are exactly the reverse of the correct answer, suggesting that many children had difficulty coordinating the self-space-representation relation when their body provided a competing frame of reference. An ANOVA on the number correct revealed a significant interaction between age and alignment condition, showing that even when children have mastered the aligned condition (by Grade 2) they continue to have difficulty in the unaligned condition.

College Students' Performance With Campus Maps.   A third illustrative study (see Liben, Kastens, & Stevenson, 2002) was also addressed to the relation among self, space, and map; it used a much larger space, this one the Penn State campus. First-semester students were taken individually to five locations, given a campus map, and asked to place an arrow sticker on the map to show where they were and which direction they were facing. At five additional locations, they were given a map containing a marked location, and they were asked to use a spinner to point toward the indicated location (beyond view) in the real space. Dependent measures included the accuracy of the placement of the arrows and spinner as well as the speed of responses. In addition, we collected data on observable strategies, noting, first, whether the participant turned the map physically while doing the task, and, second, at what orientation participants held the map when making their final responses. Our interest was whether participants would spontaneously attempt to align the map and space.

As in the other studies described previously, we also studied the impact of stimulus variables. One variable again concerned the viewing angle of the map—specifically, the contrast between plan and oblique maps. The second variable was map shape. Maps were either rectangular or round. This factor was manipulated to address another question about the physical relation between map and space: would participants given a round map (which does not privilege a direction with respect to paper space) be more likely to align the map and the space? These variables were crossed so that each participant used one of four map types derived from crossing viewing angle with map shape. Finally, we again administered a number of individual difference measures (discussed later).

Only a few results are mentioned here—not only because of space constraints, but also because this research is still in progress. One clear finding, however, is that the task was hard. Figure 12.9 is a composite map showing where one sample of college students placed their stickers on the map for one item. These data suggest that even college students do not

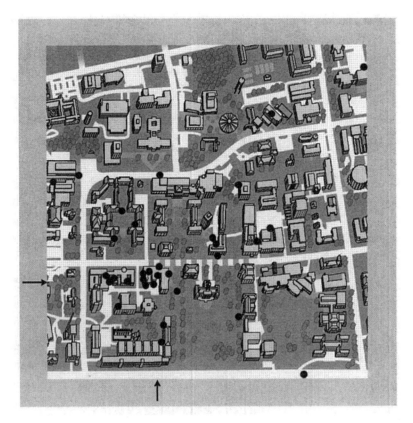

FIG. 12.9. Composite of college students' sticker placements to show their current location on campus. Participants' responses are shown by black circles; the actual location is at the intersection of the two arrows. Reproduced from Liben, Kastens, and Stevenson (2002).

find it a trivial task to figure out where they are on the map, at least when they are escorted to a location without having the opportunity to follow along on the map. (It remains unknown whether their performance would have been dramatically better if they had been allowed to use a map during the walk to the target locations or, if after they arrived, they had been given the opportunity to explore more of the environment to formulate and test hypotheses about their location.)

A further demonstration that the task was challenging is that even our research assistants experienced difficulty in running the study. That is, although all five assistants had reached an initial learning criterion showing that they knew the procedure (including the target locations and orientations), when we checked at the end of the study to make sure all procedures were still being followed correctly, we discovered errors. Spe-

cifically, although testers showed perfect consistency in taking participants to the correct locations, they did not always orient them in the right
direction, meaning that the directional data from this study had to be dis-
carded. (Recent data collection has allowed us to obtain new directional
data and address some additional questions, but these data are not yet
available to describe here.)

Despite the difficulties experienced by some participants and research
assistants, the tasks were not inherently unsolvable. Performance was
normally distributed, with some participants performing correctly on every item. This distribution set the conditions needed to examine the effects
of stimulus type and strategy. Data from the location measure (i.e., the
data that were not problematic) were consistent with the hypothesized
relevance of map format. Although accuracy did not differ significantly
across map types, speed did. Interestingly, the slowest performance of all
occurred on the map that was most like the ones typically used—that is, a
plan view map on a rectangular piece of paper. Consistent with the hypothesized relevance of the physical orientation of the map in relation to
the space, data showed a significant correlation between the number of
items on which the participant turned the map and the number of items
answered correctly. It is necessary to conduct additional research in which
map-rotation instructions are experimentally manipulated to test whether
the observed correlation reflects an advantage of map alignment or instead reflects different qualities of participants who versus do not spontaneously employ an alignment strategy. Although this particular question
has not yet been addressed, some of our research has been designed to
identify qualities that distinguish individuals who perform at different
levels of success on self-space-representational tasks. The empirical review thus closes with a brief discussion of some of this work.

Group and Individual Differences in Understanding Place Representations

Preface: Examining Group and Individual Differences. Although the empirical work discussed previously leaves many intriguing questions unan-
swered, two clear generalizations emerge. First, the research shows that
tasks used to assess participants' understanding of the relations among
self, space, and representation are challenging. These challenges are evident across a wide age span (from preschool to college) and in contexts
that are much like those found in the natural ecology (e.g., using a campus
map to figure out one's current location). Second, the research reveals
variations in performance in relation to grouping categories (such as gen-
der) and in relation to individual difference variables (such as the spatial
abilities studied in the psychometric tradition; e.g., see Eliot, 1987).

By themselves, data on group and individual differences do not allow conclusions about causal mechanisms because the data are correlational in nature. For example, one could not randomly assign a given participant to the category of "male" and another to the category of "female" and then examine the outcomes of these assignments. Data on performance in relation to group membership and individual cognitive profiles are, however, extremely valuable because they provide potential clues about the developmental factors that foster representational understanding and set the context for identifying component processes that underlie skilled performance (Liben, 2002). Once hypothetical developmental factors and component processes are identified through correlational work, experimental investigations may be designed to test their efficacy. Resulting data may be useful not only for contributing to basic research on processing of self-space-representation relations, but also for motivating educational programs to facilitate the understanding of representations needed for instructional, occupational, and everyday tasks (see Liben & Downs, 2001; Liben et al., 2002).

At the group level, the key characteristics we considered in our empirical work are participant sex and age. In and of themselves, however, neither chronological age nor biological sex is explanatory. Thus, when possible, we have supplemented demographic data on group membership with potentially relevant variables associated with that group membership. For example, with respect to age, we have assessed individuals' positions on the developmental trajectory along which projective spatial concepts progress. With respect to sex, we have assessed individuals' participation in culturally defined masculine activities that may encourage spatial skills.

At the individual level, the factors we focused on are spatial abilities (as conceptualized in the individual differences literature) and cognitive capacity variables (such as measures of working memory). We also conducted some experimental research in which we examined success on representational tasks as a function of whether participants were or were not given some theoretically motivated intervention. The two sections that follow provide illustrations, respectively, of our correlational and experimental work.

Illustrative Correlational Studies.   As mentioned in the course of describing empirical studies in earlier sections, several of our investigations included measures of developmental and individual difference variables thought to be linked to representational competence. One illustration is the classroom mapping study in which elementary school children were asked to place arrows on their aligned or unaligned maps to show the location and pointing direction of a person in their classroom (Liben & Downs,

1993). The individual difference measures were designed to explore the hypothesis that the age-linked differences in success on the mapping tasks would be linked to children's developmental mastery of projective spatial concepts (Piaget & Inhelder, 1956). Projective understanding, which involves understanding "point of view," was expected to be particularly relevant to children's performance under the unaligned testing condition (see earlier description and Fig. 12.8). Children were thus given modified Piagetian projective measures (see Liben & Downs, 1993). In addition, children were given a standardized measure of spatial skills (the Block Design subtest of the age-appropriate Wechsler Intelligence Scale). The latter was included to permit us to test whether any relation between mapping performance and projective concepts would hold over and above whatever relation might be attributable to higher spatial skills in general.

As already described, the data revealed the expected age-linked differences in interaction with alignment condition. The pattern of findings with respect to the individual difference measures was consistent with the hypothesized importance of projective concepts. That is, as expected, scores on the mapping and projective tasks were significantly correlated, particularly under the unaligned condition. More important, the correlation held even when performance on the general spatial abilities measure was statistically removed. Although the data were consistent with the hypothesis, they did not provide dramatic support for it. First, the predicted correlations were significant but not high. Second, children who performed at the highest levels on the mapping tasks generally performed well on the projective tasks, and children who performed at the lower levels on the mapping tasks rarely performed well on the projective tasks; nevertheless, there were notable exceptions to this pattern. Clearly projective concepts cannot provide a complete explanation of mapping performance.

In another illustrative study, we (Liben, Carlson, Szechter, & Mararra, 1999) asked high school students to complete the correspondences task described earlier in which participants were shown arrows on one representation and asked to place corresponding arrows on another representation. Several individual difference measures were administered. To test our hypothesis that the correspondences task would be related to mental rotation skills, we administered a mental rotation task (from the Primary Mental Abilities [PMA] test of Thurstone, 1962). To test whether that relation—if found—might simply reflect spatial skills in general, we administered another spatial task unrelated to rotation (the water level task; see Liben, 1991). A third measure was given to test our hypothesis that individuals' understanding of the view specificity of any given image would be related to participants' general knowledge of their own place in relation to the larger environment. In this "direction awareness" task, individuals were asked to point toward unseen target locations, both near and far (e.g., the school flagpole, Miami). Also included were measures of spatial working memory, including an orientation span measure drawn from Shah and Miyake (1996) requiring that participants remember a series of letter orientations, and a spatial premise integration task drawn from Byrne and Johnson-Laird (1989) requiring that participants remember and integrate orally presented spatial premises.

A regression analysis of these data showed that performance on the correspondences task was best predicted first by mental rotation and second by direction awareness. Once these variables were entered, there was no further role of performance on the water-level task nor on either spatial working memory task. Although the correlational nature of these data precludes conclusions about causality, the findings are at least consistent with the hypothesized role of understanding of changing viewpoints in images and of attention to one's place in space.

Individual difference data were also collected as part of the study in which college students were asked to show their location on a campus map. As noted earlier, map-location performance was higher among participants who used a map-turning strategy. In addition, map performance was correlated with scores on two of the standardized spatial tasks (the mental rotation task of the PMA and the ETS Paper Folding Test; see Ekstrom, French, Harman, & Dermen, 1976). Performance did not correlate with the water-level task nor with a more general measure of cognitive functioning (SAT scores).

Additional individual difference data are also being collected in ongoing research with children and adults. Although it is too early to draw many definitive conclusions from the correlational work to date, the data in hand do argue for the value of including measures of specific concepts or processing components hypothesized to underlie successful use of place representations, rather than merely trying to generalize about performance of children and adults as monolithic groups. Furthermore, the correlational data linking map performance to performance on mental rotation and projective tasks are, overall, consistent with the hypothesized importance of participants' understanding the view-specific nature of depicted and real spaces seen from any given vantage point. Do experiences that foster participants' awareness of this view-specificity enhance their success in understanding space representations? The next and final section of this empirical review discusses experimental work relevant to answering this question.

Illustrative Experimental Studies. We used two approaches to provide experimental data bearing on the hypothesis that interventions designed to enhance individuals' appreciation of view-specificity will enhance their successful use of place representations. The first was designed to provide children with experience in seeing that images of an environment differ in relation to one's own position in that environment (see Liben, 2003; Liben & Szechter, 2002). In this work, children produced the environmental images themselves by producing photographs. (The argument that experience in producing spatial graphics will enhance understanding of spatial graphics has been made elsewhere; see Liben, 1999.) Given our interest in individual differences, we also addressed the possibility that experiences in image production would have different effects for children with different spatial abilities.

In a first implementation of this approach, we provided 7- and 8-year-old children with three private lessons. In Session 1, all children received a pretest designed to assess entry-level spatial skills (the Landscape Task described in Liben & Downs, 1993). For children who had been randomly assigned to the control group, Session 1 was also used to administer a number of measures of spatial-graphic understanding. All children were then given instruction in the mechanics of using a 35 mm camera. A tour of campus followed, during which children were invited to take photographs of their own choosing. Film was developed and printed for Session 2, during which the instructor and child discussed the prior week's photographs, and then proceeded to take another campus walk during which children took additional photographs. These photographs were discussed in Session 3, which—for children in the experimental group—was also used to administer the spatial-graphic measures. Of interest was whether children who had photography experience prior to taking the spatial-graphic measures would show better performance and whether changes would interact with entry-level spatial skills.

In brief, the data showed no evidence that lessons affected children's spatial graphic performance positively. In fact there was a marginal interaction suggesting that, although lessons had little affect at all on children with relatively high-level spatial abilities, lessons may have had a negative effect on performance among children with relatively low spatial abilities. We hypothesized that this pattern of findings might be explained by the fact that the lessons had not explicitly been designed to teach about the relation between vantage point and resulting image. Thus, children who have difficulty picking up or understanding spatial information on their own might simply have been confused by the whole experience.

A second study was therefore conducted in which the photography lessons were redesigned to provide explicit experiences in linking movement in space to resulting images. First, the film camera was replaced by a digital camera that allowed far more immediate feedback to the child about how self-movement in the space resulted in a different image. Second, although we retained some opportunities for children to take photographs of their own choosing, we also included activities that were explicitly designed to highlight the relation between spatial position and image. In one such activity, children were asked to take photographs of particular referents to accomplish some goal that could be solved by moving in the space. For example, at the campus art museum, children were asked to take a picture that would include only one of the two lion's paw sculptures that flanked the museum entrance. This request could be satisfied by moving close to the sculptures so that a single paw would take up the entire image, moving to the side or back of one paw, and so on. In another such activity, children were given model photographs and asked to take another precisely like it. After taking an initial photograph, children were shown the resulting image on the camera display, asked to compare it to the model photograph, and then asked to take a second picture to produce an even closer match to the model.

The data from this study provided some, although limited, support for our hypotheses: Children's performance on some table-top spatial-graphic tasks was better among children who had been given the photography lessons, and it was the children who had entered with lower spatial skills who profited more. However, the intervention effect did not enhance children's success in identifying referents in aerial photographs.

The second major experimental approach reviewed here is part of a broader educational initiative designed to teach children to use maps. As discussed elsewhere (Liben et al., 2002), although map education and map research are common, relatively little past work has addressed direct links between a map and the actual environment it represents. Instead the emphasis has been on relations *within* a single represented space (e.g., asking or teaching children to show on a map how one would get from one location to another) or relations between two symbolic representations of the same referent space (e.g., asking or teaching children to indicate locations or routes on a map that are described verbally). A major reason is undoubtedly the practical difficulty of taking pupils or research participants to field sites for instruction or testing.

Motivated to find some means to address the instructional difficulty in linking representational and real environments, Kastens (2000) developed a curriculum entitled *Where Are We?* A core component of the curriculum is computer software that provides simulated perceptual experiences of an environment in conjunction with a map of that environment. More specifically and as illustrated in Fig. 12.10, the software provides a plan view map of a park and an inset that displays a color video of eye-level views recorded on walks through the park. Clicking the center arrow beneath the inset starts a video taken while walking straight ahead; clicking the left or right arrows, respectively, displays the videos taken while turning to the left or right. Although seeing a video is not, of course, identical to experiencing a real environment (particularly from a Gibsonian perspective;

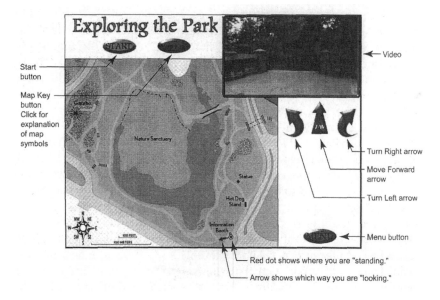

FIG. 12.10.   Annotated screen from *Where Are We?* in "Exploring the Park" mode (Kastens, 2000). (Actual display was in color.) Reproduced from Liben, Kastens, and Stevenson (2002).

see e.g., Gibson, 1979; Reed, 1988), it is at least closer to such an experience than that provided by still photographs or verbal descriptions. Until it is possible for schools to overcome the practical difficulties of field trips or the technical and financial challenges of offering virtual environments, the software from *Where Are We?* offers a practical compromise (see Liben et al., 2002).

The software offers several different modes. In *Exploring the Park,* users move around the park by clicking on the arrows while a red dot with a directional arrow moves simultaneously on the map to show changing locations directions. In *Are We There Yet?*, users are shown their initial location and orientation on the map and are asked to reach a specified location by walking through the park via arrow clicks. In *Lost!*, users are dropped somewhere in the park and are asked to discover where they are by moving around via arrow clicks. Once they believe they know their location, they click on the map and are greeted by "Sorry, try again," "You're close," or "You got it!" Finally, in *Add to the Map*, users travel through the park looking for certain objects (e.g., lamp posts) not yet indicated on the map and then place symbols on the map to show these objects' locations.

A study is in progress to investigate the impact of the *Where Are We?* curriculum on children's understanding of the links between real and representational spaces (see Liben et al., 2002). To date we have enrolled and tested children from five 4th-grade classes, with data collection from additional classes in progress. All children were given pre- and posttests designed to test their understanding of map-space relations. In the experimental but not the control classes, intervening between the two test sessions was the *Where Are We?* curriculum as implemented by the classroom teacher. Children were also given a variety of spatial measures, again as a means to examine possible interactions between the curriculum and student characteristics.

Of particular interest here is children's performance on a field mapping task. Children were taken to either a nearby urban or suburban university campus at which eight colored flags had been placed. Children were given a map and asked to place colored stickers on their maps to show the flags' locations. A point was assigned for any sticker placed correctly within a margin of error defined by sticker size. Even within this single-grade sample, scores ranged from 0 to 8. Most important, an ANOVA on the scores of children tested to date revealed a significant interaction between group and time, such that the improvement between pre- and posttests was significantly greater in the experimental group than in the control group.

In recognition of the practical difficulty of using field tests like these as part of curriculum implementation in real classrooms, we are also attempting to develop classroom tasks that may be used to assess these mapping skills. One such task is the photo-map task, in which we project a photograph of some scene on a screen, give participants a map of the area depicted in the photograph, and ask them to place an arrow sticker on the map to show where the photographer was standing and which direction the camera was pointing when the photograph was taken. Figure 12.11 provides an illustrative item and two sets of responses—one from a sample of college students and the other from a sample of fourth-grade students. What is evident from these figures is that, in general, adults are far better than children, although—not surprisingly given all the evidence of individual differences already reviewed—there is variability even among adults. From the perspective of the experimental manipulation being reviewed here, however, the most important finding is that, as on the field flag location task, we again found a significant interaction of group and time: Improvement was greater among children who had participated in the *Where Are We?* curriculum than among those who had not.

Although far more work is needed to assess the impact of the curriculum, to gather data about how the curriculum is actually being implemented by classroom teachers, and to examine how the curriculum interacts with characteristics of individual students, the preliminary findings are encouraging with respect to both theory and application. With respect to the former, the experimental data are consistent with the view that an

FIG. 12.11.   Sample item from photo-map task with maps showing composite of responses by a sample of college students (left) and fourth-grade students (right). Actual photograph was in color. Reproduced from Liben, Kastens, and Stevenson (2002).

important aspect of understanding and using place representations is understanding that views of environments change with position in space. With respect to the latter, the experimental data suggest that children's mapping skills may indeed be improved by theoretically motivated instruction.

CONCLUSIONS, AND A CALL *TO* ACTION

In closing, I return to the theme of this volume—that is, the role of action. Other contributors have focused on actions with real objects in real spaces: grasping objects or catching them, walking in situations that offer differing kinds of physical supports, anticipating locations of objects by tracking object movement and the position of barriers, and so on. In the current chapter, I instead focused on human understanding of *representations* of real spaces. I join the ecological heritage in rejecting the idea that representations provide information that is equivalent to what is provided in the actual world, but propose that experiences of human action may nevertheless influence how easily the represented world is understood. Representations that provide information that is closely related to what humans perceive as they act in real environments appear to be more easily under-stood than those that provide information collected via amplifiers of hu-man locomotion and perception. Although the program of research dis-cussed in this chapter was not driven by ecological theory, many of the findings are compatible with and illuminated by it.

In addition to revealing variation in performance in relation to stimulus variables (e.g., plan vs. oblique maps), the data reveal dramatic levels of variation among individuals. Even among adults who are successful in maneuvering in the environment that they can see and grasp, many ap-pear to struggle when they confront self-space-representation challenges. There is evidence that these struggles occur not just in our psychological laboratories, but also in the real world. Anecdotes abound about people becoming hopelessly lost or erecting fences or driveways in wrong loca-tions because of an inability to read maps. Illustrative is a report of a large financial settlement awarded to a couple who had suffered property dam-age when a logger felled trees in error. When defending his behavior to the court, the logger wrote: "The way the map was shown to me didn't help, as it should have been turned the other way" ("Pair Awarded," 1989).

We and others are only beginning to conduct research that is aimed at trying to understand the pathways by which individuals develop the skills to understand and use place representations successfully. The re-search we conducted to date is compatible with the notion that action plays an important role in understanding many kinds of place representa-tions. However, naturally occurring action and perception of the environ-ment are not enough. This is not surprising given that representations go *beyond* action. We can use representations to communicate, remember, re-duce cognitive load, see things that would never be available to unaided human perception, and see data patterns that emerge when information is displayed simultaneously (Liben, 2000, 2001; Tversky, 2001; Uttal, 2000). To understand representations fully, it is imperative that the viewer rec-ognize that the appearance of the representation is driven not only by the referent, but also by the way it has been represented. Recent work has been directed to conceptualizing ways in which representational under-standing may develop (e.g., see Callaghan, 1999; Liben, 1999) and to em-pirical investigations of how children's success in interpreting images may be enhanced through parental guidance (e.g., Gauvain, de la Ossa, & Hurtado, 2001; Szechter & Liben, 2004) and through experience in creating representations (e.g., Callaghan & Rankin, 2002; Liben, 2003). It may well be that fostering an understanding of how actions in real spaces are linked to concrete representations of those spaces may provide an especially good foundation for children's understanding of spatial-graphic repre-sentations more generally (Liben & Downs, 2001).

That education in such realms is important becomes clear when we pause to consider the central (and increasing) role that spatial-graphic representations play in education, work, and daily life. As educators, we would thus be wise to *take* action to ensure that all individuals develop a sophisticated understanding of what representations do and do not mean about their real worlds, near and far. As researchers, we would be wise to consider how our human actions affect, and are affected by, our interactions with the concrete representations that exist in all our ecological niches irrespective of the theoretical land in which we reside.

ACKNOWLEDGMENTS

Portions of the research described here were supported by grants from the National Institute of Education (G-83-0025) and from the National Science Foundation (RED-9554504 and ESI 01-01758), although the opinions expressed here are not necessarily those of these institutions. I appreciate the permission of Yann Arthus-Bertrand to reproduce the photograph shown in Fig. 12.3. I am grateful to the editors for their insightful comments and, more generally, to both Anne and Herb Pick for their intellectual guidance and support, and for their graciousness in welcoming me into their worlds.

ENDNOTES

The photograph by Yann Arthus-Bertrand reproduced in Fig. 12.3 is taken from *Earth from Above: An Aerial Portrait of Our Planet*. Below, respectively, are Arthus-Bertrand's (verbatim) descriptions of (a) the goals of his project, (b) the particular photograph in Fig. 12.3, and (c) the need for this project. Both photograph and text appear with permission of the photographer.

(a) Since 1990, Yann Arthus-Bertrand has flown over hundreds of countries. His aerial photographs cannot be dissociated from their captions, invite all of us to reflect upon the Earth's evolution and the future of its inhabitants. A report through words and images which makes us aware that, not only are we individually responsible for our planet, we must also decide what we bequeath to future generations, together.
http://www. yannarthusbertrand.org

(b) **NEW OLIVE PLANTINGS, Zaghouan, Tunisia (N 36°24′ E 10°23′).** These olive groves at the foot of the 4,250-foot-high (1,295 m) Jebel Zaghouan in northeastern Tunisia are planted in curved embankments to retain water and limit erosion, which viewed from above look like the lines on a relief map. A symbol of peace, the tree is native to the Mediterranean basin, where 90 percent of the planet's olive trees grow. An olive tree can live as long as 1,000 years, producing 11 to 65 pounds (5 to 30 kg) of olives yearly. In the past its oil was used in small clay lamps, but it has been replaced by petroleum. Today we consume both table olives and olive oil, which is renowned for its dietetic and medicinal properties and also exploited in cosmetics. It takes 11 to 13 pounds (5 to 6 kilograms) of olives to produce a liter (a bit more than a quart) of olive oil. Tunisia produced 1 million tons of olives in 2000, doubling its 1997 production and becoming the fourth-greatest producer, after Spain (4.2 million tons), Italy (2.8 million), and Greece (2 million). These countries are also the principal consumers of olive oil: 20 liters per capita each year in Greece, 15 liters in Spain and Italy, and just one-half liter in France.

(c) **Toward a sustainable development.** Since 1950, economic growth has been considerable, and world production of goods and services has multiplied by a factor of 7. During this same period, while the world's population has only doubled, the volume of fish caught and meat produced has multiplied by 5. So has the energy demand. Oil consumption has multiplied by 7, and carbon dioxide emissions, the main cause of the greenhouse effect and global warming, by 4. Since 1900, fresh water consumption has multiplied by 6, chiefly to provide for agriculture. And yet, 20% of the world's population does not have drinkable water, 40% lacks access to improved sanitation, 40% is without electricity, 826 million people are underfed, and half of humanity lives on less than $2 a day. In other words, a fifth of the world's population lives in industrialized countries, consuming and producing in excess and generating massive pollution. The remaining four-fifths live in developing countries and, for the most part, in poverty. To provide for their needs, they make heavy demands upon the Earth's natural resources, causing a constant degradation of our planet's ecosystem and limited supplies of fresh water, ocean water, forests, air, arable land, and open spaces.

This is not all. By 2050, the Earth will have close to 3 billion additional inhabitants. These people will live, for the most part, in developing countries. As these countries develop, their economic growth will jockey for position with that of industrialized nations—within the limits of ecosystem Earth. The Earth's situation is not irreversible, but changes need to be made as soon as possible. We have the chance to turn toward a sustainable development, one that allows us to improve the living conditions of the world's citizens and to satisfy the needs of generations to come. This development would be based on an economic growth respectful both of man and the natural resources of our unique planet.

Such development requires improving production methods and changing our consumption habits. With the active participation of all the world's citizens, each and every person can contribute to the future of the Earth and mankind, starting right now.

REFERENCES

Acredolo, L. P. (1978). Development of spatial orientation in infancy. *Developmental Psychology, 14,* 224–234.

Byrne, R. M., & Johnson-Laird, P. N. (1989). Spatial reasoning. *Journal of Memory and Language, 28,* 564–575.

Callaghan, T. C. (1999). Early understanding and production of graphic symbols. *Child Development, 70,* 1314–1324.

Callaghan, T. C., & Rankin, M. P. (2002). Emergence of graphic symbol functioning and the question of domain specificity: A longitudinal training study. *Child Development, 73,* 359–376.

DeLoache, J. S., Uttal, D. H., & Pierroutsakos, S. L. (2000). What's up? The development of an orientation preference for picture books. *Journal of Cognition and Development, 1,* 81–95.

Downs, R. M., & Liben, L. S. (1988). Through a map darkly: Understanding maps as representations. *Genetic Epistemologist, 16,* 11–18.

Downs, R. M., & Liben, L. S. (1993). Mediating the environment: Communicating, appropriating, and developing graphic representations of place. In R. H. Wozniak & K. Fischer (Eds.), *Development in context: Acting and thinking in specific environments* (pp. 155–181). Hillsdale, NJ: Lawrence Erlbaum Associates.

Ekstrom, R. B., French, J. W., Harman, H. H., & Dermen, D. (1976). *Kit of factor-referenced cognitive tests.* Princeton, NJ: Educational Testing Service.

Eliot, J. (1987). *Models of psychological space, psychometric, developmental, and experimental approaches.* New York: Springer-Verlag.

Gauvain, M., de la Ossa, J. L., & Hurtado, M. T. (2001). Parental guidance as children learn to use cultural tools: The case of pictorial plans. *Cognitive Development, 16,* 551–575.

Gibson, E. J., & Pick, A. D. (2000). *An ecological approach to perceptual learning and development.* New York: Oxford University Press.

Gibson, J. J. (1966). *The senses considered as perceptual systems.* Boston: Houghton-Mifflin.

Gibson, J. J. (1971). The information available in pictures. *Leonardo, 4,* 27–35.

Gibson, J. J. (1979). *The ecological approach to visual perception.* Boston: Houghton-Mifflin.

Gombrich, E. H. (1961). *Art and illusion* (2nd ed.). Princeton, NJ: Princeton University Press.

Hagen, M. A. (1986). *Varieties of realism: Geometries of representational art.* Cambridge, England: Cambridge University Press.

Hardwick, D. A., McIntyre, C. W., & Pick, H. L. (1976). The content and manipulation of cognitive maps in children and adults. *Monographs of the Society for Research in Child Development, 41,* Serial No. 166.

Harley, J. B., & Woodward, D. (Eds.). (1987). *The history of cartography: Volume 1. Cartography in prehistoric, ancient and Medieval Europe and the Mediterranean.* Chicago: University of Chicago Press.

Harrison, R. E. (1944). *Look at the world: The fortune atlas for world strategy.* New York: Alfred A. Knopf.

Kastens, K. A. (2000). *Where are we?* Watertown, MA: Tom Snyder Productions.

Kennedy, J. M. (1974). *A psychology of picture perception.* San Francisco: Jossey-Bass.

Kubovy, M. (1986). *The psychology of perspective and Renaissance art.* Cambridge, England: Cambridge University Press.

Liben, L. S. (1981). Spatial representation and behavior: Multiple perspectives. In L. S. Liben, A. H. Patterson, & N. Newcombe (Eds.), *Spatial representation and behavior across the life span: Theory and application* (pp. 3–36). New York: Academic Press.

Liben, L. S. (1991). The Piagetian water-level task: Looking beneath the surface. In R. Vasta (Ed.), *Annals of child development* (Vol. 8, pp. 81–143). London: Jessica Kingsley Publishers.

Liben, L. S. (1997). Children's understanding of spatial representations of place: Mapping the methodological landscape. In N. Foreman & R. Gillett (Eds.), *A handbook of spatial research paradigms and methodologies* (pp. 41–83). East Sussex, England: Psychology Press, Taylor & Francis Group.

Liben, L. S. (1999). Developing an understanding of external spatial representations. In I. E. Sigel (Ed.), *Development of mental representation* (pp. 297–321). Mahwah, NJ: Lawrence Erlbaum Associates.

Liben, L. S. (2000). Map use and the development of spatial cognition: Seeing the *bigger* picture. *Developmental Science, 3,* 270–274.

Liben, L. S. (2001). Thinking through maps. In M. Gattis (Ed.), *Spatial schemas and abstract thought* (pp. 44–77). Cambridge, MA: MIT Press.

Liben, L. S. (2002). The drama of sex differences in academic achievement: And the show goes on. *Issues in Education, 8,* 65–75.

Liben, L. S. (2003). Beyond point and shoot: Children's developing understanding of photographs as spatial and expressive representations. In R. V. Kail (Ed.), *Advances in child development and behavior* (Vol. 31, pp. 1–42). San Diego: Academic Press.

Liben, L. S., Carlson, R. A., Szechter, L. E., & Mararra, M. T. (1999, August). *Understanding geographic images.* Paper presented at the meetings of the American Psychological Association, Boston.

Liben, L. S., & Downs, R. M. (1989). Understanding maps as symbols: The development of map concepts in children. In H. W. Reese (Ed.), *Advances in child development and behavior* (Vol. 22, pp. 145–201). New York: Academic Press.

Liben, L. S., & Downs, R. M. (1991). The role of graphic representations in understanding the world. In R. M. Downs, L. S. Liben, & D. S. Palermo (Eds.), *Visions of aesthetics, the environment, and development: The legacy of Joachim Wohlwill* (pp. 139–180). Hillsdale, NJ: Lawrence Erlbaum Associates.

Liben, L. S., & Downs, R. M. (1992). Developing an understanding of graphic representations in children and adults: The case of GEO-graphics. *Cognitive Development, 7,* 331–349.

Liben, L. S., & Downs, R. M. (1993). Understanding person-space-map relations: Cartographic and developmental perspectives. *Developmental Psychology, 29,* 739–752.

Liben, L. S., & Downs, R. M. (2001). Geography for young children: Maps as tools for learning environments. In S. L. Golbeck (Ed.), *Psychological perspectives on early childhood education* (pp. 220–252). Mahwah, NJ: Lawrence Erlbaum Associates.

Liben, L. S., Dunphy-Lelli, S., & Szechter, L. E. (in preparation). *Interpreting aerial photographs: The role of vantage point and context.* Unpublished manuscript, The Pennsylvania State University.

Liben, L. S., Kastens, K. A., & Stevenson, L. M. (2002). Real-world knowledge through real-world maps: A developmental guide for navigating the educational terrain. *Developmental Review, 22,* 267–322.

Liben, L. S., & Szechter, L. S. (2002). A social science of the arts: An emerging organizational initiative and an illustrative investigation of photography. *Qualitative Sociology, 25,* 385–408.

Liben, L. S., & Yekel, C. A. (1996). Preschoolers' understanding of plan and oblique maps: The role of geometric and representational correspondence. *Child Development, 67,* 2780–2796.

Linn, M. C., & Petersen, A. C. (1985). Emergence and characterization of sex differences in spatial ability: A meta-analysis. *Child Development, 56,* 1479–1498.

Loomis, J. M., Da Silva, J. A., Fujita, N., & Fukusima, S. S. (1992). Visual space perception and visually directed action. *Journal of Experimental Psychology: Human Perception and Performance, 18,* 906–921.

Nelson, B. D. (1994, March). *Location and size geographic misperceptions: A survey of junior high through undergraduate college students.* Paper presented at the annual meeting of the Association of American Geographers, San Francisco.

Overton, W. F., & Müller, U. (2002). *The embodied mind and consciousness.* Introduction to the 32nd annual meetings of the Jean Piaget Society, Philadelphia.

Pair awarded $51,000 for trees felled in error. (1989, March 29). *The Los Angeles Times* [Southland Edition: National Desk], p. 14.

Piaget, J. (1952). *The origins of intelligence in children.* New York: Norton.

Piaget, J. (1954). *The construction of reality in the child.* New York: Ballantine Books.

Piaget, J., & Inhelder, B. (1956). *The child's conception of space.* London: Routledge & Kegan Paul.

Pick, H. L., & Lockman, J. J. (1981). From frames of reference to spatial representations. In L. S. Liben, A. H. Patterson, & N. Newcombe (Eds.), *Spatial representation and behavior across the life span: Theory and application* (pp. 39–61). New York: Academic Press.

Proffitt, D. R., Creem, S. H., & Zosh, W. D. (2001). Seeing mountains in mole hills: Geographical-slant perception. *Psychological Science, 12,* 418–423.

Reed, E. S. (1988). *James J. Gibson and the psychology of perception.* New Haven, CT: Yale University Press.

Rieser, J. J. (1979). Reference systems and the spatial orientation of six month old infants. *Child Development, 50,* 1078–1087.

Shah, P., & Miyake, A. (1996). The separability of working memory resources for spatial thinking and language processing: An individual differences approach. *Journal of Experimental Psychology: General, 125,* 4–27.

Spencer, C., Harrison, N., & Darvizeh, Z. (1980). The development of iconic mapping ability in young children. *International Journal of Early Childhood, 12,* 57–64.

Stea, D., Blaut, J. M., & Stephens, J. (1996). Mapping as a cultural universal. In J. Portugali (Ed.), *The construction of cognitive maps.* The Netherlands: Kluwer Academic Publishers.

Szechter, L. E., & Liben, L. S. (2004). Parental guidance in preschoolers' understanding of spatial-graphic representations. *Child Development, 75,* 869–885.

Thurstone, T. G. (1962). *Primary mental abilities.* Chicago: Science Research Associates.

Tversky, B. (2001). Spatial schemas in depictions. In M. Gattis (Ed.), *Spatial schemas and abstract thought* (pp. 79–112). Cambridge, MA: MIT Press.

Uttal, D. H. (2000). Seeing the big picture: Map use and the development of spatial cognition. *Developmental Science, 3,* 247–286.

13

▼▼▼▼▼▼▼

Mental Representations as Explanatory Constructs: A Discussion of the Chapters by Keen and Liben

Janellen Huttenlocher
University of Chicago

I have been given the assignment of commenting on chapters by Keen (chap. 11) and Liben (chap. 12). I discuss the chapters in the context of a concern, expressed by several participants at this conference, with theories that invoke mental representations in explaining behavior. The point of view expressed by these participants startled me because the notion of mental representation is vital to the study of cognition and its development. Although the notion lacks precise definition, the idea conveyed is one of internal processes that preserve information about the world and underlie a wide range of behaviors. For example, a person may remember the locations of various places in a familiar city and use this information to travel efficiently from place to place, comprehend and produce verbal descriptions of particular routes, and interpret and construct maps of the area. To banish mental representation from the explanation of human behavior seems implausible, but it may be valuable to reexamine the notion in considering the chapters assigned to me.

This conference provides a good setting for a discussion of mental representation. First, the conference was organized to honor Herb and Ann Pick, and it has been natural to focus to some extent on the beliefs of *their* mentors—James and Eleanor Gibson. In the Gibsonian (ecological) tradition, as Liben notes, mental representation is "a construct that is greeted with suspicion." The Gibsons argued that intelligent behavior should be explained in terms of "affordances" existing in the environment (J. J. Gibson, 1979). They believed that psychological theories should focus on the role of environmental information in explaining behavior and avoid positing internal processes. Second, the topics discussed in the Keen and Liben chapters concern important but different issues that raise questions about the role of mental representation in the study of cognitive development.

In its earliest stages, psychology was mainly concerned with internal processes. People's mental states were studied by obtaining reports of their experiences (e.g., did they think in words or images?). However, it soon seemed that introspection did not provide a satisfactory basis for scientific study. Not only was there no objective way to establish the accuracy of people's reports, but the approach made a claim that seemed philosophically dubious—that mental events (thoughts) could cause physical events (bodily movement). In dealing with these problems, psychology became a science of behavior rather than a science of mind. The goal was to predict behavior, and the data were relations between observable behaviors (responses) and the events that preceded them (stimuli). For complex tasks, where it did not seem possible to explain behavior without positing internal processes, those processes were conceptualized as implicit behaviors, a constraint on psychological explanation that was severely limiting.

Although observable behavior has continued to provide the main data of psychology over the last half century, the goal has become one of explicating the processes that underlie the behavior. Issues of mind–body relations no longer seem troublesome. After all, it is possible to construct a robot, a physical device, that exhibits intelligent behavior. Because the construction plans for animate creatures are not available, inferences about underlying mechanisms are arrived at on the basis of observable behavior. In psychology, these mechanisms are specified at the level of logical description. However, it is possible to augment the investigation of underlying mechanisms by direct study of neural processes. Finally, it is also possible to revisit questions about people's conscious experience. That is, introspective reports can be examined in relation to conclusions about mental processes based on behavioral data, and they may even provide a source of hypotheses about mental processes that can then be tested objectively.

So what could be the problem with positing mental representation in explaining intelligent behavior? Bill Warren argues that "the problem with representations is that there is a steep philosophical price to pay for them." Let us consider two well-known "deep" philosophical problems that have been discussed. One of the problems concerns the question of how states of the mind (representations) are related to states of the world. The other problem concerns the question of whether, if there are mental representations, there must be a being (a homunculus) inside the mind to interpret those representations.

If one treats mental representations as theoretical entities within psychology, posited to explain the relation between stimuli and responses, I would argue that these philosophical issues do not arise. Questions about the relation of mental representation to the actual world are of great interest, but they are epistemological questions, distinct from questions concerning the use of mental representation as a theoretical notion in psychology inferred from behavior. Although the study of mental representation in psychology is not concerned with the relation of inner states of the organism to the nature of the world, it would seem that successful adaptation requires that important features of the world be captured in memory (represented) and honored in behavior. As we see later in this discussion, psychology may indeed provide information relevant to epistemological questions. Further, the question of whether an inner interpreter is required to "read" mental representations is only a problem if mental states are conventional (arbitrary) "internal languages." Then indeed an interpreter would be required, potentially leading to an infinite regress in which there would have to be an interpreter of that interpretation, and so on. In the context of psychological theory, however, inner states are not mental texts that must be interpreted by subjects. They are scientific notions posited to explain the relation of stimuli to behavior.

Even when philosophical/conceptual issues are set aside, there remain problems for psychological theories that posit mental representation. Those problems concern the evaluation of theories of inner states and processes. It is often difficult to evaluate one model against alternative formulations. At this conference, questions have been raised about the adequacy of theories that posit general knowledge states to account for wide ranges of intelligent behavior, versus theories that explain behavior on various tasks in terms of more specific processes. Not only is it difficult to choose among theories, but, more generally, it is not clear to what extent it is possible for behavioral data to provide definitive information allowing one to distinguish among alternative theories.

In the context of the considerations just raised, there may seem to be attractions to the position presented by Rod Brooks (1991) in an article called "Intelligence Without Representation." Brooks argues that cognitive science has vastly overemphasized mental representation in explaining intelligent behavior. He suggests that one should seek explanations of behavior in terms of simple perception-action systems rather than conceptualization; the latter, he argued, has appeared only recently in evolution. As he put it,

> problem solving behavior, language, expert knowledge and application, and reason, are all pretty simple once the essence of being and reacting are available. That essence is the ability to move around in a dynamic environ-

ment, sensing the surroundings to a degree sufficient to achieve the necessary maintenance of life and reproduction. This part of intelligence is where evolution has concentrated its time. (p. 140)

The injunction to seek simple explanations of behavior is most straightforward in the study of early development, and I deal with the explanation of infant and toddler behavior in discussing Keen's chapter. In particular, I examine to what extent it is necessary to posit internal states to explain the behavior of infants and very young children. In the study of more complex behavior in older children and adults, it is often critical to posit mental processes so the injunction to seek simple explanations must accommodate such processes. Liben's chapter deals with spatial behavior. Such behavior is not simply based on "the ability to move around in a dynamic environment." Rather, it draws on stored information about the spatial environment individuals have encountered. Liben's topic is map use. Because maps are physical devices, it might seem possible to study them without considering mental representation. To do so would be misleading, however, because only creatures who possess the ability to represent space mentally would ever construct maps or be able to interpret them. I begin with Keen's work with toddlers, and I then turn to spatial behavior in older children and adults.

REPRESENTATION AND EARLY COGNITIVE
DEVELOPMENT

Keen describes a program of research in which she has explored toddlers' behaviors toward objects. Seeking simple explanations of behavior seems especially appropriate in studying infants and toddlers. They do not yet exhibit complex learned behaviors, nor do they report compelling introspections about their inner states. Nevertheless, investigators of cognitive development have avoided positing internal states in their explanations of young children's behavior. For a long period, starting before modern cognitive psychology, theory and research in the field were dominated by Piaget. The notion of mental representation was central to his theoretical framework.

In Piaget's theory, mature humans interpret events in terms of internal logical structures (Piaget, 1952). His view of the nature of mental representation was in many ways similar to that of Kant, except that the explanation of its origin was different. In Kant's view mental structures are innate and constitute preconditions of human thought, whereas in Piaget's view mental structures emerge from experiences during the life of each individual. According to Piaget, image-like representations in young children are transformed into logical structures in adults via action in the world. Ideas of permanent objects existing in a spatiotemporal framework and of physical causation arise during the first 2 years of life, shaped by infants' interactions with objects and events. Given this source of mental representations, they necessarily capture actual features of the world. In contrast, innate mental structures would not be shaped by an individual's experience, so correspondences with features of the world could only result from evolutionary processes, reflecting the adaptive importance of accurate information in the survival of the species.

Later investigators have had difficulty integrating their findings into Piaget's theoretical framework, as well as with finding ways to falsify his theory. Further, the idea that abstract logical structures emerge from simpler mental states has seemed to some investigators like alchemy. The chief quarrel with Piaget has not been about whether to posit mental representation, but rather with whether to posit that mental representation is acquired or innate. Recently, it has been argued that certain fundamental ideas are innate—notably, "core" physical principles such as that objects are solid and cannot pass through other objects (cf. Spelke, Breinlinger, Macomber, & Jacobson, 1992).

What empirical data can be obtained to support claims of conceptual understanding in infancy? In the early months of life, infants do not exhibit intentional behaviors that can reveal complex underlying processes. However, they *do* show variations in visual attention, and differences in looking times have been used as evidence for conceptual knowledge. The idea is that if infants understand that objects are permanent and do not pass through solid barriers, they should look longer at "impossible" events where objects seem to pass through barriers than at "possible" events where they do not. Infants *do* look longer at events that (seemingly) violate physical laws, and the results have been interpreted as showing knowledge of physical principles.

However, the finding of behavior that is consistent with a particular interpretation—in this case, innate core principles—does not necessarily imply that those principles explain the behavior. There may be other possible explanations. Before accepting a theory that posits innate core principles, it is important to try to falsify the theory. This is especially important for a theory that makes important claims, such as that infants possess innate ideas about the permanence and solidity of objects. Possibly differences in looking times might be explained in terms of simpler processes such as recognition of visual discrepancies from situations that were observed earlier (cf. Haith, 1998). Hence, the findings reported in the infancy literature are only a first step toward evaluating the notion of innate core principles as proposed by Spelke et al., and the possibility of explaining infant behavior in terms of simpler processes should lead to caution in inferring complex innate principles.

Keen's research provides a start in allowing us to evaluate whether core physical principles exist at the start of life. She notes that if infant behavior were guided by the conceptual principle that objects are permanent and unable to pass through solid barriers, then 2-year-olds should act according to that principle. After all, by this age children can retrieve objects, open doors, and so on. Keen presented 2-year-olds with an inclined runway apparatus that had barriers and a wall to obscure the runway. Children saw a ball released at one end, and the question was whether they would retrieve the ball at a point where it would have been stopped by a barrier. The apparatus had doors into which children could reach.

What Keen studied was children's choice of a door in attempting to retrieve the ball. In a set of carefully designed studies, she could find no evidence that children's reaching behavior reflected knowledge of physical principles concerning solid objects and barriers. The children often reached for the ball past the barrier. Thus, there was no reason to argue that reaching behavior in 2-year-olds is based on a mental representation that honors core physical principles. Keen found some suggestion that looking behavior might indicate a degree of sensitivity to barriers, but that is uncertain at the present time.

It is not yet clear how Keen's findings can be explained. The choice is not merely between models which posit that mental representation is innate or that it emerges through interactions with the world. It is at least possible that a quite different explanation may be called for. If looking time indeed shows sensitivity to object solidity and continuity, and reach does not, it might be that different processes control behaviors of looking and behaviors of reaching. That is, there might be no reason to posit the existence of a general knowledge of objects that controls various relevant behaviors, but only more specific perception–action connections. The notion that different processes may control different aspects of behavior has been of great interest to some recent investigators. For example, Cutting and Vishton (1995) and Creem and Proffitt (1998) proposed two-system accounts of information processing even in adults. In their work, they distinguished mechanisms involved in action from those involved in conceptualization. The perception–action system, they argued, operates without conscious awareness to support rapid precise responding, whereas the conceptual system operates consciously and more slowly to support longer term multipurpose representations.

Multisystem explanations have been invoked by developmental psychologists in explaining observed dissociations between looking and reaching behaviors by 1-year-olds in object permanence tasks (Diamond, 1998, 2001; Smith, Thelen, Titzer, & McLin, 1999). With respect to the Keen findings, however, she notes that it is not clear yet whether reaching and looking actually show reliable differences. If not, her findings might indicate that infants may possess neither core physical principles nor clearly distinguishable perception action pairings. In short, Keen's studies indicate that more research is needed to determine the extent to which there are differential looking times and reaching behaviors in early childhood and, consequently, how they should be explained. However, her work clearly indicates that investigators should seek models that posit simple processes and test them before considering models that posit complex processes that are difficult to test.

REPRESENTATION AND THE SPATIAL DOMAIN

Liben's chapter deals with spatial development—in particular, with maps. Maps are external devices that, for people who are able to interpret them, provide knowledge about geographic locations. The spatial information they encode may guide behavior in traversing unfamiliar territory, make it possible to answer questions about the distances between places they have never traversed, and so on. Because maps are external devices, it may seem possible for investigators to set aside issues of mental representation in studying their use. However, maps are only produced or interpreted by creatures who can preserve spatial information in memory. Thus, it is reasonable to start this discussion with a more general consideration of the mental representation of spatial information.

The spatial domain provides an excellent ground for examining issues of mental representation. Mobile creatures must store information about particular places to survive—to know the locations of their nests, food supplies, and so on. They must retain such information in a form that allows them to return to those locations from a variety of different starting positions. Epistemological issues concerning the relation of mental structure to the actual structure of the world have seemed especially salient in the spatial domain. During the behaviorist era, the notion of a cognitive map, which captured spatial information, was invoked to explain spatial behavior in rats (Tolman, 1948). Given the necessity for some degree of accuracy of stored information with respect to the actual world, together with the fact that many species retain spatial information, the conclusion that spatial information is mentally represented can be reached from logical considerations alone. Questions arise as to whether more detailed models of the nature of the spatial representation can be developed and tested.

Although the field of cognitive science is relatively new, it seems reasonable to suppose that we can develop theories to explain the nature and function of spatial representation. One sort of question is whether people form what could be called *integrated representations* of spatial information—namely, representations that would relate all the locations in a set. For example, consider a person who has just moved to a new city and has learned a set of paths between pairs of locations in the city by directly traversing them. Each path connects home with a particular other location (home and store, home and office, and home and dentist). The person can use the shortest paths in both directions for each pair. From such findings, one would not have reason to argue that the person has constructed an integrated mental representation that includes all the points. Suppose, however, that having gotten a toothache at the office one day, the person takes a direct (shortest) path to the dentist from the office—along a path that was not previously traversed. Stated more generally, what should be said about a person who has learned specific pairs of locations and can use the information to go directly between any combination of the points by the shortest route? That person might be said to have formed a unified mental representation of the points—a maplike mental structure. This unified representation might then support a variety of kinds of behaviors that could be derived from a map of the region.

Thought experiments reveal any number of other cases where it is clear that objects and/or events are mentally represented. Consider a hypothetical example like many experiences a person might report. The person is trying unsuccessfully to disassemble a puzzle involving several interlocking pieces. After putting the puzzle aside and taking up another activity, the person realizes what the solution is. Seeing the puzzle again, the person disassembles it immediately without trial and error. Such behavior strongly suggests that the critical aspects of the puzzle and the movements of its pieces were mentally represented.

In addition to thought experiments, there are of course actual experiments that demonstrate that objects and events in the world are mentally represented. There is evidence from the work of Shepard (e.g., Shepard & Metzler, 1971) concerning imagined actions on objects. People were asked to judge whether a standard figure was identical to a comparison figure shown in a different orientation. In making the judgment, people reported that they imagined rotating one of the figures until its major axis matched that of the other figure and then compared whether the figures were identical. Behavioral findings supported these introspective reports; decision times increased linearly with the angle of separation between the major axes of the two figures, as if actual rotations were being carried out.

Findings like those of Shepard are consistent with the claims of investigators who argue that problems involving imagined actions on objects are solved using the same cognitive and neural processes as are used for actual spatiomotor processing (Barsalou, 1999; Glenberg, 1997). There is preliminary support for this claim in cognitive neuroscience findings, which indicate that common neural regions may be activated both in imagining acting on objects and in actually carrying out those actions (e.g., Carpenter, Just, Keller, Eddy, & Thulborn, 1999; Richter, Ugurbil, Georgopoulos, & Kim, 1997). Insofar as mental processes involved in thinking about objects and action are parallel to processes in actual perception and action, there would not be a problem where a homunculus must interpret the language of thought. The internal processes would be grounded if indeed they draw on the same mental structures as perceptual processing.

Let us turn now to map use—the focus of Liben's chapter. Maps can depict places in a variety of ways, and the manner of depiction has the potential to affect the mental representation of geographic information and, hence, human behavior. Maps provide an external way to preserve knowledge obtained previously by the map maker. In addition, maps can be used to create new knowledge, providing information about location that goes beyond what is available from direct observation, such as features of space that cannot be simultaneously observed—whole neighborhoods, cities, states, or countries. In addition, variation in the kind of map used may affect people's understanding of space (e.g., route maps vs. aerial depictions of a region). Clearly, differential information provided by variations in the symbolic devices used can have profound effects on people's behavior in space.

Liben's work on maps is based on developmental assumptions she shares with Piaget. She believes that the spatial representations that accommodate scalar and rotational transformations develop slowly over childhood. Her work shows that the nature of conventional forms of presenting information in maps can affect behavior and judgment. For a person who knows how to interpret maps, they can guide action, enabling new ways to think about space. They vary in how they portray the world; some maps show spatial environments in a way that is closer to real-life experience than others. Lynn argues that the closer the map is to real-life experience, the easier it is for children to interpret. For example, she argues that aerial views are harder to interpret than oblique views. Yet children are able to acquire certain types of spatial information from maps, such as the shapes and sizes of particular regions. The use of physical representations, as Liben notes, can have substantial effects on behavior that is guided by such representations of space.

Finally, departing from Liben's chapter, I want to point out that mental representations involving imagined spatial displays, such as diagrams and graphs, are critical in nonspatial as well as spatial thought. The use of spatial representations in syllogistic reasoning provides powerful tools for reasoning. For example, class membership syllogisms can be solved by using enclosed spaces to represent classes (Venn diagrams). Ordering problems may be solved through construction of spatial arrays in which objects are laid out in order along any sort of dimension. A single dimensional spatial array can be used to preserve information about, for example, their relative aesthetic value (e.g., Huttenlocher, 1973). There is behavioral evidence that such imagined displays are used in reasoning—the evidence includes disruption of performance from doing visual activities while solving ordering syllogisms, and the appearance of a similar order of difficulty for ordering syllogisms and parallel tasks in which they construct actual arrangement of objects.

These comments are intended to alert investigators who deal with processes that may be conceptualized without positing mental representation that, in handling many problems in human psychology, the notion is essential. However, the advice of skeptics is important to cognitive psychologists because some of us posit mental representations too readily without seeking alternative explanations based on simpler processes. All of us should scrutinize the models we propose to determine whether alternatives are possible and evaluate those alternatives before presenting them in the literature.

REFERENCES

Barsalou, L. (1999). Perceptual symbol systems. *Behavioral and Brain Sciences, 22*(4), 577–660.

Brooks, R. (1991). Intelligence without representation. *Artificial Intelligence Journal, 47,* 139–159.

Carpenter, P. A., Just, M. A., Keller, T. A., Eddy, W., & Thulborn, K. (1999). Graded functional activation in the visuospatial system with the amount of task demand. *Journal of Cognitive Neuroscience, 11*(1), 9–24.

Creem, S. H., & Proffitt, D. R. (1998). Two memories for geographical slant: Separation and interdependence of action and awareness. *Psychonomic Bulletin and Review, 5,* 22–36.

Cutting, J. E., & Vishton, P. M. (1995). Perceiving layout and knowing distances: The integration, relative potency, and contextual use of different information about depth. In W. Epstein & S. J. Rogers (Eds.), *Perception of space and motion. Handbook of perception and cognition* (2nd ed., pp. 9–117). San Diego, CA: Academic Press.

Diamond, A. (1998). Understanding the A-not-B error: Working memory vs. reinforced response, or active trace vs. latent trace. *Developmental Science, 1*(2), 185–189.

Diamond, A. (2001). Looking closely at infants' performance and experimental procedures in the A-not-B task. *Behavioral and Brain Sciences, 24*(1), 38–41.

Gibson, J. J. (1966). *The senses considered as perceptual systems.* Boston: Houghton-Mifflin.

Glenberg, A. M. (1997). What memory is for. *Behavioral and Brain Sciences, 20,* 1–19.

Haith, M. M. (1998). Who put the cog in infant cognition? Is rich interpretation too costly? *Infant Behavior and Development, 21*(2), 167–179.

Huttenlocher, J. (1973). Language and thought. In G. Miller (Ed.), *Communication, language, and meaning: Psychological perspectives* (pp. 172–184). New York: Basic Books.

Piaget, J. (1952). *The origins of intelligence in children.* Madison, WI: International Universities Press.

Richter, W., Ugurbil, K., Georgopoulos, A., & Kim, S.-G. (1997). Time-resolved fMRI of mental rotation. *Neuroreport, 8*(17), 3697–3702.

Shepard, R. N., & Metzler, (1971). Mental rotation of three-dimensional objects. *Science, 171,* 71–703.

Smith, L. B., Thelen, E., Titzer, R., & McLin, D. (1999). Knowing in the context of acting: The task dynamics of the A-not-B error. *Psychological Review, 106*(2), 235–260.

Spelke, E. S., Breinlinger, K., Macomber, J., & Jacobson, K. (1992). Origins of knowledge. *Psychological Review, 99*(4), 605–632.

Tolman, E. C. (1948). Cognitive maps in rats and men. *Psychological Review, 55,* 189–208.

Author Index

Subject Index